The Lost Paradise

CHICAGO STUDIES IN ETHNOMUSICOLOGY
A series edited by Philip V. Bohlman, Ronald Radano, and Timothy Rommen

The Lost Paradise

Andalusi Music in Urban North Africa

JONATHAN GLASSER

The University of Chicago Press
Chicago and London

Jonathan Glasser is assistant professor of anthropology at the College of William and Mary.

The University of Chicago Press, Chicago 60637
The University of Chicago Press, Ltd., London

Printed in the United States of America

25 24 23 22 21 20 19 18 17 16   1 2 3 4 5

ISBN-13: 978-0-226-32706-8 (cloth)
ISBN-13: 978-0-226-32723-5 (paper)
ISBN-13: 978-0-226-32737-2 (e-book)
DOI: 10.7208/chicago/9780226327372.001.0001

Publication of this book has been aided by the AMS 75 PAYS Endowment of the American Musicological Society, funded in part by the National Endowment for the Humanities and the Andrew W. Mellon Foundation.

Library of Congress Cataloging-in-Publication Data

Glasser, Jonathan, author.
The lost paradise : Andalusi music in urban North Africa / Jonathan Glasser.
pages cm — (Chicago studies in ethnomusicology)
ISBN 978-0-226-32706-8 (cloth : alk. paper) — ISBN 978-0-226-32723-5 (pbk. : alk. paper) — ISBN 978-0-226-32737-2 (e-book) 1. Music—Algeria—History and criticism. 2. Music—Morocco—History and criticism. 3. Arabs—Algeria—Music—History and criticism. 4. Arabs—Morocco—Music—History and criticism. I. Title. II. Series: Chicago studies in ethnomusicology.
ML350.G63 2016
781.62′927061—dc23

2015024745

♾ This paper meets the requirements of ANSI/NISO Z39.48-1992 (Permanence of Paper).

When Moses went up to the sky he found the Holy One, blessed be He, sitting and connecting small crowns to letters.

He said before Him: "Master of the world, who is keeping you [from finishing]?"

He said to him: "There is a man who will come to be in some generations, his name is Akiva ben Yosef; he will one day expound layer upon layer of laws on each and every tip [of the letters]."

He said before God: "Master of the world, show him to me."

He told him: "Turn around."

[Moses] went and sat in the last of the eight rows of the class, and even there he did not understand what they were saying. His strength drained. When [the teacher] came to a certain point, his students said to him, "Master, how did you arrive at this?" He said to them, "It is a law given to Moses from Sinai." And [Moses'] mind was quieted.

BABYLONIAN TALMUD, *Gifts 29b*

Contents

Figures

Acknowledgments

It is fitting to begin a book about a century-long musical memory project by recalling the people who over the past decade have allowed me to write this book and to carry out the research from which it emerged. But as the following pages show, complete recollection is impossible no matter how strong the desire. With this humbling fact in mind, I would like to name some of the people who have helped me along the way, with the hope that those I do not name here will nevertheless recognize themselves in the broad spirit of these thanks.

As the coming pages show, Andalusi music enthusiasts are frequently described by others, and sometimes even by themselves, as a closed community that is protective of its secrets. My own lived experience, however, has suggested much the opposite. This book would not have been possible without the openness and generosity of countless musicians and enthusiasts, initially in Morocco and subsequently in Algeria, France, and North America.

In Rabat, Mohamed El-Haddaoui and Hadj Ahmed Piro gave generously of their time and knowledge in the early stages of this project, and Mohamed Alaoui and the Association Ryad el Andalous have given me, my colleagues, and students a gracious welcome in more recent years. In Oujda, I was warmly welcomed by the late Cheikh Ahmed Azzemouri, Mouhcine Azzemouri, Mohamed Benabdellah, Amina Bensaad, Mohamed Chaabane, Nasr Eddine Chaabane, Kheira Dali, Dr. Esseddiq Fadhil, Dr. Taha Haddam, Abdelhay Lotfeallah, Nasreddine Ouahidi, Tahar Salamy, Ahmed Tantaoui, and the local representatives of the Ministry of Culture. In addition, I would like to acknowledge the cooperation of the following associations and institutions and the generosity and kindness of their members: Ahbab Cheikh Salah, Andalusiyya, Huwāt al-ṭarab al-gharnāṭī, Ismaïliyya, Moussilia, al-Qudama, Riyad Gharnata, Tarab, and Ziryab, as well as La Cicada and the circle of Riyad el Andalous

In and around Algiers, my warm thanks to Hadj Mamad Benchaouche, Brahim Benladjreb, Abdelhadi Boukoura, Fazilet Diff, Hadi Kheir, Waïl Labassi, Salima Maadini, Mourad Ouamara, Nour-Eddine Saoudi, Youcef Touaïbia, Yacine Touati, and Zakia Kara Terki, as well as the teachers and students at the Algiers Municipal Conservatory, the Association des Beaux Arts, the Association El Fen El Acil (Koléa), and Association Essoundoussia. I would acknowledge my indebtedness to the late Sid Ahmed Serri, who passed away as this book went to press. His personal generosity was crucial to its writing, and it is his words that bring it to a close. In Oran, I would like to thank Mokhtar Allal, Rachid Gaouar, and the many members of Association Nassim el-Andalous who have welcomed me there. In Tlemcen, a special thanks to Fayçal Benkalfat, Nacreddine Baghdadi, Bilkacem and Redouane Ghoul, Benali El Hassar, Fawzi Kalfat, and the members of Association Ahbab Cheikh Larbi Bensari, Association Gharnata, and S.L.A.M. In Paris, I would like to thank Noureddine Aliane, Nassima Chaabane, Brahim Hadj Kacem, and Beihdja Rahal; in Marseilles, Maurice El-Medioni; and in Montreal, Sid-Ali Hamouche and the late Samy al-Maghribi. And although there are many others whom I have not had the chance to cite here, my acknowledgments would not be complete without mentioning Bouziane Zaid, who explained to me in New York that what Salim Hilali was singing on the cassette was something called *gharnāṭī*.

This book would not have been possible without the support of a variety of institutions, including the American Musicological Society, which aided in its publication. The ethnographic and archival research on which this book is based was supported by the Wenner-Gren Foundation; the Fulbright Fellowship Program; the University of Michigan's Center for Middle Eastern and North Africa Studies, Rackham School of Graduate Studies, and Frankel Center for Jewish Studies; the American Institute for Maghrib Studies; and, at the College of William and Mary, the Reves Center for International Studies, the School of Arts and Sciences, and Swem Library. Overseas archival and library research was carried out at the National Library of France, the National Library of Algeria, the Bodleian Library, the Algerian National Archives, the Centre d'Études Diocésain-Les Glycines, the Institut méditerranéen Mémoire et archives du judaïsme in Marseille, the Centre des archives d'outre mer in Aix-en-Provence, the Centre des archives diplomatiques in Nantes, the Khizāna al-ʿāmma and Archive coloniale in Rabat, and the Maktaba Daūdiyya in Tetuan. Many thanks to the individuals at these institutions who have helped me, including Konrad Antczak, Nassim Balla, Daoud

Casewit, Patrick Johnson, Bouzeid Khelili, Akli Kidji, Jean-Marie Leclercq, Saadia Maski, Naima Mehareb, Guillaume Michel, Marie-Thérèse Mounier, Kerry Murphy, Karim Ouaras, Robert Parks, Ali Rachedi, Ute Schechter, Tom Trovato, Monika Van Tassel, Bill Vega, and the staff at the Centre d'études maghrébines en Algérie and the amazing Interlibrary Loan Office at the College of William and Mary. A special thanks to Mallory Moran for preparing the maps and figures that appear in the following pages.

In addition, I would like to thank a few of the many people on several continents who have helped bring this work to fruition through their feedback and encouragement, including the late Mohamed Aboq, Catherine Darmellah Andouard, Rachid Aous, Kathryn Babayan, Fiona Balestrieri, Beth Baron, Rachid Bellahsene, Tuska Benes, Abdelfettah Benmoussa, Sabeha Benmansour, Michael Bonner, Eric Calderwood, Driss Cherkaoui, Julia Clancy-Smith, Joshua Cole, Rachel Colwell, Andy Conroe, Fred Corney, Mohamed Daoud, Carl Davila, Ahmed Amine Dellai, Aditi Deo, Daho Djerbal, Dmitrii Dorofeev, John Eisele, Mohamed Farraji, Bill Fisher, Rebecca Fulp-Eickstaedt, Izza Genini, Mustapha al-Ghadiri, Denise Elif Gill, Jane Goodman, Aron Gutman, Yasmeen Hanoosh, Rima Hassouneh, Jane Hill, Jim House, Brian Hulce, Marcia Inhorn, Judith Irvine, Deborah Kapchan, Ayfer Karakaya-Stump, Brian Karl, Max Katz, Simon Keeling, Skye Keene-Babcock, Tony Langlois, Hasna Lebbady, Josiane Le Bescond, Erica Lehrer, Michelle LeLièvre, André Levy, the late Simon Lévy, John Lucy, Derek Mancini-Lander, Mohamed El Habib Mansouri, Scott Marcus, Caitlin Marsh, James McDougall, Neil McMaster, Omar Metioui, Hadj Miliani, Deborah Morse, Philip Murphy, Ali Neff, Dard Neuman, Mustapha Nezzari, Ben Nickels, Frédéric Nortes, Asmae Otmani, Gul Ozyegin, Jann Pasler, the late Christian Poché, Vijay Prashad, Sara Pursley, Nejma Rahal, Ann and David Reed, Fawzi Sadallah, Maya Saidani, Marlene Schäfers, Ron Schechter, Edwin Seroussi, Jonathan Shannon, Chris Silver, Amy Stillman, Martin Stokes, Deborah Spitulnik, Ted Swedenburg, Mag Tayar, Eli Thorkelson, Samuel Thomas, Rachid Toumi, the late Linda Trucchi, Susanne Unger, Lucia Volk, Susan Waltz, Brad Weiss, Christopher Witulski, Sibel Zandi-Sayek, Chitralekha Zutshi, and the members of the Anthropology of Europe Workshop at the University of Chicago, the Departments of History and Near Eastern Studies at Princeton University, the Department of Anthropology at Yale University, and my students, colleagues, and fellow Middle Eastern Music Ensemble members at the College of William and Mary.

Finally, I would like to acknowledge the invaluable mentorship of Ammiel Alcalay, Kelly Askew, Carol Bardenstein, Ross Brann, Ron Kuzar, Anne Rasmussen, Dwight Reynolds, Benita Rose, Anton Shammas, and Andrew

Shryock. At the University of Chicago Press, the patient support of Elizabeth Branch Dyson, the expert guidance of Nora Devlin and Richard Allen, and the generous comments of anonymous reviewers have seen this book into the world, and for this I am grateful. The research and life experience that went into researching and writing this book would have been far less fun without the hospitality of Esther Bitton, Jacob and Rachel Bitton, the Boughalem family, the El-Khayat family, Raphael Elmaleh, the Glassers of Saint-Ouen, the Glasser-Skogs of Blackeberg, the Kejji family, Sheila Levitan, Marie-France Mathoulin, Lionel and Béatrice Rotenberg, and the late Fifine Sciarrino and Adam and Inka Weber. Finally, I would like to acknowledge the sustaining presence of my friends Zeid Hanania and Will Kabat-Zinn; my brothers Jason, Nathaniel, and Raphael and my cousin Francine Glasser; my loving parents, Irene and Morton Glasser; and, most especially, my partner, Kathrin Levitan, without whom none of this would have been possible. I lovingly dedicate this book to our children, Azalea and Selma.

Note on Transliteration

Like the Andalusi repertoire itself, the terms used to talk about the repertoire can be highly localized in time and space. I am wary of unwittingly contributing to a standardization project, but for the sake of consistency I have chosen certain terms over others unless I am directly quoting a text. For example, I refer to the final movement of the *nūba* as the *khlāṣ* rather than as the *mukhliṣ*, following the Algiers convention over the Tlemcani convention, and write *ṣan'a* rather than the alternate *ṣanā'a*. With regard to plural nouns, I have followed particular conventions: for example, *shghālāt* rather than *ashghāl*, *tūshiyyāt* rather than *tawāshī*, and *khlāṣāt* rather than *khulāṣāt*, *akhlaṣa*, *akhlāṣ*, or *mkhāliṣ*.

It is challenging to find a way to transliterate both spoken and written Arabic in a way that does not favor one over the other. When quoting directly from a written Arabic text, I have transliterated from standard Arabic; when discussing terms used in everyday speech, I have transliterated from spoken Maghribi Arabic. Hence I usually write *nūba* rather than *nawba*, *m'allim* rather than *mu'allim*, and *ḥsīn* rather than *ḥusayn*. I also write *qṣīda* rather than *qaṣīda* when discussing the colloquial strophic song tradition in the Maghrib, as opposed to the non-strophic classical Arabic poetic tradition. Likewise, I have preserved the initial *m* in such terms as *mṣaddar*, instead of rendering it as either *muṣaddar* or *amṣaddar*, and I generally present *ẓ* as *ḍ*. For the *hamza* in the case of broken plurals, I have preferred *y* over ': *qṣayid*, not *qṣā'id*. However, in a few cases, I have opted for a spelling that reflects the standard written form over the spoken one: for example, *inṣirāf*, not *nṣrāf*; *inqilāb*, not *nqlāb* or *niqlāb*; *muwashshaḥ*, not *mūshshaḥ*; *shuyūkh*, not *shyūkh*; and *al-diyūr*, not *ad-diyūr* or *ddiyūr*.

For proper nouns, I have followed the standard English-language mapping conventions for places, and, in an effort not to make the text look alien for those familiar with some of the people I am writing about, I have selected one of the French orthographic conventions in common use with regard to persons—in other words, Cheikh Larbi Bensari, not Cheikh Larbi Ben Sari or Shaykh al-ʿArabī Bin Ṣārī, and Cheikh Sfindja rather than Shaykh Sfīnja. Again, the exception is when I cite names drawn from an Arabic text.

Introduction

Somewhere around 1900, in the western Algerian city of Tlemcen, a young schoolteacher named Mostefa Aboura embarked on a remarkable musicological project. Equipped with a mastery of staff notation and a fine sense of musical relativism garnered from his years as a clarinetist in the local symphonic band and as a student in Algiers, Aboura began to transcribe the Andalusi musical repertoire of his beloved city in an effort to document it, analyze it, and safeguard it from loss.[1] It was an ambitious project, unprecedented in scope. Centered on a long, complex suite form known as the *nūba* said to have originated in al-Andalus (medieval Muslim Spain), with each *nūba* organized around one of roughly a dozen melodic modes and divided internally into five vocal movements linked by a range of instrumental forms, the repertoire added up to many hundreds of individual pieces. What is more, knowledge of this repertoire was distributed among diverse people and venues: humble professional musicians known as *shuyūkh*, middle- and upper-class amateurs like himself, music cafés, artisans' workshops, festivities in private homes, and informal gatherings of friends. Competing versions abounded, and, in what might seem like a paradox, each new generation in the chains of *shuyūkh* seemed to be working with a dwindling stock of repertoire and peers, making Aboura's efforts an ingathering of scattered, unruly, endangered musical knowledge.

Aboura was not alone in his efforts. There were parallel, overlapping projects in turn-of-the-century Tlemcen and Algiers, and these had a few nineteenth-century precedents, including among French intellectuals close to the ruling colonial apparatus. Aboura also came to find a lifelong collaborator in a fellow schoolteacher from a well-to-do Tlemcani family, Mohamed Ben Smaïl, some nine years his junior. The project soon took on a new scale.

Aboura and Ben Smaïl methodically transcribed the repertoire of leading *shuyūkh* of Tlemcen, amassed a vast library of printed materials and phonograph recordings, and wrote reports that to all intents and purposes resembled government documents. Their efforts were exported westward with Ben Smaïl's work-related move to Morocco following the establishment of the French Protectorate there. In 1925, taking his cue from the rise of an amateur association devoted to Andalusi music in the Algerian capital just prior to the First World War, Ben Smaïl established a musical society called l'Andaloussia in the border city of Oujda, just across the frontier from Tlemcen, with the explicit aim of "bringing back to life the Andalusi music imported to Africa by the Moors expelled from Spain"—a music that he compared to "those beautiful pieces of silk and gold textiles gnawed at by time and conserved at the Museum of Ancient Silks at Lyon."[2]

Yet although aspects of Aboura's and Ben Smaïl's project were taking on an increasingly public cast, the vast collection of transcriptions and reports that undergirded it remained curiously out of view. With the exception of several pages published by Ben Smaïl in a French-language journal, neither of the men published their observations, even as some of the parallel projects saw the light of day and were widely cited.[3] During a triumphant visit of the Oujda association to Rabat to play before the colonial authorities in 1928, French Protectorate officials publicly lamented that Aboura's and Ben Smaïl's "labors, which remain in manuscript form, hide themselves with too much modesty in notebooks, and risk becoming lost."[4] In 1939, four years after Aboura's death, Ben Smaïl prepared to present his late collaborator's transcriptions during the opening session of the Congress of Moroccan Music in Fes. But despite the Oujda association's participation in the gathering, the scheduled presentation did not take place, and Ben Smaïl died eight years later without having transmitted them to the authorities.[5]

Hidden away in Tlemcen, the collection lived on, now enriched by the efforts of Mostefa's son Kheireddine Aboura. And as the collection grew over the two generations, the Andalusi musical world shifted around it, leaving its traces in the archive's accumulating layers. *Shuyūkh* died and new ones arose, even as the social category was said to be fading; lineages continued, died out, divided. Meanwhile, the revivalist project that the elder Aboura helped inaugurate came to full flower. By the time of his death, amateur associations on the model of l'Andaloussia were proliferating in Tlemcen, Constantine, and especially Algiers, where the repertoire came to be taught in the municipal conservatory. One could hear Andalusi music in concert halls and public squares, through phonographs and the radio. The field of musical genres expanded and changed shape. Learned aficionados discoursed on the repertoire in lecture halls and reformist circles, and published compilations of *nūba* song texts. And although decolonization saw the loss of many performers and listeners to war and exile, in the aftermath of independence Algerian intellectuals took up the cause of Andalusi music as a national classical musical patrimony (*patrimoine, turāth*) that was central to the desire of the Algerian people to "'become itself again' after 130 years of depersonalization."[6] New generations of amateur associations arose, including one named after the city of Granada over which Kheireddine Aboura presided until his death in 1977. National and regional festivals provided young men and, increasingly, women opportunities to perform; state-supported research projects undertook the work of safeguard on a national scale; and novel timbres, venues, and documentation efforts multiplied, even as the national political scene moved from centralist to liberal models, turned upside down in the face of the social protests of 1988, and descended into civil war in the 1990s.[7]

Yet even as the spirit of Aboura's and Ben Smaïl's work lived on among a wide range of devotees through these varied times, there were only glimpses of their work now and then, largely confined to the years just after independence: a display of ephemera and musical instruments at a municipal cultural festival in 1966, and a few facsimiles in a short book on Andalusi music printed two years later.[8] It was not until a full century after Aboura's project started that the transcriptions began to shift into view. A new generation of aficionados emerging from the civil war years, aided by the internet and spurred on by a renewed sense that the Andalusi musical repertoire was in danger, began to seek out recordings, manuscripts, and other documents that might expand the sense of the musical past. In Tlemcen, one leading scholar and devotee of the repertoire was able to negotiate the transfer of the bulk of the collection from Mostefa and Kheireddine's descendants to the Ministry of Culture. As of this writing, the work of sorting through the trove and piecing together the history of its constitution and migrations is ongoing. But it is already clear that at the deepest layers of this century-old accumulation are hundreds of transcriptions, among them dozens of pieces that were circulating in Mostefa Aboura's day but that have since disappeared from the musical stream. It is as if Aboura's project has come full circle, finally divulging that which he sought to document and which, for a century, had become doubly lost.

✶

One need not know much about Andalusi music to find this tale of twice-buried treasure intriguing. But for habitués of the Andalusi musical milieu, this is a dramatic variation on a familiar theme. For the lost—in Arabic, the *mafqūd*—is a central conceit of Andalusi musical practice in its various regional forms in Morocco, Algeria, Tunisia, and Libya. Its trajectory begins with a narrative of musical origins in al-Andalus, medieval Muslim Spain, what is often referred to in Arabic as *al-firdaws al-mafqūd*, "the lost paradise," where the *nūba* form is said to have originated in courtly life, perhaps through the legendary figure of Ziryāb, a ninth-century musical migrant from Baghdad to Cordoba. According to what Carl Davila has termed the "standard narrative" of Andalusi musical origins, the *nūba* was originally linked to twenty-four melodic modes, each tied to a specific hour of the day, each carrying its own humoral powers.[9] After 1492, the year of the fall of Granada, the last of the Muslim states in Iberia, this repertoire was exported to the Maghrib by Muslims and Jews fleeing Christian rule, a fugitive relic of the civilizational splendor of the lost paradise.

Yet built into this narrative of rescue from loss is another narrative of loss: despite the passing-down of the *nūba* repertoire over the centuries through manuscript poetry collections and face-to-face transmission of the melodies, and despite the addition of new, specifically Maghribi songs and forms to the performance practice, the core *nūba* repertoire attenuated, so that the twenty-four *nūbāt* corresponding to twenty-four modes were reduced by roughly half. The named cause of this loss varies: the persecutions in Spain, French colonialism, rural-to-urban migration, new media and musical genres, and state negligence have been commonly identified culprits. But by far the favorites in the Andalusi musical milieu are oral transmission and the hoarding of musical knowledge. According to many practitioners of the past hundred years and more, oral transmission carries within it certain built-in failures, so that pieces have changed, blurred, and disappeared. And in a related fashion, it is said that the penchant of *shuyūkh* to hoard their knowledge—whether out of professional competition, lack of disciples, or sheer irrationality—likewise ate away at the repertoire. In the words of a contemporary of the elder Aboura in Algiers, each musician "goes to the grave with words and melodies which those who remain do not know and do not conserve . . . such that these melodies remain their captive."[10] It was this state of affairs that prompted figures like Aboura, Ben Smaïl, and their turn-of-the-century peers to undertake the project of safeguard and revival by way of various forms of inscription and externalization—what contemporary practitioners narrate as the bringing out of Andalusi music from the private (*min al-diyūr*, "from the houses") into the public sphere.

And indeed, Andalusi music in its various regionally distinct forms did become public, in Algeria as in Morocco, Tunisia, and Libya, taking on a new status as a national and transnational "classical music" in the independence era.[11] Yet the story of Aboura's collection also suggests that the movement from private house to public square was less complete and straightforward than is commonly told. Even at the heart of the revivalist movement, some things remained hidden from view, or became more hidden, or even went into hiding after having been out in the open. Archives could come to resemble the hoards they allegedly were meant to combat. Things became lost even as associations, printed compilations, and festivals multiplied—some would even say because they multiplied. One hundred years after revivalists rushed to record the last *shaykh*, aficionados of Andalusi music who I have encountered in Oujda, Tlemcen, Oran, Algiers, and Paris continue to speak passionately of the need to document the last *shaykh* before his passing. The patrimony, it is said, is still in danger.

This book attempts to think critically about these ironies while taking them seriously as a form of social practice that is deeply compelling for its devotees. In particular, this is an inquiry into the place of the lost within a more than century-long project of musical salvage and revival that stretches across a network of Algerian and Moroccan cities and into the Maghribi diaspora. The contours of this question and of this temporal and geographic envelope emerged from ethnographic research that began in Oujda in 2004, chiefly among the members of the contemporary incarnation of l'Andaloussia and its various offshoot associations. While this research focused on living practitioners whose activities centered on Oujda, the things that performers and aficionados said and left unsaid pointed both backward in time toward the early decades of the twentieth century and eastward toward Tlemcen and Algiers, the twin capitals of the particular *nūba* form that is practiced in Oujda. The temporal dimension hinged on practitioners' discussions of lineages of *shuyūkh*, most of whom combined a resolute localness with close connections to other places, and few of whose lineages reached before 1900 with any specificity. Tlemcen and Algiers stood out among these other places as sources of musical authority, repertoire, sound recordings, and written texts; through ethnographic and archival research that eventually expanded to Algeria and France I came to understand Oujda as one of many musical satellites of these two Algerian cities, a part of a formally and socially defined musical network of circulation. Another aspect of temporality, however, was the revival movement itself, which had emerged a century before I started my research, and which stood in a complex relationship with the genealogies of the *shuyūkh*: revival seemed to coincide with the outer limits of genealogical memory, and at the same time treated genealogically embedded musical authorities as objects of salvage and reform. In other words, I came to understand what I was encountering as a tradition in the sense articulated by Talal Asad: an ongoing debate over the "apt performance" of a practice that is highly attuned to the intertwining of the present with both a past and a future.[12]

If the contours and conditions of the genre formation gave rise to this book's attempt to grapple with what revival in fact names, they also came to shape the narrative and analytic strategies I pursue here, including the movement between multiple places and historical moments.[13] The contours and conditions of the genre formation can likewise be seen in the tacking back and forth between insights and questions derived on the one hand from ethnographic fieldwork rooted in musical participant-observation and semi-structured interviews, and on the other hand from close reading of written documents. While some of these documents stand at a remove from Andalusi musical practice in the sense that they embody scholarly approaches that are distant from practitioners' concerns, in many cases they are closely tied to those concerns. As will be seen, Andalusi music is a deeply textual and scholarly tradition, and the production of texts and their archivization are central to the twentieth-century project of revival. Outsiders' scholarship has often been created in close dialogue with musical practitioners and has frequently been integrated into musical practice.[14] A significant proportion of the literature on Andalusi music has been written by scholars who are themselves serious practitioners.[15] And for many practitioners, making Andalusi music is itself a form of scholarship. This state of affairs confounds any attempt to definitively separate history from memory, secondary sources from primary sources, the past from the present, the "ethnographic" from the "historical," the academic from the nonacademic, and the observer from the observed.[16] Thus this book emerges from an engagement with genre as a historically extended "orienting framework for the production and reception of discourse," but one that also serves to orient the shape of this book[17]—a framework that has unavoidably fuzzy edges and blind spots, but that also exists in particular places, in activities carried out among particular people, that works upon and through musical sound, and that has a variegated, fateful, still growing past.

It is this past and its relationship to the present and the future that I suggest practitioners are talking about when they speak of the lost. In the following pages, I treat the longevity of the revivalist project not as a sign of failure but rather as evidence of the vitality of a longstanding genealogical ethos that treats the Andalusi repertoire as a precious inheritance embodied in authoritative performers and listeners.[18] This genealogical ethos is finely attuned to what practitioners sometimes call "the passage of time and its people." This awareness of temporality and loss is both a part of the practice and a commentary on the phenomenal texture of that practice. Yet despite its age, the practice is not hermetically sealed. The lost as a form of commentary on the temporality of tradition has taken on new powers and qualities as the ground of Andalusi musical production shifted through the rise of new technologies, institutions, and forms of politics, among them the revivalist project itself. This book is an exploration of the territory of loss that is coterminous with the Andalusi musical project.

*

For students of nationalism, loss and defense against its threat are familiar tools in the construction of the nation—tools that help make the very thing they seek to protect.[19] As a child of the nineteenth century, these nationalist imaginings can in turn be situated within a broader move since the end of the eighteenth century to define the difference between the present ("the modern") and the past as a qualitative rupture that brings about loss and, with it, an impulse toward salvage and restoration.[20] The understanding of nationalism and modernity as intertwined discursive projects that have the trope of loss at their center has been deeply influential for a wide range of scholars, among them historians of North Africa. In recent years, the work of George Trumbull IV has underlined the centrality of salvage ethnography to French rule in Third Republic Algeria before the First World War.[21] In a different fashion, the work of James McDougall has pointed out that despite the allure of the narrative of a primordial Algerian nation's persistence and revival in the face of colonialism, revival is not an objective phenomenon but rather a discursive construction that twentieth-century Algerian Muslims under colonial rule deployed to diverse ends and that historians have too readily adopted when narrating the broad sweep of modern Algerian history.[22]

Similar insights have shaped scholarship on processes of musical revival. The work of Katherine Bergeron on the "restoration" of Gregorian chant in nineteenth-century France has mapped the ways in which revivalists of medieval plainchant grappled with profoundly modernist concerns and inscriptual technologies in their constructions and reconstructions of the ostensibly ancient.[23] Among students of American and English folk revivals, the emphasis has been on transformations and transfers, with revival naming what is in fact a partial appropriation of a musical practice by a group of people who were previously unassociated or only loosely associated with it.[24] Like much of the literature on nationalism, these approaches have a complex relationship to notions of rupture and rescue. On the one hand, they are skeptical of revivalist narratives of loss and near-loss. On the other hand, they often suggest that rupture is there but simply not where revivalists say it is: rupture takes the form of a profound social dislocation to which revivalist discourse is in fact responding, or which arises from the powers and problems of new technologies, or which revivalists themselves help to create through their own actions.

These ironic dispositions have been helpful in approaching the Andalusi musical case that is examined in this book. They draw attention to the elements of struggle that have often entered into the relationship between middle- and upper-class revivalists and working-class *shuyūkh*, and they attune us to the acts of reform, redefinition, and inscription that have frequently attended revivalist activities. In addition, they help situate some of the tropes of Andalusi musical revival within broader historical trends and sensibilities whose center of gravity often lay in France. Indeed, Andalusi revivalist discourse borrowed heavily from the movement to "restore" Gregorian chant in nineteenth-century France, and echoes of this connection circulate in the conversations of aficionados today. Likewise, the discourse of patrimony as it developed in the Maghrib and came to be applied to Andalusi music leaned heavily on post-1789 French models.[25] The patrimonial origin narrative about the conversion of a private, royal hoard of treasure into a public, national one was closely tied to the post-French Revolution attempt to reconfigure the collective relationship to the remnants of the past in an era of unprecedented turbulence.[26] Exported to colonial Algeria, the discourse of vandalism and salvage took on new meaning as the French seizure and destruction of Algerian cities occasioned the uncovering and in many cases creation of vast numbers of ruins.[27] Hence the metaphor of uncovering ruins and engaging in architectural restoration came to be ubiquitous in the North African musical milieu, with the *nūba* standing as a decayed edifice in demand of rescue and reconstruction. And alongside this archaeological and architectural metaphor came the image of hoarded musical knowledge as buried treasure, rumors of which multiplied in the decades following the French conquest of Algiers in 1830, when the last Ottoman Dey was said to have hidden his wealth.

There are many ways in which we can productively think of Andalusi musical revival as a classically nineteenth-century philological project that continues in the twenty-first century. But followed through, the problem of rupture raises thorny questions for thinking about Andalusi musical revival. It has become easy to treat phenomena such as this one as the internalization of a hegemonic colonial discourse. But what exactly is the relationship between revival and its before? Is it possible to locate a before? What if revival as a particular stance is older than we thought, and is only visible to us because of changes in the forms in which revivalists worked? As Isabelle Grangaud and M'hamed Oualdi have coyly asked, is everything colonial in the Maghrib?[28] What is our archive, and how was it made? These are also questions about what happens after revival: if we are still in revival, was revival "always" there? Is something like revival simply a part of what we mean by performance, as in Richard Schechner's notion of performance as "restored behavior"?[29] In other words, is there a way to think about revival as something other than a self-ratifying narrative without falling back on a naive understanding of the term?

In asking these questions, I am inspired both by Jean During's work on the urban art music tradition of Iran in *Quelque chose se passe: Le sens de la tradition dans l'Orient musical* and by Burt Feintuch's more recent reconsideration of musical revival.[30] For During, restoration and renewal constitute the temporality of a tradition that seems to share a great deal with North African Andalusi musical practice, all the way from the master-disciple relationship down to the very size of the repertoire.[31] The "something" that "passes" or "takes place" in the title of During's work captures a crucial element of the "meaning" or "direction" (*sens*) of the Iranian practice: transmission and loss are two sides of the same coin, just as revival is a recurring and often ambiguous part of a genealogical chain that points toward both the past and the future.[32] In similar fashion, Burt Feintuch writes of musical revival not so much as a question of transformation, transfer, or invention but as a discourse whose efficacy depends upon the "shape-shifting" nature of musical phenomena: "worlds of music" are both real, material practices and practices that "wax and wane," with revival standing as "one of the words we use as we talk about that waxing and waning, that shape-shifting."[33]

To say that revival may be the default mode for certain musical practices and an idiom for talking about their in-built evanescence is not to brush aside the questions of power that are particularly important for making sense of social practices (including musical ones) in colonial and postcolonial contexts. But During's and Feintuch's placement of rupture within the continuous micropractices of transmission, circulation, and perception that connect closely to Asad's notion of tradition, rather than primarily within the realm of large-scale sociopolitical processes, allows us to pay attention to elements of Andalusi musical practice that are otherwise difficult to notice.[34] I am not suggesting that these micropractices are divorced from discourse or politics, or that we should return to a starry-eyed, precritical, Orientalist-tinged essentialism. Rather, I am arguing that our understanding of processes of social construction will be much richer if we attend to the strands of continuity, alternate temporalities, and problems of periodization entwined in such processes. It may very well be that in today's amateur associations and Andalusi music festivals we encounter the remainders not only of modernist revival but also of a larger practice that embraces modernist revival in its stream.[35]

*

One of the things that attention to the micropractices of circulation permits us to notice is the Andalusi musical repertoire's status as an inalienable possession.[36] For Annette Weiner, whose work focused on the Trobriand Islands off Papua New Guinea, inalienable possessions are a category of objects intimately tied to persons and collectivities.[37] Their importance to the sense of individual and collective self can give rise to elaborate strategies for keeping them from the demands of exchange and thereby loss; these strategies include the exchanging of what she calls alienable objects, in an effort to engage in "keeping-while-giving." It is in light of these valuations and existential conditions that Weiner described inalienable possessions as heavy, dense objects, meaning that they circulate far more slowly (if at all) and to greater social effect than alienables such as commodity goods.

As Elizabeth Ferry has pointed out in her work on silver mining in Guanajuato, Mexico, the idiom of patrimony that is so ubiquitous in nation-state contexts is a way of talking about inalienable possession: something named as patrimonial belongs to a collective, is inherited from past generations, and should be transmitted intact to future generations.[38] Viewed in terms of the literature on nationalism, patrimony names objects and practices, either emblems of "the folk" or (as in this instance) paragons of exogenous high culture that act as focal points for the definition of the nation and for its defense against alleged threats to its integrity, whether that be oblivion, the foreign, individualism, crassness, or deracination. The wear and tear that the precious object faces, the problem of protection against loss, mirror the national self: both object and nation are valuable, unique, venerable, but also vulnerable and therefore in need of the solicitude of the state.[39]

A prominent part of the story traced in these pages is the attempt to delineate Andalusi music as a national and transnational patrimony, beginning in the colonial period and solidifying in the years after independence. As will be seen, the figure of the hoarding *shaykh* who carries repertoire to his grave was and is an important part of the discursive project of rescuing Andalusi music. For someone living in Aboura's day, it was an image that was already familiar from nineteenth-century political economy: a collective, national, modern, enlightened state hoard of wealth arrayed against the antimodern, individualistic, antisocial hoard of the miser.[40] Musically speaking, then, the project of securing a national patrimony would necessarily involve the externalization of the Andalusi repertoire, turning it out from the spaces in which it is said to be confined—whether those are the home of the patron, the commodity relations governing musical production and consumption, or the body of the *shaykh*. The printing press, staff notation, sound recording, and radio have been the primary media in this project that is often known as *tadwīn* (writing, inscription, documentation, codification, fixation, compilation).[41]

Alongside this concern for externalization come questions about the proper way to ensure repertorial continuity. These questions have carried many of the anxieties and fantasies about evanescence, continuity, and decay that Jonathan Sterne has suggested were central to the introduction of early sound recording.[42] And in many respects, the responses to these concerns have conformed to classic nineteenth-century positions regarding the merits of conservation versus restoration: for conservationists, the task is to maintain for posterity what was left in all its incompleteness, while restorationists advocate the creation of a perfected, rationalized whole that may never have fully existed in the first place.[43] These debates in turn hinge on the question of musical authority. After all, in order to pursue either a conservationist or restorationist track, one has to take stock of and evaluate the multiplicity of versions in circulation. And if one is to engage in a project of restoration, one also has to come up with a notion of what rationalized perfection sounds like.

All of these tropes and debates thread their way through the pages of this book. However, despite the resilience of these conversations and figures of speech, I am wary of treating this as a story of a discourse that simply arose, developed, and persisted. The hoarding *shaykh* is both a trope and a lived reality. Not only have devotees passionately complained to me of hoarding masters living in the present, but I have spent time with individuals who have told me that they are keeping repertoire permanently to themselves. And as the story of the Aboura collection suggests, projects of conserving inalienable possessions for posterity can themselves come to resemble the kinds of hoards that their creators decry.[44] What, then, is the relationship between the "antisocial" hoard and the "social" hoard? How does one turn into the other, or fail to do so? And what happens when we understand the hoarding *shaykh* as reality as well as trope—a reality that may in fact sometimes blend seamlessly into the revivalist project?

Thinking through these questions in the context of this book requires a few musical revisions to Weiner's thought. The beauty of Weiner's work on inalienable possessions lies partly in its attention to the material qualities of the various kinds of object she discusses—qualities that in her view make a difference for value creation and the objects' maintenance over time. But in the case of a musical practice, what is the equivalent of the non-equivalences of cloth, banana-leaf bundles, and stone adzes that Weiner wrote about?[45] When thinking about Andalusi music, it can be tempting to place this materiality in the various tools of the revivalist movement: transcriptions, sound recordings, printed books. Yet this technologist temptation misses the fact that any value these tools have rests upon a notion that musical knowledge is ultimately embodied in persons. In this sense, notions of materiality in the Andalusi instance are very much centered on the idea of people as media: vessels, texts, conduits.[46] Furthermore, musical materiality cannot be separated from the question of musical form, such as the *nūba* as a suite, its component parts, the combinations it demands and forbids, and the hierarchy of values that is embedded within it and its larger genre configuration. In this light, extending Weiner's thought musically requires attention to questions of temporality, form, and evaluation that in turn closely dovetail with questions of production.[47]

Students of music as a social practice have struggled with how best to conceive of the process of musical production.[48] For the nineteenth-century political economist Jean-Baptiste Say, who was writing well before the rise of sound recording, music was an example of what he called "immaterial products . . . values consumed at the moment of production."[49] But while Andalusi music practitioners of the past century and a half seem to have talked about the *nūba* repertoire as a rare, precious, endangered inheritance embodied in a handful of master musicians tied to one another in genealogical fashion, much of this repertoire has been conceived as being far from transient. If anything, it has been understood to perdure through these genealogical linkages, a product whose performance is consumed at the moment of production, but that, to the degree that it is replicable, exists beyond that immediate moment of display.[50] This replicability in turn relies upon the skill of the performer, as well as the judgment of the listener that what was performed was "a display of communicative competence"[51] that conforms to an established "orienting framework"—in other words, that it was an "apt performance" within the genre tradition.[52]

This temporally evanescent yet recurring formal aspect of the performed object has a number of ramifications. First, there is a social accumulation that takes place in this process of recurrence, as well as an opportunity for transformation, for making what Steven Feld calls "new lives, new circulations, permanence-through-transience."[53] Second, something that perdures beyond the moment of performance can also perish over the long term. This means that one of the values that may be realized in the regular performance of a piece or repertoire, particularly in the absence of sound recording and transcription, is its maintenance over time—in other words, the act of display is simultaneously an act of sheer realization of the sonic object. Finally, there is a transferability of the product that goes beyond the momentary production-consumption nexus, since, contra Say, the "immaterial product" may indeed be appropriated by the consumer, stored by the producer for future use, accumulated, and shared with a third party.[54] This is a reading of performance as a form of display or mode of circulation, with displays "function[ing] as tokens of value whose visual images [read 'sonic forms'] circulate in the public domain without the objects displayed being exchanged."[55] In the musical case, display or performance is crucial to the moment of production and consumption, even if the potential to be produced and consumed is not exhausted in that moment. In fact, in many respects it is the opposite of exhaustion, since display is ideally the basis for further display. Musical performance—which in this instance is a way to display without necessarily relinquishing control—is a variation on the challenge of "keeping-while-giving" that Weiner viewed as central to the maintenance of inalienable possessions.

In turn, Say helps us to connect Weiner to Marx by way of the hoard. The assembling and withholding of musical materials resembles the hoarding of money that Marx saw as a primary means for individuals in precapitalist and early capitalist societies to build up wealth.[56] Hoards of money stand "in constant tension with circulation" in that they constitute accumulations of things that have meaning only through circulation but that in being kept from circulation take on potent, latent value.[57] Marx's discussion of the hoard is particularly focused on money in the form of gold, which differs from corn, sheep, or slaves in that it is the embodiment of exchange-value, unsullied by use-value.[58] Musical repertoire in this sense dwells in the world of use-value. At the same time, musical repertoire is very much like money in that circulation is its modus vivendi, even as the forms remain lodged in its performers. In these sense, music has currency and is currency.

Together, Weiner, Say, and Marx allow us to identify several strategies, not necessarily mutually exclusive, at work in the Andalusi musical milieu for addressing the dilemma of keeping while giving. One is what Mourad Yelles describes as the official, state-centered "patrimonial ideology"[59]—the delineation and maintenance of a collective treasure that, like the bank notes and gold said to shore up the fiscal health of the nation, is to be guarded vigilantly by the state.[60] Viewed through the lens of nationalism, this can be seen as a metaphor for the notion of a collective spirit as inalienable possession. Musically speaking, this is a "keeping" that relies on the full but controlled "giving" of the repertoire to a national public, and it uses tools of diffusion and vulgarization to make the repertoire widely available to the public. This often involves a call for standardization in the face of the allegedly problematic proliferation of versions. Such a reaching toward unity recalls the valuation, particularly before the twentieth century, of Arabic verse (*naẓm*) over prose (*nathr*), in that *naẓm* is about the order or organization (likewise *naẓm*) that allows for words to travel as coherent text, while *nathr* evokes scattering or dispersion. On the side of *naẓm* stand inventories of song texts, archives, printing, the establishment of associations, and robust, clearly delineated genealogical chains—indeed, the entire project of documentation and inscription often known as *tadwīn*. But taken to its extreme, *naẓm* turns immobile, something "so weighty, ponderous and immovable" that "it finally comes to rest."[61]

Other strategies that we will encounter in the following chapters evince a range of orientations vis-à-vis the state but involve a different balance between keeping and giving. For the mass of Andalusi music practitioners, including both performers and nonperforming aficionados, the way the repertoire ought to go is a profoundly contested concept that is the subject of passionate debate.[62] If the stewards of Andalusi music are keepers of forms that then get instantiated in performance, the "keeping" lies in the assertion of a monopoly over the means and standards of performance and evaluation, whether that hinges on genealogical authentication, a notion of musical coherence, a sense of the beautiful, or attunement to listeners' musical desires over time. In other words, engaging in tradition in the sense of debate is itself a declaration of commitment to the attempt to maintain the patrimony. The "giving" happens in the realm of performance and in the realm of transmission of the standards of evaluation to the next generation of stewards.

There are also strategies that involve keeping a part of the repertoire buried. A teacher might transmit only a part of his knowledge; a singer might deform a melody or leave out a verse, or simply refuse to perform something. Implied in these moves is a holding back of some repertoire while allowing some other part of the repertoire to circulate. These are the moves that are closest to the notion of the lost and the trope of the hoarding *shaykh*, and that are also most given to an economic argument focusing on what they might do for a person's reputation as a possessor of rare knowledge.[63] Viewed over time, and particularly in relation to the narrative of loss, these kinds of keeping can add up to the sense that the past itself is what is kept from the present. Such an understanding can inflate the importance of individuals who have a link to that past. It can encourage a sense of struggle vis-à-vis the past, and it can accentuate the notion that there was an originary act of giving or transmission in the past that is precious.

Still another form of keeping-while-giving can be read into the shape of the repertoire itself. As will be explored in depth in chapter 3, Andalusi music as a genre is organized around a notion of a heavy center occupied by the *nūba* in turn surrounded by a periphery of lighter song forms in colloquial Maghribi Arabic. Together, these forms constitute what I refer to as

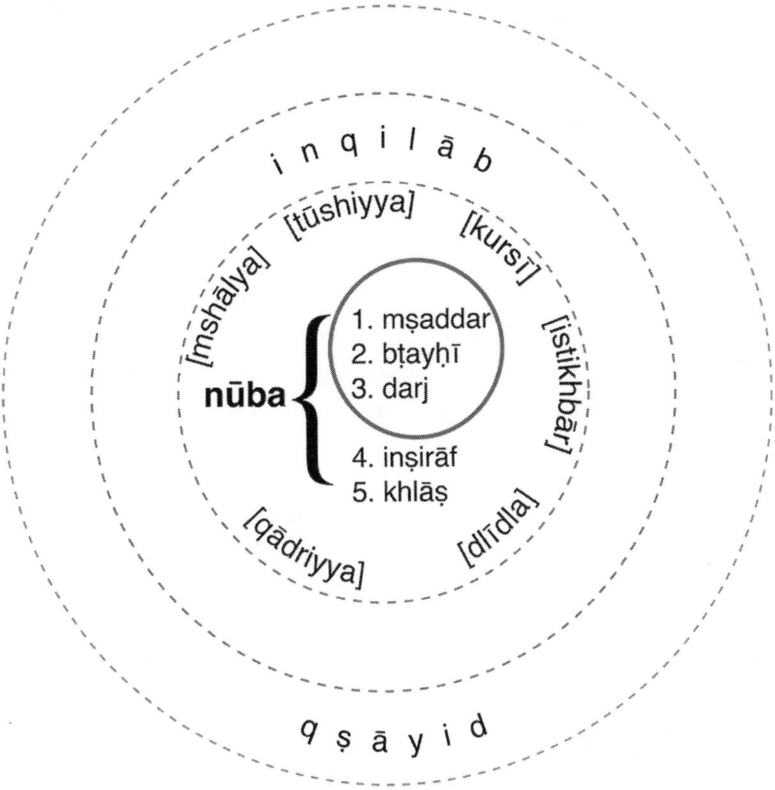

FIGURE 1. The Algiers-Tlemcen Andalusi music complex, with the *nūba* form at its center. Figure by Mallory Moran.

the Andalusi complex or the *nūba* complex (see fig. 1). In the case of the Algiers-Tlemcen tradition that is the focus of this book, some of the adjuncts to the *nūba* are known as *qṣāyid* (sing. *qṣīda*) or *malḥūn* (or more specifically by the name of two of their subcategories, *ḥawzī* and *ʿarūbī*). Furthermore, even within the *nūba*, the first three core movements are relatively slow and serious—they are characterized as *thaqīl* or heavy—while the final two are relatively faster, more dance-like, and characterized as *khafīf* or light. In addition, there are song forms that tilt toward classical Arabic (*inqilāb*) and song forms that tilt toward colloquial Arabic (*qādriyya* and *dlīdla*) that can be added into a *nūba* performance, alongside instrumental preludes (*tūshiyya*, preceded in the Tlemcen tradition by an unmetered section called *mshālya*), interludes (*kursī*), and unmetered vocal and instrumental improvisations (*istikhbār*). Many of these "light" forms and framing sections circulate beyond the circle of *nūba* specialists who are the focus of this book. Thus the notion of a heavy portion that is kept and a lighter portion that is given is immanent within the genre configuration itself.

I sketch these strategies here as ideal types that might orient the reader to the range of possibilities that enter into the patrimonial practice. As will be seen, Andalusi music practitioners engage in many different combinations and versions of these strategies, and contradictory approaches often exist in the same person. The notion of the lost emerges from within this variegated terrain, taking on many shades of meaning as a result, appearing and reappearing in changing forms, oscillating between extremes of concentration and dispersion. Nestled in the sense of genre, in the narrative of origins, and in musical models of personhood, the lost is, to borrow old metaphors and mix them, the buried treasure on which the ruin of the *nūba* stands.

*

This book is organized into two parts. Part 1, titled "The People of al-Andalus," is about Andalusi music as a social formation: a historically extended, self-aware, cosmopolitan, yet intensely localized collectivity that has made Andalusi music in Algeria and its borderlands, and in so doing has made itself. Over the course of three chapters, I try to convey the shape of this social formation taken as a whole, including the senses of place, temporality, personhood, and genre that have characterized it over a century and a half. Even though I talk about transformations in the practice over this period, my emphasis in part 1 is on tracing broad continuities. It starts out from the present in order to communicate a sense of the practice as a heterogeneous but coherent tradition.

The first chapter of part 1, "An Andalusi Archipelago," explores the senses of place and historicity that are central to Andalusi musical practice. For its practitioners, Andalusi music is an urban repertoire that comes in city-specific and regional versions. This sense of localness is closely tied to the fact that practitioners understand the repertoire to be embodied in genealogically embedded, place-specific musical authorities. At the same time, the sense of an archipelago of distinct urban musical centers is tied to the origin narrative of Andalusi music, which claims that the repertoire emerged from specific Iberian cities and was brought to the Maghrib through particular waves of Muslim and Jewish migrants. This chapter demonstrates the way in which this origin narrative is reproduced within contemporary conversations about place, genealogy, and genre, and how senses of place and historicity are central to practitioners' understanding of transmission, accumulation, authority, and collectivity.

Chapter 2, "The *Shaykh* and the *Mūlū*," maps the two central positions by which practitioners approach Andalusi music: the *shaykh* or musical master, and the *mūlūʿ* or devotee. The relationship of *shaykh* to *shaykh* over time is what makes Andalusi music an embodied genealogical practice. Yet when we start to think about the figure of the *shaykh* in relation to the figure of the *mūlūʿ*, several elements of ambiguity come to the fore regarding the flow of musical authority and the contours of musical community over time. By considering the relationship between *shaykh* and *mūlūʿ* alternately as one of patronage, pedagogy, and discipleship, this chapter teases out longstanding tropes regarding social class, genre boundaries, and transmission that are embedded within practitioners' notions of genealogical authority. As a key element of a long-lasting participant framework, the relationship of *shaykh* to *mūlūʿ* is central to the dialectic of rupture and continuity that helps animate the Andalusi musical project.

Place, historicity, and personhood are crucial to understanding what it means to speak musically of the people of al-Andalus. Ultimately, however, this social formation rests upon a sense of Andalusi music as a genre within a larger genre field. The final chapter of part 1, "Heavy and Light: Andalusi Music as Genre," thinks through Andalusi music as a complex of genres. At its center is the *nūba*, the five-movement instrumental and vocal suite organized by melodic mode that highlights the *muwashshaḥ*, a poetic form with roots in al-Andalus. At the margins of this genre complex lie the several other song forms, cited above, that listeners understand as lighter Maghribi derivatives of the Andalusi *nūba*. Thus this genre complex encapsulates much of the urban Arabic-language repertoire that Algerians and other Maghribis often describe as patrimonial, with the *nūba* standing as the heaviest, oldest, most authoritative center of the complex. While this genre complex stands in sharp contrast to a variety of generic "others," the *nūba* itself recapitulates aspects of this wider genre field within the sequence of its movements, which end with a shift toward rhythms marked as light, popular, and feminine. This chapter treats the sense of Andalusi musical genre as a durable framework for negotiating and maintaining a hierarchy of musical values.

While part 1 starts from the present in order to take in Andalusi musical practice as a tradition, part 2, titled "Revival," takes as its starting point the period of Mostefa Aboura and his peers, and traces the ways in which the innovations that revivalists introduced have since shaped and been absorbed by Andalusi musical practice in Algeria and its borderlands. Thus in some respects part 2 is oriented toward change over time, both at the turn of the century and since. In other respects, part 2 treats revival as a historically specific idiom that emerged from a particular configuration of the musical field but that then became an integral, longstanding part of the social formation, and not always on the terms of its authors. In this way, the exploration of revival delves into what came to be a key element of the social formation and asks what we should make of revival as a claim and project. Ultimately this section is not so much an injection of change into an earlier image of stability as it is a deeper exploration of a particular stance and of its ambiguous place within the broader practice.

The first chapter in part 2, titled "Ambiguous Revivals," considers the origins of the project of Andalusi musical revival in turn-of-the-century Algeria. An examination of coinciding efforts to publish and transcribe elements of the Andalusi genre complex shows revival to have emerged from vigorous dialogue between indigenous music aficionados and a range of government officials and settler intellectuals. These efforts made use of new print and recording technologies; at the same time, these technologies were central to revivalists' anxieties about the future of Andalusi music. This dynamic becomes particularly apparent through the story of the collaboration between the Algerian Jewish musician Edmond Yafil and the French journalist Jules Rouanet, and their subsequent dispute regarding their relationship with the late *shaykh* Mohamed Ben ʿAli Sfindja, the leading performer of the repertoire in turn-of-the-century Algiers. This microhistory demonstrates the degree to which the revival of musical patrimony was tied together with problems of embodiment, genealogical authority, and the powers and problems of new technologies.

Chapter 5, "Texts, Authority and Possession," examines the printed song text compilation, a central medium for Andalusi musical revivalists to materialize the repertoire and engage in the work of *tadwīn*. Because a major impetus for the creation of compilations is the desire to correct other compilations, *tadwīn* through print leads directly into a key question of musical authority: how does one authenticate a version of a song text, and of the repertoire more broadly? By tracing the intertwined trajectories of several printed compilations of *nūba* texts over the past hundred years, this chapter highlights diverse strategies for asserting textual and musical authority, as well as recurring dilemmas with regard to the limits of genealogical authority. These instances of textual building underline the fluid relationship among texts, persons, authors, and the concept of hoarding in the Andalusi musical domain, thereby demanding an understanding of printed compilations as metonymic parts of a wider symbolic field of musical inscription and storage.

Chapter 6, "The Associative Movement," explores the key institutional framework for the Andalusi musical revival: the amateur association. Created as a vehicle for modernist pedagogy and public performance at the beginning of the twentieth century, the association has been an important way for amateur music-lovers to exercise their passion for Andalusi music while differentiating themselves from the professional, often working-class *shaykh*. At the same time, associations have been closely tied to the *shuyūkh* through both the integration of professionals in their ranks and the production of new authorities within their framework. By tracing the development of the associative movement since the early twentieth century, including the notorious fractiousness of associations, this chapter argues that similarly to printed texts, associations need to be understood as a technology of *tadwīn* that tends to reproduce and even embody the genealogical ethos and the mystique of the hoard alongside its dominant discourse of science.

The final chapter of part 2, "The Politics of Patrimony," considers the relationship of musicians, aficionados, the state, and the concept of patrimony in Andalusi musical practice in the modern period. While the state has been closely involved in Andalusi musical revival since the beginning of the twentieth century, revival has rarely been a top-down project. Instead, state officials and agencies have generally been drawn into musical revival through the inroads made by aficionados into the state orbit, in some cases through their creation of para-state archives and institutions. This chapter examines several fraught instances of state interaction with non-state musical actors in the colonial and postcolonial periods to argue that the concept of Andalusi musical patrimony constitutes a special kind of subject: impassive yet powerful, simultaneously national and profoundly other, continually shifting its locus between the centers of power and its margins.

PART ONE

The People of al-Andalus

Prologue: An *Istikhbār*

The musicians sitting under the lights of the outdoor stage have hit upon a pause. Among the percussionists, the goblet-shaped *darbūka* has stopped its galloping, the tambourine, the *ṭār*, has dropped into its handler's lap. The audience of a few hundred people, seated on folding chairs and separated from the stage by a small fountain and the sound crew and photographers, is attentive. A clearing has been reached, an open space in the middle of density, a pavilion of stasis amid movement.

The repose is mixed with suspense. A few of the violinists, their instruments perched on a knee, draw forth a quiet drone. An *'ūd* player gently, persistently provokes a low string on the instrument's pear-shaped body. Out from this backdrop, a violist pulls forth a spare, unmetered melody from the instrument that resembles a small double of his upright posture. His gaze rests on the middle distance in serious concentration. The bow weaves its way through the austere progression, appearing to waver in space at the quiet height of the tension. When he closes the statement, the focus turns to the young woman sitting in the front arc of musicians. A *kuwītra*, like a smaller, elongated, more delicate *'ūd*, rests in her arms. She leans slightly forward so that her lips are at the microphone. Her forehead furrows into an expression of intense pathos. Slowly, starting on a fifth and meandering her way toward tonal home, she intones, in elevated, classical Arabic:

Yā ahla andalusin li-llāhi darrukum
O people of al-Andalus! How God did shower you . . .

A ripple of recognition runs through the crowd, as if she has addressed them directly or given voice to a deep, half-forgotten, collective desire. A mandolin traces the contour of the melody the singer just offered. The suspense persists, even though most everyone knows what will come next. The singer leans forward again, and repeats,

O people of al-Andalus!

A murmur from the instruments.

How God did shower you . . .

She takes her time. A few of the instrumentalists follow along the path she has marked, resuming their drone once they have caught up with her. The list builds on itself, one at a time:

. . . mā'un wa-ḍillun wa-ashjārun wa-anhārun
. . . with water . . . and shade . . . and trees . . . and rivers!

She falls silent. Affirmative murmurs rise from the audience—admiration, satisfaction, perhaps even relief. An *'ūd* elaborates on the melody, quietly reaching higher than did the singer, the long pick adding its distinctive click to the strings' liquid tones, while the other instruments lay down their soft bed of sound and offer gentle responses to the soloist's turns of phrase. When the *'ūd*-player has finished his exploration and the singer begins again, the stage is set for the height of intensity. She sets out from the top of her range:

The Garden of Paradise is nowhere . . .

Again, the instrumentalists' murmured response to her call. And again she sets out from the top:

The Garden of Paradise is nowhere if not in your land.

An instrumental echo. Then, resolving the melody back to home:

Given the choice, I would have chosen it myself.

A banjo takes its turn, summarizing the two lines the singer has just sung. Like the other instruments, it is in no hurry; it calls the listener in rather than stepping out with a grand gesture. Finally:

After it, you would not be afraid . . .

An echo.

After it, you would not be afraid to enter Hell—

A murmur from the instruments.

After Paradise—
After Paradise, the fire does no harm.

Abruptly riding an open syllable, she sets off in a new direction, an adjacent set of colors. The instrumentalists seem ready to follow. But no sooner has she has marked out this alternate sonic space than she returns, her voice descending the well-worn spiral staircase with a flourish:

After Paradise, the fire does no harm.

More murmurs of approval, even applause here and there. The percussionists are poised, the instruments back in position. When the full ensemble takes launch again, the music seems triumphant, perhaps even joyful. The singer has returned to her *kuwītra* and blended back into the group. The musicians and listeners have come out from the clearing.

*

This moment of high formal drama—called an *istikhbār*, literally an inquiry into the character of a melodic mode—took place in the Moroccan border city of Oujda in the summer of 2006 during the performance of a *nūba* in the mode *zīdān*. Within the formal, metered structure of the *nūba*, the *istikhbār* is a contrasting moment of truth, when a singer might momentarily break free from the group to display her or his musical prowess while giving the percussionists a well-deserved rest. To an outsider it may sound like a free, meandering improvisation tossed back and forth between vocalist and instrumentalists, intricately embellished with spontaneous ornaments and occasionally punctuated by bursts of passion. But although a good performance is distinctive and fresh, the *istikhbār* in the context of a *nūba* is highly formalized with regard to many elements: the relationship between textual and melodic phrasing, the alternation of instrument and voice, the calculus of repetition, elaboration, and forward movement, the melodic motifs that should be drawn upon for a given mode at specific junctures, and more. As two veteran musicians explained in the context of another *istikhbār* rehearsal in which I participated six years later, one is "imprisoned," required to stay "on the tracks." It is this treacherous topography and its soloistic nature that make the *istikhbār* the keep of advanced performers, and an object of intense rehearsal and refinement behind the scenes. Likewise, it is the experienced, assiduous listener—the *connaisseur*, literally "one who knows," the *mélomane*, the *mūlūʿ*, the aficionado—who grasps what makes a good *istikhbār*.

Not all the groups that performed in this state-sponsored festival of *nūba* performances in the tradition of Tlemcen and Algiers—a genre that is often known in the Moroccan-Algerian border region as *gharnāṭī* or Granadan music—met the standards of the *mélomanes*. When I was not playing violin in the ensembles on the stage, I spent much of my time amidst a group of older men sitting nearby, close to the sound crew. During a performance by a group that played a harmonized *nūba* from scores perched on music stands, one seasoned aficionado leaned over to say to me, "This is not our *gharnāṭī*, the one that we know." Since I was onstage for the *nūba* that featured the *istikhbār* on the words "O people of al-Andalus," I did not know what this aficionado made of our performance: although we had played in the usual semi-unison, heterophonic style, without reference to a notated score, the performance had been an experimental fusion with an ensemble from Tetuan. But even if this attempt to erect a temporary bridge to a formally contrasting Maghribi-Andalusi musical practice teetered between fidelity and dangerous innovation, I like to think that in the *istikhbār*, the *mélomanes* could discern "their *gharnāṭī*": the singer confidently followed the basic framework without ever seeming to imitate anyone in particular. What's more, she hit the right note of restrained and sorrowful passion.

The choice of text, too, was pleasing, one of the best loved within the repertoire, an evocation of the abundance and ease associated with the lost paradise. Not only did these particular lines invoke al-Andalus, but they happened to originate there as well, from the pen of Ibn Khafāja, a famed poet born in the eleventh century near Valencia. It is one of a handful of canonical texts performed in the *nūba* tradition that has a known author (or, for that matter, that mentions al-Andalus), yet few performers or listeners are aware that Ibn Khafāja composed these lines. Instead, for most people, no doubt including the bulk of the festival audience and the musicians, the words, like the unwritten, authorless melodies to which they are sung, are examples of *turāth* or *patrimoine*—heritage, patrimony, a collective inheritance.[1]

For those who mobilize this powerfully resonant concept in their speech, patrimony hardly requires an explanation. In Algeria, Tunisia, and Morocco, *patrimoine* and *turāth* are ubiquitous terms, used to talk about architecture, crafts, and literature, among other things, and they are especially prominent in Andalusi musical circles, including at festivals such as this one.[2] The master of ceremonies repeatedly reminded the audience to guard this musical patrimony from loss, and such admonitions lurked backstage as well, including in the rehearsals during which the soloist prepared her *istikhbār*. During a run-through in the days before the festival, the head of the ensemble had interrupted the singer, worrying that she was embellishing too much and in the process straying too far from the basic form. "You need to guard the *aṣāla* [the authenticity or originality of it]," he counseled all of us by way of the singer. "This is *turāth*, and with *turāth* you can't all go off and do your own thing. If I did my thing and you yours and him his, then it would go away, it couldn't be passed on. It's gotten here because people conserved it as it was, and now we need to do the same." And with that, he instructed the singer to begin again.

With this in mind, we might hear the words of the *istikhbār* not only as an invocation and relic of a storied civilizational past but also as a paean to the concept of patrimony itself: something of great value given in the distant past and fragmentarily reconstituted in the present through the act of performed recollection. But in the process of invoking the image of an old gift, practitioners also invoke the intervening links in the chain—the people and places that are nearer at hand. In the instance of this particular performance, with its partial loyalty to the form and aesthetic of Algiers and Tlemcen, the musicians pointed east, toward the other side of the border, as well as westward toward Tetuan. The *mélomanes* seated in the audience in their turn could compare what they heard to what they knew from their own experience in the local associations, their regular tuning-in to the radio and old recordings, and the time they had passed in town during the soirées of the departed *shuyūkh* of their younger years. Individual *shuyūkh* were present in other ways as well. The association to which the soloist belonged is named in memory of Cheikh Salah, a renowned performer of Andalusi music in Oujda, Tlemcen, and Oran during the middle decades of the twentieth century, and father to the association's president and musical director. And the biography of Cheikh Salah in turn could point to Cheikh Larbi Bensari of Tlemcen, the paragon of Andalusi music in the tradition of that city and of the region as a whole.

Thus for those in the know, the *istikhbār* could be heard as emerging from and speaking to a network of interconnected places, times, and concepts: al-Andalus, Maghribi cities, the medieval past, the living memory of young and old, and the capacious, high-prestige category of patrimony. We might even go so far as to suggest that "the people of al-Andalus" were not only past but included as well the *mélomanes* themselves, these local guardians of taste sitting in a modest municipal park, with its small fountain, clusters of date palms and cypress tress, and the illuminated outer walls of the old city in whose presence the evening's performances unfolded.

The following three chapters attempt to elaborate this interpretation of "the people of al-Andalus" as a far-flung, cumulative, but finite network of passionate listeners and performers—one that embraces a chain of Algerian and Moroccan cities, linked together through devotion to a common genre configuration that is rooted in Algiers and Tlemcen and that includes the memory of earlier generations of practitioners. By drawing on contemporary practice and the threads of communal memory that are its fiber, these chapters work through questions of place, people, and genre. How exactly does this chain of places and generations work? What is its geographic and temporal shape and texture? What is being transmitted, across place and across time? What kinds of people make Andalusi music? And what kinds of people does Andalusi music make?

1

An Andalusi Archipelago

In 1934, in the Moroccan city of Tetuan, a collection of Arabic poems appeared under the title *Anthologie d'auteurs arabes / Kitāb nafḥ al-azhār* (Anthology of Arab Authors / The Book of the Scent of Flowers).[1] Although printed in the capital of the Spanish Protectorate in northern Morocco, home to its own longstanding Andalusi musical tradition, the book was decidedly a product of Algeria and specifically of the far western city of Tlemcen. Gathering poems from Tlemcen's *nūba* repertoire as well as Moroccan poems known in Algeria as *gharbī* or "western," its editors were two young Tlemcanis from well-off families, Abderrahmane Sekkal and Mohamed Bekhoucha, the former a leading amateur performer then living in his native city, the latter a professor of Arabic at the Lycée Lyautey in Casablanca. In turn, the audience they invoked was comprised of their fellow Tlemcanis. Writing just four years after the centenary of the French invasion of Algeria, they suggested that

> after a century of French domination, thanks to the influence, direct or indirect, exercised by the médersas [government-run Arabic-language schools], high schools, colleges, discs, and radio, people's spirits have turned toward the Arabic language and its unsuspected treasure of music and poetry. We have often heard in the streets of Tlemcen children singing "The Dewdrop," "The Setting Sun," "Morning," and other pieces of real artistic value. An ardent desire to revive the glorious past of the Muslims appears to have been born from this influence, and we have seen fit to respond by grouping in this collection Andalusi poems, in an Andalusi idiom, together with their child: Maghribi poems in a Maghribi idiom.

Closely echoing other such printed collections of *nūba* poetry, they stated that their "only aim was to save an entire literature from total loss."[2]

There was another way in which *Nafḥ al-azhār* was deeply Tlemcani. In both the French and Arabic versions of the introduction, the compilers acknowledge their "old friend," the Tlemcani musician Moulay Djellali Ziani as the most immediate source for the poems. In turn, this great musician learned these poems from his teacher Moulay Mounaouar Benatar (also known as Bin ʿAttū), a renowned performer who split his time between Fes and Tlemcen, where he helped to "revive" the *gharbī* repertoire. It was these two masters, one the teacher of the other, who served as "the intermediaries" for the collected poems.[3] The link of these poems to the past of Tlemcen by way of particular Tlemcanis, and in turn the link of Tlemcen to al-Andalus by way of this embodied art, is telescoped and elaborated in a passage from the Arabic introduction:

> Tlemcen—may God guard it—was of the highest rank in this wondrous Granadan art, and there was no place like it anywhere in the world since the existence of al-Andalus. There is nothing surprising about this, because her people were accomplished in poetry and the serious pursuit of learning. The age looked kindly upon them in every respect, and they lived the good life, so that they were able to attain their desires, including complete mastery of the practice of this musical science, until it was as if Tlemcen were itself part of the islands of al-Andalus. Its inhabitants willingly put themselves at the service of belles-lettres, refined love, and intense musical devotion [*wullāʿa*] to the point that both love and understanding suffused their spirits. Men passed on from their ranks who continue to be widely remembered and praised (may exalted God have mercy on them). The first of them is Shaykh al-Ḥājj Ḥammādī al-Baghdālī, who died in Tlemcen [1867] and was buried there. Second after him is Shaykh al-Munawwar Bin ʿAttū, who died in Fes and was buried there [1899]. Third is Shaykh Muḥammad Bin Shaʿbān, known as Būḍalfa [Boudelfa], who is buried in Tlemcen [1914]. Their student is the revered and distinguished musician Mūlāy al-Jilānī al-Zayyāni [Moulay Ziani], who today is still alive at about eighty years of age. He has played a part in writing the biographies of these *shuyūkh*, all of whom he recalls as very eminent, and until today a class of people exists who devote themselves to musical knowledge and performance.[4]

Though not particularly dramatic on first reading, this passage condenses a great deal about Andalusi music considered as a social practice. Some of it concerns the connection between cosmology, genealogy, and genre, what Mikhail Bakhtin might have called the chronotope (the time-space) of Andalusi music: it highlights North African places and their connection to al-Andalus, vividly demonstrates the logic and ethos of genealogical authority, and hints at the intertwining of "Andalusi" music with other musical forms marked as "Maghribi."[5] The passage also raises questions of historical context: its appearance in a collection of *nūba* poetry printed at the high watermark of European colonial rule in the Maghrib intimates the nesting of Andalusi musical connoisseurship within a project of musical reform that was itself nested within wider sociopolitical currents, including the ones that passed through the government-run Arabic colleges known as the *médersas*. Finally, the passage hints at the temporal and geographic reach and texture of the collectivity that forms itself around Andalusi music: Bekhoucha and Sekkal were situating themselves within generations of musical practice stretching outward from Tlemcen, pointing westward to Fes and northward and backward to medieval Granada. Implied in their list is a blurring of temporal hierarchy with qualitative hierarchy: the best, they seem to be saying, comes first, or rather, the good of the last derives from the good of the first. In turn, their retrospective glance came to be taken up in later retrospections, so that eighty years later I found tattered copies of *Nafḥ al-azhār* in the archives of devotees who traced their own genealogies through some of the same people cited in the above passage, and even through Sekkal himself.

This passage, then, is a fragment within a still living tradition, and this chapter begins to draw a map of this tradition.[6] In doing so, it introduces a network of sites that for Andalusi music practitioners are linked by people, history, narrative, genealogy, movement, musical form, and affect. In orienting the reader to these linkages—to what we might call the spatial poetics of Andalusi music—this chapter aims to address several questions. How is it that Andalusi music is both intensely local and part of a transnational network of cities? How does its status as an import from al-Andalus make it deeply Maghribi? And what is the relationship between musical genealogies, contemporary musical practice, and this temporal, geographic, and narratival map? The following pages approach these questions first by considering the relationship among mobile people, immobile place, and the notion of musical treasures. It then turns toward a discussion of the palimpsestic relationship between the Maghrib and al-Andalus—in other words, the layering of al-Andalus onto the map of North Africa. In the final section, I consider the way in which this palimpsest is reinscribed and in many respects produced in everyday musical practice.

A Treasure Map

Contemporary scholars draw on a panoply of terms to talk about musical collectives, ranging from communities to scenes to publics and well beyond.[7] While Bekhoucha and Sekkal were working with a more limited palette, it was one that held great expressive powers for their readers. Their primary medium was place: Tlemcen. Yet the power of their home city as a locus of musical prestige rested on their evocation of a link to al-Andalus, and specifically to the city of Granada, the last bastion of Muslim sovereignty in the Iberian peninsula. In their text, the link is two-sided, in that Granada is presented as the immediate source for the *nūba* tradition of Tlemcen and other cities (hence the term *gharnāṭī* or Granadan), and Tlemcen is described as having lived up to its music's fabled roots. In this way, the Andalusi musical imaginary upon which they draw and which, in the process, they reproduce places Tlemcen and its parallel North African cities within a geographic and temporal framework that includes al-Andalus as a potent, storied, yet nearly palpable point of origin.

But let us look more closely at the claim in *Nafḥ al-azhār* that "it was as if Tlemcen were itself part of the islands of al-Andalus." Instead of the usual *jazīrat al-andalus*, "the peninsula [literally the island] of al-Andalus," it reads *jazā'ir al-andalus*, "the islands of al-Andalus."[8] *Al-jazā'ir*, the islands, is also the Arabic name for Algeria (even if the etymology is disputed), so that another way of reading this felicitous slip is as "the Algeria of al-Andalus." We will shortly see that this is not the only way to read the passage. But for now, such verbal play suggests how Andalusi music could stand as a potent signifier of Algeria as a whole and serve as a pathway for communion with al-Andalus and its spirit. It also suggests a useful conceptual term for conceiving the site of this study, a site that is both multiple and singular in the sense that its component localities can be imagined as constituting one large, internally differentiated, noncontiguous territory. There is no established insider term for this terrain, even if it is intimated on those fairly rare occasions when people speak of *la musique andalouse* or *al-mūsīqā al-andalusiyya*, "Andalusi music" in its broadest sense. Riffing on the slip between island and islands, let us call this site the Andalusi archipelago.

It is worthwhile to briefly think about this archipelago's geological age. According to what Carl Davila terms "the standard narrative," it began in al-Andalus, fashioned in large part by the legendary ninth-century Baghdadi musical migrant and courtier known as Ziryāb, and was transplanted to the Maghrib whole-cloth by Andalusis after 1492.[9] Viewed through a more scholarly lens, this narrative poses some problems. For Mahmoud Guettat, the musical connection of al-Andalus to the Maghrib long predated 1492 thanks to the social and political melding of these lands over many centuries.[10] A close reading of the documentary evidence also raises some doubts about our ability to connect various swathes of contemporary practice to medieval al-Andalus. Although the musical term *nūba*, for example, shows up in several medieval sources, it is difficult to clearly attach it to its contemporary meaning in the Andalusi musical milieu, and we can find several other meanings for it in the modern period, including melody and even the military fanfare in the Ottoman Algerian court.[11] The earliest manuscript that uses some of the terminological and organizational elements of the *nūba* as known in the modern Maghribi traditions likely dates to the beginning of the sixteenth century and was probably compiled in the region of Tlemcen.[12] Other than this exciting rediscovery, however, as well as an early eighteenth-century description of an urban musical genre in Algiers that strongly resembles the *nūba* and eighteenth-century Moroccan manuscript collections, our knowledge of the repertoire dates to the nineteenth century.[13] It is particularly in the second half of the nineteenth century that we begin to find descriptions of the *nūba* repertoire in the works of both European and Maghribi writers, and it is also at this time that we see the fairly widespread production of *nūba* songbooks that follow the basic modal and movement organization that the repertoire takes today.[14] At the very least, something formally close to the modern *nūba* traditions has existed in Morocco, Algeria, and Tunisia since the eighteenth century, with an apparently sharp increase in the production of songbook compilations in the nineteenth century.

Using the archipelago metaphor to talk about the modern configuration of Andalusi musical places is attractive in a number of ways. The image of an island conveys the sense of local coherence and distinctiveness that is often associated with individual cities where Andalusi music is practiced: in what may at first seem paradoxical, Andalusi music is always from a specific North African locale. Furthermore, not all the islands are the same size, and there are groupings within the archipelago itself, so that Constantine serves as a sort of Andalusi musical capital for eastern Algeria for much of the twentieth century, Tlemcen for western Algeria and eastern Morocco, and Algiers for central Algeria as well as for Mostaganem and Béjaïa. In many cases there are distinct names for the music characteristic of these somewhat smaller configurations: *mā'lūf* is often used for the *nūba* tradition of Tunisia and eastern Algeria, *āla* is generally reserved for the dominant *nūba* tradition of Morocco, *gharnāṭī* is today frequently used for western Algeria and its Moroccan offshoots, and *ṣanʿa* is used for Algiers as well as for Tlemcen, even while the Algiers and Tlemcen traditions are largely compatible (fig. 2).[15] In order to further specify, one can speak of the *mā'lūf* of Testour versus the *mā'lūf* of Annaba, the *ṣanʿa* of Mostaganem versus the *ṣanʿa* of Blida, or the *āla* of Fes versus the *āla* of Tangier.[16] In addition, the term *andalusī*, *andalous*, *andalou*, or *andalus*, all translatable as simply Andalusi, can be used to refer to both the pan-Maghribi musical form as a whole and to its local instantiations.

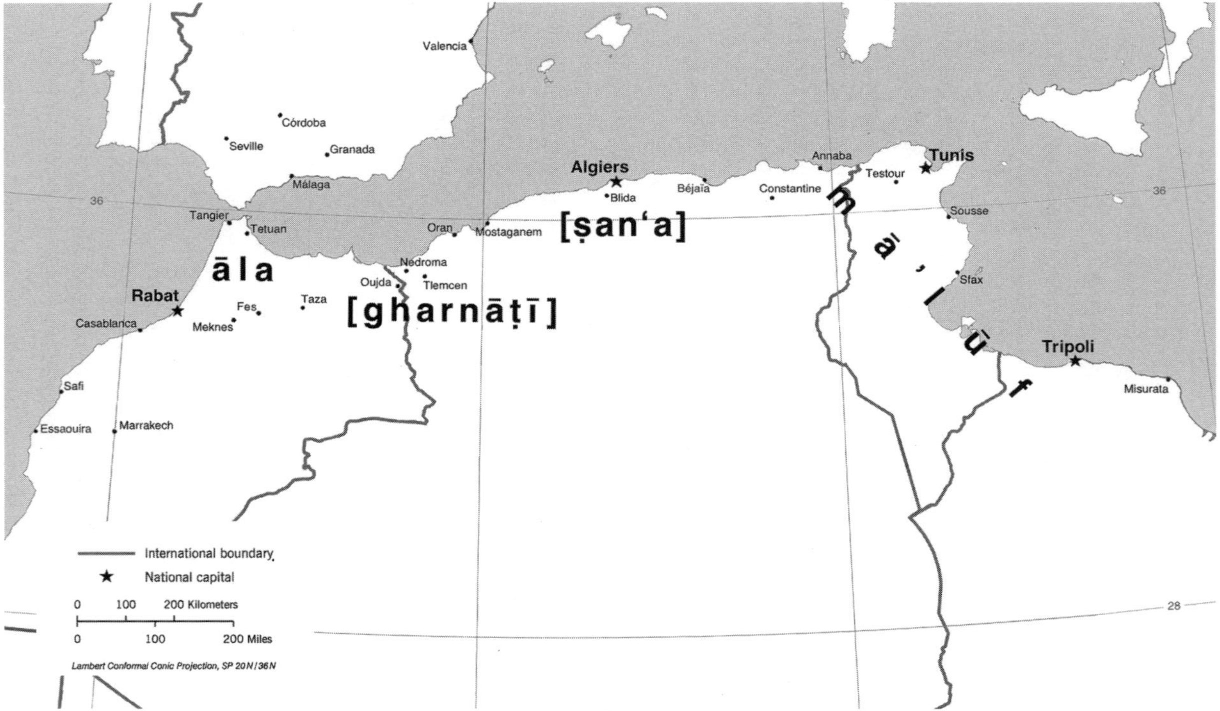

FIGURE 2. The Maghribi-Andalusi genre map. The term *ṣan'a* is common in western Algeria and in Oujda, alongside *gharnāṭī*. All of the localized terms may on occasion be replaced by the terms that mean Andalusi music (*andalou, andalous, andalusī, andalus, al-ṭarab al-andalusī, al-mūsīqā al-andalusiyya, la musique andalouse*). Map by Mallory Moran.

Islands are also necessarily sharply divided from the water around them, and to speak of Andalusi music is to speak of a quintessentially urban music that is mainly discontinuous from its non-urban surroundings. As will be explored further in chapter 3, Andalusi music is a genre complex whose edges invoke the urban hinterland, particularly through the colloquial Maghribi song repertoire sometimes known as *ḥawzī*, which etymologically points to the *ḥawz* or outskirts of a city.[17] But at the center of the genre complex, which is to say with regard to the *nūba*, we are talking about an urban, urbane music—*une musique savante*, a "learned music" that acts as the classical pinnacle for what in French is called *la musique citadine*, urban music. Ideologically speaking, such urban music stands in maximal contrast to the musical and more broadly social space of the countryside—a space that in predominantly Berber-speaking regions often stands in linguistic contrast to the urban center as well.[18] And not just any city will do: the places most closely associated with Andalusi music are also associated with the Arab-Islamic conception of *ḥaḍāra* or civilization, or else are home to communities closely connected to those old centers of learning, trade, government, and urbanity. Hence for Tlemcen, Oujda, Nedroma, and Oran but not Maghnia or Berkane; for Algiers, Blida and Mostaganem but not Bouira; for Constantine, Annaba but not Souk Ahras; for Fes, Meknes but not Sefrou.[19]

Furthermore, the urbanness that Andalusi music invokes is not the urbanness of the present. Instead, it recalls the urbanness of the era before massive rural-to-urban migration, when only a very small percentage of Maghribis lived in urban centers. Thus for many practitioners I have encountered, Andalusi music is properly the preserve of "old families," "noble families," or "pure families," whose roots reach back to a time before the cities were inundated with people from the countryside and hence became "mixed." For some aficionados who are able to lay claim to old urban roots, such a pedigree is a weapon in the act of self-differentiation, and it can even be turned on fellow practitioners, as when devotees quietly use their rivals' purported rural roots (and the lack of erudition and respect that such roots allegedly entail) to criticize their musical efforts. Similarly, I know practitioners who reserve their highest praise for those amateur associations that at one time were known for their refusal to admit any members from outside the local elite. But for those who do not lay claim to such roots, there are alternative ways to invoke urbanity. For Nour-Eddine Saoudi, for example, a leading figure in the Algiers scene whose family originally came from the southeastern oases, *citadinité* or urbanness is something that can be taken on by choice and is not the keep of particular families. And in the associative realm, many people credit the growth of populist, non-elitist amateur associations, particularly in the late

1970s and the 1980s, with improving the level of pedagogy and performance in a variety of cities. There is, then, a tension between a notion of *citadinité* in the blood and *citadinité* as a sensibility that can be cultivated. The value of *citadinité*, however—the marriage of urbanism and sophistication—is not up for dispute.

Musically speaking, the city-islands that make up the broad Maghribi archipelago are linked. Thus certain modes, instruments, founding myths, musical-poetic forms (in other words, the *muwashshaḥ*), texts, forms of subjectivity, terms of art, and organizing frameworks (namely a *nūba* as a modally defined compound form) are common denominators throughout the archipelago. But the flip side of this connectedness is that, to varying degrees, the constituent cities contrast with one another with regard to some of these same elements. Several of these contrasts work at the level of region, so that the bulk of Moroccan *nūba* practices are close enough to carry the common name of *āla*, the bulk of the Tunisian, Libyan, and eastern Algerian practices are close enough to be mutually recognizable as *mā'lūf*, and the central and western Algerian practices to be known as either *ṣan'a* or *gharnāṭī*. This sense of a broad, tripartite regional coherence and interregional contrast comes down to questions of the terminological and rhythmic identity of the *nūba*'s core movements, the poems themselves and their melodies, the content and naming of the melodic modes, and questions of instrumentation and performance style. Thus most of the song texts that *mā'lūf* practitioners draw upon are not the same as the song texts that *āla* practitioners draw upon. What is arguably a single mode can be known by different names, as in the case of the Algerian *zidān* and the *ḥijāz kabīr* of Moroccan *āla* practitioners. Or a term may be used for very different things, as in the case of the *mṣaddar*, which is a vocal and instrumental movement in the Algerian *nūba* but is a nonvocal instrumental overture in the *nūba* of Tunisian *mā'lūf*.[20]

This grouping of the archipelago into three broad regions has come to be a sort of official codification of Maghribi-Andalusi music, but it is likely at least a partial result of the long-term localization of musical practice, the sort of "history of recurrent interactions" that Humberto Maturana and Francisco Varela term "structural coupling."[21] In turn, such localization likely reinforced itself, in that it delineated a "congruent" framework for continued musical interaction and development. Thus, logically speaking, for an innovation in the performance of a particular poem to spread to an alternate location, that poem must already be part of the performance practice of this alternate location. In this sense, the Algiers-Tlemcen section of the archipelago, including their satellite cities, hold together as a unit in that they constitute a formal space within which a repertoire, broadly conceived, can circulate.[22] The flip side of this sense of regions within the archipelago is that they are in turn internally differentiated by city or sub-region. Thus in Moroccan *āla* practice, Fes and Tetuan are conceived as two distinct schools of performance, while a similar contrast holds in Algeria between Tlemcen and Algiers. These are insider contrasts, in that in gross morphological terms the *nūba* of Tlemcen is the same as that of Algiers, and that of Fes is the same as that of Tetuan. Practitioners generally speak of these differences as coming down to the existence of alternate versions, interpretations of rhythmic cycles, styles, placements of song texts within the *nūba*, understandings of modal classification, and senses of the song text canon.

Such differentiations between neighboring musical localities can be the stuff of intense loyalty, including in the Algiers-Tlemcen section of the archipelago that is our focus here. While mobile connoisseurs have long commented on the differences in performance practice between these two cities in fairly dispassionate terms, many performers and aficionados express a strong attachment to one of the twin capitals.[23] Interestingly enough, there is broad agreement about the qualities that are said to musically differentiate the two cities—the differences in opinion tend to hinge on which qualities are desirable or deserving of support.[24] For many practitioners, Algiers is new, light, fast, virtuosic, modern, flashy, derivative of Tlemcen (and secondarily of Constantine), influenced by Ottoman music, rhythmically somewhat simplified, relatively incomplete with regard to the full *nūba* structure, yet rich in sung repertoire. Tlemcen, on the other hand, is characterized as old, authentic, slow, heavy, serious, conservative, austere, even soporific, workmanlike, un-virtuosic, self-sufficient, richly detailed with regard to rhythm, relatively complete with regard to *nūba* structure, yet paradoxically more limited in terms of sung repertoire.[25] Of course, these are not neutral descriptions, but in many ways are prescriptions for how "Algiers" and "Tlemcen" ought to sound—in other words, they are discursive constructions of musical place.

The attribution of a certain authenticity to a geographically remote city such as Tlemcen has a counterpart in the way in which practitioners talk about secondary cities within the archipelago. In some cases, there is the sense that at one time there was a distinctiveness that has since been lost to the influence of a dominant city: for example, *āla* practitioners in Tangier speak of a specifically Tangier school of performance that has since been covered over through the influence of Tetuan, and enthusiasts in Oujda lament the loss of the locally distinctive repertoire to the influence of recordings and Radio Algiers.[26] Alternatively, practitioners from one of the central places sometimes speak of practitioners in peripheral areas as retaining knowledge that has been lost in the center, as claim certain Tlemcanis who visit Oujda, thereby mirroring the Algerois ascription of authenticity to "remote" Tlemcen. Alongside this, and in some respects in tension with it, is the notion that the secondary cities carry a lighter genre valence that tilts away from the *nūba* core. Thus Mostaganem follows the *nūba* practice of Algiers but is known for its specialists in *ḥawzī*, and a similar pattern holds for Annaba vis-à-vis Constantine and Oujda vis-à-vis Tlemcen. In other words, the center of the genre complex, with its emphasis on classical Arabic and heaviness, is weighted in central places, while the colloquializing, lighter edges of the genre complex subsist in their periphery.

There is no doubt that the sense of difference between Algiers and Tlemcen, and in turn between these and other cities, is intensified through various political conditions and forms of contact. In the case of Oujda, the closing of the frontier with Tlemcen and the power of Radio Algiers led to a generational shift in loyalty from Tlemcen to the Algerian capital. And as the frequency and intensity of musical interactions have increased with the advent of radio, recordings, the internet, festivals, musical touring, and quicker transportation, the occasions to note, construct, and reinforce differences have multiplied. In particular, the bringing together of distinct traditions within a single national framework raises questions of distinction and melding. On the one hand, ensembles from Constantine have been known to adjust the format of the *nūba* to approximate the practice of Algiers and Tlemcen when performing outside their home city. On the other hand, the national space can give rise to a desire to demarcate and protect the sense of local distinctiveness. The creation of compilations of *nūba* texts, for example, necessarily leads to comparison and the resulting delineation of which texts are specific to which regional tradition. And the creation of a national Andalusi music orchestra in Algiers in the early 2000s has given rise to dissension among observers (and even some orchestra members) regarding the wisdom of bringing together the traditions of Constantine, Algiers, and Tlemcen in a single ensemble.

The tensions over melding and distinctiveness within the Andalusi archipelago are best summarized in the contrast between two terms for mixing: *mazj* and *khlāṭ*. Practitioners usually use the colloquial *khlāṭ* or the French equivalent *mélange* to negatively refer to what is usually an unintentional blurring of the lines between regional schools. For example, in Oujda, where the Algiers and Tlemcen versions are in competition with one another, I have heard a musical authority whose allegiance is with Tlemcen reprimand an adult student for doing an *inqilāb* in the Algiers style. A *mazj*, on the other hand, is a knowing, temporary blending of regional schools, two compatible modes, or, according to Maya Saidani, genre registers that are not usually paired.[27] Such a fusion, done with the right skill and intentionality, is an important way to introduce a sense of newness and experimentation into a repertoire that in many respects is fixed. Done correctly and with the understanding that it is temporary, such fusion can in fact promote distinction rather than blurring, in that to fuse two things is also to assert that they are distinct in the first place and will remain so once the experiment is finished. But *mazj* is hardest to do when one is dealing with closely neighboring practices, as opposed to a fusion between Andalusi music and flamenco, or between Moroccan *āla* and Algerian *ṣanʿa*. The more subtle and meaningful the differences, the more difficult it is to bridge them, even if only temporarily.

The conviction that the Andalusi musical practices are rooted in distinct places, and that these should remain separate, finds an echo in the challenges of embodying the repertoire itself. The pieces that make up a *nūba* often closely resemble one another. As I quickly discovered as a novice performer, a challenge greater than learning a piece is finding a way to keep it separate from another piece that resembles it. This is particularly difficult and important in a practice in which most musicians memorize what they play through close listening and repetition phrase by musical phrase—a process that musicians refer to in Arabic as *ḥifḍ*, which can be translated as both memorization and preservation. Indeed, for many aficionados, part of the impressiveness of a figure like Sid Ahmed Serri, the leading living practitioner in Algiers, is his ability to maintain control of literally hundreds of pieces without confusing them with one another.

The notion of distinctive places also dovetails closely with the notion that this is music associated with "old," "pure" families. Just as such families are said to guard their purity by refusing to mix and by holding fast to their sense of place, the Andalusi repertoires are said to guard their purity by remaining rooted in a distinct place. This homology between purity of blood and musical purity is particularly accentuated among Tlemcanis, who are particularly well-known in the region for parallel cousin marriage. As one young Tlemcani living in Oran explained to me, Tlemcanis have a sense of "race," which this particular individual referred to not so much as racism but as an idea of genealogy (*silsila*), a desire "to protect ourselves" and preserve things as they are. This helps to account for the seeming paradox that Tlemcen is considered "the source" yet is also said to be comparatively poor with regard to vocal repertoire: the implication is that such relative poverty is a sign that Tlemcanis have not artifically enriched their repertoire by drawing on others.

The sense of distinctive places that act as containers of repertoire is closely tied to a particular model of musical personhood. The repertoire does not reside in Tlemcen, Algiers, or Constantine but rather in people who have come from those places and who embody that sense of place. These people are the *shuyūkh* of the past and their modern inheritors—authoritative musical persons to whom practitioners based in the association movement turn for musical authentication and guidance, even as claims of discipleship do not go unchallenged. These people themselves are embodiments of the commitment to the local tradition. Take, for example, Larbi Bensari, who died at an advanced age in 1964. As conveyed in countless photographs, posters, and book covers, Larbi Bensari is the prototype of Tlemcani Andalusi practice—a status that he achieved within his own long career and that has only grown since his death. His performance practice, which was recorded but which also lives on in the memory of Tlemcani aficionados whose forebears served as Cheikh Larbi's patrons and disciples, is said to embody many of the conservative, traditionalist musical qualities associated with the Tlemcen school of the first half of the twentieth century, and virtually all musicians playing in the Tlemcani tradition link themselves to Cheikh Larbi as an embodiment of these values. In turn, Cheikh Larbi derived his musical knowledge and authority from other Tlemcanis, including Boudelfa, the immediate genealogical link that Sekkal and Bekhoucha provided for their source, Moulay Ziani. In this way, Cheikh Larbi was an eminently local figure, someone who lived, worked, and died in Tlemcen, and who derived his musical weight from there.

At the same time, professional musicians of Cheikh Larbi's day and before were not stationary, as the case of Bin 'Attū, who split his time between Fes and Tlemcen, points out. The great success of a leading female singer of turn-of-the-century Fes, Khaddūj al-Sibtiyya, was due in part to her performance of Algerian songs, which became the rage of Fes in her day and which she learned during her years living in Tiaret in central Algeria.[28] One of the leading singers of the *nūba* in the Algiers region at the end of the nineteenth century, Cheikh Qaddūr Bin Gālī, spent time in Tangier in an effort to expand his collection of song texts—collections that appropriately enough for an archipelago are sometimes known as "vessels" (*safā'in*; singular *safīna*).[29] Similarly, Cheikh Larbi traveled widely, both in Algeria and abroad. His travels to the Arab and Ottoman East are said to be the source for various songs, including "Al-bulbul ghannā 'alā ghuṣn al-bān" (The nightingale sang on the willow branch), which he brought back to Tlemcen and where it came to find a place on the outer edge of the Andalusi complex. Thus, like various predecessors, Cheikh Larbi helped to enlarge his repertoire through travel, and his personal authority as a representative of the Tlemcani tradition gave him the power to domesticate these pieces.[30]

For Cheikh Larbi, travel was not only an act of ingathering. Through his recordings and performances in places like Cairo, Constantine, Oujda, and Taza, as well as the fact that he was himself an object of pilgrimage for musical devotees from elsewhere, Cheikh Larbi came to make the Andalusi music of Tlemcen known beyond its borders. One practitioner from Oujda suggested to me that the *shaykh* had "left lots of pieces" in Tangier, which had been one of the cities that he visited repeatedly. In other words, in his travels, Cheikh Larbi both gathered up repertoire and left tokens of his core repertoire behind, waiting to be discovered like half-buried jewels and effectively extending the musical reach of his home city.[31] Finally, travel helped to distinguish the Tlemcani *nūba* from other instantiations of the *nūba*, both for listeners and no doubt for Cheikh Larbi and his supporting musicians: through circulating in the archipelago, whether at the level of the individual musician or the modern amateur association, one's place in it might become clearer. But while there is mobility here, the image of the musical *shaykh* in the Andalusi archipelago is the very opposite of the old Maghribi image of the ambulant musician moving from market to market: Cheikh Larbi always returns home, back to the source, the immobile archive.

If we return to another disciple of Boudelfa, Moulay Ziani, we can discover another aspect of the place-person link. For Sekkal and Bekhoucha, Moulay Ziani was as Tlemcani in his genealogy as was Cheikh Larbi. Yet not only was Moulay Ziani similarly connected to Fes (by way of Bin ʿAttū, in whose ensemble Moulay Ziani had played as a child and young adult), but he also spent time in Algiers. Thanks to his time in the capital, Moulay Ziani came to bring Algerois repertoire to Tlemcen, thereby setting up an alternative stream within the local early twentieth-century Andalusi music scene. Although Cheikh Larbi overshadowed Moulay Ziani for practitioners in the second half of the twentieth century, some musicians in the Tlemcani tradition authenticate their own practice primarily through him by way of Sekkal, rather than through Cheikh Larbi. In this case, the alternative genealogy is intertwined both with an alternative geographical trajectory and with an alternative genre valence, given the fact that Algiers provides a less conservative, somewhat more "popular" alternative to the classicism associated with Cheikh Larbi.

These brief examples from the life and lore of Larbi Bensari and his peers suggest the centrality of place to Andalusi musical practice. Although one need not be in Algiers to play Algerois, or in Tlemcen to play Tlemcani, these central places stand for a certain stability and fixedness. After all, few things are as immobile as place. At the same time, people themselves are mobile, and movement is an important way in which variety and newness may be legitimately introduced into the repertoire (or, for secondary cities, that the *nūba* repertoire might arrive in the first place). But because the success of newness is measured in whether the novel practices have the chance to grow old, the successful innovations-through-movement are in the past. Furthermore, the core of the repertoire is said to be buried locally, in particular persons who are the recognized conduits for ascertaining whether or not something actually exists or not in that place. In this spirit, one locally recognized master in Oujda explained to me that, in the old days, people only had recourse to living authorities and that the advent of cassette tapes and the radio have allowed for a dangerous mixing. At the same time, the unhinged, dangerous mobility afforded by the rise of broadcast media and sound recording can be counteracted by selectivity: in the case of this master, he is known for listening exclusively to recordings and radio from Tlemcen, the city of his musical allegiance.

Let us think of the musical map, then, as an archipelago of buried hoards. Ideally, these treasuries are located in particular places, and they require close contact with these places in order to access some of their riches. The point of entry, of mediation, with these treasures is the *shaykh*. The *shuyūkh* pass from the scene, entering the immobile landscape, in some sense themselves becoming the treasure and not merely its vessels.

The Maghribi-Andalusi Palimpsest as Charter Myth

For some practitioners, it is possible to talk about the archipelago in entirely Maghribi terms, with reference to a key *shaykh* and his teachers and students: perhaps Cheikh Larbi in Tlemcen, or, for Algiers, the turn-of-the century Cheikh Mohamed Ben ʿAli Sfindja, or today's Sid Ahmed Serri. But for most practitioners, the archipelago is inseparable from the mythos of al-Andalus and its medieval and early modern migrants. This act of drawing upon al-Andalus results in a palimpsestic framework, in which the Maghribi map overlays an Andalusi one or vice-versa. One tradition, for example, holds that refugees from Cordoba brought their music to Tlemcen, refugees from Seville brought theirs to Tunis, and those from Valencia and Granada brought theirs to Fes and Tetuan.[32] Another tradition identifies Algeria with Granada, and Tunisia and Morocco with Seville.[33] Thus the regional groupings within the larger archipelago get explained by matching them to particular places of origin in al-Andalus.

The overlaying of the Andalusi map onto the Maghribi one is a major part of what we can call al-Andalus talk, a speech genre that often goes along with membership in the contemporary Andalusi archipelago. Although a very widespread practice among practitioners, such talk is not uncontroversial, particularly in scholarly circles. For some researchers who are deeply involved in Andalusi musical practice, such as Youcef Touaïbia from the Algiers-based website Groupe Yafil, al-Andalus talk is an unsubstantiated distraction from the verifiable but relatively unexplored more recent history of the practice.[34] In a somewhat related vein, several scholars writing in the post-independence period have suggested that the Andalusi label for the *nūba* repertoire originated at the turn of the twentieth century, and that emphasis on its Andalusi origins and character served colonial, or, in some readings, anticolonial ends by emphasizing the European roots of North African "high culture."[35] In a similar way, some post-independence Maghribi intellectuals have militated for alternative appellations that either privilege already existing regionally specific names, such as *āla* or *mā'lūf*, or that emphasize the Maghribi and sometimes specifically national quality of the music, as in "Algerian classical music," "Moroccan classical music," or "Maghribi classical music."[36]

The textual materials from prior to 1900 suggest a more complicated story. In some cases, there is little to suggest that practitioners thought of the repertoire as coming from al-Andalus.[37] In other cases, there are strong indications that musicians and listeners thought of the repertoire as having a close link to al-Andalus, and even more specifically to Granada.[38] Nevertheless, since 1900, the Andalusi mythos has become more firmly entrenched and foregrounded in musical practice. At the same time, the tenor of this mythos has clearly shifted, even if its broad outline has remained fairly stable. For example, the image of al-Andalus as a vanished tri-religious utopia of tolerance is a fairly recent development that has come to enter musical discourse, but it is calqued on an older, arguably more potent Maghribi sense of al-Andalus as a paragon of Arab-Islamic civilization that was lost to Christian powers.[39]

Taken in its broad outlines, talk about al-Andalus as I have encountered it among contemporary practitioners and in the written record of the past century serves as what Bronislaw Malinowski called a charter myth, a story of origin that provides a constitution for the current social order.[40] For practitioners, the Andalusi charter myth can do a great many things. For example, it naturalizes musical difference through the narrative of multiple exiles. It provides a back-story for the rise of the *nūba* by focusing on certain great personages from the Andalusi past, in particular Ziryāb, the court musician who fled from 'Abbāsid Baghdad to Cordoba due to the jealousy of his teacher, Isḥāq al-Mawṣilī. Such a narrative links the repertoire to a prestigious Andalusi past that is in turn connected to the Arab-Islamic (and, in Ziryāb's case, Persian) heartlands. It suggests that the repertoire existed as a coherent whole in the place of its birth and represents it as a noble, courtly music. Furthermore, the narrative accentuates the notion of a high-prestige, urban music in that the repertoire is traced back to Andalusi exiles, paragons of urbanity and sophistication who are said to have brought a range of arts to the Maghrib before eventually blending into the wider social fabric of Algeria's cities during the early nineteenth century.[41] One non-Tlemcani musician explained to me that for the elites of Tlemcen, listening to this music makes them feel like they themselves are the monarchs of Spain. A highly educated connoisseur told me, "I am in al-Andalus during Muslim rule when I listen to this music. It is not a question of nostalgia. They did something in the Middle Ages that had never been done before. . . . It was nighttime in Europe, and for us it was day."

In addition to these broad identitarian claims, the origin narrative is sometimes deployed to account for highly specific aspects of the repertoire. Several writers have documented the rich lore that invokes medieval courtly protocol to account for the five-movement structure of the Algiers-Tlemcen *nūba*, with the sequence of movements following the entry, audience, and exit of the sultan.[42] In everyday interactions, such use of al-Andalus to account for repertorial specificities abounds. One Tlemcani devotee of the genre suggested to me that the current rhythmic interpretation in the Algiers school of *nūba* performance had to be mistaken due to its simplicity: if one goes to the Alhambra and sees the complexity and refinement of Andalusi civilization, he argued, it will be clear that today's interpretation of the rhythms is a deformation of what was originally intended, likely arrived at by the simplifications of the "simple artisans" who were historically the performers of this music. Thus al-Andalus can simultaneously account for what exists today and serve to outline what has been allegedly lost through the passage of time and therefore stands to be regained through effort.

A related aspect of the charter myth is that it projects near histories into a mythic past, like the Nuer myths described by Evans-Pritchard.[43] As will be examined in detail in the second part of this book, starting at the turn of the twentieth century self-conscious efforts at musical revival and reform led to the introduction of sound recordings, printed collections of *nūba* poetry, and the amateur association form—all of them crucial media through which the Andalusi archipelago assumes its current form. Yet there is also a tendency to assimilate the changes wrought in the past hundred years into the grand narrative of Andalusi origins. For example, the employment of musical revivalists from Tlemcen in the French Protectorate apparatus in Morocco was important for the introduction of Algerian Andalusi styles to Rabat, Tangier, and other Moroccan cities. Yet in Morocco, more than one person has told me that the presence of *gharnāṭī* in Rabat and Oujda, and the past presence of *gharnāṭī* in Tangiers and Tetuan, was due to the passage of Granadans through these cities or their settlement there. Conversely, the absence of *nūba* traditions in locations close to *nūba* centers is sometimes explained by an absence of Andalusi migrants. Consider comments from Nasreddine

Chaabane, a leading Oujdi performer and teacher of Andalusi music, riffing on whether there was *gharnāṭī* in Oujda before the arrival in the 1920s of an Algerian *lycée* teacher, Mohamed Ben Smaïl, who founded the city's first Andalusi music association:

> One day, you take some onions. You've been told that it is impossible to grow onions in Michigan. . . . But you try one day. You plant the onions on a farm near you, and it grows. "This can't be true! They said it won't work here, but it did." There is someone who will come to you and say, "A long time ago, they grew onions here. That's why this succeeded." . . . I come back to *gharnāṭī* . . . it existed in Oujda, it existed in Taza, it existed in Tetuan, it existed in Rabat, it existed in Marrakesh, it existed in Fes, it existed in Salé—why didn't it remain in all these cities, why did it remain only in Oujda? Because it found that there are very old families here. You'll tell me that we are on the frontier with Tlemcen. . . . But Maghnia . . . is twenty kilometers from us, and there is no *gharnāṭī*. But in Tlemcen, there is . . . You see? This is to say that *gharnāṭī* [survived in Oujda] because it existed here before [Ben Smaïl]. . . . If *gharnāṭī* music succeeded here . . . it's because it existed here before, and there were [old] families who loved it.[44]

The presence of migrants is also used to account for the origin and movement of instruments. The *rabāb*, a two-stringed bowed instrument that in Algeria is played hanging from the shoulder, has a central role in some Andalusi music ensembles, and the form it takes in the *nūba* repertoire is popularly traced to al-Andalus; indeed, it is sometimes referred to as the "sultan of the instruments," and today stands as a sort of icon for the repertoire as a whole, in that it is understood to be a difficult, neglected, rare, and preternaturally sonorous instrument that, in this particular form, is unique to the Andalusi musical ensemble. More controversial is the contention that its competitor, the violin, usually understood as a modern import to North Africa, in fact originated in al-Andalus and diffused northward into Western Europe and southward into the Maghrib.[45] The explicit presence of actual migrants can in some instances be dispensed with for the invocation of sheer proximity to al-Andalus to explain features of contemporary musical practice. For example, when I asked one connoisseur why there are so many women in the Oujda ensembles as compared to the *āla* orchestras of the Moroccan center, he drew a map of northern Morocco and southern Spain, marking out Granada, Oujda, Rabat, and Fes. Pointing out the relative distance of Oujda, Fes, and Rabat to Granada, he said, "See? Oujda is closer to Granada, so there is more civilization [*ḥaḍāra*]."[46]

Andalusis are also understood to have left their traces within the repertoire itself. One longstanding explanation for the vocables *yā lā lān* that are inserted into many of the *nūba* song texts is that they refer to a small river called Lalán that is located in Spain.[47] Many practitioners also take the words of the handful of song texts that make reference to al-Andalus as clear evidence that these particular poems originated in al-Andalus—in other words, the traces of Andalusis are evident in the pathos of the words and melodies of parts of the repertoire itself. Cheikh Zemmouri of Oujda, speaking of the *inqilāb jarka* "Yā asafī 'alā mā maḍā" (O my sorrow, alas, for what has passed!), explained that the open syllable *āh* that begins the piece is a remainder of the sorrow of the departure from al-Andalus, an affective proof that the words of this *inqilāb* indeed originated there.

This Maghribi-Andalusi palimpsest that enters even into the song texts themselves can in turn bring into play the spatiotemporal figure of modern Spain, which offers for many practitioners a palpable way of bringing the charter myth into the present. Visits to contemporary Spain are a crucial way in which a sense of the repertoire's historical reality takes personal shape. In many instances, performers and enthusiasts speak of visits to sites such as the Alhambra as revelatory pilgrimages. The sense that one can find a musical connection to the Andalusi past in the landscape of modern Spain also informs the many efforts to engage in musical fusion with musicians from Spain and southern France. Just as many European and North American early music enthusiasts have turned to the North African Andalusi music traditions as a site of contact with the medieval past, North African Andalusi music enthusiasts have turned to flamenco performers, Spanish early music ensembles, and traditional music groups from southern France as musical partners and potential sources for acts of musical "restoration."[48]

How are we to make sense of these moves, as well as the place of the broader Andalusi origin narrative within the musical practice? Given the intensely localized sense of musical practice that seems to guide Andalusi music practitioners, the narrative of exile from al-Andalus is certainly convenient. It provides a way to naturalize the sense of localized traditions while asserting that they all come from the same venerable source—that we really are talking about an archipelago rather than an assemblage of islands. It writes loss directly into the musical discourse: the *nūba* was once complete, but it is a repertoire that has deteriorated in its passage to the Maghrib and into the present. It also points to a purported source for all these genealogies: we may not know who Cheikh Larbi's teacher's teacher's teacher was, but if we accept the standard narrative, we can be sure that somehow there is a link back to Ziryāb, which in turn might link Cheikh Larbi to other acknowledged authorities whose repertoire sounds different from his own.[49] Particularly in explanations of how Andalusi music arrived in specific places, al-Andalus helps account for or ratify the success of the known genealogies—perhaps Ben Smaïl brought the association form to Oujda, but perhaps Boabdil, last king of Granada, stopped through there in his exile. Thus genealogies, even if they peter out as one reaches into the past, point toward a deeper presence or ultimate cause, putting al-Andalus and North Africa into a relationship of mutual doubling. In this way, the al-Andalus narrative is the backbone of the sense of an ultimate authority. Given the ubiquity of this notion of an Andalusi musical palimpsest, for many practitioners there is something deeply satisfying and efficacious about this explanation of difference, and this in part comes from the way in which the narrative naturalizes the current terrain and provides tools for shaping one's own musical vision.

Reterritorializing through Names

So far I have presented the al-Andalus narrative as an apparatus that is often brought in to enrich a more basic ideology of personhood and place rooted in the Maghrib's more recent past. But the success and efficacy of this marriage is unimaginable without considering a key way that the narrative is reproduced and extended: the reinscription of al-Andalus talk within the genre's name. One way to get at this is to return to *Nafḥ al-azhār* and interpret Bekhoucha and Sekkal's *jazā'ir al-andalus* as a full-fledged pun.[50] For while al-Andalus is primarily a past place that lives in memory, practitioners sometimes use it to talk about Andalusi music as a genre, alongside the Arabic and French adjectival forms *andalusī* and *andalous*. Enthusiasts sometimes half-jokingly refer to themselves as *ahl al-andalus*, the people of al-Andalus, on the model of the term *ahl al-ṣan'a*, "the people of *ṣan'a*," understood as "the people who love *ṣan'a*." Thus we can stretch our reading of *jazā'ir al-andalus* to mean not just "the Algeria of al-Andalus" or "the archipelago of al-Andalus" but also "the Algeria or archipelago of Andalusi music." Such a reading conjures an important aspect of Andalusi musical practice understood as a site of inquiry: that there is a "people of al-Andalus" who exist by dint of their engagement with Andalusi music, a social formation placed within a particular musical geography. This is a Maghribi-Andalusi musico-geographic palimpsest, but it is a version in which al-Andalus is domesticated as genre, as a sort of "second nature" or reterritorialization of al-Andalus within the genre field.[51]

In other words, we might productively ask, what is Andalusi about Andalusi music? As the preceding section showed, the Andalusi label is widely embraced as a reference to medieval Iberia and its migrants to the Maghrib. But when we look more closely, it becomes clear that the longstanding association of this music with the term has partially detached the term from its grounding in al-Andalus. In part, this alternative understanding of al-Andalus is connected to the question of ethnicity, or perhaps non-ethnicity. The embedding of Andalusiness within traditional Maghribi notions of urbanity means that its sense as a marker of ethnicity is partially disentangled from involvement in Andalusi music; in other words, one need not be of Andalusi origin to be devoted to this kind of music, and not all people who claim an Andalusi origin are particularly interested in the *nūba* repertoire. This disentanglement of ethnic or genealogical Andalusiness from involvement in Andalusi music is only partial both because there are some prominent performers who lay claim to Iberian origin, and because the Andalusiness of the repertoire becomes available to practitioners in a roundabout way that reintroduces a quasi-ethnic form of identification.

Consider, for example, the framing banter of an announcer at an Andalusi music festival in Algiers that I attended in May 2009. The context was the finale in a month-long festival sponsored by a municipal organization featuring performances from the *nūba* repertoire by Algerian associations, as well as statements from various Andalusi music luminaries. During his comments, the announcer veered into an unscripted discussion of the merits of Andalusi music and the festival's success, and began to engage in a speech genre unto itself: a contrast of Andalusi music with *raï*, an Algerian popular music genre associated with working-class youth and disdained by many Andalusi enthusiasts. As will be explored further in later chapters, this is a widespread form of social critique in such circles, but most interesting for our purposes is the announcer's use of a form of appellative play: repeatedly, he contrasted *aṣḥāb al-rayy*, "the devotees of raï," with *ahl al-andalus*, "the people of al-Andalus," here redirected to the devotees of Andalusi music.

The basic form of the linkage is also exemplified in a friendly argument I was party to at an association headquarters in Oran. The dispute pitted two young Andalusi music practitioners against an outsider to the scene who teaches piano performance and Western music theory on the premises. The latter was arguing that Andalusi music changes because of failures in the transmission of melodies. Western classical music of the past centuries, on the other hand, she said, has not changed substantially thanks to notation. "Just wait thirty years until you have kids and they're playing in the association, and you'll hear how different it all sounds," she chided. And in response, one of the two young men laughed while quoting a famous line from the Andalusi repertoire of the region: *ahl al-andalus yafhamū al-ishāra*, "The people of al-Andalus understand the meaning." That is to say, "Andalusi music lovers get it, and you don't."

The comprehensibility of such lighthearted but ultimately quite serious verbal play rests upon the listener's ability to hold in mind the two valencies of *ahl al-andalus*: as the standard name of the inhabitants of (and exiles from) al-Andalus and their descendants, and as the name for the devotees of a musical genre. Such talk performs a generic and social differentiation in the present by invocation of a quasi-ethnic distinction rooted in past place and movement. The potential implications of the parallel go far: if there is an analogy between "the people of al-Andalus" then and now, today's enthusiasts are the paragons of sophistication and are beleaguered, doomed, or lost. And indeed, Andalusi music practitioners are proud of their cause, intensely focused on narrating their past, convinced that their numbers have diminished, and protective of an ostensibly endangered repertoire.

The performative force and wit of the statement here hinge on the use of *andalus* to refer chiefly but not exclusively to the musical genre. Yet the fuller significance of such verbal play lies not only in the pun but also in the way the pun involves a quotation from the repertoire—in this case, the line *ahl al-andalus yafhamū al-ishāra*, which together with the *istikhbār* lines by Ibn Khafāja is one of a few well-known song texts that directly invoke "the people of al-Andalus." In this particular instance, these claims are not simply being asserted but are being performed through an act of quotation. In other words, as in the case of the *āh* in the famous *inqilāb jarka*, the Andalusiness of Andalusi music, and we can also say of al-Andalus itself, is partly stored within forms of address internal to the musical canon, and these forms get rearticulated through use. Redirecting these references works toward several ends: it blurs al-Andalus and the current social-generic terrain while skillfully exploiting and reproducing their distinction, and it performs a mastery of the repertoire while playfully intimating that the repertoire speaks directly to the present.

Yet the seriousness of this analogy cannot be accounted for simply by recourse to word play. There has to be some notion of Andalusi music being from al-Andalus—to make the analogy at all convincing, it cannot just be a situation in which *andalusī* is simply a placeholder within a generic field, emptied of its historical associations. As the previous section demonstrated, it is the historical association—the idea that the repertoire came from there—that lends such invocations weight. In turn, this historical association works because of the element of movement that is woven into the figure of al-Andalus; in other words, al-Andalus is not simply a mirror for the contemporary musical order but is a figure whose specific qualities matter for those who engage it. It is through the notion of al-Andalus as a historical place, and as a source of people and their treasures, that the characteristics imputed to it become available for re-diffusion into Andalusi musical practice.

In a way, the reinscription of the al-Andalus narrative into the genre-naming practice is a continuation of the process of musical place-making by reference to such central sites as Tlemcen and Algiers, although one that casts musical authority into a more remote sense of place than can be provided even by Tlemcen. In all these instances, there is a locating of musical practice in particular authoritative places. In turn, this location is then musicalized: it becomes the ground of musical practice, either through senses of personhood, genre frameworks, or naming. Brought into the ligaments of the practice, internalized, these reterritorializations make these senses of place oddly inescapable: despite individuals' scattered doubts regarding the veracity of the al-Andalus narrative it has been written into the practice, and to find a way out of it involves a directionality that has not yet been discovered. Thus the al-Andalus narrative is not simply an apparatus that is brought in so as to enrich a more basic ideology of place and personhood; rather, for many, the al-Andalus narrative is an integral part of that ideology and a vehicle for its elaboration.

In the end, what does this reterritorialization through genre mean for thinking about the Andalusi archipelago? When we look at the modern map of North Africa, we can see that the Andalusi musical public is a noncontiguous collectivity rooted in particular localized practices and institutions, which in turn are rooted in particular individualized musical authorities who are rooted in place yet mobile. These practices are said to have been brought to the Maghrib by Andalusi refugees in the medieval and early modern period, and this longstanding origin narrative provides a powerful way to naturalize the current musical terrain and project its qualities, patterns, and more recent historicity into the deep past. This narrative is not only explicitly transmitted from practitioner to practitioner but also reproduces itself through the genre names that link the *nūba* traditions back to al-Andalus. This situation gives rise to a community of practitioners who understand themselves and their music as sharing a great deal with the reputed qualities of al-Andalus itself: they are rare, valuable, sophisticated, and endangered.

We come back, then, to the soloist's *istikhbār* that we evoked in the prologue. "O people of al-Andalus" happens to be one of a handful of canonical texts performed in the *nūba* tradition that has a known author or that mentions al-Andalus. For most performers or listeners, however, these words are no different from most other texts that wind up in *nūba* performance: like the unwritten, authorless melodies to which they are sung, they simply come from the *turāth*. But if Ibn Khafāja's words come to this scene as if they are a bird flown in from al-Andalus, they also come by way of other, more tangible routes: the sweat and tears of the rehearsal process, the layered histories of the association system, the project of revival, and the genealogies of the *shuyūkh*.[52]

But having arrived in the mouth of the soloist, the words of Ibn Khafāja, buried as they are in a patrimonial embrace, are an animation of a medieval invocation of Iberia's inhabitants—animation being understood in Erving Goffman's sense of a relaying of discourse that originates from someone (or, in the case of patrimony, something) else.[53] This animated stretch of discourse brings to mind for many contemporary listeners the notion of a lost paradise remembered in the present. In the words of the anthropologist and *nūba* performer Nadir Marouf, "The aim [of singing] is not to please—it is not artistic in the literal sense of the term. It is the carrier of a message of restoration of a patrimony, in such a way as to be able to reveal some of the spirit, lustre, and passion that presided over its initial elaboration."[54] As the preceding pages suggest, Ibn Khafāja's words are also an invocation of the listeners themselves, these select "people of al-Andalus" who have come together—from different neighborhoods, cities, countries, generations, social classes, walks of life—in this charged performative moment. It is an animation that comes out of the mouth of the singer, but that is understood to spring from a golden past, and which, for the initiated, might sound like a mutual speaking of the past to the present. How God has showered them with riches, riches rescued from the past, but very much alive.

2

The *Shaykh* and the *Mūlūʿ*

When Cheikh Salah died in 1973 at the age of 62, the Algerian-Moroccan border region lost one of its major performers of the *qṣīda* repertoire, and Oujda lost a key pedagogue in the perpetuation of the *nūba* tradition. For his family, it was the loss of the patriarch and the main breadwinner: over his lifetime, Salah had worked as a postal worker, a businessman in retail and the coffee trade, an attendant at the Shell fuel station, a radio electrician, and a shoemaker, but by the end of his life he was able to rely on his renown as a wedding performer, particularly in Tlemcen, the birthplace of his mother and of his wife.

For one son in particular, Cheikh Salah's death prompted a sort of musical and existential crisis. Mohamed Chaabane was born in 1948. As a child he would fall asleep listening to his father playing mandole and *ʿūd* after dinner. Mohamed's formal initiation into music began at the age of twelve when his father brought home an upright piano, and, without any prompting, the child began to pick out melodies. He became obsessed with playing the piano—a fixation that at one time even threatened his school studies. Under his father's strict direction, he soon learned the basic building blocks of the *nūba* repertoire, beginning with the short vocal *inqilābāt*, moving on to the instrumental *tūshiyyāt* that can open a *nūba*, and concluding with the unmetered *istikhbārāt* for each of the modes. With this base, Mohamed was able to quickly learn the melodies of the repertoire while playing in his father's ensemble in Tlemcen.

Mohamed soon became known as a piano prodigy, and even appeared on the cover of a major media magazine published in Rabat. The Andalusi repertoire was not his only musical passion: he took piano lessons in the European classical tradition at the municipal conservatory, and he had a boogie-woogie band that played hits from the U.S. But his father's musical specialties took the lead, and through his parents and his frequent visits to Tlemcen he came in contact with the leading musical figures of the day, including Larbi Bensari and Abdelkrim Dali, the latter a cousin of Cheikh Salah's wife. It was thanks to Cheikh Salah's regular engagements in Tlemcen that Mohamed absorbed a great deal of his father's repertoire and performance idiom. Starting in 1965, Mohamed was also a member of the Association Andalouse, which his father was then directing. By now, Mohamed was a student at the Lycée Victor Hugo, finishing his studies in 1968. Two years later, Mohamed moved across the border to Oran, where he found good work as a technical agent at the Algerian electricity and natural gas utility. By this time, his musical activities were largely on hold, although he would occasionally go to the center of Oran to observe rehearsals of the recently formed Association Nassim El-Andalous, comprised of Tlemcanis living in Oran.

Mohamed's new life in Oran was disrupted by his father's death. On his return to the family house in the working-class neighborhood of Boudir, Mohamed began to furiously develop his musical skills. He had always been a pianist, but now he devoted himself to learning the *ʿūd*, which was his father's instrument of choice and which, unlike the piano, enjoys an unquestioned place in the Maghribi musical imagination. Mohamed also began to try to learn to sing his father's repertoire, which he had heard many times but, as an instrumental accompanist, had never fully internalized. His father was well-known for his refusal to record or to allow others to record him, but Mohamed had assumed that his father would discreetly leave behind some recordings in their house in Boudir. All he found was a few old reels, Cheikh Salah's copies of songbooks from the *gharnāṭī* and *āla* traditions, and his manuscript notebooks in French orthography. In the face of this paucity of documents, Mohamed suddenly faced the challenge of recuperating his father's sung repertoire with the aid of just a few scratchy recordings and the notebooks, whose contents might jog his musical memory.

And so Mohamed launched himself into a massive project of recuperation through the painstaking restoration and embodiment of his father's repertoire. Starting in September 1973, just a few months after Cheikh Salah's death, and working through the following summer, Mohamed worked incessantly to recover this body of musical knowledge. He would work from 1:00 in the afternoon until the early morning, drinking coffee, smoking cigarettes, listening to the old reels, and playing *ʿūd*. Music took over his psychic world, and he eventually became exhausted. He broke from this schedule when it became clear that his own wellbeing was in danger.

I came to hear this narrative over a series of meetings with Mohamed

Chaabane in 2006, some of them in the Association Andalouse, which he was directing (and which he still directs as of this writing), others in a classroom at a municipal youth center where he was teaching music and French on a part-time basis. During our informal meetings in the latter space, we would often be joined by a caretaker who we usually referred to as the Ḥājj. The Ḥājj is some years older than Mohamed and is a music aficionado who is particularly passionate about *qṣāyid*; he conserves a vivid memory of Cheikh Salah, and he loved to listen to Mohamed's playing and participate in our conversations. One January day, in the course of a response to a question I had posed regarding his father's repertoire during weddings and his attitudes toward such performances, Mohamed began to speak of how his father had had knowledge of "many things that were lost" when he died. With his *'ūd* in his arms, Mohamed suddenly lowered his voice, and in hushed tones he recounted something that had happened to him more than three decades earlier:

> One day, there was a *qṣīda* in one of these books that my father had written in French—"My torments have worn on, my misfortune has worn on, bearing it has worn me out—O my father, what a state I am in!" A *ḥawzī*. In my youth we used to play it. . . . I kept thinking about the melody but couldn't find it. I didn't want to go get it by sucking up to [one of the *shuyūkh* who played with Cheikh Salah], I just didn't want to go to him. . . . I assure you, this is the truth. How do you sing it, "My torments have worn on, my misfortune has worn on," how do you sing it, how do you sing it? I went to sleep. At night, I saw him in his suit, with his red *ṭarbūsh*, in a robe, in what was like a garden, like the *ḥarṭūn* [in Tlemcen] . . . [which is] like the park in Oujda, but better, with trees, and flowers, and water.
>
> In the morning, when I opened my eyes, the note rose up. Laaaaaaa! When I woke, the note . . . the scale that my father used to sing it in was in my head . . .

He began to coax the lilting melody from the strings of his *'ūd*, and sang:

> My torments have worn on,
> my misfortune has worn on,
> bearing it has worn me out—
> O my father, what a state I am in . . .
>
> "This happened to me, in the morning when I awoke, I don't know how, when I woke from the dream . . . How do you explain this?" he asked me.
>
> The Ḥājj answered, "This is your father. He loves you."

*

So far, we have explored the Andalusi archipelago as a temporally and geographically extended sociological and discursive formation. We turn our attention now to the subjectivities or forms of personhood that permeate such spaces and arrangements. Where the previous chapter asked where "the people of al-Andalus" live, the current chapter inquires further into the kinds of people they are, and how they imagine themselves to be.

We already have a hint of an answer to these questions. Axiomatically, the people of al-Andalus are defined by their close engagement in the project of making Andalusi music, both in performance and in the realm of connoisseurship. I have also suggested that viewed over at least the past hundred years, this community or public is animated by a self-image that closely mirrors the mythos of the music itself: these are urbane, cosmopolitan-yet-local, rare, even threatened folk, latter-day musical incarnations of a Maghribi image of Andalusis after the fall of Granada. Finally, I have pointed out that an important part of the Andalusi musical ethos is the notion of genealogical authority embodied in locally authenticated masters. For practitioners, these masters or *shuyūkh* constitute routes, sources, and means of circulation, production, and consumption that tie cosmology to more concrete near histories in substantive ways. They are also the primary medium for picturing the temporality of the practice: through such genealogical figures, who in the mainstream narrative theoretically point back from afar to al-Andalus, the archipelago testifies to a transgenerational, *longue durée* project.

This chapter takes a closer look at the musical master or *shaykh* as a central kind of person within Andalusi musical practice. I am interested in thinking through what it means to speak of somebody as a *shaykh* and how a person becomes recognized as one. But while the *shaykh* is a central form of musical personhood, to speak only of *shuyūkh* would be to miss another crucial kind of musical person: the enthusiast, devotee, connoisseur, fan, or aficionado, often known in Maghribi Arabic as the *mūlūʿ*. Thus I am also interested in thinking through what it means to speak of somebody as a *mūlūʿ*, and again how an individual becomes one. Although there are many people who encounter Andalusi music in a more peripheral fashion, for the "people of al-Andalus," the figures of the *shaykh* and the *mūlūʿ* cover the primary recognized "discursive subject positions" or forms of personhood.[1]

The exploration of the *shaykh* and the *mūlūʿ* as subject positions is also necessarily an exploration of the relationship between them. In exploring these relationships, I invoke the notion of a participant framework that the end of the previous chapter touched upon—an arrangement of possible relationships toward discourse within a given context.[2] The context is the Andalusi musical milieu as a whole, and the discourse includes both talk about music and the sonic elaborations that we typically think of as music itself. It is in these relationships that we will encounter much of the dynamism of these terms. For while the *mūlū'īn* constitute the ideal audience for the *shaykh*, they also provide a pool from which new *shuyūkh* arise. In addition, the field of musical practice is charged with various sorts of tensions between the *mūlū'* and the *shaykh*, so that from some angles the *shaykh* is in fact an ambiguous figure—one who mingles quasi-spiritual authority with avarice and even vulgarity. Hence while the *shaykh* is more central and visible than the *mūlū'*, it is also the more enigmatic and contested of the available subject positions.

The discursive relationship of *shaykh* to *mūlū'* shows a strong continuity over the past century and a half, despite the many institutional changes that the second part of this book explores. But in order to account for such continuity, it is necessary to pay close attention to the social and economic processes in which the subject positions and discourse exist—what we might call the accumulated political economy of the participant framework. This process of accumulation also contains elements of real change that help to give credence to the frequent claim that the *shuyūkh* are a phenomenon of the past: some kinds of professional musicianship that existed in the first half of the twentieth century no longer exist in robust form.[3] Yet the concept of the *shaykh* persists, carrying with it the residue of earlier formations. Thus this chapter highlights the link between the socioeconomic order and the notions of *shaykh* and *mūlū'* while at the same time recognizing their distinctiveness from one another. In other words, the latter notions are not unmediated reflexes of the socioeconomic order, but neither are they entirely independent of that order. This chapter is therefore about both longstanding discursive tropes and what Bourdieu might call the durable structures of music-making from which these tropes emerge and upon which the deployers of these tropes act. These discursive and relational structures are also deeply meaningful for practitioners, whose consciousness and experience live upon but are not reducible to the subject positions. To map the broad contours of these subjectivities is to begin to get at the meaning of the lost paradise.

The Semantic Web

The concepts of *shaykh* and *mūlū'* (occasionally written as *mulū'*) are far from simple, but it is useful to initially gloss them in fairly straightforward terms. *Shaykh* is an honorific that is roughly translatable as master or teacher, not unlike the term *m'allim* with which it is often interchangeable. There are alternative ways to refer to a musician in the Maghribi context—for example, one can reference the instrument a person plays (such as a *kamānjī* for the *kamān* or *kamānja*, the viola or violin), or talk about someone as a singer (*muṭrib/muṭriba*; *mughannī/mughanniyya*), artist (*fannān/fannāna*), ensemble member (*ālī*), or simply a musician (*mūsīqī*). More than most of these, however, *shaykh* implies a certain standing. In a musical context, it sums up a person's social position as a fully adult male vocalist and instrumentalist who has mastery of a repertoire that is understood as traditional, and who might lead other musicians in an ensemble and act as a reference in the musical community. The *shaykh* is not necessarily a virtuoso—in fact, some have been known for not having particularly sweet voices or advanced instrumental technique. Instead, the crucial requirement to be considered a *shaykh* in the Andalusi archipelago is to have mastery over a vast amount of repertoire.

Mūlūʿ, which can be interpreted both as an adjective and a noun, is roughly translatable as fan, devotee, music-lover, aficionado, connoisseur, or amateur (in the latter's literal sense of one who is in love). It is largely interchangeable with the Arabic term *dhawwāq* (derived from the verb for taste) and the nineteenth-century French neologism *mélomane* (literally a person who is manic for melodies, just as "fan" likely derives from "fanatic"), and it resembles the *sammīʿa* or devoted listeners of Egypt and the Levant.[4] It likely derives from the somewhat unusual classical Arabic passive participle *mawlūʿ*, someone who is in love with or aflame with passion for someone or something.[5] Unlike *shaykh*, *mūlūʿ* is not available for use as a title or address term. In Andalusi musical circles, it is typically used for an aficionado who may or may not also play an instrument or sing. If the *mūlūʿ* is also a musician, then it is typically in an amateur, nonprofessional capacity.

These two terms can cover the vast majority of the inhabitants of the Andalusi archipelago, in that a *shaykh* is a musical authority and a *mūlūʿ* is a devotee of the repertoire, a person who we might say is interpellated by music as a listener—in this case, by Andalusi music.[6] I should point out that on occasion practitioners have described me to one another as a *mūlūʿ*, which, as will be seen, is not incompatible with the more common identification of me as a *bāḥith* or researcher. In addition, *shaykh* and *mūlūʿ* form a pair, in that *mūlūʿīn* constitute the *shaykh*'s ideal audience and entourage. Of course, there are also people who are more occasional or passive listeners to Andalusi music, but it is telling that such people are outside the self-made boundaries of the musical milieu. Implicit in the insider lexicon is the notion that Andalusi music demands passionate devotion.

The power of these terms lies partly in their connection to extramusical spheres—as one member of a Tlemcen association explained to me, *shaykh* as used in the musical milieu is a metaphor that draws on other domains. *Shaykh* is widely used in Arabic as an honorific that recognizes a person's political, social, generational, or religious authority. It connotes age, wisdom, leadership, and mastery, and is often used to refer to the teacher in a teacher-student relationship or, in the Sufi context, to the master in a master-disciple relationship. Its alternative in the Maghribi musical context—*m'allim*—in fact comes from *mu'allim*, the standard Arabic term for teacher or for the master in an artisanal apprenticeship context.[7] *Mūlū'* likewise has a connection to the spiritual realm: derived from a root meaning burning, glowing, or passionate love, in the Maghrib its nominal form, *wullā'a*, is occasionally used in Sufi poetry to refer to the desire to unite with God or with the Prophet.

But before we embrace a quasi-Sufi interpretation of the *shaykh–mūlū'* relationship, it is important to briefly touch on the class associations of these terms in the musical context. Although we can find the term *shaykh* being used for musicians from middle-class and elite social backgrounds, the prototypical *shaykh* is from the traditional urban artisanal class, and various classic *shuyūkh* had training in an artisanal occupation other than music—Cheikh Larbi Bensari, for example, was trained as a barber, Cheikh Sfindja of Algiers as a shoemaker, and until the middle of the twentieth century there were many examples of small-scale textile producers and silversmiths with such musical specializations. Similar occupational and class associations can be made for the prototypical *mūlū'*. Although there are many historical and current examples of Andalusi music lovers from modest social backgrounds, the prototypical enthusiast is from the elite, and indeed there are long traditions of elite families renowned for their *mélomanes*. All of this becomes quite a bit more complicated when we start to look at the *mūlū'* not simply as a listener but also as a potential *shaykh* in training. However, for the time being, we can say that the discursive stereotype presents the *shaykh–mūlū'* relationship as crossing a class divide, and sometimes a very sharp one at that. As one Tlemcani musician explained to me, the *shuyūkh* of the past used to sleep in their patrons' stables, not in their houses.

Gender is another important thread in the semantic web: both the *shaykh* and the *mūlū'* are gendered as male. Although there are female musical authorities and aficionados in the Andalusi milieu, especially since the late 1960s in the Algerian context, women are clearly the marked category. Before the entry of women into the association system, female performers were mainly linked to the professional categories known as *msemma'āt*, *meddāḥāt*, and *fqīrāt*.[8] As the following chapter will explore, the genres associated with these names touch on the outer edges of the Andalusi complex and have traditionally been heard in all-female gatherings; like the *nūba* repertoire and its *shuyūkh*, today these genres and their bearers are often described as either having disappeared or being in the course of disappearance.[9] Particularly with regard to the term *shaykh*, female performers present an acute problem. While the term *shaykh* can be feminized as *shaykha*, in this form it becomes indistinguishable from the Algerian and Moroccan term for a professional female performer of erotically charged repertoire—charged in part because of the *shaykha*'s willingness to perform before men.[10] In practice, some early twentieth-century female performers in the Andalusi musical complex took on the term *shaykha* or *mʿallma*, but their status as female performers presented certain dilemmas with regard to genre and propriety that we will explore further. For the time being, we can say that the question of the *shaykha* brings otherwise latent questions regarding professional musicianship to the fore.

In addition, gender and generational difference enter into the way in which musicians within the Andalusi milieu have talked about sound and genre. Practitioners have sometimes spoken of the low (and therefore thick) strings and low vocal registers as the *shaykh* or the male, and the high register as the *shabāb* (youths) or the female—a mapping of gender and generation onto the voice and instrument that also gestures toward the singularity of the *shaykh* and the multiplicity of the *shabāb*, the soloist versus the chorus that responds.[11] Similar distinctions have also entered into the naming of professional musicians in *raï*, where *shaykh* has been upended by the titles *shabb* and *shabba* (young person, male and female; in francophone transliteration, *cheb* and *chebba*). In addition, the vocal style of *raï* tends to pitch the male voice far higher than is the norm in the Andalusi complex, and, as will be explored further in the next chapter, *raï* is often attacked by its detractors, including among devotees of Andalusi music, for its challenge to conservative notions of sexual propriety.[12]

Thus the threads of this semantic web suggest some of the richness of these terms and at the same time raise questions about how best to conceive of the relationship between the *shaykh* and the *mūlūʿ*. Are we dealing with artisanal apprenticeship, or with spiritual discipleship, or with market exchange, or something else? How can we account for some of the contradictory qualities associated with the musical *shaykh* over the past hundred years? How can we make sense of the question of social class as it relates both to the discursive tropes and the actual practice of musical production and consumption over time? In order to think through these questions, let us turn first to the question of professional musicianship and patronage before considering apprenticeship and discipleship in their turn.

Master and Patron

In very general terms, we can say that it is by being a *mūlūʿ*, a person who is taken with Andalusi music, that one is initiated into the Andalusi musical sphere, and that the *shaykh* occupies a central place of power within this sphere, serving as the primary animator of the musical patrimony. However, this initiation, both as a process and as a point of eventual arrival, works very differently depending on one's social position. To begin, let us consider the relationship of *shaykh* to *mūlūʿ* as the relationship between a professional musician and a musical patron or client. In this formulation, the *mūlūʿ* is a person who desires a certain kind of music—in this case, the *nūba* and its allied repertoire—and the *shaykh* is a person who ideally can satisfy that desire.

As will be seen momentarily, the relationship between professional and patron can become quite fluid once we start to look at amateur music-making. For the time being, however, let us think through those instances when the relationship of *shaykh* to *mūlūʿ* can be conceived as one that ties a professional musician to a paying client. In the Andalusi milieu, this is an old form of relationship that hinges on the notion that musicianship is a specialized knowledge, and that it is a knowledge whose exercise is a form of service toward an individual or group of higher status than the performer. In other words, as has been described for North Indian classical music, this is a high-prestige music, but, at least from the elite point of the view, the bulk of its prestige redounds to the music-loving patron rather than to the musical performer who in some respects serves as the patron's proxy.[13] Viewed in regard to the participant framework, the patron is a co-animator of the musical discourse, alongside the paid performer, and one who in some respects carries the greater weight in this process of animation. In the words of Abdelmajid Merdaci, "The favored figure in the musical field is that of . . . the *mélomane*, who shares the savoir-faire with [the professionals] without sharing their social status."[14]

There are many examples of such a dynamic in the Algiers-Tlemcen archipelago beginning from some of the earliest available descriptions of musical practice. According to the early nineteenth-century traveler Filippo Pananti, music-making in urban Algeria was a service provided to wealthy clients, some of whom kept instruments for use by the performers they contracted.[15] The turn-of-the-nineteenth-century Mrs. Blanckley, wife of the British consul to Algiers, describes a similar pattern for high-status female patrons and their female entertainers, whose singing and dancing acted as both pleasure and proxy for their audience.[16] After the French invasion in 1830 and into the first decades of the twentieth century, performers within the *nūba* complex were sometimes described as working in cafés, where they were responsive to the requests of the audience members. Specialists in the Andalusi repertoire were also hired to perform in private homes, a practice that continued into the twentieth century, even as the venues for both professional musicianship and amateur performance shifted and expanded in various ways.[17] In the late nineteenth century and throughout much of the twentieth, many musicians specializing in the Andalusi repertoire found regular work as entertainers in the context of all-night wedding parties, often hosted by the father of the groom in his own home in honor of his male guests, but in many cases for more mixed audiences as well. Although the practices around weddings have shifted radically since the 1970s, with the introduction of rented wedding halls, compacted sequences of ritual events, and a shift in taste regarding musical genres, even today, particularly in Tlemcen, there are professional musicians specializing in the Andalusi repertoire who are hired for performances within homes or in wedding halls, as well as families of *mélomanes* who are known for performing such patronage.

This is not to say that either the professionals or the patrons of today are the same in sociological terms as the professionals of earlier eras. Indeed, as the second part of this book explores, the institutional and media channels of musical production have markedly shifted since the turn of the twentieth century. In particular, there has been an upward shift in the class status of professional performers: the days of sleeping in patrons' stables are long past, as is, according to some, the time of the "true *shaykh*." Yet it is possible to point out certain continuities regarding the general sociological features associated with the subject positions of *shaykh* and *mūlū'* over this period. Of the people who in recent decades have made at least some of their livelihood from performing the Andalusi repertoire and who have been referred to as *shuyūkh*, many are able to place themselves within a musical lineage of masters reaching back to the nineteenth century, even if these lineages are often characterized by upward socioeconomic mobility. In some cases, as in the case of Cheikh Larbi and his son Redouane, or Mohamed and Nasreddine Chaabane and their father Cheikh Salah, these lineages overlap with filial kinship. Likewise, there are Andalusi music-lovers who come from long lines of aficionados. On occasion, lines of *mélomanes* can even be linked to lines of *shuyūkh* over multiple generations. Cheikh Salah of Oujda, for example, was patronized by a prominent *mélomane* doctor; their sons have followed in their respective footsteps, one a doctor and *mélomane*, the other a professional musician patronized by him, thereby reproducing the particular configuration of *shaykh* and *mūlū'* that their late fathers formerly embodied. As was repeated to me again and again, for many devotees, Andalusi music is "in the blood."

In addition, because this kind of relationship of *shaykh* to *mūlū'* rests upon the patronage of professional musicians, there is a built-in element of class differentiation. The *shaykh* thus understood is an artisan of sorts, while the *mūlū'* who hires him axiomatically has the economic power to do so, as well as the lack of either knowledge or willingness to engage in such performance. Viewed in less ideal-typical terms, there is indeed a broad class differentiation that becomes clear in historical hindsight. With a few exceptions, such as the turn-of-the-century musician Chaouel Durand (known as Mouzino), who was the son of a successful merchant originally from Constantine, most of the professional musicians known for the Andalusi repertoire in the nineteenth and twentieth centuries came from families of mainly modest artisans and small-time businessmen. The people who were known for hiring such musicians, on the other hand, included some of the most prominent figures in Algeria. Mohamed Ben 'Ali Sfindja, for example, the doyen of Andalusi music in turn-of-the-century Algiers who was also a shoemaker, was patronized by the leading scholars, lawyers, and businessmen of his era. Many of the latter-day patrons of Andalusi music are doctors, lawyers, engineers, and businessmen, in some cases descended from some of the same people who were patrons of Andalusi music in earlier generations.

This class dimension of the patronage relationship quickly becomes more complicated on closer inspection. There have long been cases of accomplished amateurs from well-off backgrounds performing for private gatherings, although in many instances these were *en famille*—that is to say, for members of the musician's close kin network. In addition, although falling outside the prototypical image of the Andalusi music patron, enthusiasts of more modest means found ways to patronize *shuyūkh*, sometimes through attendance at cafés that featured live music and likely through the hiring of musicians for their own festivities. In some instances, to be a member of an elite was to speak of a status rather than a class per se, in that some members of the old Algerois *mélomane* families were small artisans even if they could claim deep local roots. In addition, patrons of professionals did not typically host musicians for one-on-one audition. Rather, the *shaykh*'s audience was made up of a plurality of *mūlū'īn* who were guests of the patron. While most of these were audiences made up of people of roughly equal status, some musical occasions could in fact assemble a diverse crowd, including women, servants, and people of the neighborhood.[18] In other words, while the prototypical *mūlū'*-as-patron is a person of ample means, there have always been ways for enthusiasts of more modest means to access the Andalusi repertoire.

In addition, among professional musicians themselves, the question of social class has long been quite subtle. Writing in the early 1860s, the Russian traveler and musical commentator Alexandre Christianowitsch suggests that there was a well-developed hierarchy of musicians in Algiers, with the musicians of the café scene, most of whom were Jewish, being ranked far below *nūba*-specialized musicians, most of them Muslim, who frequented private soirées.[19] According to Christianowitsch's primary informant, a musician by the name of Hammoud Ben Mustapha, the high-prestige performers specializing in the Andalusi repertoire account were largely artisans who, like himself, had training in a craft other than music.[20] This description is in keeping with the evidence for the milieu of *shuyūkh* in the later nineteenth century and the early twentieth century. Thus although we can find many Jewish professional musicians who identified themselves as such (including Mouzino of Algiers, the Amsili brothers of Oran, and Maklouf Rouch and Maqshīsh of Tlemcen), we can find some professional musicians (both Muslim and Jewish) who identified strongly with their nonmusical métier.[21]

The co-occurrence of musical craftsmanship with other forms of craftsmanship, both in self-representation and everyday practice, is not only a question of the greater acceptability of nonmusical crafts or even of the difficulty one faced in pursuing a decent living solely from music. Rather, the overlap of musical specialization and the artisanal milieu was many-sided and all-encompassing. Particularly in Tlemcen, there seems to have been a longstanding connection between textile producers and musical production, particularly in the Andalusi musical milieu. The evidence is not only anecdotal but is also woven into the lexicon in that there is a fair amount of semantic overlap between musical and craft vocabulary.[22] In the glossary of textile terms from Tlemcen compiled by the colonial officials Alfred Bel and Prosper Ricard in the early years of the twentieth century, for example, the *rabīb*, a particular ornamental tie made along the edges of textiles, is a diminutive of the *rabāb*, the bowed fiddle traditionally central to ensembles specializing in Andalusi music that the *rabīb* closely resembles in miniature.[23] And, likely flowing in the opposite direction, the textile term *barwal*—which in turn-of-the-century Tlemcen could designate a kind of thick white wool thread[24]—names a movement in the Tunisian-based *nūba* tradition, a rhythm used at the end of the *nūba* in the Algiers-Tlemcen tradition, and a popular song form (*barwala*) that is part of the Moroccan *nūba* practice. Taken together, the overlap between the names of the instruments and agents of *nūba* and textile production in Tlemcen gives substance to the frequent claim in Algeria that the traditional textile industry and the *nūba* are historically linked.[25]

More broadly speaking, the vocabulary around Andalusi music draws quite directly on the vocabulary of artisanal production. We have already touched upon the use of *m'allim*, a generic term for teacher or for master in a master-apprentice relationship, to refer to a professional musician. A more elaborate example of a semantic linking of the *nūba* with the artisanal spheres is the term *ṣanʿa* (pl. *ṣanāyiʿ*), which is widely used to refer to the *nūba* as a repertoire. More generally, *ṣanʿa* means craft, skill, art, and workmanship. It is often used in connection with the artisanal activities that are associated with the precolonial Maghrib, including textiles, silver- and goldsmithing, tilework, and leatherwork. In Andalusi musical circles, it is also used on rare occasion to mean mode, as in *ṣanʿat al-māya*.[26] At the same time, as will be explored further in the following chapter, *ṣanʿa* can be used to refer to each individual sung poetic text constituting the *nūba*. Musicians in both the Algiers and Tlemcen traditions also sometimes speak of *ṣanʿa* as finesse or sophistication, as when a group leader adds an ornament or a novel instrumental arrangement. In this vein, Redouane Bensari is said to have been fond of musically contrasting Algiers and Tlemcen with the adage, "The art of Algiers makes *ṭarab* [musical excitement or pleasure], while the art of Tlemcen is *ṣanʿa*." Finally, the trilateral root *ṣ-n-ʿ* can be used as a verb for musical performance, and occasionally appears in *nūba* texts, as in "wa-l-ʿūd yaṣnaʿ tawāshī" ("and the *ʿūd* fashions [plays] embroideries," *tūshiyya* or "embroidery" being the term for the introductory instrumental form that opens the *nūba*). The semantic richness of the term *ṣanʿa* intimates the broader ways in which musical and artisanal traditions have been knitted together in discourse and in wider social practice.

In a variety of ways, then, we can think of the *shaykh* as an artisan in the employ of the *mūlūʿ*-patron. Yet in thinking about the *shaykh–mūlūʿ* relationship as one of a professional to a patron, we are not dealing with the raw extraction of high-prestige musical product from a low-prestige producer. Instead, we are dealing with a relationship in which there is a sort of collusion and isomorphism between patron and musician, in that the musician partakes of some of the prestige of the music and of its patrons. In addition, there is ideally a complementarity between musician and patron, which can shade into competition. Because of the repertoire's complexity, and the tradition of requesting particular pieces and modes, there is a need for both an educated audience and musicians who are able to meet the demands of that audience. Indeed, until today, professional musicians speak of the need for refined listeners in order to perform satisfactorily.[27] The notion that patrons are indispensable to the life of Andalusi music is particularly vivid in anecdotes of a breakdown in patronage. The connoisseur and musical commentator Mohamed Zerrouki, writing in 1952, told of an exchange with Cheikh Larbi Bensari, in which he asked the master why he was lately neglecting to play the *rabāb*. Zerrouki reports Cheikh Larbi having replied, "Ah, my *rabāb*—it is in the storeroom in my house, hanging among the onions of my winter provisions."[28] That is to say, Cheikh Larbi suggested that he was just getting by, and that the *rabāb* demanded a different level of patronage, security, and human thriving.

Another aspect of this ideal complementarity concerns melodies and words. In a tradition in which the words of the *nūba* poetry but not the melodies themselves have traditionally been written down, musicians provide the musical skill and, quite literally, the musical dimension itself. Nineteenth-century patrons, on the other hand, were known for compiling collections of *nūba* poetry. While musicians often memorized the poetry and kept their own notebooks, the compilations of the wealthy *mūlūʿīn* were often highly elaborate and extensive. Indeed, nineteenth-century enthusiasts seem to have specialized in compiling and correcting such compilations and may have furnished them to hired musicians for use in their performances. Based on the sheer elaborateness of some of these aficionados' compilations, as compared to the more ad hoc texts kept by literate professional musicians, it would seem that patrons viewed themselves as guardians of the poetic content of the repertoire, while they turned to professional musicians to provide its sonic, performative body.[29] Something of this spirit shows up today as well. As one elite *mélomane* explained to me, "This music, it has two things: there is the art, and there is the science. I am not an artist [*fannān*], so I try to follow the science end, read the history, the theory."

Beyond the question of melodies versus words and art versus science, this ideal of complementarity or co-production—the sense that *shaykh* and *mūlūʿ* provide two pieces of a whole—becomes most visible when it is not met. The mismatch between musician and client can come from either term in the dyad. The musician and musicologist Rachid Guerbas, who helped found Algeria's national Andalusi music orchestra, recounts one such instance stemming from the first half of the twentieth century:

> The incomparable *kwitra* player, the late *Mohammed Bahar*, told me that these peripheral pieces within the *Nawba* [ie, the *dlīdla*, the *qādriyya*, and the *inqilāb*] were the portion of novices, and for performing an *inqilāb* during a musical salon, a singer might be vigorously pursued by the hosts, sticks in hand, who could not countenance the affront done them by causing them to hear such "light" pieces in the presence of an audience of fine connoisseurs.[30]

The mismatch could also go the other way. Bouali wrote as follows at the turn of the twentieth century, when the *nūba* seems to have been a much longer and more loosely constructed affair:

> On each night, if [a musician] begins in a mode/*nūba* [*ṣanāʿa*], he does not leave it for another, because each mode/*nūba* has a *tūshiyya* and many *inṣirāfāt* and *mṣāddir*. Because of this, if some of the listeners send a request

> to the singer to perform a particular poem or *muwashshaḥ*, and it is not in the mode/*nūba* that they are in (so that performing it would bring them out of one mode/*nūba* and into another), it quickly becomes apparent to the singer that the person making the request is completely without taste, refinement, or knowledge of this art. If others agree with his request to sing a particular poem or *muwashshaḥ* in that mode/*nūba*, then the singer will become embarrassed and will tune his strings and perform his poems, with the fear that someone present with him who is knowledgeable will reproach him for doing so.[31]

When the match was a good one, however, the relationship of patron to *nūba* specialist could be strong indeed. Writing at the turn of the twentieth century, musical reformer Edmond Yafil hinted at a kind of collusion between professional musicians and *mélomane* keepers of poetic compilations in excluding perceived outsiders from access to their knowledge.[32] In this sense, *shaykh* and *mūlū‘* has historically been a cross-class relationship that can carry within it the seeds of exploitation and domination, but that also potentially forms a circle closed to encroachment from a variety of outsiders who might threaten the purity of the musical object.

Master and Apprentice

Understanding the relationship of *shaykh* to *mūlū‘* as one of patronage uncovers an important facet of this longstanding dyad. An alternative way of conceiving the relationship of *shaykh* to *mūlū‘* is on the master–apprentice model. Such an approach brings us to the question of how a *shaykh* comes into being, as well as the role of musicianship among nonprofessionals.

Thus far, we have treated *shaykh* as a title associated with a particular occupation. However, it is also an honorific, and one that can be applied to professionals and nonprofessionals alike. Since at least the turn of the twentieth century, there have been amateur musicians who have attained high levels of mastery, usually through close contact with a professional who has acted as both paid performer and as teacher. In some cases, amateurs were even known to surpass the knowledge and skill of professionals.[33] In other words, being a high-status *mūlū‘* could eventually lead to being considered a *shaykh* in its honorific rather than its occupational sense. In some cases, such as Abderrahmane Sekkal, amateur performers have played before nonmusicians, though usually in *en famille* settings in which the performance could not be easily mistaken for an engagement before strangers. In addition, the rise of the amateur association provided a venue for amateur musicians to perform publicly, but in a setting that was explicitly (and juridically) nonprofessional. In many such instances, the amateur with mastery of the repertoire has been referred to as a *shaykh* and has come to take on a more formalized pedagogical role vis-a-vis the members of the association. For most heads of associations of today and of the past, the main pedagogical technique has consisted of transmitting by ear the melody of a given piece phrase by phrase, with the students echoing the teacher both on their instruments and vocally. This form of internalization on the part of the student is often referred to as *ḥifḍ*—memorization, safekeeping, or preservation.

Because the term *shaykh* is both an honorific and a marker of an occupation, some high-status amateurs who have achieved mastery eschew the title, and commentators sometimes take pains to clarify what it means in a given context. For example, one musician, seeking to differentiate the *shuyūkh* of Oujda from the *shuyūkh* of the major Algerian *nūba* centers, explained to me that in Algeria *shaykh* is a master, while in Oujda it is simply a job title. In the case of Abderrahmane Sekkal, the ambiguous class associations of the title *shaykh* could be neutralized by his learning in respectable literary arts, which likewise could merit such an appellation. Again, the dilemmas of such a title become exceptionally clear when we move from men to women. In the case of *shaykha*, whose dominant meaning in the musical context is not an honorific but instead a low-status occupation and genre marker, many urban female performers since the mid-twentieth century working in and around the Andalusi complex have been known either by their full name (Maryem Fekkai, Alice Fitoussi) or by a stage name (Reinette l'Oranaise, Fadhela Dziria, Line Monty), even though they usually came from a social milieu similar to that of the prototypical male professional. A similar pattern holds for professional female performers in the contemporary moment who come from higher-status families and grew up through the amateur association and conservatory system rather than in the circles of working-class *msemmaʿāt*, such as Beihdja Rahal, Zakia Kara Terki, Lamia Maadini, and Nassima Chaabane.

In the case of high-status male amateurs like the early twentieth-century disciple of Sfindja named Mohamed Benteffahi, the move toward mastery traditionally required close contact with a *shaykh*, but through settings and forms of relationship that sheltered the amateur from being mistaken for a professional. Yet for many people, the road toward mastery involved a much closer rubbing of shoulders with the *shaykh* in professional settings. Particularly for musically inclined people from the urban artisanal milieu, being a *mūlūʿ* was potentially a path toward becoming a *shaykh* not just in the honorific sense but in the occupational one as well. In a Maghribi Arabic reader that Mohamed Bekhoucha wrote for use at the Lycée Lyautey in Casablanca, he described a *mūlūʿ* as someone who is taken by a song, starts memorizing it by listening to a *mʿallim*, learns to play an instrument, and then, having mastered it, might join a group, play at festivities, and make "a living from this craft."[34] In other words, for Bekhoucha, a *mūlūʿ* is a professional-in-the-making. Indeed, practitioners sometimes describe the subordinate members of the professional ensemble as the apprentices or students (*mutaʿallimīn*) of the *shaykh*.

Although there may have been private lessons between professionals and aspiring professionals in the period before the rise of the amateur associations, instruction seems to have followed the model of practical learning through peripheral participation that characterizes Maghribi craft apprenticeships, and indeed apprenticeships more generally.[35] Musicians came to master their instrument and to know the repertoire by repeatedly performing alongside the *shaykh* in the ensemble, and by being asked to take on increasing musical responsibility along the way. The shift from apprenticeship to mastery does not appear to have been formalized, but the moment when a musician was able to lead the ensemble or form his own ensemble seems to have been a landmark: to be the head of an ensemble is axiomatically to be its *shaykh* or *mʿallim*.[36] This process is not radically different from the association practice, in which the teacher invites the student into participation, first by demanding the repetition of musical phrases, and then, once these have been imprinted in the student, through playing through the pieces and whole *nūbāt* as a group, with the teacher at its head.

It is chiefly through such apprenticeships via professional performance that many of the prestigious lineages of *shuyūkh* were formed, particularly in the era before the advent of the amateur association. For example, in multiple accounts of the Algiers scene, there was a direct chain of transmission from Hadj Brahim, who had been the favorite singer of the last Dey of Algiers, to Mohamed Mnemmeche to Sfindja and beyond, as well as from Mnemmeche to several other fin-de-siècle singers. But while the notion of apprenticeship was there, we should be wary of the image of an exclusive, stable, or especially formalized relationship. If the turn-of-the-century circles of professionals in Algiers and Tlemcen were not a radical departure from the nineteenth-century milieu, musicians on the pre-1900 scene learned their repertoire and trade through contact with multiple musical elders, both in one-on-one situations and through live performance contexts. Similarly, acknowledged musical masters like Mnemmeche had multiple disciples who are said to have inherited their repertoire. But even if the image of a strict allegiance to a single teacher is untenable, close contact with a master is an object of nostalgia for many contemporary practitioners, for whom "sitting" with a *shaykh* and treating music as "a way of living" cannot be replaced by listening to recordings or reading books. And even though veterans of wedding performances complain of the noise, drunkenness, and inattention that plagued some parties, many musicians and listeners lament the loss of the wedding as a major site for paid performance and apprenticeship.

Given the importance of on-the-job apprenticeship to the attainment of musical mastery, there are many stories of conflict between *shuyūkh* and their students, particularly when students reached a high level and came to be potential competitors to the teacher. As far as I know, specific stories of antagonism between master and apprentice in the nineteenth century do not come down to us, but there are many later examples of rivalry and betrayal, arguably best embodied in the famous split between Cheikh Larbi Bensari and his son Redouàne, who went into exile in Casablanca in the 1950s following a crisis in their relationship whose cause is a source of much speculation. In addition, there are many accounts of *shuyūkh* who failed to transmit parts of the repertoire to their students, so that it is fairly common to hear people speak of the typical *shaykh* as avaricious and closed, or even to invoke the notion of *l'esprit cheikh*, "the shaykhly spirit," meaning the tendency of some musicians not to share their musical knowledge; indeed, according to Abdelmadjid Merdaci, writing of Constantine, the shaykh "does not serve to diffuse knowledge but rather to withhold it."[37] Although contemporary practitioners often speak of the *shuyūkh* as primarily having existed in the past, the concept of the *shaykh* and *l'esprit cheikh* continues to exist. As one musician explained to me, the conflict between Ziryāb and Iṣḥāq al-Mawṣilī, the teacher whom Ziryāb had surpassed, was the first example of hoarding (*iḥtikār*) in Andalusi music, and a practice that is very much still alive.

Such rivalries are of course also generational struggles. If the *nūba* is a coveted repertoire that takes a great deal of time and social interaction to master, then it is not surprising that older musicians should figure prominently among the ranks of its bearers, and that younger aficionados interested in learning to play the repertoire should be drawn to them. A *mūlū‘* in this sense ideally migrates into the position of master over time. However, it is also possible to see how a certain anxiety might enter into the relationship. From the student's point of view, a number of potential questions arise. Does the master have full control of the repertoire? Is the master giving all that he knows, and how would one know such a thing? Is there enough time, and enough ability on the disciple's part, to absorb the master's knowledge? In similar fashion, the master might consider whether the disciple is capable of absorbing the musical knowledge, and the effect that sharing this knowledge might have on the master's reputation for uniqueness and desirability.

The potential for distrust and betrayal between teacher and student, and even between the *shaykh* and the more prosaic, nonperfoming *mūlū‘*, is mirrored in the relationship between *shuyūkh* themselves. Writing of the turn-of-the-century milieu, Jules Rouanet wrote of singers who were known to mangle the words or melodies on spotting a competitor in the audience.[38] Writing in 1904, the young Algerois aficionado Edmond Yafil recounted how in his efforts to compile the *nūba* poetry in printed form, he had been given manuscript texts that bore truncated or deformed poems, as if he was the recipient of intentionally damaged goods.[39] Thus eavesdropping was a known method of knowledge acquisition, as well as a threat to be guarded against. Even the notion of theft entered into musical parlance, so that when around 1860 Christianowitsch played a *nūba* that he had learned from Ben Mustapha on the piano for Hadj Brahim, the elder musician jokingly exclaimed, "You stole the *nūba* [*saraqt al-ṣanʿa*]!"[40] A similar notion of stealing repertoire is current among some practitioners today. One Moroccan singer explained to me that his visits to Larbi Bensari in Tlemcen were opportunities to "steal" pieces from the venerable performer. Sid Ahmed Serri, the doyen of Andalusi music in Algiers, has spoken of standing by the synagogue door off Bab Azzoun in central Algiers in order to eavesdrop on the singing that was taking place during prayer time. Thus such on-the-sly transmission speaks to a broader ideology of musical possession, secrecy, rarity, and competition. [41]

With respect to the alleged miserliness of *shuyūkh*, people often point out that as individuals who earned their living through musical performance, professionals had an economic interest in preserving the exclusivity of their knowledge. In many ways, this is a sensible explanation, but it bears some qualification that in turn brings us back to the relationship between professionals and amateurs. The notion of *l'esprit cheikh* is applied not only to professionals who rely upon performance for their living but also to master musicians who do not require musical performance for their livelihood, and even to nonperforming aficionados who allegedly withhold sonic and written documents from circulation. We will explore this topic further in later chapters, but for now the difficulties that it introduces to the economic explanation can be resolved in most respects by invoking Bourdieu's notion of social and cultural capital: the Andalusi repertoire constitutes a polymorphous form of capital that may be converted into money for professionals, and into nonmonetary prestige for nonprofessional masters or collectors.[42]

Such an explanation suffices for the time being. However, it raises one final consideration that we need to make with regard to musical apprenticeship. For *mūlūʿīn* of a certain social class who come to be known as *shuyūkh* in the honorific rather than the occupational sense—in other words, who can be referred to in nearly the same breath as *shuyūkh* and as "great amateurs"—there is the conceit that their performances are not necessary for them to make a living. Yet there are examples of such *shuyūkh* who have been able to supplement their income through professional engagements. Indeed, for some of the late nineteenth-century *shuyūkh*, it was not entirely clear if musical performance was necessary for their livelihood, and some of them continued to practice their nonmusical trade alongside music. Furthermore, there were *shuyūkh* from well-off families who discreetly supplemented their income through paid performances. Thus even if there were clear barriers to the musically skilled son of an elite family earning money through musical performance at the turn of the century, in slightly less wealthy circles the possibility for ambiguity—in other words, for the blurring of *shaykh* as honorific with *shaykh* as occupation—was far greater.

The potential for status anxiety regarding professionalism became more acute after the mass entry of more elite individuals into musical performance through the amateur association movement in the twentieth century. In some cases, accomplished musicians from well-off backgrounds have become acutely aware of the problems this could pose. Sid Ahmed Serri, who came to prominence through the amateur association system in the post-Second World War years, stopped his wedding engagements as mixed dancing became more common, and also as his nonmusical professional life began to overlap with musical performance in uncomfortable ways:

> I was a functionary in a bank, I was the head of personnel. It so happened that while I was singing [during a professional engagement, I noticed that] there were colleagues, lower-ranking than myself, for whom I was in a way responsible, who had come to listen. I was not at ease. I was not at ease. There was even a time when there was a reception at SONATRACH [Algeria's state hydrocarbon corporation]—there was even the director general of the bank who had come. I did not feel comfortable. I said no, I must stop, stop completely.[43]

From this time on, Serri confined his public appearances to amateur festivals and concert hall performances—settings that fall outside the traditional venues of the occupational *shaykh*. Furthermore, for Serri, the term *shaykh* is not necessarily desirable, both because it is too common and, one suspects, because of its occupational residue. In his terms, the honorific *sīd*, as in Sid Ahmed, is sufficient.

Master and Disciple

We have considered the relationship of *shaykh* to *mūlūʿ* in terms of patronage and in terms of artisanal apprenticeship. Each model reveals an aspect of the dyad, even if the models cannot be entirely disentangled from one another.

We turn now to the final aspect of the relationship that we will examine here: the element of spiritual apprenticeship on the Sufi model. We have already touched upon the potential of the term *shaykh* to be understood as a marker of religious authority, and the possibility of using *wullāʿa* in a Sufi context as a term for spiritual rather than specifically musical passion. We can now take this observation a step further and suggest that the relationship of the *shaykh* to the *mūlūʿ* parallels and partakes of the relationship of the Sufi *shaykh* to his *murīd* or disciple.

On the whole, the Sufi parallel is not something that is raised by devotees of Andalusi music. Although there are religious sub-genres and song texts, the main body of the repertoire is not explicitly religious. In fact, the themes of wine and erotic love that frequently recur in the poetry have led some people to criticize the Andalusi repertoire on religious grounds and to link it to a time of decadence that, according to them, ultimately resulted in the downfall of the Muslims in al-Andalus. Nevertheless, many Andalusi music practitioners approach the repertoire in ways that work against the notion that this is a secular music. Some singers interpret the poetic references to wine and love as spiritual metaphors. Some religiously conservative music-lovers speak of Andalusi music as an acceptable form of music, in contrast to other, more "vulgar" styles: one musician told me that he had not "opened the door of music very much" for his four daughters, but that Andalusi music is acceptable in his house, alongside the Qur'an, instrumental music, the Egyptian singer Umm Kulthūm, and several other singers he identified as "classics." In such a view, Andalusi music is part of the *turāth*, and as such the patrimonial is distinct from the crassness of "the music of the market," thereby linking morality, religion, and patrimony in one fell swoop. Another working-class devotee criticized those who play Andalusi music just for the sake of money, rather than out of love for the patrimony, as well as those musicians who drink; for him, "the people of *gharnāṭī* are like the people of *gnāwa* or the *ʿīssāwa*"—in other words, members of a religious brotherhood.

An overlap between musical and spiritual terminologies is not at all surprising given the historical ubiquity and importance of Sufi orders in the Maghrib. Particularly in the same artisanal milieu from which many musical practitioners have come, association with a Sufi order was common well into the twentieth century. Turn-of-the-century textile workers who belonged to the same brotherhood were even known to recite their brotherhood's *dhikr* (ritual recitation of God's name) while working.[44] In addition, there was feedback between the melodies, modes, and poetic forms used in devotional contexts (Jewish as well as Muslim) and those used in the Andalusi repertoire, thanks in large part to the overlap between those who engaged as vocalists in these varied institutional spheres.

The quasi-Sufi aspects of the *shaykh–mūlūʿ* relationship are more a continuation of the themes of apprenticeship than they are of the themes of patronage. A key facet of this resemblance lies in the way in which the notion of authority is reproduced. In Sufi circles, the term *shaykh* is usually applied to a spiritual master around whom disciples congregate. The *shaykh* may act as a ritual guide and teacher who initiates disciples into the practices of the particular Sufi order of which he is part and whose store of knowledge he carries. This *shaykh* might in turn look to a higher-ranking *shaykh* who has wider geographical and deeper institutional reach. In addition, a living *shaykh* is necessarily linked to a deceased spiritual authority. In the Maghrib, a common model for such a link is the maraboutic lineage, in which a founding *shaykh* is understood to have performed miracles, and whose tomb and lineal descendants are said to retain and potentially transmit some of the grace, charisma, or blessing (*baraka*) embodied in the founder. In turn, many such lineages build upon much older, geographically more diffuse genealogies, often eventually meeting up with genealogies of sharifian descent (in other words, descent from the Prophet Muhammad).[45]

In Andalusi musical circles, the reproduction of the *shaykh* follows a similar pattern. One does not reach the status of *shaykh* out of thin air; rather, it is through practice and the building up of relationships with *shuyūkh* that one can go from simply being a *mūlūʿ* to being a *shaykh*. In this sense, the *shaykh* is always both singular and collective, an individual but at the same a member of a collectivity, both in the sense that the *shuyūkh* constitute a category of persons and in that the *shaykh* always exists within a genealogical chain. As one Tlemcani physician who moonlights as a performer explained to me, "The *shaykh* is one who designates his successor." These relationships are all about the "face-to-face" and the act of reproduction-through-transmission: as one aficionado said of someone whose musical authority he does not respect, the problem is that this figure had just listened to some recordings, read some transcriptions, but had "never really had a master, he never lived inside this music." And thus the *shaykh* necessarily implies a lineage leading to him, and at least potentially away from him as well. Mokhtar Allal, a student of Abderrahmane Sekkal, recalls his teacher telling him that no matter how much a musician knows, someone who "did not learn from a master is empty inside."[46]

The invocation of a *shaykh* or, better, a lineage of *shuyūkh*, is widespread in Andalusi musical practice. It has become commonplace to name amateur associations after well-known musical authorities, and the walls of associa-

FIGURE 3. At Café Malakoff, Algiers, 2014, the genealogical ethos in a musical place of memory: a wall of images of Hadj Mohamed El Anka, former proprietor of the café and among its most famous performers. The round percussion instrument in the upper left is a *ṭār*.

tion headquarters are often graced with images of *shuyūkh* of local significance, in some cases arranged in genealogical form (see fig. 3). The invocation of a lineage by Sekkal and Bekhoucha in *Nafḥ al-azhār* is reflected in contemporary practice, as in Sid Ahmed Serri's photographic self-placement within a line leading back to Mohamed Fekhardji and his brother Abderrezak, from them to Mohamed Benteffahi, from him to Sfindja, and finally to Mnemmeche.[47] Such invocations can also be seen in the old photographic practice of positioning association members around images of deceased *shuyūkh*, and in the practice of mounting performances "in homage to" masters, whether living or deceased. In the case of the journey of members of the Oran-based association Nassim El-Andalous to Casablanca to visit the expatriate *shaykh* Redouane Bensari, estranged son and musical inheritor of Cheikh Larbi, the contact with the living *shaykh* can even take on the quality of a religious pilgrimage.

There is a further Sufi parallel in the stories of how individuals became *shuyūkh*, in that the biographies of many *shuyūkh* feature an originary contact with an established authority. In some cases, these are stories about the establishment of a teaching relationship; in other cases, they tell of simple proximity to such a figure; in still others, they are charged moments of discovery. Often they blend into the realm of kinship, and there are tales of a relationship of descent that establishes, reinforces, or ratifies a musical connection. For example, some narratives feature a father who is also the son's *shaykh*, or a musical master who takes on the role of a sort of "spiritual father" to the student. Finally, there are numerous stories of the musician hiding his musical practice from what he expects to be a disapproving father (often himself a musician), who turns out to be impressed and supportive once the son's talent is discovered.[48]

For an example of a mixture of elements of discovery, kinship, and proximity, let us return to a story about Cheikh Salah recounted by his son Mohamed. Cheikh Salah's Tunisian-born father was employed in Rabat, and he would meet his son on occasion in Taza, part way between Oujda and Fes. A lover of music from a young age, Salah constructed a *guembri* (*ginbrī*), a string instrument used in *gnāwa* music, and he learned to play it with facility. One day, while visiting Taza, young Salah climbed a tree to watch a military parade. Cheikh Larbi happened to be in town with his musicians, during one of their regular tours of Morocco. He spotted the boy and called him down from the tree, explaining that he had noticed him in these parts before and wondered who he was. The *shaykh* soon realized that he was related to Salah through the boy's mother, who was from Tlemcen. The musicians who were with the *shaykh* asked the boy to play his *guembri*, and were shocked to find that he had a great deal of talent.

This story of an auspicious initial encounter with the great Tlemcani *shaykh* contains several features that place Salah's legend within a larger tradition of stories of encounters between masters and disciples, both musical and spiritual. First, there is a chance meeting during which the *shaykh* recognizes his disciple. Second, there is an accompanying recognition of a deeper kinship between the young boy and the *shaykh* (this is reinforced and complicated by the fact that Taza was a place where Salah would meet with his absent biological father). Third, there is an element of testing, in the course of which the boy demonstrates his musical gift to the gathered elders. This tale thus establishes Salah's own path to becoming a *shaykh*. The story is in fact far from sufficient for explaining Cheikh Salah's later musical career as an adult, which involved intensive interaction with Tlemcani *shuyūkh* and *mélomanes*. Yet it is a fitting origin narrative, for it ratifies a musical gift through multiple routes: kinship, talent, and actual contact with a prestigious figure.

If *shuyūkh* resemble Sufi saints in terms of the process of their reproduction, they also resemble them in terms of the affective content imputed toward them. Many accomplished performers speak of the great love they feel for their teachers, and of the deep patience, compassion, and musical absorption they were capable of. One performer told me of how her late teacher, whom she described as her "spiritual father," was able to sense disputes amongst his students and foster reconciliation with just a few words. *Shuyūkh* are also remembered for their miraculous memories and stamina. In a sense, it is the *shaykh*'s musical ability and uniqueness that most closely resembles the power of the Sufi saint. Because of the reverence commanded by such musical power, *shuyūkh* are sometimes said to elicit behavior from listeners that would otherwise be unacceptable, as in the story of the late nineteenth-century Jewish musician known as Maqshīsh, whose performance was said to be so absorbing that guests would fail to return their friends' greetings while he played, and one woman suffocated her baby in an effort to keep its cries from disrupting the concert.[49] In death, too, *shuyūkh* can take on powers that recall Sufi masters, as in the case recounted at the beginning of this chapter of the recovery of the melody of the *qṣīda* through a dream. A student of Abderrezak Fekhardji recounted how a picture of the *shaykh*, who was the leading figure in Algiers in the two decades after independence, suddenly fell from the wall and shattered after the student and his fellow association members returned from the master's burial. More prosaically, some musicians pay yearly visits to the graves of their *shaykh*, and "paying homage" to the *shaykh*, alive or dead, is a common feature of contemporary festivals and association concerts that we will return to in chapter 6.

If the musical repertoire is a quasi-sacred, esoteric body of knowledge that is passed down through individuals, then some of the qualities of avarice and secrecy discussed earlier in relation to apprenticeship can also be read in spiritual terms. The musical *shaykh*, whether he is said to hoard his knowledge or not, is understood to be an heir to secrets. Some of these secrets may be transmitted to disciples, but others may be lost with his passing. Because the *shaykh* literally embodies a precious repertoire, the loss of the *shaykh* can mean the loss of valuable musical goods. This rupture helps to explain some of the pathos of the *shaykh*'s passing, and some of the ambivalence in which the *shaykh* is sometimes held—the way he may be an authority but at the same time be someone who is held in reproach by those around him, as in the story of a musical *shaykh* who died alone in his house, with his body lying undiscovered until its stench alerted the people of the neighborhood to his passing. The notion that the *shaykh* is closed or avaricious comes back to the notion that the *shaykh* refuses to share the full extent of his knowledge. So while part of this trope can be understood as a function of the occupational *shaykh*'s precarious position as someone who must make at least some of his living from musical performance, another part of the trope draws its power from elsewhere, beyond the brute demands of livelihood.

Thus the genealogical ethos that gives rise to the *shaykh* also gives rise to the question of genealogical continuity past the lifetime of the *shaykh*. Just as the death of the Sufi saint often gives rise to ambiguity about rightful succession, the passing of the musical *shaykh* can be fraught with tensions and the threat of dispersion. For many turn-of-the-century reformers, the perceived crisis in Andalusi music arose from the failure of *shuyūkh* to appoint successors.[50] Similar anxieties circulate in contemporary practice. One musician recounted to me how his dying *shaykh* said that he would have designated him as his successor if he did not think that this would go unrecognized by the student's contemporaries.[51] And for some people, such as the Tlemcani physician cited above, the age of *shuyūkh* is definitively past:

> What is a master? It is knowledge. . . . Right now, today, truly speaking, one must be logical: there is no master. Today, there are no more masters. . . . Why? Because . . . these people here [in the association], they are amateurs . . . they do their jobs, they have their work. Take me, for example: I don't dedicate myself entirely to music, therefore I cannot be a master. They [the *shuyūkh*] had nearly their entire existence basically devoted to music. That is not the case now. We don't have the true professionals who might become musical masters. . . . I say that a master is a musical professional—that is the definition for me.

Yet even if not everyone agrees that the age of the true *shuyūkh* is past, the loss of the *shaykh* is, to invoke the work of Jean During, always a loss of something—a loss of the *shaykh*'s person, which may include repertoire but is also about the loss of that which is distinctive about that musical individual. In this way the *shaykh* stands for unrealized value—value that may be recuperated in part through contact with the living *shaykh* and in part through genealogical contact with the deceased *shaykh*. *Shuyūkh* are concentrations of value, and the trope of loss or near-loss accentuates this sense that they are actual hoards. Hence the way that the power and pathos potentially summarized in the person of the *shaykh* can verge into the realm of the supernatural. And hence the way in which contact with the deceased *shaykh* through a dream goes beyond the question of repertoire per se: it is not the melody that is being recovered in Mohamed's telling (after all, colleagues of Cheikh Salah knew it) so much as the actual connection with the genealogical forebear, a connection that in this instance is lodged in the circulation of the melody itself. What is transmitted, in a sense, is the originary act of giving.

This also brings us back to the image of al-Andalus, the lost paradise. When we consider Mohamed's narration of the dream, the park in Tlemcen, with its fountains and trees and water, resembles the al-Andalus of Ibn Khafāja's beloved lines. In a sense, the dream is all about the return to the still-living source, the miraculous recovery of lost knowledge. Most of the time, however, this ultimate source is out of reach. In a way, we can think of al-Andalus as standing for the pathos of transmission: the repertoire is always being saved from loss, an attenuated treasure that existed in more perfect form at the root. Thus there is a homology between al-Andalus and the genealogical transmission of musical valuables. The repertoire is the *bagage* from al-Andalus, a cargo that is also an individual's body of musical knowledge, a body that is sometimes interchangeable with the term *patrimoine*, used here in the sense of an individual's (rather than a collective's) body of knowledge. The term for lost repertoire, *al-mafqūd*, of course resonates with *al-firdaws al-mafqūd*, the lost paradise, the standard euphemism for al-Andalus. Practitioners have long spoken of saving the repertoire "from shipwreck" when talking about the work of safeguard, revival, and defense of a collective, anonymous patrimony through the creation of textual "vessels."[52] In this largely unconscious metaphor, al-Andalus and the genealogical ground of generic reality are so closely aligned as to freely flow into one another, so that in such an instance it is difficult to talk about genealogical and al-Andalus talk as ontologically separate speech genres.[53] Rather, together they constitute a modality for conceiving ideologies and actual instances of gift, movement, transmission, value, danger, and loss. Here, al-Andalus is not about a static spatiotemporal figure, but rather about a trajectory of movement from a place to another place, an irreversible transmission across water and land that closely resembles transmission of musical knowledge from master to disciple.[54]

✶

We will have occasion to return to these resonances. But for the time being, it suffices to say that the three facets of the *shaykh–mūlūʿ* dyad cannot be entirely disentangled. Ultimately it is difficult, and likely not worthwhile, to separate craft apprenticeship from spiritual discipleship, or to rigidly demarcate performers who allegedly need the money they are paid from those who allegedly do not. Yet identifying these facets of the relationship is helpful in marking out some of the broad patterns and apparent contradictions that arise for the inhabitants of the Andalusi archipelago. They suggest some of the continuity in the subject positions themselves, and the way these positions have been able to accrete specific, diverse qualities and a broad robustness over time and across space. At the same time, they suggest how it is that these continuities have been able to weather the many changes in the mode of producing and reproducing Andalusi music over the past hundred or more years: patronage, apprenticeship, and discipleship might be quite different from one another, but their points of overlap allow what appear to be but two subject positions to accommodate a wide range of people coming from varied directions.

Taken as a complex whole, the relationship of *shaykh* and *mūlūʿ* speaks to the primacy of a genealogical ethos in the Andalusi musical community. This ethos rests upon two main foundations. First, musical knowledge is held to reside chiefly within individual master performers; in this sense, it is believed to be embodied knowledge. Second, this embodied knowledge is derived from and flows (even if only barely or incompletely) to other individuals who likewise become repositories of such knowledge. Hence each master musician ideally stands at a crossroads of overlapping dyadic relationships, and, when the musician passes along repertoire to younger generations, he or she constitutes a link in further chains of relation. Such an idealized structure of transmission requires that the core repertoire be conceived as fixed, and it means that its primary medium of existence is passage through people. But we should not simply conceive of *shuyūkh* as transmitting musical pieces. Rather, as I suggested above, they transmit the act of transmission, and, like Marcel Mauss famously described in his theory of the gift, they transmit something of themselves in the process.[55] In other words, the repertoire is not in fact separable from the persons who embody it. But when *shuyūkh* transmit something of themselves, this happens through the transmission of repertoire that gave rise to them in the first place. It is to the form and substance of this repertoire that we now turn.

3

Heavy and Light: Andalusi Music as Genre

In a vivid account of his musical convalescence in Algiers in 1861, the Russian military officer and music enthusiast Alexandre Christianowitsch recounts the way in which his encounter with the *nūba* was entangled with his developing relationship with the musician Hamoud Ben Mustapha:

> One evening while walking, having already notated around fifteen melodies, I bumped into my friend, who convinced me to go hear a famous Jewish musician who, he told me, played *qānūn* very well. The offer accepted, I went to hear the great artist. Having arrived in a little Moorish house full of music-lovers [*amateurs*] who surrounded the *qānūn* player, Hamoud said to me, "Listen closely, I am going to have him play the tunes that you notated." With that, I heard the songs that I already knew, but which nevertheless sometimes seemed strange to me, so abundant were the ornaments that choked the melody. "He plays well," my friend told me, "but he only plays Arbi [*ʿarbī*], Insiraf [*inṣirāf*], and street songs, and he does not know how, he cannot know how to play the *nūba*," he added, raising his finger meaningfully. "What is the *nūba*?" I asked him. "The *nūba*," he responded, in a tone that meant to say, What, you don't know the *nūba*? "Oh, it is the greatest music in the world!" And why had he not spoken to me of it? "Because it is too difficult! You would not be able to play it. The *nūba* is too difficult," continued Hamoud, becoming more and more animated and fixing me with a passionate glance. Then, taking me by the hand, he added, "In Algeria, there are only three individuals who can play the *nūba*: Hadj-Brahim, Sid-Ahmed-ben-Seliem and Mohamed-el-Menemmech. Aside from these three old men, no one, no one knows the *nūba*."[1]

The essay in which this passage is found provides a vivid, tantalizing account of musical connoisseurship and tourism in mid-century Algiers. For the purposes of thinking about genre, however, I would like to juxtapose

Christianowitsch's quotation of Ben Mustapha with the comments of an Algiers shopkeeper who I encountered in May 2009. I had stepped into a small bookstore that I had noticed several times before while walking down Didouche Mourad, the main shopping boulevard in downtown Algiers, in the hope of tracking down a songbook compiled by Sid Ahmed Serri. The proprietor of the bookstore, a thin man somewhere beyond sixty, wearing a button-down cap, shook his head:

> People nowadays, they're not interested. There was a time when every Friday it was Serri on the radio. We would sit down as a family and listen, to Serri and the others, back in the '50s. Today it's *raï* [music]. If I were in the government, I would ban *raï*. It's vulgar. The other music, of Serri and those, that's classical—classical music. With *raï*—I went to a wedding, I was with my family, and there was a *raï* singer. What did he sing? "You, girl, are for everybody." I said to myself, What is this? For shame! You, girl, are for everybody?? For shame. With classical music, you could listen to it as a family. You see what's happened to Algeria today?

Several things are striking about setting these two musical narratives side by side. Despite the obvious differences in terminologies, frames of genre reference, texture of everyday life, and time period, these are both statements about the *nūba* repertoire and its others. Those others vary: in one case, it is a set of song forms and performance contexts associated by Ben Mustapha primarily with Jewish professional performers (and, if we read the rest of the essay, with women and children), while in the other it is a popular music genre associated with working-class urban youth, sexual impropriety, and a world turned upside-down. Yet despite the changing identity of those generic others, the generic self that Ben Mustapha and the shopkeeper champion is in certain respects the same.

This chapter attempts to map that generic self. But as this juxtaposition implies, and as Bakhtin and his readers have taught us, to describe genre is always to describe genres.[2] Those genres include symbolic opposites, such as Ben Mustapha's street songs and the shopkeeper's *raï*. They also include "marginal genres" that often go along with a genre, the proximate genres that exist at a genre's porous borders.[3] In the Andalusi case, those neighboring genres, including the *inqilābāt* and *qṣāyid*, are what make Andalusi music more than the *nūba*. The following pages seek to map the particular genre configuration upon which rest the kinds of collectivities, narratives, and subjectivities described in the previous chapters, while simultaneously drawing attention to the inherent plurality and contestability of that configuration.

There are a number of analytic traps to avoid along the way. One is the objectivist, formalist trap in which genres are neat packages distinguished from one another by clearly observable features. At various moments I draw attention to ambiguities and disagreements regarding genre—the way in which genre is a subjective social construction, frequently contested, whose lineaments must be discovered "over the shoulder" of practitioners.[4] In particular, I explore the broad categorization of genres into the categories of the *thaqīl* (heavy, slow, serious) and the *khafīf* (light, fast, playful) that runs through listeners' and performers' discourse about music. In this way, the collectivities, narratives, and subjectivities described in the previous two chapters do not simply rest passively upon a genre configuration but in fact arise from a genre configuration that itself gets made and negotiated by the members and bearers of those same collectivities and subjectivities.

But while listening to practitioners' own generic "boundary work" is crucial, I also emphasize elements of a formalist analysis.[5] These formal elements are important not only because practitioners themselves draw attention to them but also because they are embedded in the musical practice in such a way that they do not seem to surface in everyday awareness. This is to say that musical self-fashioning is not an act of pure volition on the part of "the people of al-Andalus": the formal attributes of the genre configuration often have a solidity and otherness about them. These formal attributes are just as social as the boundary work that is evident in discourse, but they tend to emerge from older, more temporally extended patterns of social labor and for this reason often appear to be fixed, quasi-natural facts. Consideration of this historical dimension of genre in the following pages means paying attention to both continuities and discontinuities, including the emergence and disappearance of genres and attributes over time. Therefore, this chapter adds a historically minded element to constructionist approaches to genre, as well as to Steven Feld's broader critique of the traditional analytic division between musical structure and social structure: in the following pages, musical structures, including the ones that add up to a sense of genre, are in fact social structures, although not in a form consistently homologous to what is traditionally understood as social structure in the anthropological and ethnomusicological literature.[6]

The following description begins with the *nūba* and moves outward to include the wider complex and its surround, using the past century-and-a-half of musical practice as its general time frame. It can be daunting to describe what is sometimes called "the vast edifice" of the *nūba* to a novice. A good guide, however, is the sort of songbook that I was looking for on Didouche Mourad, the kind of compilation that typically serves as the proximate source for the poetic texts sung in the *nūba*. Alongside the scholarly commentators themselves, songbooks are one of the things that make Andalusi music a *musique savante*, "a learned music."[7] In the Andalusi scene, songbooks are practical guides for musicians and listeners, but along the way they are also sites for articulating a musical vision. They are, in a sense, devices for storing and shaping the words and formal logic of the *nūba*, and I would argue that making them has been a central part (rather than simply a representation) of the genre practice at least since the early nineteenth century. Leaving aside the songbook as a social practice in itself for chapter 5, here I use the standard printed songbook as used in the past hundred years to walk through some of the formal aspects of the repertoire. The songbook's structure serves as an excellent guide to practitioners' own conceptualizations of the Andalusi musical complex, and this chapter explores three aspects of the structure that go a long way toward explicating the *nūba* as a musical form: poetic text, mode, and movement.

At the same time, what the songbook leaves out is of great importance. These aporia include much of the melodic and instrumental substance of the *nūba* form, as well as many of the aspects of the Andalusi musical complex that go beyond the *nūba*. In the later sections of this chapter, such gaps lead us outward from the genre core to explore the fuzzy boundaries of the practice—boundaries that we will see are closely connected to the structure of the *nūba* itself. This map will suggest that the sense of Andalusi music as a genre closely articulates with its position within a genre field in a way that goes beyond simply being situated within a system of contrasts and similarities.

Ṣanʿa: From Poem to Song

Songbooks in the Algiers-Tlemcen tradition are usually organized along two axes: melodic mode and movement within the *nūba*. Thus they typically begin with all the song texts associated with the mode *dhīl*, starting with the *mṣaddar*, then moving to the *bṭayḥī*, the *darj*, *inṣirāf*, and *khlāṣ*, before starting again with the *mṣaddar* of the next mode. Because mode and movement are so central to the organization of the songbook, and, by extension, to the insider's map of Andalusi music as a genre, we will look at each of these elements in turn. But first, we need to look at the song texts (*ṣanʿa*, pl. *ṣanāyiʿ*) themselves that are seemingly the "stuff" that is being organized in the songbooks. In fact, the notion that the song texts are what the songbooks organize is not quite the way some practitioners conceive it: one professional musician, for example, explained to me that these song texts are really the third element by which the *nūba* materials are classed. In order to make sense of such a statement, we need to first think through the place of the song text within Andalusi musical practice.

The Andalusi traditions of the Maghrib, like many Arabic-language musical traditions, privilege the voice and the sung text.[8] While the *ʿūd*, *kuwītra*, *rabāb*, *ṭār*, mandolin, violin, viola, piano, and *darbūka* have been central to the Algerian Andalusi tradition over the past hundred years (and many more in the case of the first four instruments), they are very much accompaniments to the voice. More specifically, they frame the voice and respond to the vocal line itself through the instrumental *jawāb* or response that repeats the melody at regular intervals.[9] Even the substantial sections of the *nūba* that are purely nonvocal, such as the opening *tūshiyya* or the *kursī* that introduces the first four movements, serve to frame vocally centered pieces. The privileging of the voice, not only in the Andalusi traditions but in a range of urban Arabic-language repertoire, can be heard in the way in which contemporary musicians often refer to nonvocal material: these sections are *mūsīqā ṣāmita*, "silent music." As we will explore further in chapter 4, some commentators even suggest that the poetry in the *nūba* traditions functions as a vessel for the transmission of melodies, as if the poems themselves constitute melodic notation—a reasonable proposition given the fact that the general structure of the song form maps closely onto the poetic structure.[10] The melody is an absent presence, the crucial aspect of the repertoire that is invisible yet implied in the songbook's form and content. At the same time, many practitioners assert that compared to the *qṣīda* repertoire, for example, the words of the *nūba* poetry are not a central focus for listeners—the *nūba* is lyrical rather than topical. As a radiologist *mélomane* put it to me, just as one can take an x-ray in which the ribs are not visible, one can remove the words from one's musical memory and take pleasure in the melody alone.

It is widely known among practitioners, educated North African outsiders, and scholars that much of the poetic material featured in the *nūba* is in the strophic form known as *muwashshaḥ* or *tawshīḥ*, and that in the Maghrib this form is largely confined to the *nūba* traditions.[11] This form is one of the major links of the *nūba* tradition to al-Andalus, in that the *muwashshaḥ* is quintessentially Andalusi.[12] Likely emerging as a distinct form in both classical Arabic and in Hebrew in the eleventh century, the *muwashshaḥ* soon became a much-loved poetic framework in Andalusi courtly life as well as among literati in medieval Egypt, the Levant, and the Maghrib. Much of the attraction of the *muwashshaḥ* lay in the novel elements that it introduced to the repertoire of poetic forms available to medieval men (and occasionally women) of Arabic letters. Among these was its subject matter, which intertwined with the affective repertoire of courtly aesthetics: union with the beloved, separation, desire, wine, and the natural world as embodied in the garden. In turn, such themes could be diverted into praise for patrons. While themes of love and praise had certainly been present in the *qaṣīda* repertoire that preceded the *muwashshaḥ* and that remained the preeminent Arabic poetic form even in al-Andalus, the *muwashshaḥ* introduced a distinctive cast of characters, forces, and images that tended to go together: the beloved (*ḥabīb*), the cup-bearer or wine-pourer (*sāqī*), desire (*ʿishq*), meeting or union with the beloved (*waṣl*), and the watcher or censor (*raqīb* or *ʿādhil*) who menaces such union.[13]

Notwithstanding these novelties, what has received a larger share of attention in the work of literary historians is the formal innovation that the *muwashshaḥ* represented and that sharply distinguishes the *muwashshaḥ* from its predecessors in both visual and aural terms. Unlike the canonical classical Arabic *qaṣīda*, with its single rhyme throughout the poem, the *muwashshaḥ* is strophic—that is, it is made up of a pattern of strophes or verses, which in this instance introduce contrasting rhymes, replacing the visual sense of long, dense, straight columns with the sense of wide, airy, extended checkerboards.[14] Aside from the consistency of the number of lines and verses (the typical classical *muwashshaḥ* is made up of five main blocks consisting of five lines each), the *muwashshaḥ* is also held together by a returning rhyme, on the model AABBB, AACCC, AADDD, AAEEE, AAFFF. The prototypical *muwashshaḥ* in the literary tradition ends with a restatement of the rhyme AA, as if to provide a lock to what threatens to be a never-ending pattern (indeed, "lock" is the meaning of one of the Arabic terms, *qufl*, used to refer to such an ending).[15]

The contrast between two elements—the common rhyme and the changing rhyme—may explain the derivation of the word *muwashshaḥ* from *wishāḥ* or *wushāḥ*, the medieval Arabic term for a women's embroidered, multicolored belt, collar, or sash.[16] Although the specific material form of an Andalusi *wishāḥ* is unclear, the connection to the *muwashshaḥ* makes sense in that the poetic form is based on an alternating pattern, in this case an alternation that also contains further elements of end-rhyme contrast as one moves from strophe to strophe. The suggestion of a connection to such a wearable object is further encouraged by the use of the term *simṭ*, a string on which pearls are strung, to describe the common rhymes. In this metaphor, the common rhyme is the thread upon which are strung the changing rhymes (traditionally referred to as the *aghṣān* or branches).

From its beginning, the *muwashshaḥ* was a deeply musical form. After half a century of lively scholarly debate about its relationship to other Arabic,

Romance, and Hebrew poetic forms, it is clear that the *muwashshaḥ* was conceived as a poem intended for singing. Although we know very little about the melodic forms associated with the *muwashshaḥ* in the medieval period, the strophic nature of the poem would suggest some kind of melodic repetition, perhaps on the model of verse-chorus.[17] Furthermore, it is clear that the *muwashshaḥ* in al-Andalus interfaced with song forms in colloquial Arabic and in Romance.[18] A formally similar, nearly contemporaneous sung poetic form, the *zajal*, was primarily in colloquial Arabic. In addition, the final two lines in the common rhyme in the medieval Andalusi *muwashshaḥ*, sometimes known as the *kharja*, often shifted from formal Arabic (or, for the Hebrew *muwashshaḥ*, from Hebrew) to colloquial Arabic or Romance, while simultaneously shifting from the voice of the poet to the quoted voice of another. James Monroe has suggested that the *kharja* in fact represented a quotation from a popular song and perhaps even functioned to provide the reader with the appropriate melody.[19] While the *kharja* introduces many tantalizing uncertainties regarding linguistic register, intertextuality, quotation, and song that have given rise to a lively scholarly subfield unto itself, even the main body of the classical *muwashshaḥ* suggests that poets who engaged the form were closely attuned to music.[20]

In the many centuries after its emergence, the *muwashshaḥ* came to be central to a range of Arabic-language song traditions that continue into the present day. In Yemen, Syria, and Egypt, the *muwashshaḥ* has long been a favorite poetic form for urban singers and composers, who often draw upon the works of medieval and post-medieval poets working in this form.[21] In the Mashriq, the *muwashshaḥ* is so closely associated with music that some composers can speak of composing a *muwashshaḥ* without words—that is to say, a melody that is understood to be an appropriate vehicle for a *muwashshaḥ* text.[22] In the Maghrib, the *muwashshaḥ* is not only central to the *nūba* traditions but also shares many formal elements with the texts that make up the body of urban colloquial repertoire sometimes known as *qṣāyid* or *malḥūn*, of which *ḥawzī* and *ʿarūbī* are part. Some Maghribi scholars treat such poetry as North African versions of the medieval *zajal*, transformed in this instance to reflect the diction and landscape of the Maghrib rather than of al-Andalus.[23]

Most of the scholarship on the *muwashshaḥ* has focused on the question of its origins, with little attention to its afterlife in North Africa. The rare discussions of the *muwashshaḥ* in its contemporary musical context, whether Mashriqi or Maghribi, have usually focused on what it might tell us about medieval musical practice, and in turn what medieval musical practice might contribute to a primarily literary history.[24] Alternatively, attention is placed upon the usually fragmentary survival of Andalusi poems at the expense of the later, Maghribi compositions that follow the old model. But once we start looking at Maghribi musical practice in its own right and not simply as an adjunct to Andalusi literary history, we begin to be presented with an orientation to poetic form that is in some respects distinct from what is found in the scholarly literature on the *muwashshaḥ*.

First, as is clear from a cursory examination of a songbook in the Maghribi Andalusi traditions, no authors are listed. A user of a songbook has no immediate way of knowing if the poem is from al-Andalus or from the Maghrib, or whether it is very old or relatively new. The very anonymity of the songbook *muwashshaḥāt* may have helped to expand this poetic repertoire, since it has been suggested that authors of erotic poetry in later periods sometimes attributed their creations to the poets of al-Andalus as a way to protect their own reputations.[25] Unlike a classical Arabic *dīwān*, in which authorship is the logic of the collection, and unlike the thematic and biographical organization of poetry in the Arabic *adab* or belles-lettres literature, the *nūba* songbook orders its poetic contents along the two eminently musical axes of mode and movement. Thus a poem may appear more than once in the same songbook, a reflection of the fact that the same poem may be used in more than one mode and movement and, by extension, that it may be sung to more than one melody. The focus upon musical practice brings the poems away from the literary historian's concern with authorship, historical and geographic provenance, and theme. Instead, the poems come from the songbook and from the tradition, which itself stands as a kind of author. As a tradition, the repertoire is necessarily an object that comes from the past—a past that is metonymically conceptualized as al-Andalus, even if many musicians are aware that not all that they sing was actually written there.

Another key difference from the literary-historical understanding is that the songbook texts rarely follow the fully elaborated five-strophe form associated with the prototypical *muwashshaḥ*. Samuel Stern, a founding figure in *muwashshaḥ* studies, pointed out that within the North African musical context many old *muwashshaḥāt* appeared in truncated form, and the parts that tended to be shed were those sections that were in praise of a specific ruler. Stern pointed out that as a result of such shedding, "the whole repertoire comes to consist of love-poetry."[26] He also noted that the truncated poems could become even shorter in the hands of musicians. Take his discussion of "Al-ʿūd qad tarannam" (The *ʿūd* resounded). Stern pointed out that in North Africa, the poem came to lose those sections that were written in praise of the ruler al-Māʾmūn of Toledo. But, in addition, "when, during my visit to Tetuan eight years ago [1954], Sr. Valderrama had arranged for a concert by the orchestra of the [municipal] conservatory, I asked the musicians whether they were acquainted with the poem *al-ʿUdu qad tarannam*. They were indeed, and intoned it without further ado: but they only knew the first lines."[27]

For Stern, "Al-ʿūd qad tarannam" was a poem that had attenuated in its passage into modern North African musical practice. For the practitioners of Andalusi music with whom he was interacting, however, it was a song—in the words of Carl Davila, writing about *āla* performance in Morocco, it is the "text-as-sung" rather than the text-as-written that is the model.[28] The compilations to which many of the musicians likely had access may have had many more lines than the ones they sang, and the performers may have been well aware of this fact (although they probably were unaware of the lines in praise of al-Māʾmūn). But it is unlikely that the musicians conceived the lines they sang as an excerpt of anything, whether written in the songbook or existing in a complete version in some other location. Instead, what they sang was probably for them a whole unto itself. Or rather, if it was in fact conceived as a fragment, it was not a fragment of a larger poem but rather a fragment of the *nūba* repertoire as a whole, a fragment from the patrimony. In similar fashion, even the more elaborated sung texts that one can often hear in the Algiers-Tlemcen tradition do what from Stern's perspective might seem a certain violence to the prototypical *muwashshaḥ* form, including the form in which they often appear in the songbooks: frequently lines and whole strophes are omitted. In practice, the poem on the page is something that is drawn upon for the creation of a sung object—a highly partial selection that is made possible in part by the fact that the poems are rarely obviously narrative in tone, even if some practitioners can intuit a story developing over the course of a *nūba*.[29] Furthermore, there are unmarked repetitions of lines, as well as non-referential vocalizations (often on the syllables *yā lā lān*) known as *tarāṭīn* that are not written on the page but that enter into many of the sung texts as a crucial component, often stitching together the halves of a single poetic line.[30] In other words, the page contains both more and less than what goes into its musical version.

The contrast between a literary-historical perspective and a musical-practical one sharpens further when we turn to the terminology used in the *nūba* traditions for these sung objects. While printed and manuscript songbooks sometimes make reference to the *muwashshaḥ* and *zajal* forms in their titles, in the Algiers-Tlemcen tradition these terms are not the standard way to talk about the sung text, even if practitioners are often capable of identifying a particular text (*naṣṣ*) as a *muwashshaḥ* or, on occasion, as a *zajal*. Instead, among Andalusi music practitioners, the sung text is a *ṣanʿa*, or alternatively a *shghul* or *shughl*.[31] Both these terms denote a work; in the case of *ṣanʿa*, the term overlaps strongly with craft or a crafted product, a made thing.

As described in the preceding chapter, in the Andalusi musical context *ṣanʿa* can be used to refer to a sung text, to a sense of musical finesse, to an act of performance, and even occasionally to a mode. It can also lend its name to the *nūba* as a musical genre, particularly in the Algiers-Tlemcen tradition. It is the polyvalent centrality of the term *ṣanʿa* (not to mention the musical encounter embedded within the colonial encounter) that has occasionally led Algerian commentators to refer to this musical genre as the Maghribi equivalent of "opera": as Nadir Marouf has pointed out, opera is Italian for "a work," in the same way that *ṣanʿa* or *shghul* can be glossed as "a work."[32] These are genre-specific terms: one does not use them to refer to sung texts that are clearly outside the Andalusi musical framework, just as one does not refer to the *nūba* song texts as *qṣīda*. Nor is it conventional practice to use the standard Arabic term for song, *ughniyya*, to refer to the Andalusi sung texts.

Just as *ṣanʿa* brings us away from a notion of poetic form abstracted from musical practice, the way in which musicians and listeners talk about the structure of a given *ṣanʿa* represents a transformation of the formal terminology used in the *muwashshaḥ* tradition. This is most obvious in the meaning of the term *maṭlaʿ*. In *muwashshaḥ* scholarship, the *maṭlaʿ* (which literally means opening or top) refers to the common-rhyme couplet that sometimes opens the poem, thereby acting as a sort of mirror to the *kharja* that ends the prototypical Andalusi *muwashshaḥ*. In the Algiers-Tlemcen tradition, in contrast, the *maṭlaʿ* primarily refers to a secondary melodic motif that contrasts with the melodic motif used for the bulk of the lines in a given *ṣanʿa*. This secondary melodic motif is indeed linked to lines that, when viewed in prototypical *muwashshaḥ* form, are in the common rhyme. However, among musicians, the term *maṭlaʿ* is generally used to refer only to the initial line of the common-rhyme couplet, this initial line being the one that is sung using the secondary melodic motif. Furthermore, in most sung texts in the Algiers-Tlemcen tradition, the common-rhyme couplet, as well as the *maṭlaʿ* in the sense of the secondary melodic motif, appear not at the beginning of the text but rather after the non-common rhyme lines, so that the rhyme scheme is usually AAABB.[33] The second line in the common-rhyme couplet has its own musical term: it is not a continuation of the *maṭlaʿ* but rather the *rujūʿ*, the "return" to the primary melodic motif. Thus, in the following song text (which in current Algerois practice can be a *darj* in *nūbat mjennba* or an *inṣirāf* in *nūbat ṣīka*, and in Tlemcen a *darj* in *nūbat ṣīka*), lines 4 and 5 together constitute the *maṭlaʿ* in poetic terms, but are respectively a *maṭlaʿ* and a *rujūʿ* musically speaking (the spacing approximates that typically found in songbooks, and the nonstandard, colloquializing vowels reflect the songbook and performance convention):

1. Yā sāqī lā taghfal	*	qum fāyyiq sulṭānī
2. Imlā l-kās wa-nāwil	*	wa-asqi ḍīyā ajfānī
3. Khadduh jīt nuqabbil	*	bāsh tanṭfā nīrānī
4. Wa-nqūl luh yā badrī	*	li-amrak samʿān wa-ṭāʿa
5. Mā ykhallaf shī dahrī	*	yā sāqī dhī al-sāʿa

O cupbearer, do not forget to rise and awake my sultan!
Fill the cup and serve it, pour out the light of my eyes!
I came to kiss his cheek so as to extinguish my fire.

And I tell him, "O full moon, I am at your command!"
No one can replace you for me, O cupbearer of this moment![34]

While *maṭlaʿ* has a musical meaning distinct from its literary meaning, it also in some respects resonates with the formal aesthetics of the *muwashshaḥ* as a whole. If it has been theorized that *muwashshaḥ* derives its name from the contrast of the common-rhyme couplets with the sets of three rhyming lines whose rhymes change from strophe to strophe, in the manner of an embroidered, multicolored *wishāḥ*, then the melody introduces yet another element of contrast. The primary melodic motif establishes the coherence of the whole, while the secondary melodic motif marks the departure from the preceding rhymes. But rather than separating the common-rhyme couplet from the lines that precede it through the consistent use of the secondary melodic motif, the second line of the couplet in fact returns to the primary melodic motif through the *rujūʿ*. In this way, the melodic contrast represented by the *maṭlaʿ* in its musical sense represents a knot that creates a braid in the sung text. Another way of conceiving this is that the primary melodic motif functions in precisely the same manner as the common-rhyme couplets, the "strings" on which the pearls of the changing rhymes are strung. But rather than duplicate the work of the *simṭ*, the primary melodic motif works against it, thereby using both melody and rhyme to create an interlocking structure.[35]

We are now better placed to consider what the musician meant when he told me that *ṣanʿa* is one of three ways in which the *nūba* material gets classed in the songbooks. My initial understanding was that the songbooks class the song texts according to mode and movement. But the claim that there are in fact three axes of classification gets at an important aspect of the practice: it is the *nūba* that is the primary content of the songbook, and *ṣanʿa* is one of the building blocks of the *nūba*, one of several ways in which the *nūba* material is given shape and organized. This building block is not a mute poem but rather is ideally a sung text, one that exists in luxuriant potentiality through its written form—a written form that is often drawn upon only partially in the movement from written page to performance. We might say, in keeping with a venerable metaphor within the Andalusi musical tradition, that the *nūba* is the "edifice" that gets built, the *ṣanāyiʿ* are the building blocks that are extracted from poems in the songbooks, and mode and movement are guidelines for the assemblage of these blocks. The blocks are distinctive from one another in certain respects, but they are made of similar elements. There is no conceit of author or other sort of provenance to stand in the way of the practitioner's act of making use of these words. Rather, the texts are conceived as coming from a single author, whether that is identified as a single mode-specific *nūba*, the *nūba* repertoire as a whole, al-Andalus, or the patrimony. To "make" these texts in performance is to give voice to this other's words.[36]

Ṭabʿ: The Nature of Mode

Ṭabʿ—literally "nature" or "stamp," here translated as "mode"—is one of the crucial organizing logics for the arrangement of the poetic texts that get mined for the making of *ṣanāyiʿ* or *shghālāt*. As mentioned in the introductory chapter, there are sixteen named modes in current practice, with seven of them being treated as the root modes (*uṣūl*) and the rest as their derivatives (*furūʿ*). Of these sixteen, twelve have enough song texts from the various movements to constitute more-or-less complete named *nūbāt*. Which derivatives match up with which root modes is a point of disagreement between those who follow the practice of Tlemcen and those who follow that of Algiers. Hence on the left below are the root modes, followed by their derivatives to the right, marked with a T for a Tlemcen-specific classificatory practice and with an A for Algiers-specific ones (those modes that "have" a more-or-less complete associated *nūba* are in bold):[37]

Roots	Derivatives
jarka	[none]
raml al-māya	***ḥsīn*** (T), ***raṣd***, *ghrībat ḥsīn* (T), ***ghrīb*** (T)
zīdān	***mjennba, raml***
ʿaraq [*ʿarāq*]	***ḥsīn*** (A), *ghrībat ḥsīn* (A), ***ghrīb*** (A)
ṣīka	[none]
mazmūm	[none]
muwwāl	***dhīl, māya, raṣd al-dhīl***

The modes in bold that are able to lend their names to a *nūba* are usually presented in the songbooks in a set order. In the Algiers-Tlemcen songbook tradition, the particular order of the modes is a convention that does not have an obvious link to performance practice of the past century and a half;

in other words, although most songbooks begin with *dhīl*, this has no bearing on the placement (or lack of placement) of that mode and *nūba* within a performance or set of performances.[38] Instead, the written ordering of modes simply provides a modicum of standardization in the songbooks' layout. In the context of modern performance, a *nūba* remains within a single mode or, on occasion, within a set of complementary modes. Thus a *nūba* in the mode *raṣd*, called *nūbat al-raṣd*, draws most of its *ṣanāyiʿ* from the section of the songbook devoted to *raṣd*, and one in the mode *ṣīka* (called *nūbat ṣīka*) draws its texts from the section devoted to *ṣīka*.[39] The term *nūba* applies to the entirety of texts and accompanying melodies associated with a given mode; it also applies to what is actually performed from this pool of potential texts. Thus *nūbat ṣīka* as a whole always exists in potential, but because of the limits of knowledge, skill, time, and patience, the *nūbat ṣīka* one actually hears is an instantiation, and one that will usually at least partially vary from other instantiations with regard to the selection and execution of poetic texts.

The focus on a central mode in any given performance is in fact a wider feature of a conceptually, historically, and in some instances terminologically related set of traditions, including the ancient Greek modes and much of the modern urban art music of the Middle East, Central Asia, and South Asia. As in the case of Middle Eastern and Central Asian *maqām* and South Asian *rāg*, *ṭabʿ* refers to a set of sonic relationships that go beyond the abstracted concept of a stepwise scale in modern Western European tradition to include certain recurring, not-necessarily-stepwise melodic motifs or gestures.[40] The connection between the North African Andalusi modes and other modal systems is not lost on practitioners. For example, the Mashriqi *maqāmāt* and Maghribi *ṭubūʿ* in some instances share names but not internal sonic relationships, and in other instances share internal sonic relationships but differ in their names. Likewise, the points of connection to the ancient Greek modal system, and in turn to Western European plainchant, were of great interest to colonial-era commentators like Salvador Daniel, for whom the North African modes seemed to encapsulate musical systems that in Europe were lost with the move toward harmony and equal temperament in the early modern period.[41] Mode continues to be a favorite medium for speculation about the deep past and high civilizational crosscurrents.[42] It also provides a framework through which musicians orient themselves to other musical practices and other performers. One Tlemcani musician explained to me that in order to improvise well with a group of Spanish musicians, he simply had to find the mode in which they were playing and join in. Mode, like the concept of key and chordal progressions in the European tradition, is thus a basic way through which practitioners find their bearings, both within the Andalusi tradition and in relation to other traditions.

As in many modal musical practices, the concept of *ṭabʿ* in the North African Andalusi traditions is connected to a theory of humoral medicine, with various modes traditionally being associated with a range of bodily effects and times of the day. Writing in the early eighteenth century, English observer Thomas Shaw wrote of the modal system in Algiers that "if the account be true, (which I have often heard seriously affirmed,) that the flowers of *mullein* and *mothwort* will drop, upon playing the [mode] *mizmoune* [*mazmūm*], they have something to boast of, which our modern *musick* does not pretend to."[43] Most Maghribi discussions of such theories written in the past hundred years treat the humoral connection, particularly in its medicalized form, as a form of knowledge that is no longer current at the moment of writing.[44] Yet the notion of a connection of certain modes to specific hours of the day does circulate among some performers and listeners and is sometimes also relevant to performance practice outside the concert stage context.[45] In addition, the notion of a connection between *ṭubūʿ* and hours of the day connects very closely to the notion of an attenuated repertoire. According to the widely circulated origin narrative, there were once twenty-four modes and *nūbāt*, corresponding to the hours of the day, and these modes and *nūbāt* have attenuated to roughly half that number. Such a narrative posits a sense of modal, humoral, and even cosmological completeness in the Andalusi past, and it institutionalizes the sense that what remains today is a mere fragment of a larger whole. It also introduces the possibility that certain modes might be recovered, by recourse either to neighboring, ostensibly more complete traditions, or to individuals with knowledge of them. Writing at the turn of the twentieth century, Bouali reported evidence that "in the lands of al-Andalus this art contained twenty-four modes, while in our age what remains of these are only twelve modes, and this among the strongest singers. There was in Tlemcen a Jew named Maqshīsh who I used to spend evenings listening to, and he had command of sixteen modes, and today we have those who are deemed praiseworthy and skilled for knowing but four."[46]

For the initiated, most of the modes are immediately recognizable, often even in those instances where the listener encounters a *ṣanʿa* or instrumental section that is otherwise entirely new. Intimate familiarity with the character of a *ṭabʿ* is also crucial to the performance and evaluation of the unmetered, improvisatory *istikhbār* that is ubiquitous in the Andalusi musical complex and that parallels the kinds of improvisation that are so crucial to Mashriqi *maqām* and North Indian classical music. In a related manner, listeners often have strong loyalties to particular *ṭubūʿ*, so that the modes themselves can become objects of devotion and of musical requests. Like the Egyptian *ṭarab* enthusiasts described by Racy, some listeners and performers of Andalusi music attest to a love of particular modes and speak of specific emotions that certain modes embody or express.[47] For example, some practitioners speak of *mazmūm* as carrying a special note of sadness that recalls the loss of al-Andalus and makes this mode a specialty of Jewish singers in the Algerian tradition (Jews being frequently identified by Muslim listeners as specialists in the emotion of deep sadness or *shajan*). Some notions of mode-specific affect seem to be linked to the past or present performance context, even if it is impossible to say whether it was affect or context that came first: for example, there are practitioners who say that *ṣīka* carries a martial spirit, and it is believed to have been the mode used by the last Dey of Algiers' military band.[48] Affection for a certain mode is also tied up with the ability to engage in connoisseurship. So, for example, the practice of making musical requests to a performer can sometimes take the form of a request for a particular *ṣanʿa*, but particularly when the repertoire is drawn from the *nūba* repertoire, the request can also be simply for a particular mode. Indeed, the ability to make an appropriate request is itself part of a connoisseur's musical competence, just as performative competence lies in the ability to respond to such requests.[49]

The identity of the modes and their relationship with one another provides a basis for musical interaction not only between performers and listeners but also between teachers and students. For example, the seven primary modes provide the basis for the *inqilāb* repertoire, a *muwashshaḥ*-based song form on the model of the *ṣanʿa* that in some cases gets integrated into the *nūba* as a prelude but that in many instances stands apart, and can even be strung together into what is sometimes called *nūbat al-inqilābāt*. The *inqilāb* is marked as somewhat lighter than the primary forms that make up the *nūba* proper and is often used to initiate a student into the Andalusi complex. In addition, learning an *inqilāb* in each of the primary modes can become an opportunity to learn the basics of the *istikhbār*, since such an unmetered improvisation is often used to introduce the song form. The *istikhbārāt* in the Andalusi tradition, like the *inqilābāt*, correspond to the seven primary modes and can then be extended to apply to pieces (including whole *nūbāt*) in the secondary modes.[50] The *istikhbār*, like the Mashriqi *taqsīm*, is a crucial site for instrumental virtuosity as well as for exploration of the subtleties of a particular mode, not to mention for display of the very ability to engage in such exploration. In the Algerian case, it is also a musical space in which sonic relationships that are difficult to access on fixed-pitch instruments like mandolin and piano, and that tend to recede in metered, nonsoloistic parts of the Andalusi repertoire, may be preserved, even if they usually remain untheorized.

The identity of the modes provides an occasion for debate over the theoretical foundations of the repertoire itself. As mentioned a few pages earlier, some of this falls along the lines of regional schools, with Algiers and Tlemcen attaching certain derivatives to divergent root modes. Despite attempts to codify the practice over the past century, or perhaps precisely because of such attempts, the localized nature of modal theorization has persisted and perhaps in some ways even intensified. Indeed, it is precisely in moments when aficionados from different locales meet that an attempt to assert modal coherence can come to the surface. Bouali, writing at the turn of the twentieth century, intimated this precise situation in his explanation of why a book such as his was needed:

> Although I am Tlemcani by residence and origin, I spent two years in Algiers in pursuit of greater learning at the upper *madrasa*. Among my classmates there were people from all the regions in Algeria and from parts of Tunisia. We could not help but speak about what we know or have heard is used in our respective regions, either by eyewitness or by hearsay, and we would say, "Agreement is found with God."[51]

Even within a specific locale, however, the solidity of the modal categories can come into doubt among advanced performers and listeners.[52] The occasions for such conversations are manifold. Coaching a performer on how to do an *istikhbār* can spark a discussion of the actual modal contours and possibilities and the relationship of modes to one another, so that performance practice can make modal theory an object of explicit theorization and contestation. Even in the absence of an object of evaluation, aficionados are often invested in making definitive pronouncements about the theoretical underpinnings of the repertoire. Such investment is closely tied to the widespread desire to demonstrate mastery before peers and would-be competitors, as well as to the repertoire's status as a *musique savante*, a learned music that is complex and, ideally, coherent. The sense that there is a lack of modal coherence can cause considerable anguish. For example, some advanced practitioners have difficulty locating a modal distinction between *zīdān* and *mjennba*, or between *ḥsīn* and *raml al-māya*, or between *dhīl* and *raṣd al-dhīl*. Modal ambiguity opens up an important avenue for the merging of material from two different *nūbāt*, particularly for those *nūbāt* that are understood to be structurally incomplete. In the Algiers practice, for instance, elements from *ʿarāq*, which lacks a complete five-movement *nūba* despite the existence of poems for all five (most of these poems are understood to have lost their melodies), are routinely integrated into *nūbat ḥsīn*, a process that is evident in some of the nineteenth-century collections.[53] The Andalusi musical ideology tends to treat incompleteness of *nūbāt* and vanishing distinctions between modes as evidence of loss over time—in other words, that what we see today are the ruins of earlier, more complete and distinctive structures. While the existence of classed song texts that have no known melody certainly suggests a process of decay, the loss of modes is more ambiguous. It may be that modes were reorganized, renamed, and reinvented. Furthermore, in some cases there is evidence that modes that are today treated as distinct from one another were in the nineteenth century sometimes combined into a single *nūba*, which would suggest that the sense of a modal canon is more recent than is usually supposed.[54] For most practitioners, however, the fact that there are written traces of modal names that are no longer current is taken as evidence of progressive sonic blurring over time.

We will explore this ideology of lost completeness further in the coming chapters. For the time being, we can simply say that these fuzzy boundaries are the site of various forms of anxiety and ideological work that are central to the Andalusi musical mythos. At the same time, there is broad agreement about the centrality of mode, and of specific modes, to the organization of the *nūba* and the para-*nūba* repertoire such as the *inqilābāt*. Indeed, in the absence of a notion of composer or poet, *ṭab'* provides a key organizing framework at a level of specificity beyond that provided by repertoire, genre, and patrimony.

Movements as Hierarchy: The Heavy and the Light

While *ṭab'* or mode is one axis along which the songbooks are organized, and *ṣan'a* is arguably another, the third axis is movement, or the component parts that make up the *nūba* as a sequence. Within each mode, the poetic texts are grouped according to the part of the *nūba* to which they belong. As laid out in the introductory chapter, there are five parts to the *nūba* in the Algiers-Tlemcen tradition, which follow one another in performance and within the songbooks themselves, and even small collections of poems that do not present a complete *nūba* respect the general order of the movements.[55] The etymologies of the movement names themselves trace an arc, with the term *mṣaddar* suggesting setting out, the term *bṭayḥī* evoking a plain, *darj* bringing to mind a step-by-step advance, and *inṣirāf* and *khlāṣ* pointing toward escape, departure, or liberation.

These five sections are the central building blocks of the *nūba* and follow one another in the songbook tradition for each mode. However, just as the two halves of a poetic line can be bridged by *tarāṭīn*, and the vocal lines are tied to one another by the instrumental *jawāb* or response, the five main sections of the *nūba* are held together by a range of other mode-specific forms, often without words, that do not appear in the traditional songbook. There are, for example, the *mshālya*, an unmetered instrumental prelude that gives the outline of the mode; the *tūshiyya* or metered overture, as well as an alternative metered overture form known as the *tshanbar*; the *kursī*, the short metered instrumental interlude or overture that introduces the *mṣaddar*, *bṭayḥī*, *darj*, or *inṣirāf* sections of the *nūba*; and even for some *nūbāt* a closing instrumental piece known as *tūshiyyat al-kamāl*, the *tūshiyya* of completion or perfection. There is also the *istikhbār*, the unmetered, mode-specific improvisation, which can be both instrumental and vocal, and can be inserted between two of the central sections of the *nūba* (though not between the *inṣirāf* and *khlāṣ*). In the case of a vocal *istikhbār*, the text is usually a rhymed couplet in classical Arabic drawn from outside the *muwashshaḥ* corpus; in fact, selection of *istikhbār* texts has been less tied down to a sense of a textual canon, and a given text may be used for any mode. In a related manner, *istikhbār* texts have not traditionally been included in the songbooks, although some recent published songbooks have included a separate section for them.[56] Finally, there are several kinds of texts that can be integrated into a *nūba* but that are not part of the central five sections. One of these is the *inqilāb*, which several of the twentieth-century songbooks include in an appendix. In Algiers, the *inqilāb* can replace the *tūshiyya* as a way of beginning a *nūba*. There are also the short colloquial verses known as the *qādriyya* (sometimes paired in popular women's repertoires with a melodic form known as *zindānī*) and the *dlīdla*, both of which can be inserted between the *inṣirāf* and *khlāṣ* in contemporary practice or, in the case of the *dlīdla*, inside a series of *inṣirāf* texts. Like the *istikhbār* texts, these short forms have traditionally not been part of the songbook but have started to show up in some recent printed versions.[57] We will return to these auxiliary elements of the *nūba* and their lives beyond the confines of the *nūba* form momentarily.

The five central sections of the *nūba* are often written about as movements (*ḥarakāt*, singular *ḥaraka*), en par with the movements in a symphony or sonata—a parallel that is frequently pointed out in written commentaries.[58] But in everyday discourse, performers and listeners speak of each poetic text sung in performance as a freestanding instantiation of the section. In other words, an *mṣaddar* in the context of a *nūba* performance is not just a formal position within the larger structure but is in fact the actual *ṣanʿa* that is performed in that setting. The difference this makes becomes clearer in the *inṣirāf* and *khlāṣ*, where multiple *ṣanāyiʿ* are often strung together. In such an instance, one is in fact performing multiple *inṣirāfāt* and *khlāṣāt*. In some respects, it is better to think of these sections as actual musical forms that, in the *nūba* context, appear in a set order or succession (recall that *nūba* can be translated as alternation, succession, or turn).

This point raises the question of what, if anything, distinguishes these putative forms from one another. In terms of poetic form, they are essentially the same, in that one could not tell a *darj* from an *inṣirāf* by comparing the texts on the page—in fact, as noted earlier, in some cases the same text can be used for a *darj* in one *nūba* and for an *inṣirāf* in another. Likewise, there is no obvious, consistent differentiation with regard to the relationship between broad melodic structure and poetic form, or with regard to the vocal range they demand or the elements of the mode that are highlighted.[59] Instead, the difference lies in the underlying rhythmic pattern, relative tempo, and the formal position of the parts relative to one another as enshrined in the songbooks and in performance practice.

With regard to *mīzān* or rhythmic pulse as elaborated by the percussion, the Algerois practice has been to treat the *mṣaddar*, *bṭayḥī*, and *darj* alike as a grouping of four beats. The Tlemcani practice has been to treat the *mṣaddar* and *bṭayḥī* as a four-beat pattern, but one that is syncopated and sometimes broadened to eight or sixteen beats in the *mṣaddar*; the Tlemcani *darj*, on the other hand, has a broad sense of three or six beats.[60] In both the Algiers and Tlemcen traditions, the usual sense is that there is a very slight step-by-step acceleration in the rhythmic pulse as one moves from *mṣaddar* to *bṭayḥī* to *darj*; indeed, in Algerois practice, slightly increased tempo is sometimes the only metric differentiation between the first three movements.[61]

In both traditions, the *inṣirāf* marks a further densification of the rhythmic pulse, with its move to a limping 6/4.[62] The transition to the *khlāṣ* evens out the syncopation of the *inṣirāf* into a typically Maghribi 6/8 polyrhythm, with its bidirectional possibility of being felt as a group of three or a group of two.[63] As is the case for the first three movements, the transition from the *inṣirāf* to the *khlāṣ* is usually felt as an acceleration of tempo.

Taken as a whole, then, the five movements or stations are characterized by a broad increase in speed. This overall impression is reinforced by the fact that the *nūba* often ends with a chain of several *khlāṣāt* that increase in tempo one after the other, so that the *nūba* can seem to hurtle to a close. Despite this sense of an overall acceleration, there are some important internal differentiations that lend the acceleration of the *nūba* greater complexity. The first three movements are usually talked about as *thaqīl*, the Arabic term for heavy or slow, and the second unit is usually talked about as being *khafīf*, the Arabic term for light or fast. This transition from one unit to another is audible as an increase in rhythmic energy and is sometimes formally reinforced through the placement of an *istikhbār* between the *darj* and the *inṣirāf*, which has the effect of momentarily suspending the metric pulse entirely. At the same time, there is a sense of acceleration internal to each of these two units, so that the overall movement from *thaqīl* to *khafīf* is replicated within the units, with the *mṣaddar* being the most *thaqīl* of the *thaqīl* and the final *khlāṣ* being the most *khafīf* of the *khafīf*.

The concept of the *thaqīl* and the *khafīf* has great importance beyond simply being a way to talk about relative tempo. As the semantic range of these terms makes clear, speed is inseparable from the question of weight and seriousness. In other words, the *nūba* represents a temporalized hierarchy, with the *mṣaddar* standing in a privileged, initial place—a concept that is echoed in the use of the root to talk about giving a guest the seat of honor. This notion of a hierarchy has long been current within the Andalusi musical milieu. Consider, for example, the dual meaning of *nūba* as a suite form and as a military formation. Consider, too, the Arabic saying cited at the turn of the twentieth century by the musicologist Jules Rouanet: "The *nūba* is a government and the *mṣaddar* is its king."[64] In other words, the *mṣaddar* has pride of place through its position within the *nūba* sequence. Furthermore, because of the frequently soloistic vocal nature of the *thaqīl*, these movements have tended to be in the control of the leader of an ensemble, while the *khafīf* movements, and particularly the *khlāṣāt*, have tended to be opportunities for collective singing. In this respect, primacy of the *thaqīl* was reiterated in the primacy of the *shaykh*.

The primacy of the *thaqīl* becomes still clearer once we think about what is required to talk about a *nūba*. Although a complete *nūba* in the Algiers-Tlemcen tradition includes all five movements, as well as their relevant framing material, performances have often abbreviated the sequence to include only certain sections. Such performances typically include more than one movement and are presented as excerpts from the *nūba*. To perform an *inqilāb* with a *khlāṣ* or with a set of *khlāṣāt*, on the other hand, is not to perform excerpts from a *nūba* at all but rather to follow the performance convention associated with the *inqilāb* as a minor genre. Conversely, when an abbreviated performance includes an *mṣaddar* followed by an *inṣirāf* and *khlāṣ*, many would agree that one could legitimately speak of such a performance as a *nūba*, though not a fully elaborated one. That is to say, *nūba*-ness is weighted in the *thaqīl*.

The contrast of *thaqīl* and *khafīf* carries with it a variety of associations regarding gender, sophistication, propriety, social class, genre boundaries, and the body. As touched upon in the preceding chapter, there is a link between the figure of the *shaykh*, Andalusi music as a patrimonial genre, and the lower register of the voice and of stringed instruments, suggesting an image of gravitas in keeping with the notion of the *thaqīl*. What might seem to be simply a suggestive link can become quite vivid in performance. In contemporary settings, female listeners sometimes take the onset of the *inṣirāf*, and especially the full rollicking *khlāṣ* rhythm, as an opportunity to ululate, and it is not uncommon for male and female listeners to clap, sing along, or even get up and dance. In Turino's terms, this is a shift from presentational to participatory performance.[65] And onstage, the shift to the *khafīf* has often also been a shift from solo voice to chorale, thereby duplicating the shift from the presentational to the participatory. Privately, some male performers and aficionados have expressed doubts to me about the ability of women to successfully perform an *mṣaddar*, *bṭayḥī*, or *darj*. And performers, both male and female, sometimes complain about audiences that are unable to appreciate an *mṣaddar* or *bṭayḥī*, and who are only interested in the *khafīf* elements as if, in the words of some critics, they are at a wedding. The *thaqīl* and the *khafīf* are, then, moral judgments as well as musical categories.

The Children of the *Nūba*

These claims and valuations are inexplicable if we conceive the distinction of *thaqīl* and *khafīf* as purely internal to the *nūba*. The popular cast of the *khafīf* is closely tied to the fact that these are elements that have circulated and continue to circulate beyond the confines of the *nūba*. The *inṣirāf* and *khlāṣ*, as well as the *inqilābāt*, *qādriyyāt*, and *dlīdlāt*, have long been central to the repertoire of urban female performers, including those known as the *msemma'āt* (see fig. 4); the *inṣirāf* and *khlāṣ* have likewise been central in the male-coded, twentieth-century popular repertoire known in Algiers as *chaabi* (*sha'bī*).[66] Similarly, some of the *tūshiyyāt*, *krāsī* (singular: *kursī*), and *istikhbārāt* show up in these popular urban repertoires. This is not to say that the elements shared by the *nūba* repertoire and the popular urban repertoires are identical. In fact, there are many differences in instrumentation, rhythmic interpretation, timbre, and vocal diction that are immediately recognizable to practitioners. Such differences are frequently policed by Andalusi performers, so that I have heard aficionados criticize an *istikhbār* performance for being too *chaabi*; in similar fashion, integration of a *qādriyya* into the *nūba* at one time led practitioners and observers to distinguish between an ordinary *qādriyya* and a *qādriyyat ṣan'a*—that is to say, a *qādriyya* of or for the *ṣan'a* genre.[67] But while the *nūba* raises up that which is integrated into it, in a sort of musical hypergamy, such integration establishes a connection to repertoire

FIGURE 4. Two record covers from the 1960s. Note that the same group of *msemma'āt* are shown on the two recordings, one of which is presented as "light" repertoire and the other of which is presented as "classical music."

that is understood to be outside its purview—a connection that of course is simultaneously a condition for the elaboration of difference.

Commentators on Andalusi music often conceptualize the relationship between the *nūba* and its others as a relationship of parentage. The *inqilāb*, *qṣāyid*, *qādriyyāt*, and *dlīdlāt* are often spoken of as "related to" or "derived from" the *nūba*. This is a typical genealogical move: the *nūba* is presented as the oldest and most refined, an import in "clear" Arabic, and it has various offshoots that are treated as newer, lower, more colloquial, and more local and Maghribi, even as they share many modes, poetic forms, rhythms, and instrumental and vocal practices with the *nūba*. This should be understood in large part as an ideological move that brings various genres into relationship with one another, and that brings them together in a hierarchical fashion in which the *nūba* is presented as the "base" of urban music more generally.

In many ways, this conception is similar to the conception of the movement from the *thaqīl* to the *khafīf* in the *nūba*: in both instances, the *khafīf* comes later, as the completion or ornament of the more substantive musical core.

Our understanding of the relationship of the *nūba* to these popular urban repertoires deepens when we start to notice that many of these shared elements act as framing material both within the *nūba* and outside of it. For the popular urban repertoires, many of these instrumental and vocal forms take place within a larger performative sequence whose centerpiece is occupied by the long, strophic, colloquial song form known as *qṣīda*, also known by the terms for two of its subcategories, *ḥawzī* and *ʿarūbī*, or by the general term *malḥūn* (meaning "colloquial").[68] In such a context, the *qṣīda* is very much like the *thaqīl* elements of the *nūba*: it is central, serious, relatively slow, and marked as male for both performers and listeners, even if some prominent female performers have staked a claim to it in the twentieth century. Furthermore, the *qṣīda* blurs into the *khlāṣ*, first through a transition from a square rhythm to the rollicking, 6/8 pulse of the *khlāṣ* in the latter part of the *qṣīda* text, and then in some instances through a further transition to a set of *khlāṣāt* derived from texts independent from the *qṣīda* itself. Here again, such a transition often elicits ululations, clapping, and dancing from audience members, particularly in a wedding context. In a related manner, an *inqilāb* outside the *nūba* context is often followed by a *khlāṣ* or a set of *khlāṣāt*, again with the *inqilāb* occupying the relatively heavier performative center, and the *khlāṣāt* occupying the lighter after-frame.[69]

In the context of the *nūba* performance as it has been known over the past century, the *qṣīda* cannot be integrated into the *nūba* structure. But among performers of the Andalusi complex, *qṣāyid* are frequently performed alongside a *nūba*, usually after the *nūba* has been completed—in fact, one association member told me that that "one cannot imagine a music association that only does Andalusi music [i.e., the *nūba*]," without *ḥawzī*. In this respect, the *nūba* has pride of place in the larger performative event in the same way that the *mṣaddar* has pride of place within the *nūba*. In many concert settings, one gets the distinct impression that audience members are in fact more interested in the *qṣāyid*, and some performers who emphasize the *nūba* express resentment over such a preference. This connection between the *nūba* repertoire and the more popular repertoires, such as Algerois *chaabi*, the music of the *msemmaʿāt*, and the *qṣīda* repertoires more broadly, can lead to a blurring of the genres and to the strategic introduction of friction in order to enforce generic separation. One musician in Oujda, for example, in responding to my question about who he felt to be the most important figure in *gharnāṭī*, named the great Algerois *chaabi* artist Hadj El Anka, only to be corrected by the nearby head of his ensemble, who asserted that El Anka performed *qṣāyid* rather than *gharnāṭī*. This comment left the musician in disbelief: didn't El Anka do *bṭayḥī* and *mṣaddar*? The ensemble leader responded with an emphatic no.

Of course, El Anka did have mastery over a great deal of *nūba* material, in large part because the *nūba* material provided a pedagogical base for many musicians of his day. In other words, if we take practitioners at their word, the *nūba* is the foundation of urban musical art—it both has gravity and is gravity. Furthermore, El Anka's performances drew on shared repertoire and forms such as the *inṣirāfāt*. In fact, both the musician and the association head were correct: El Anka both specialized and did not specialize in the *nūba*, and this is because the *nūba* needs to be understood as part of a complex that can be approached from both its inside and from its edges. This particular kind of ambiguity—which, by the way, is by no means confined to Oujda—is a central part of Andalusi musical practice, and likely of genre practice more widely. In this respect, Andalusi music is an "essentially contested concept."[70] And such contestation does not only work in the direction of denying someone's expertise in the Andalusi repertoire—I have encountered similar arguments from people trying to assert that a person specializing in *chaabi* is in fact a specialist in the *nūba*. It is in this way that a decidedly high-brow art can on closer inspection have low-brow connections. Furthermore, this helps to explain the way in which "the people of *ṣanʿa*," "the people of *ḥawzī*," and "the people of *chaabi*" can from one angle be three "peoples" in competition with one another, while from another angle they can appear to overlap or perhaps even constitute a single "people."

The *Nūba*'s Others and the Question of *Turāth*

Just as there are repertoires that can be understood to be part of the Andalusi complex, whether at its center or margins, there are also repertoires that are understood to be outside the Andalusi complex.[71] These include mainly rural musical genres that are marked as folkloric; new, politically conscious Kabyle song; *music-hall* and other varieties of Franco-Arab song dating to the interwar period and the post-Second World War era; *raï* and other forms of popular, allegedly commercial youth music of the past several decades; various forms of popular music from Europe, the Americas, and the Middle East; *sharqī*, the Maghribi name for the urban art music of Egypt and the Levant; and European classical music.[72]

This list could go on, and in some respects it is an open set. For our purposes, however, it is useful to think about what places these musical forms definitively outside the Andalusi musical complex. One axis of difference has to do with newness and novelty versus oldness and fixity, and in particular the question of patrimony. The ultimate orienting framework within which the *nūba* and its "children" are embedded, patrimony as a category takes in that which is understood to have an old pedigree and, usually, unknown authorship. That which is more or less unambiguously outside the patrimonial category is the new, the current, that which is not yet proven to be anything other than ephemeral. In this sense, patrimony is what Michael Frishkopf refers to as "a temporally moving target observed, nostalgically, as those genres or styles preceding—by a generation or two—music popular among those who are presently young."[73] Another axis of difference hinges on the geographic origin of the music in question, whether that be the eastern Arab world, Western Europe, or rural spaces within the Maghrib itself. But not all these senses of difference carry the same quality. In some instances the difference is threatening, while in other instances it is nonthreatening. In some cases the difference is understood to exist alongside a quality of similarity or even compatibility. Thinking through a few of these generic relationships will be helpful in delineating the scope of the Andalusi complex.

Let us first consider *raï*, which is the most loaded other for Andalusi music enthusiasts. We have already touched on some of the associative contrasts between Andalusi music and *raï*: the old versus the new, the high versus the low, the proper versus the improper, the permanent versus the ephemeral. Indeed, *raï* in many respects represents an inversion of Andalusi music, down to the very way in which musical authority gets conferred: not only does the *raï* singer take the title of *shabb* or *shabba* rather than *shaykh*, but the concept of the *khafīf* is central to the aesthetic values of *raï* aficionados.[74] But these contrasts in themselves do not entirely account for the opprobrium in which *raï* is often held—after all, there are other forms of new music associated with allegedly crass young people that are not the focus of sharp critique. I would argue that the special attention meted out to *raï* stems from three elements: the success of *raï* in garnering widespread attention, its relative newness and emphasis on novelty, and *raï*'s relationship with the edges of the Andalusi complex.

Raï's success among working-class youth contrasts sharply with the bounded, more middle-class, and multigenerational nature of Andalusi music's audience, in spite of the ongoing efforts to make the public more aware of and interested in the *nūba*. As a product of low-fi cassette production that flew beneath the state's radar during its formative years, *raï* is diametrically opposed to the quasi-official, state-oriented Andalusi musical milieu. And despite the fact that it took some years before the state authorities began to pay attention to *raï*, for many Andalusi musical practitioners the fact that the state paid *raï* any attention at all is scandalous. As the bookstore owner who I quoted at the beginning of the chapter asserted, *raï* ought to be banned rather than tolerated or promoted.

But this is in a way a restatement of the problem we need to address. The problematic nature of *raï* lies more in its emphasis on novelty and in the way that it connects to the complex's outer edges. *Raï*'s association with newness and the positive valuation of novelty contrast sharply with the logic and ethos of patrimony. Both in terms of its production values (particularly during its early period) and in the ephemerality of its hits, *raï* embodies the notion of a "music of the market" that comes and goes. At the same time, however, the opprobrium cast on *raï* moves well beyond that cast on some other musical styles marked as commercial. To account for this, the association of *raï*'s predecessors with the outer edges of the Andalusi repertoire must be taken into consideration. The standard narrative of *raï*'s roots is that it emerged from the repertoires of the *meddāḥāt* and of the rural *shuyūkh* of the Oran region, as well as from the urban cabaret music known as *wahrānī* (meaning Oranais). The repertoire of the *meddāḥāt* included *inqilābāt* as well as *qādriyyāt* using the *zindānī* melody, while both the rural *shuyūkh* and the *wahrānī* performers touched on the *qṣīda* repertoire. In turn, *raï* stars such as Cheb Khaled have recorded *wahrānī* classics as well as some classics from the Algerois *chaabi* repertoire. What I would suggest, then, is that for many Andalusi music practitioners, *raï* is understood to descend in part from the hinterlands of the complex. In this way, it is both an embarrassment—a poor relation of sorts—and a latter-day incarnation of the *nūba*'s definitional other.

This approach helps to explain why *chaabi* has not typically been the target of *nūba* practitioners' wrath, even if one can find a sense of competition between some devotees of each. Aside from the fact that *chaabi* never took on the mass youth appeal of *raï* and tends to be associated with some of the same central urban places as the *nūba*, I would also suggest that *chaabi*'s focus on the *qṣīda* sets up a parallel between the *qṣīda* and the heavy elements of the *nūba*. The *qṣīda* is heavy and traditionally male relative to other elements of the Andalusi complex's outer edge. Thus the *qṣīda*, even if in some instances it stands as a competitor to the *nūba*, in some respects resembles the *nūba*.[75] It stands closer to the core of the complex. Furthermore, it combines an openness to new compositions with a strong emphasis on maintaining a repertoire of classic *qṣāyid* that are closely linked to genealogically embedded male musical authorities. *Chaabi* partakes of the same sense of a "lost paradise" as we find at the heart of the Andalusi milieu.[76]

Something similar can be said for *sharqī* and European classical music.

Andalusi music practitioners have frequently spoken and written of the *nūba* as a classical music on a par with the European tradition. The entry of Andalusi music into the Algiers conservatory in the 1920s was understood as a revindication of indigenous Algerian expressive culture, and, as I will explore further in chapter 7, the understanding of the *nūba* as a national classical music played an important role in post-independence discussions of cultural policy, including efforts to standardize, reform, and textualize Andalusi musical practice. Unlike the case of the *qṣīda* in *chaabi*, the sense of European classical music's parallel to the *nūba* is uncomplicated by the notion of a genetic connection, despite the longstanding tradition of supposing a distant link by way of ancient Greece and medieval Europe, including al-Andalus.[77]

A similar pattern holds in the case of *sharqī*. As used in the Maghrib, the term *sharqī* refers to a range of urban musical styles, some of which are old and anonymous and others of which are connected to known twentieth-century Egyptian composers and performers such as Muḥammad ʿAbd al-Wahhāb, Riyāḍ al-Sunbāṭī, and Umm Kulthūm. Together, this body of repertoire belongs to the patrimonial category as defined by Frishkopf, in that it is understood to be a canon of classics derived from a prestigious though varied past. Like Western European classical music, *sharqī* is understood to be not native to the Maghrib, even if there are again distant connections by way of al-Andalus, particularly in the Levantine *muwashshaḥ* tradition. The grand twentieth-century figures in *sharqī* had a devoted following in the Maghrib in their own lifetimes, and there continue to be devotees of *sharqī* classics today. For some Andalusi music practitioners, *sharqī* represents a potential competitor, and one that, unlike Andalusi music, is a favorite of supporters of Arabization at the expense of French. However, this is very much a competition between dissimilar equals or near-equals. One *sharqī* enthusiast who also plays the *nūba* repertoire explained to me that *sharqī*'s greater reliance on notation is something that Andalusi music practitioners ought to aspire to, since notation gets rid of all kinds of vagueness that afflict the Andalusi repertoire. Some musicians have also commented on the relative openness of *sharqī*: as a musician whose father was a fan of *sharqī* said to me, *sharqī* is very rich, largely because of its openness to composition, while the *nūba* repertoire is by definition limited. At the same time, some practitioners admit that *sharqī* is vast and rich as compared to Andalusi music, but hold that it is in fact too rich, and has lost some of its substance as a result.

Despite the apartness of *sharqī*, somewhat on the model of European classical music, there is the simultaneous notion that *sharqī* is partly compatible with the Andalusi repertoire thanks to overlapping instrumentation, modes, poetry, aesthetics, sophistication, and patrimoniality. Redouane Bensari, the famed son of Cheikh Larbi, was accomplished in both the Andalusi repertoire and the *sharqī* repertoire, as was Abdelkrim Dali. *Muwashshaḥāt* are a beloved genre in Egypt and the Levant, and there are devotees and practitioners of the *sharqī* version of this poetic form throughout the Maghrib. And although rare, elements of *sharqī* repertoire have at times been integrated into Andalusi practice. The eastern *ʿūd*, for example, has come to predominate over its Maghribi version in most places; as mentioned earlier, several *inqilābāt* were borrowed directly from the Levant; and in Morocco, *sharqī* vocal improvisation has partly displaced the traditional unmetered vocal improvisation in the *nūba* of the *āla* tradition. Recent Andalusi music performers have also occasionally found ways to integrate instrumental (but not vocal) pieces from the *sharqī* repertoire whole cloth. For instance, the Association des Beaux Arts in Algiers, which specializes in the Algerois *nūba*, sometimes introduces a *longa* or another *sharqī* instrumental piece in a compatible mode at the tail end of a *nūba*. Note, however, that this is an addition at the end of the sequence, a supererogatory musical gesture. Furthermore, this is something that is reserved for musical functions outside the realm of official, state-sponsored festivals.

What this suggests, then, is that the Andalusi complex opens out onto other musical practices in cautious ways that are attentive to patrimoniality, formal constraints, and the protocol of the *nūba*. This caution is evident in conversations about innovation and composition in the *nūba* form. As the prologue to part 1 pointed out, performers walk a fine line between the introduction of positive novelty and desecration of the patrimony, even as one can trace many generations of innovations in timbre, instrumentation, and general performance practice. As one association leader explained during a rehearsal in which I participated, blending foreignness and age with patrimonial authority, "[*Qṣāyid*] we can change around. But with *gharnāṭī* . . . we can't change it. The *qṣāyid* are from here. *Gharnāṭī* is from al-Andalus. We don't have the right to change it. The *qṣāyid* we have a right to change. *Gharnāṭī*, no, because it comes from the old days [*min al-qadīm*]."[78] Despite such views, there have also been many generations of experimentation with orchestral composition, though none of them actively sought to expand the canon.[79] Nevertheless, such compositions can raise controversy among practitioners. As one musician told me in explaining his refusal to be involved in the production of a French composer's work inspired by the Algerian *nūba* tradition, "I only work *turāth*."

Yet for experimenters coming from inside the Andalusi milieu, new composition is not always entirely separate from the concept of patrimony. In 2007, for example, Nour-Eddine Saoudi, a leading voice on the Algiers scene, released his *Nouba Dziria*, with original song texts and melodies on the model of the *nūba*, and a strong influence from *chaabi* and mid-century popular Algerian song.[80] For Saoudi, this composition is not an attempt to expand the *nūba* canon. Rather, it is simply a treatment of the *nūba* as a compositional form. This is not to say that he is indifferent to whether it is accepted. In his words, "It might be integrated into the repertoire or it might not be." This is a question to be answered by the larger community of practitioners beyond his own person and his own lifetime. Not surprisingly, compositions such as Saoudi's can be highly controversial. For Beihdja Rahal, a leading Algerois performer of the Andalusi repertoire in France and Algeria, composition is simply not possible:

> I am completely against composition, because there we are no longer dealing with the safeguard of the patrimony, in the preservation of that which was transmitted to us. Composition means that we are doing something new, and the new is no longer the preservation of patrimony. In this case, if we speak of composition, then we can in this case also think of reconstructing Roman ruins, for example. Here we are no longer in the domain of what is archaeological patrimony. We demolish, and say yes, let's construct on this site, and say we have built something in the old style. Or else we reconstruct things from scratch and say there, we have finished. So I think that composition is not preservation. One is no longer in [the domain of] patrimony. Why not compose? Yes, why not, we are free to do it, but we are not in this well-defined domain of the preservation of a patrimony transmitted from generation to generation.

Yet Saoudi's comments point toward an important aspect of the way in which Andalusi musical patrimony works in the *longue durée*. Take, for example, Cheikh Sfindja, who is today remembered as the paragon of the Algiers tradition at the turn of the twentieth century. Few contemporary practitioners are aware that Sfindja composed the melody to the well-known *inqilāb* in the mode *ṣīka*, called "Al-qadd alladhī sabānī" (The form that captivated me), using an old poem that had "lost" its melody. Although known to be Sfindja's melody in his day, knowledge of his role quickly atrophied as it was integrated into the *inqilāb* repertoire.[81] In other words, its successful uptake into the musical practice led it to resemble any other old song text, and the anonymity of its poetic content predominated over the notion of a composer.

In turn, the drawing in of Sfindja's *inqilāb* helps us to make sense of broader historical processes regarding the *nūba* and its relationship to the patrimony concept. It is not simply that patrimony is a meta-genre to which the *nūba* and various "children" belong and "others" relate. Rather, in important ways, the *nūba* is a patrimonial structure, technology, or vessel. Although it appears that the *nūba* as a performative event in the nineteenth century was a longer and in some respects looser affair, with the enchaining of many *mṣaddarāt* one after the other, the primacy of the precious and rare *thaqīl* movements was crucial.[82] The *nūba* was an occasion to display these pieces, but they were also presented alongside pieces that were somewhat less rare and patrimonial. And there was even the integration of "lighter" elements such as the *qādriyya*, which in Ben Mustapha's terms any "urchin" knew. Yet inclusion within the *nūba* practice was understood to elevate it, as in the old distinction between *qādriyya* and *qādriyyat ṣanʿa*. Furthermore, in being drawn in by the gravitational pull of the *nūba* form, some of these shared or semi-shared pieces came to be drawn into a canonical repertoire and written into songbook compilations, shedding some of their ephemerality in the process. In some cases, such integration has allowed pieces to outlive their currency in popular urban repertoires. In this respect, the *nūba* can be conceived as a net that captured elements of the wider, variegated musical field of the nineteenth-century and early twentieth-century scenes, and in so doing has recapitulated aspects of that field's hierarchy within its precincts. Or better, in keeping with the notion of the *shaykh* as the lower register, we can think of it as a depression that was able to build up a sedimentary layer, or, in keeping with the Aboura collection, an archive.[83]

In considering the question of genre from a historical perspective, the musical field of the late nineteenth century of course did not remain stable. New genre frameworks and notions of repertorial coherence emerged: as described earlier, *chaabi*, *raï*, and *sharqī* have each stood in a distinct relationship of difference with the Andalusi complex at various points in the past century. The new sounds that the recording industry and radio helped to usher in during the first decades of the twentieth century had the important effect of setting off the Andalusi repertoire as distinctively local and authentic, and of giving *mélomanes* something to listen against. As Mohamed Zerrouki, a Tlemcani contemporary of Bekhoucha and Sekkal, stated before a meeting of the reformist Cercle des Jeunes Algériens in the summer of 1935:

> At the café—to finish off, no doubt, the agreeable taste of an unsweetened coffee (already a victory of modernism that succeeds in ousting the old preparation for which the European nevertheless envies us)—the phonograph, whose horn has become a modern cornucopia, lavishes us with a ringing, scratchy glimpse of Turkish folklore, Egyptian, Tunisian, and Tlemcenian. The two- or three-octave harmonium used in Tunisia follows the ghaita from the south of the Constantine region, which gives way in its turn to the piano, the flute, the violin of some "famous" artist from the Algerian capital. The Andalusi lute (Kouitra), so timid, so discreet, with its exquisite whispers, finds itself for-

> midably amplified by this barbarous servant that is the loudspeaker. . . . I am careful not to include all of our musical productions in the same observations. The dozen or so Andalusi modes that still live on certainly offer a thoroughly dilapidated sight, and if we were to make a comparison with the archaeological domain, we could not but find in them an exact similitude with the Merinid ruins of Mansourah (Tlemcen). Enthusiasts [*amateurs*], however, know how to see in these ruins the primitive splendor of pieces that were the feast of the ruling caliphs who applied themselves so diligently to being patrons of the arts.[84]

It is, then, the rarity, delicacy, and local authenticity of the *nūba* repertoire that gets accentuated in this new genre dispensation. We can start to see how it is that the expansive changes in musical soundscape can amplify already existing forms of value and differentiation. These forms are the very contours and sonic substance of the genre terrain, so that to come to know the *nūba* is to come to inhabit forms of difference, grooves of sociality that are given life through the protocol of mode, movement, and sung verse. To emphasize form is not to say that meaning is fixed, or that genre is impervious to change. But it is to say that the effect of the ruin invoked here by Zerrouki builds upon actual material and temporal practices whose shapes are fateful for what comes to overlay them. And in the process of overlay, the underlying practices retain something of their shape while changing their position and their richness. So it is that the heavy becomes heavier as what counts as patrimony expands. Circulation becomes more restrained. The patrimonial becomes even more so. Weighed down by what is over it, the buried sinks still further, drawing in some things with it, leaving others behind. The voice deepens, the plot thickens.

PART TWO

Revival

Prologue: A Photograph

Let us return to the festival stage in Oujda. At most times of year, the concrete dais on which the performers arrange themselves is an informal meeting ground for members of competing amateur associations whose headquarters, lent to them by the local representatives of the Ministry of Culture, lie off-stage. Move into one of the association headquarters during off-hours and we find a long, high-ceilinged, windowed, tiled room housing a well-worn grand piano. Low couches and tables line one half of the space, while the other half is occupied by wooden risers and chairs facing a board chalked with the *ṣanāyiʿ* for the *nūba* currently in rehearsal. Shelves in one corner hold instruments in various states of repair that association members will play when they gather: violin, viola, mandolin, *darbūka*, *ṭār*, perhaps a *kuwītra* and banjo as well. A bass and cello quietly lean upright in a corner.

The walls are hung with potbellied *ʿūd*s, a withered *rabāb*, a worn-down clock that calls out the hour, a large, glittery sign that reads in Arabic *al-jamʿiyya al-andalusiyya* ("the Andalusi association"), and many framed photos and posters. Some of these are announcements of concerts and festivals, or formal images of the association members in concert dress. Others are snapshots of association members in rehearsal, in concert, or on tour, in some instances dating back to the 1960s. A few of the photographs date back much earlier. Some are black-and-white images of Cheikh Salah and other local *shuyūkh* or of key regional figures like Cheikh Larbi and his son Redouane. One large group portrait shows members of the association dressed in matching robes, instruments in hand, at the Colonial Exposition in Paris in 1931. And one sepia-toned photograph dates back still earlier, to the earliest days of the Association Andalouse, or, as it was then known, Société l'Andaloussia, its eighteen musicians arranged in symmetrical rows that match the elabo-

FIGURE 5. L'Andaloussia of Oujda (Association Andalouse) circa 1925. The instrumentalists at top hold mandolins, Mohamed Ben Smaïl stands to the right. Courtesy of the Centre des Études et Recherches Gharnati, Oujda.

rate entrance to the building behind them, holding mandolins, violins, an *ʿūd* at either end, the child percussionists seated on the ground (see fig. 5). The formation's perfect balance draws our attention to the figure who breaks it, standing apart to the right, with one arm behind his back and the other extended straight out toward the center of the group, grasping a baton. He is the only person who does not look toward the camera. Instead, his gaze is trained on the instrumentalists.

This figure is Mohamed Ben Smaïl, the schoolteacher and *mélomane* from Tlemcen who was employed in the French Protectorate's Franco-Arab school system in Morocco and was Mostefa Aboura's close collaborator. Viewed from Tlemcen, Ben Smaïl is someone who became marginal, slipping away into a colonial frontier city, off the main musical path. But viewed from Oujda rather than from Tlemcen or even Rabat, the meaning of Ben Smaïl is somewhat different and is inflected with a set of questions that are particular to the local terrain. Practitioners ask: Was there Andalusi music in Oujda before the Tlemcani's arrival? If so, how might we know? If not, what was there, and what does this mean for making sense of Oujda's place in the Algiers-Tlemcen archipelago? These eminently local questions refract anxieties regarding the place of Algerians in Oujda, the distinctiveness and value of the local *nūba* practice, and the debate about whether this city should be viewed historically as a semi-rural backwater or as a civilizational center, a place of *ḥaḍāra*. But in other ways, the questions that the photograph raises are similar to those raised by the oldest photographs that grace the association headquarters and scrapbooks in other, more established centers of *nūba* practice. Even if practitioners in Tlemcen and Algiers do not fret about whether Andalusi music was a twentieth-century import, the local equivalents of the Ben Smaïl photograph raise related issues. What was there before these photographs? Why can't the community of practitioners easily recall a before? Is it that "revival" was an awakening to consciousness, or is this in some way an illusion? What did photography and other new technologies such as phonograph recording, staff notation, and Arabic printing actually document—a practice that was going away, or a practice that was in some sense arriving on the wings of these same technologies?

These are questions about a moment of what Karin Barber might call "instauration," a simultaneous "creating *and* preserving [of] forms" that combines both establishment and renewal.[1] Considered in this light, then, the oldest photographs that grace the walls of the amateur associations mark both a beginning and an end for practitioners. They mark an end in that these earliest figures are often described as "the last *shaykh*," the master who was the last to know the full repertoire and whose passing brought an era to a close. And they mark a beginning in that they were the ones who prompted a movement to save the repertoire from oblivion. In this movement of revival, such masters are ambiguous figures: participants in revival, but also the objects of revival, the detainers of that which requires rescue, even the barriers to that rescue. They are visually captured in the photographic process, but the photograph process itself is at first glance invisible.

As the beginning of this chain is enigmatic, so is its end. For as gestured toward already, the notion that the repertoire was under threat and required salvage did not end with the rise of revivalist instruments such as the amateur association, the phonograph record, and the printed songbook. In fact, a century later, many practitioners still speak of a repertoire that is under threat, that is disappearing, and that demands rescue. People continue to even speak of the last *shaykh*, so that in 2009 I could hear one middle-aged Algerian practitioner explain to friends visiting from the west of the country that while there were no more *shuyūkh* in Tlemcen after Larbi Bensari, "we in Algiers still have Ahmed Serri."

How might we make sense of this? Why is the *shaykh* always the last, or never the last? How can we account for the longevity of revival? What does it even mean to speak of revival? And why 1900? What beginning and end (if either) does this date mark? These questions smuggle a sense of rupture into what has thus far been a treatment of Andalusi music as a continuous though of course necessarily changing social formation reaching back to the middle of the nineteenth century and stretching to the present. The following four chapters explore the problem of revival starting from its apparent origins at the turn of the century. Beginning from a turn-of-the-century Algerois revivalist circle that paralleled and overlapped with Aboura and Ben Smaïl in the west, and moving through an examination of compilations, associations, and the state politics of patrimony, the following pages explore the way in which Andalusi musical practice over the past century and into the present has been an eminently textual practice. This is not only a question of writing, revising, and printing texts, but also a question of how the metaphor of inscribing text, of *tadwīn*, is central to the way in which the people of al-Andalus envision their practice and its dilemmas.

4

Ambiguous Revivals

Somewhere around 1900, a photographer set up his equipment in the grass in the Algiers suburb of Belcourt and arranged before him a study in symmetry. Against a verdant backdrop, a row of seven men stood facing the camera, with the oldest of them—dressed in white against the darker clothes of the others—placed at the center. Beneath them sat six others, cross-legged. Of these six, the center two held instruments, the younger man resting his right arm on the top of his *kuwītra*, the elder holding his *'ūd* as if ready to play. They held their gaze on the apparatus. The photographer peered through, and pulled the shutter (fig. 6).

The image that emerged from this moment is a veritable who's who of the Algerois Muslim elite at the turn of the twentieth century.[1] To the far right, sporting a watch chain, stands Omar Bouderba, a leading lawyer. He is next to members of the Hamoud Boualem family, who made their fortune in soft drinks that were manufactured and bottled in Belcourt, and near Omar Bensmaïa, a successful tobacco merchant who moonlighted as a visual artist.[2] The scholarly elite is represented here as well, including some of the key people who in 1903 hosted the great Egyptian Islamic reformist cleric, Muḥammad 'Abduh, during his visit to Algiers.[3] It was Omar Bensmaïa, in fact, who led 'Abduh from the Algiers port to his uncle, Abdelhalim Bensmaïa, the prominent Islamic scholar who taught at the reformist, government-funded *médersa* of Algiers, and acted as 'Abduh's key interlocutor in Algeria. Pictured to the *'ūd* player's right we find Ahmed Lakehal, son of Shaykh Lakehal, a prominent businessman who founded the Belcourt mosque and who played host to 'Abduh during his time in Algiers. Ahmed even appeared alongside 'Abduh and Abdelhalim Bensmaïa in a photographic portrait documenting the great mufti's visit.[4]

FIGURE 6. Sfindja, Benteffahi, Ahmed Lakehal, and friends in Belcourt, Algiers, circa 1900. Courtesy of Groupe Yafil and Zakia Kara Terki.

The real center of the garden image, however, are the two musicians. The *ʿūd* player is none other than Mohamed Ben ʿAli Sfindja, a shoemaker by trade and Algeria's leading performer of the Andalusi repertoire. The young *kuwītra* player is Mohamed Benteffahi, son of a prominent Algerois family, very much from the same social status as those standing behind him. Benteffahi sits to Sfindja's left, the traditional position of the student in the Andalusi professional ensembles of that era. The setting is almost certainly the garden of the Lakehal family, who regularly played host to Sfindja in Belcourt. Thus Ahmed Lakehal, seated to Sfindja's right, is host to Sfindja, and via Sfindja host to the other listeners. Likely this was a regular occurrence, and perhaps one that Lakehal decided it was time to document by calling in a professional photographer.

The resulting image can be read as a performance unto itself. The listeners are presenting themselves as listeners, assembled around the esteemed elder musician, thereby combining equality with differentiation. It is also a performance of discipleship: Benteffahi, the elite *mūlūʿ*, is shown next to his *shaykh*, and also among his social peers, the other *mūlūʿīn*. There is a certain publicness about the image, a certain impulse toward documentation and bringing music into the open. At the same time, it appears to be a private garden. If the image hints at a set of relationships between the *mélomanes* and their *shaykh*, what are they exactly in this particular historical context? What are we to make of them? And what does it mean to record these by way of the camera?

*

To start to address these questions, however, we need to leave Belcourt and head toward the heart of the city. In 1905, Algiers played host to the fourteenth meeting of the International Congress of Orientalists. Convened under the patronage of Charles Jonnart, the new reformist Governor-General of Algeria, the Congress brought together hundreds of participants from Algeria and abroad, and the organizing committee included leading Algerian Muslim scholars, colonial officials specializing in indigenous affairs, and resident Orientalists. One of the major attractions during the conference was a lecture-demonstration on Arab music. In the main hall of the Hôtel de Ville, the journalist and musicologist Jules Rouanet—already known to some in the ample audience for his contributions to "the restoration of Moorish music"[5]—presented a lecture that featured live performances by a colorful line-up drawn from the "Moorish" cafes and the apartments of the lower and upper Casbah that reached upward from just across the square: *msemma'āt* welcomed the audience with the song "Rāna jīnak" ("We have come to you"), and the talk was punctuated with musical demonstrations by the legendary singer Yamina, the venerable Mohamed Ben 'Ali Sfindja, and others.[6]

Rouanet's presentation of these musicians was laden with pathos. He introduced them as "the last musicians possessing the repertoire. They no longer have students, and soon their entire music will fall into oblivion."[7] For Rouanet, they carried the final vestiges of medieval Arab musical culture. He assured his audience that despite the lack of written records, the songs that they heard during the presentation were basically the same as those of the medieval period, thanks both to the "faithfulness—verging on fanaticism—of the Arab people regarding their musical art"[8] and the fact that Arab music had not evolved since "the great age of the Moors of Spain."[9] He voiced the hope that the assembled musicians would provide the basis on which a great work of scientific restoration would take place. Rouanet employed an extended architectural metaphor, begging the audience that he

> be allowed to compare the specimens of this music to the capital of a Roman column, to the fragments of architecture or sculpture found in the excavations of our archaeologists. The work of time has dulled the principal features; the statue has lost its arms; the head no longer has a nose; the monument has nothing but its general outline. These fragments, considered in isolation, are shapeless and signify almost nothing. However, we apply to them the known laws of Roman architecture and sculpture; through rigorous calculations, simple comparisons, the bringing together of isolated documents, the synthesis of scattered particulars, we reconstitute the missing parts; the capital or the

> base guides us to the column, the column to the peristyle, the peristyle to the temple.[10]

Although Rouanet treated the entire repertoire presented by the musicians as threatened by oblivion, he held that the Andalusi repertoire in particular was facing a crisis:

> These professionals [who know the *nūba*], whose number diminishes every day, represent the Arab music that is going away, that is flickering out, which assimilation and progress are menacing. They do not have students to gather together the old repertoire as they had done. After them, the beautiful music of Granada and the classical romances will be forgotten little by little. Only a few light popular songs will remain, a few fragments held onto by women and amateurs. But one day not very far off, all of this musical past of the Arab race will have vanished, and future generations will no longer have examples of an art that had its particular splendor and nobility, that, as much as architecture, was [a product] of its age and place.[11]

At the same, Rouanet assured his listeners that the "disaster . . . might be partly averted." Thanks to the "enlightened solicitude the honorable Governor-General of Algeria brings to all that relates to the renaissance of the native arts and industries, I have tried to save from shipwreck this Arab music that we regard with indifference, if not with disdain, contenting ourselves with comparing it to our modern music and thereby concluding an ignoble superiority in our favor." This statement also included a gesture toward a member of the audience: "Mr. Edmond Yafil, a young Algerian who professes a veritable passion for Arab music, who knows it admirably well, and who put me on the path with much zeal, giving generously of his person and of his funds to contribute to the exhuming of these monuments of musical archaeology, and to placing them under a good light hitherto gained for the history of Muslim art." Rouanet concluded with an ornate evocation of al-Andalus: "The heritage of the past centuries is still important. Oblivion has not yet cast its eternal shadow on all the music that the caliphs and their beautiful favorites listened to, and that resounded within the gilded interiors of the Alhambra and the Generalife."[12]

Rouanet's words telescope a great deal about the discourse and event of musical revival in early twentieth-century Algeria. His lecture shows the way in which Arab music, in particular Andalusi music, was becoming the object of a revivalist project in a newly emerging colonial public sphere, and how it sat at the nexus of scientific, aesthetic, and colonial discourses that went well beyond specifically musical matters. It shows the way in which such projects involved indigenous Algerians as partners, as carriers of musical repertoire, as objects of discourse, and as co-participants in the revivalist project. It also shows the way in which some revivalists were talking about such music: it was the remnant of a medieval past that was under threat by the forces of modernity and that required modern methods to save it from utter oblivion. All in all, it presents musical "restoration" as a modern project eminently at home in the colonial setting.

*

Once again, however, we cannot stay still but need to leave the Hôtel de Ville and walk over just a few streets to the lower Casbah, perhaps stopping into Edmond Yafil's father's restaurant for a plate of hot *loubia* along the way. Then, moving on, a contemporary French newspaper account describes what we might have encountered were Sfindja not occupied at Rouanet's presentation or called out to a private gathering in Belcourt:

> In a filthy alley next to a mosque hides a *café maure* where there is singing; it is called "Chez Sfindja." Sfindja is a stout Moor wearing a white jacket, seated Turkish style on a cushion. He sings very old Andalusi songs while accompanying himself on the guitar, songs from the time when Spain was Muslim, from the time of the Alhambra and Boabdil. At the center of the room, a little jet of water in a fountain trickles without sound over soda bottles, strewn with large cut flowers. Before the singer, to delight the eye, are goldfish in glass beakers. From the ceiling hang dozens of canaries in little cages; the light and music waken some of them up there, or perhaps make them dream; they mix their chirps with the notes of the guitar. The listeners, crowding all the way into the street, listen motionlessly and in silence while drinking sweet tea.[13]

Peering beyond the passage's Orientalist veneer, we catch a vivid glimpse of Andalusi music-making outside the rarefied atmosphere of the lecture hall.[14] Nested within a column about settlers who take on indigenous ways, the passage hints at Europeans among Sfindja's audience. But it also raises the question of Sfindja himself. What did he make of his music? What did he make of Rouanet and Yafil, and of his hosts in Belcourt? How did he and others like him position themselves vis-à-vis the revivalist project?

This chapter is an inquiry into the roots, shape, and implications of the discursive project known as Andalusi musical revival. It primarily addresses the question of the revivalist project's historical origins, rather than the sources of its longevity, although hints of an answer to the latter question percolate through the following pages. The strategy I pursue here is to contextualize the early twentieth-century revival within a particular moment in colonial urban life. The very first years of the twentieth century witnessed the rise of a new, tenuous colonial public sphere that included some indigenous Algerians within its purview, alongside various European colonial intellectuals. These actors could draw upon half a century of discourse on the subject of patrimony within the Algerian context, and by 1900 the notion of the need to revive various patrimonial arts and practices had become mainstream. An examination of three simultaneously published efforts to engage with the Andalusi repertoire in revivalist terms—works that coincided with the unpublished efforts of Aboura and Ben Smaïl—shows the ways in which a diverse set of actors, including indigenous Muslims and Jews as well as French officials and intellectuals, met one another around the *nūba* repertoire, modernist sensibilities, and new technologies and institutions such as Arabic printing, musical transcriptions in staff notation, wax cylinder recordings, and copyright.

At the same time, such revivalist actors did not all have the same agendas; nor were their agendas entirely consistent. By focusing on the career of one particularly successful early revivalist, Edmond Nathan Yafil, who would become a key player in the recording industry, musical pedagogy, and performance in the years around the First World War, I suggest that revival brought together multiple logics and accompanying dilemmas, and for many of its leading Algerian figures this movement was very much a continuation and transformation of older projects and relations of musical production. Yafil's relationships with figures like Sfindja and Rouanet, including the latter's very public break with Yafil over questions of copyright, demand that we situate the impulse toward revival not only in the realm of colonial and European politics of the turn of the century but also within the relationship between the *shaykh* and the *mūlūʿ* as it existed in that era. These complications introduce an element of ambiguity into the notion of revival. What was the relationship between revivalist discourse and musical practice, and what made revivalist discourse efficacious, if at all? Was revival new, or simply newly visible, and if the latter, what made it visible? Although the questions I ask focus on a particular, highly charged, constitutive moment within Andalusi musical practice, they potentially have profound implications for what we make of the revivalist project's subsequent trajectory.

The Roots of Revival

When Rouanet delivered his lecture-presentation in 1905, he used an idiom of patrimonial safeguard and restoration that was already well developed. The notion of patrimony in the modern Maghrib derives from at least two different historical sources. One of these is France and the European colonial powers more generally since 1789. Post-revolutionary France is the widely acknowledged workshop of the modern idea of national patrimony as it developed in Western Europe over the course of the nineteenth century: a body of things of such value and significance to the nation that to part with them puts national sovereignty and self at risk. The origin story of the modern French notion of patrimony is telling in this regard. Said to derive from the transformation of the Louvre from a private, royal treasure to a public, national one, the modern notion of patrimony is an inversion of what Max Weber termed patrimonial authority, the king's right to treat his entire dominion as his personal treasure and inheritance.[15] On the near side of the process of inversion, instead of the ruler treating his or her dominion (including its inhabitants) as a personal patrimony, it is the people of that nation as a whole treating specific things within that dominion as their collective patrimony (including the notion of sovereignty itself, now uncoupled from the sovereign). The contents of that patrimonial category may shift over the years, but in the French case the collection of the displaced king's most private and valued possessions is at the center. The modern notion of patrimony, then, is tied up with the founding and maintenance of popular sovereignty and nationhood. In Hardt and Negri's terms, it is the state-centered category of objects that helps transmute the multitude into a people, and that in a sense stands as a sign of peoplehood.

The other historical source is found in the Maghrib itself. For if the concept that originated in France continued to be developed and deployed in new ways in North Africa, it also became entangled with parallel concepts and legal regimes indigenous to the Maghrib. The Islamic endowments known as *waqf* or *ḥabūs* played a crucial role in urban Algerian life during the Ottoman period, and the French authorities viewed this regime of inalienable possessions in land and buildings both as a religiously-tinged threat to secular market exchange (and, by extension, to French colonization) and as a kind of kindred spirit to the French concept of *patrimoine*.[16] In addition, many North Africans already utilized forms of land inheritance and household organization that rested on the idea of inalienable collective possessions at a subnational level. Pierre Bourdieu has suggested that well into the twentieth century a concern with the integrity of the patrilineal patrimony was of prime importance in Kabylia and beyond.[17] In other words, the dominant French understanding of patrimony necessarily met other logics of inalienability.

In meeting such logics in the colonial setting, there was also tension and synergy between them. Nabila Oulebsir has shown how the idea of urban architectural patrimony and the category of the Hispano-Mauresque in nineteenth-century Algeria were closely linked to the destruction of Algerian urban space by colonial authorities as French military and political control over Algeria became firmer at mid-century.[18] Less well known is the role of looted manuscripts in the establishment of the Algiers Library, whose collection is the basis for today's Algerian National Library. The decades-long French conquest of Algeria brought with it the destruction of vast numbers of Arabic manuscripts. Some of the documents that survived were seized by scholar-officials during military expeditions, and some were bought from soldiers who had looted them.[19] The shepherding and safeguard of such objects conferred a certain prestige and aura of stability on the state elites who claimed to guarantee their inalienability. Particularly in the 1850s, climaxing with the final French conquest of Algeria, a regime of legislation and new scholarly institutions established a patrimonial framework that featured close ties between the state and nongovernmental bodies and individuals.[20]

At the same time that the delineation of a sphere of inalienable possessions in the colonial context was the flip side of a process of alienation of Algerian possessions and space, manuscripts and "Hispano-Mauresque" architecture brought colonial officials into intimate connection with Algerians. Unlike Algeria's many Roman ruins, which were often taken by colonial officials as a potent, primordially European prefiguration of their own presence, Hispano-Mauresque objects and spaces were directly associated with Algerian Muslims, and in the case of manuscripts and epigraphy often required the assistance of Algerian textual specialists to decipher.[21] Such collaborations fit well into the Second Empire "royaume arabe" policy—named for the Emperor Louis-Napoléon's 1863 plea that Algeria be considered not a colony but an Arab kingdom—that featured a strengthening of paternalistic institutions against the despoilment of Muslims at settler hands.[22] The "Hispano" part of Hispano-Mauresque also opened the possibility of a link to the medieval and early modern European past in such a way that indigenous Algerian elites could be understood as kin to European colonial elites.[23] In addition, the category of Hispano-Mauresque patrimony allowed for the extension of the patrimonial category to a variety of living practices, including poetry.

The "royaume arabe" moment from which the Hispano-Mauresque patrimonial model arose was short-lived, due to intense settler opposition and the rise of the Third Republic following the end of the Franco-Prussian War. The tumultuous transition from Second Empire (1852–70) to Third Republic (1875–1940), separated by the Paris Commune and its violent suppression, helped usher in a period of unprecedented settler control over Algerian affairs that finalized the dispossession of Algeria's rural population and the reconfiguration of the urban landscape. The military's *bureaux arabes* that had acted as a buffer and interface between settlers and indigenous Algerians were disbanded, and the Franco-Arab educational model geared toward indigenous elites abandoned. While Algerian Muslims regained and surpassed the conquest-era population figures, they faced ever-mounting economic and political marginalization, and in the capital they became a demographic minority.[24] The 1870 Crémieux Decree foisted French citizenship upon the vast majority of Algerian Jews, and French military defeat of the 1871 Kabyle uprising made it the last major challenge to French control of Algeria until 1945. The new dispensation sought to make Algeria as French as possible, and for liberals this meant drawing indigenous Algerians into the French educational and legal system.[25]

The second tenure of Governor-General Charles Jonnart (1903–11) was in some respects a continuation of these trends and in other respects a return to some of the spirit of the *royaume arabe* moment.[26] The power and permanence of the colonial state was being promoted as assiduously as ever, but the intellectuals working within the state's orbit increasingly included indigenous Algerians in addition to French veterans of the *royaume arabe* era. Jonnart himself displayed a strong interest in the indigenous arts and their promotion and was widely viewed by Algerian Muslim intellectuals as a sympathetic figure despite the fact that he did not significantly improve their legal status at this time.[27] Jonnart's efforts to promote artistic and literary activity took many forms, including the promotion of an Algerian school of painting, government support for the indigenous artisanat and for institutions of higher learning aimed at Muslim elites, and the adoption and proliferation of a style of public building that came to be known as the neo-Mauresque, or, somewhat satirically, as the *style Jonnart*. The Governor-General also oversaw a major expansion of the Museum of Muslim Art in Algiers that was cloaked in the language of reviving the dormant genius of the Arabs.[28] Jonnart's sponsorship of the International Congress of Orientalists was part of this reputation, and the event was marked by the recitation of an Arabic poem written in his praise by Choeïb Abou-Bekr (al-Shuʿayb Abū Bakr), the *qāḍī* of Tlemcen, who declared:

> Welcome to you, greetings and peace
> to all of you, O *ḥuḍḍār!*
> You performed the duty that was due you:
> you heeded the call of General Jonnart.[29]

What helped distinguish the Jonnart-era attention from the earlier colonial interest in the Hispano-Mauresque was the emphasis on revival rather than merely conservation or safeguard. The notion that the French state might revive the dormant Hispano-Mauresque genius of the Arabs was not Jonnart's personal invention. For example, the organizers of the Exposition d'art musulman at the Champs-Elysées in 1893 had framed the exhibit of decorative arts as an attempt to simultaneously gather examples of disappearing industries, point the way toward artistic renaissance in France's Muslim possessions, and provide French artists and decorators the opportunity to commune with their own medieval past.[30] The end of the nineteenth century also saw a broader mania for al-Andalus and Spain in the metropole, as exemplified by the highly successful spectacle "Andalusia in the Time of the Moors" that accompanied the Universal Exposition of 1900. Roger Benjamin has suggested that the spectacle's heady blending of images of 1492 Granada with exotica from contemporary Spanish Andalucía and Algeria reflected a broader nostalgic strain in turn-of-the-century expositions as well as a more specific lamination of current French colonial anxieties upon representations of the Spanish and Arab-Islamic imperial pasts.[31] In many ways, then, we can see the Jonnart era as an apotheosis of a broader notion of colonial patrimony in its revivalist idiom and the emphasis on revival as an exercise in colonial domination. It became commonplace at this time to speak of France's desire and ability to revive a moribund Algerian culture, and similar discourse could be found in British-ruled India.[32] In addition, the ready adoption of Hispano-Mauresque motifs seemed to state that the colonial presence was strong enough to safely integrate the Algerian Arab arts into the patrimony of French Algeria, with Algeria being treated no differently than Provence or Brittany.[33] The increased participation of indigenous Algerians could be taken as evidence that the colonial subjects were themselves coming to participate in modernist discourse and institutions. Furthermore, the turn-of-the-century revivalism cast the French state as an active agent, the reviver of a passive Arab object, in a kind of colonialist version of the Arab *nahḍa* developing in Egypt and the Levant. Thus what was sometimes known as the neo-Mauresque exemplified the ideological bent of the new politics of the Jonnart era in that it demonstrated a fresh reaching toward a modernist Algerian identity that would mix European and Algerian Arab elements to what many viewed as felicitous political effect.

But while the turn of the twentieth century in many ways was the apex of this arc of domination, Hispano-Mauresque patrimony was an inherently ambiguous site of activity. On the one hand, it was a marker of colonial triumph, whereby the past is clearly defined and controlled and residual indigenous resistance effaced. At the same time, it is clear that out of this moment grew an indigenous critique of the colonial regime, often from the very ranks of indigenous intellectuals who participated in colonial patrimonialist enterprises. It is also important to note that from the perspective of many indigenous Algerians, the objects of this project were not wholly subsumed within the power of the colonizer. Rather, these objects were part of other, older projects that in some ways could be understood apart from the colonial discourse through which they were often being approached in 1900. Finally, many indigenous Algerian intellectuals were closely attuned to modernist currents in Egypt, the Levant, and the wider Arab and Muslim lands, where al-Andalus was a potent image of Arab-Islamic civilization, loss, and futurity, and where the rhetoric of revival was ubiquitous.[34]

We should also note that while this was a quintessentially colonial predicament, it was also part and parcel of a broader predicament that was not confined to classically colonial situations. The belief that certain practices, professions, and races were doomed to disappear before the onslaught of modern European civilization was directed both to overseas colonial phenomena and to practices of the "folk" within Britain and France.[35] The image of impending disappearance and the accompanying need for "salvage ethnography," then, was a more general feature of an ideology of modernization that found special encouragement and shape in the colonial context.[36] And if "modernity" threatened a variety of "traditional" practices, then one of the constituent ironies of such a situation is that said modernity also provided the methods necessary for rescuing these practices. There is, then, a certain efficacy to the discourse of disappearance in this historical form: in some respects, talking about disappearance is a way to talk about the "modern" from within its precincts and to bring about the simultaneous effect of disappearance and rescue of the modernist ideology's "traditional" other, as well as the sense that such precincts exist in the first place. How this might be will become clearer as we look more specifically at early twentieth-century efforts to "revive" Andalusi music in Algeria.

Reviving Musical Patrimony: Contextualizing the Print Interventions of 1904

The Andalusi revivalist project in Algeria becomes historically legible first as a largely textual endeavor, with the documentary record pointing back to 1904 as the year that saw the publication of three works that treated Andalusi music in a revivalist idiom, and that for the first time presented Algerian *nūba* poetry in print. These included a series of Arabic poetic texts from *nūbat al-dhīl* published in a French-language newspaper in Blida;[37] the poetic-musical treatise titled *Kitāb kashf al-qināʿ ʿan ālāt al-samāʿ* (The book of unveiling the arts of listening) by the Tlemcani schoolteacher Ghouti Bouali;[38] and Edmond Yafil's massive compendium of *nūba* texts titled, in Arabic, *Majmūʿ al-aghānī wa-l-alḥān min kalām al-andalus* (The collections of songs and melodies from the words of al-Andalus), and in Judeo-Arabic, *Dīwān al-aghānī min kalām al-andalus* (Treasury of songs from the words of al-Andalus). These works coincided with the creation of the ambitious but ultimately unpublished work of Aboura and Ben Smaïl in Tlemcen.

To what degree should we view these publications as the inauguration of a revivalist movement? Why this year and not earlier? Addressing these questions satisfactorily is harder than one might think. Because the written word is the main way in which historians approach past contexts, and because print generally travels through time more easily than does manuscript writing and the spoken word, the existence of these works can have a self-ratifying quality about them. The spoken interactions from which they no doubt emerged and to which they responded do not come down to us in any easily recognizable form. There is in fact considerable evidence that the second half of the nineteenth century saw a flurry of ambitious manuscript compilation efforts which do not explicitly refer to themselves in revivalist terms but which may have been carried out in a revivalist spirit. Furthermore, print, like sound recordings and musical transcriptions, can cast the modes of interaction and transmission that it partly displaced as incomplete or flawed. In this sense, new technologies carry within them a critique of other, older technologies, so that the distinction between decadence and revival can be read as a discursive effect written into the self-commentary of the newer technologies. We can think of this as a revival effect that emerges from the messy, always incomplete passage from one technological modality to another.[39]

Keeping these caveats in mind, the 1904 works nevertheless provide a useful way into the phenomenon of Andalusi musical revival. Their simultaneity, and the somewhat resentful awareness of at least one of the authors (Desparmet) of the works of the others, suggest that they collectively mark an event.[40] At the same time, these printed works were not in all respects unprecedented. A collection of 117 Maghribi Arabic songs, a few of them drawn from the Andalusi complex, was published in 1902 and 1904, based on the work of Constantin Sonneck, who was for a time the director of the École supérieure musulmane in Constantine (known in Arabic as Al-madrasa al-kittāniyya) and ended his career as a professor at the École coloniale in Paris.[41] Before this, we have evidence of a series of sheet music arrangements from *nūbat ḥsīn* and an *inqilāb* in the mode *jarka*, likely dating to the years before 1894, associated with an Algerois Jew named Bouaziz and an Alsatian piano teacher named Martz Keil.[42] And to the east, there were nearly contemporaneous Judeo-Arabic printings of song lyrics associated with the Tunisian *nūba* tradition known as *ma'lūf*.[43]

In addition to these publications of melodies and song texts, there was a tradition of colonial music scholarship dating back to the Second Empire period that helped establish aspects of the turn-of-the-century revivalist discourse. One of the inaugural acts of scholarship on North African Andalusi music was a study by the composer, performer, and pioneering musicologist Francisco Salvador Daniel titled *La musique arabe: ses rapports avec la musique grècque et le chant grégorien*, published in 1862–63 in the state patrimonial organ *Revue Africaine.*[44] A resident of Algiers over more than a decade, Salvador Daniel interacted closely with Algerian musicians and music-lovers, and although less ethnographically rich than some contemporary work, *La musique arabe* offers important insights into musical practice in North Africa at that moment.[45] For Salvador Daniel, an ally of Saint-Simonian elements in the French military apparatus who would later be executed for his participation in the Paris Commune, Arab music was not barbarous cacophony, as many settlers in Algeria charged, but instead a sophisticated music deserving of scholarly attention and respect.[46] At the same time, his vision of Algeria was a classically nineteenth-century Orientalist vision of a frozen society.

These two seemingly contradictory aspects of Salvador Daniel's argument in fact leaned upon one another in supporting the central thesis of *La musique arabe*: that the modal system underlying the *nūba* reflects the ancient Greek musical system, which had been transmitted by Arabs to Christian Europe in the medieval period, where it became the basis for Gregorian chant. For Salvador Daniel, the subsequent introduction of harmonic theory in the thirteenth century led to severe modal impoverishment in European music, meaning that current harmonic practice of the nineteenth century was sharply limited in its possibilities. The existence of the modal system among the Arabs offered an opportunity to "restore" plainchant and to enrich current European compositional practice through an act of "musical archaeology"[47]—an opportunity that he would later seize upon through a series of Algerian-inspired experimental compositions for voice and piano.[48] This all may sound like colonial whimsy, but despite his eccentricities Salvador Daniel was very much within the mainstream of French musicological thought of the period. *La musique arabe* appeared precisely at the moment when French intellectuals were in the midst of an epic undertaking of "restoring" Gregorian chant. The work of Katherine Bergeron has shown how this effort lay at the crossroads of multiple political, religious, and political projects and tensions in nineteenth-century France, and exemplified certain typically modern predicaments regarding visions of the medieval and revolutionary past.[49] For Bergeron, Gregorian revival was, like that other revivalist phenomenon known as nationalism, a classically nineteenth-century movement—a resolutely modern vision of primordiality.

In addition to Salvador Daniel's Gregorian revivalist treatment, 1863 saw the publication of Alexandre Christianowitsch's *Esquisse historique de la musique arabe aux temps anciens*. Unlike Salvador Daniel, Christianowitsch, a Russian military officer and music enthusiast convalescing in Algiers in 1861, was somewhat peripheral to the official patrimonial scene.[50] However, the officer's search for the "precious traces" of "Arabian music" in Algeria brought him in contact not only with several prominent Algerian musicians but also with Hassan Ben Hammed, an employee in the Arabic manuscript collection at the Algiers Library, and with Auguste Gorguos, a teacher of colloquial and classical Arabic at the Lycée impériale in Algiers who belonged to the newly established Société historique algérienne.[51] In his text, which combines vivid descriptions of social interactions, medieval Arabic music history, illustrations of Algerian instruments, and short harmonized transcriptions of melodies drawn mainly from seven *nūbāt*, Christianowitsch invokes a classically patrimonial archaeological metaphor, treating the *nūba* repertoire that he encountered as scattered remnants of a long-decayed edifice, with ultimate roots in ancient Greece and Arabia, that begged an act of salvage. His juxtaposition of the past glory of Arab civilization with the inglorious "realities" of the present is familiar nineteenth-century Orientalist fare. However, unlike those patrimonialists who saw the danger to Algerian material culture as a result of the colonial process of which they themselves were part, Christianowitsch treats the danger facing Arab music as a result of the natural passage of time, Islamic legal mistrust of music, and the degrading effects of "the yoke of the Turks."[52]

Algerian music did not cease to be a topic of scholarly interest with the transition to the Third Republic. For example, *Notes sur la poésie et la musique arabes dans le Maghreb algérien* was printed in 1886. Written by the chief military interpreter Léon Guin and by Gaëtan Delphin—who at the time was instructor of Arabic in Oran and later became director of the Algiers *médersa*—the study covered instrumentation, the composition of professional ensembles, and the *nūba* and *qṣīda* forms.[53] Finally, the work of Si Ammar Ben Saïd Boulifa on Kabyle song, published in 1904, built upon a relationship with the Saint-Simonian colonial military official and savant Adolphe Hanoteau.[54] Thus the turn-of-the-century scene added to an already existing body of scholarship in the same way that it extended an already existing patrimonial discourse, even if a closer look starts to show up some important differences as well.

The first of this year's works began on February 27, 1904, when a series of *nūba* texts started to appear in *Le Tell*, a French-language newspaper based in Blida, near Algiers, that identified itself as "a newspaper of politics and colonial interests." The text was in Arabic and simply consisted of a single *ṣanʿa*, an *mṣaddar* from *nūbat al-dhīl*. The text was "edited" by Joseph Desparmet, a local teacher of Arabic and a specialist in colloquial poetry, and by E. Fèliu, a court interpreter in Blida, and it was "collected" from Mahmoud Ben Sidi Saïd Geddoura (also known as Mahmoud Ould Sidi Saïd), Blida's leading singer, violinist, and *rabāb*-player, and a student of Yamina, the leading female professional performer in Algiers.[55] This was the first in a series of eight installments, the last of which appeared July 2, 1904, all of them drawn from the first two movements of *nūbat al-dhīl*. Other than a notice forbidding duplication in all the installments but the first, there was no other French text—a rarity in the pages of this particular newspaper.

Desparmet had enlisted Ben Sidi Saïd at the beginning of what turned out to be the Arabist's long-term scholarly engagement with the question of meter in Maghribi popular poetry, a literature that he described in 1905 during his own talk at the International Congress of Orientalists as "lost for us from a literary point of view if European criticism does not equip it with a decent method for safeguarding and, if necessary, scientifically restoring its integrity."[56] Ben Sidi Saïd's career was in musical performance, and we can only guess at what he might have said about the columns in *Le Tell*. But it is not difficult to imagine a young performer like him, who would go on to be a pioneering recording artist, teacher, and association leader, treating Desparmet's work as an important adjunct to his own musical practice. The printing of pieces from the first two movements of *nūbat al-dhīl* exactly mirrors the form of the traditional songbook, as if these columns were the beginning of a serialization of a *kunnāsh* or notebook, a radical reimagining of a preeminently manuscript practice. Can we even read the sudden appearance of "duplication forbidden" after the first installment as evidence of second thoughts on the part of Ben Sidi Saïd, of Desparmet, or of them both?

Already there are several differences from the Second Empire works of Salvador Daniel and Christianowitsch that are worth pointing out. While Desparmet was clearly ensconced in the Franco-Arab educational successor to the Second Empire patrimonial milieu, his intervention focused on the poetic content of the repertoire. Such a focus was in fact more in keeping with the songbook-centered practice of Andalusi music practitioners. Furthermore, it was accessible only to readers of Arabic, even if it was published in a French-language newspaper.[57] In this sense, the publication took literate indigenous Andalusi music enthusiasts as a major part of its audience. Furthermore, this publication, by naming the source of the poetic texts, highlighted Desparmet's relationship with Ben Sidi Saïd. Desparmet is in essence situating the text and himself within a relationship of musical authority and transmission.

Similar patterns are visible in a simultaneous work that focused in large part on the *nūba* repertoire. On Bastille Day, July 14, 1904—less than two weeks after the appearance of the final *nūba* column in *Le Tell*—a Tlemcani teacher in the Franco-Arab school at the Great Mosque in Sidi Bel Abbès named Ghouti Bouali, recently returned from a brief sojourn at the French Legation in Tangier, completed *Kitāb kashf al-qināʿ ʿan ālāt al-samāʿ*, although it would not be available in print until 1906.[58] On its face, the work is largely about the Arabic language in its formal and Algerian colloquial varieties, and the superiority of verse (whether classical or colloquial) over prose in allowing words and ideas to endure. Although less than half the book is devoted specifically to music, much of the discussion of music concerns the preservation of *muwashshaḥāt* and *azjāl* through melodies, and in turn the need to find ways to preserve melodies through musical notation. Along the way, Bouali includes the texts for a range of poems drawn from the *nūba* and *qṣīda* repertoires. The explicit underlying logic for the writing of the work is the author's observation that "the teachers of this art [of music] were diminishing in number, and no field turned its attention to it such that is was on the verge of extinction and disappearance."[59]

Bouali's work did not appear in a vacuum, as there were several new Arabic treatises on music circulating in manuscript form in the Tlemcen region at the turn of the century, at least one of them written by Choeïb Abou-Bekr, the city's reformist *qāḍī* who had penned the celebratory verses for Jonnart, as well as the works of Bouali's fellow schoolteachers Aboura and Ben Smaïl.[60] In some respects, Bouali's work followed an old model: it appears to have been intended to work within the idiom of the Arabic manuscript treatise, both in its language and organization and in the way he later recalled its completion in 1903 as the moment of its "publication."[61] At the same time, Bouali almost immediately submitted it to the government authorities to be printed. The authorities initially refused, citing the high cost, but several factors intervened in Bouali's favor. Abdelhalim Bensmaïa, one of Muḥammad ʿAbduh's hosts in 1904, read the manuscript and gave it a favorable review.[62] In keeping with common practice, Bouali had dedicated the book to Governor-General Jonnart, "who filled our country with justice and spread landmarks and hospitals far and wide."[63] And Dominique Luciani, director of indigenous affairs for the colonial administration, who made clear his preference for aesthetic matters over religious ones, pressed Bouali's case, particularly after the author acceded to requests to add a considerable section on European staff-notation in the conclusion. In the end, the work was printed lithographically, rather than typeset, and the book's 250 copies were distributed to the author, the various Franco-Arab schools, Arabists in Algeria and Europe, and government offices in Algeria and Tunisia.[64]

In content, too, *Kashf al-qināʿ* reflects a geographically and temporally wide-ranging musical and literary consciousness that points to the broader reach of musical revival in this historical moment. Aside from a vast range of Andalusi and Maghribi poets, some of them discovered in his perusals of personal manuscript libraries, Bouali cites the Qur'an, Ibn Khaldun, Francisco Salvador Daniel, the work of contemporary Egyptian musical reformers, the modern Moroccan historian al-Nāṣirī, and a recently published Moroccan edition of an eighteenth-century biographical dictionary of musicians and poets from Fes. His sense of musical relativity with regard to *nūba* form and performance was rooted in his two years of study at the government-run *médersa* in Algiers, which brought him in close contact with Algerians from many parts of the country, and possibly with Tunisians as well, and led to many conversations about comparative musical practice.[65] This period also provided him with opportunities to observe Algerois musical events, which he juxtaposes with the practice in Tlemcen in *Kashf al-qināʿ*.[66] Finally, the discourse of musical revival evident in Bouali's text is sometimes indistinguishable from a modernist discourse of Islamic reform that could be heard in both colonial offices and in Algerian and Middle Eastern intellectual circles, with its sharp critique of the cult of saints associated with popular Sufism. In Bouali's words regarding the genesis of his book, "Some urge me on to be courageous, and some urge me to sit down in the obscure *zawāya* [Sufi lodges] and saints' tombs; I favored the first group because its origins are in the sciences, and I unsheathed the reed-pen against the wilderness."[67]

But it is the substance of Bouali's argument that is most telling with regard to his project. For Bouali, the *nūba* and *qṣīda* repertoires are an adjunct to the Arabic language that gives them their poetic substance, and it is for this reason that this treatise on music dwells on the history of the Arabic language and its grammatical rules and canonical poetic meters. According to Bouali, the rules of Arabic grammar arose as Arabic spread, as a sort of compensation for the dangers such extension in space (and exposure to foreign languages) posed to the integrity of the Arabic language.[68] In this way, the rules of Arabic poetic meter are extensions of this effort to guarantee linguistic integrity and transmission across time and space. Bouali's argument echoes the old Arabic valuation of verse (*naẓm*, synonymous with organization and order) over prose (*nathr*, related to the concept of dispersion and loss). And in this way music is presented as an essentially vocal art that is likewise governed by a body of partly forgotten rules that should allow music to serve as a reliable vessel for Arabic poetry in its classical and colloquial varieties. It is for this reason that Bouali presents the rudiments of Arabic modal theory and instrumental technique in the Algerian tradition. It is also in this area that Bouali sees the need for the introduction of further techniques for the preservation of the melodies of the musical repertoires, which for him show clear attenuation due to failures in transmission. In this vein, Bouali proposes a highly original form of staff notation that reads from right to left (in keeping with the right-to-left script of Arabic) and that allows for the representation of pitches that fall outside European staff notation.[69] Bowing to his editors at the Office of Indigenous Affairs, Bouali ends the work by introducing the basics of the standard European staff notation and orchestral convention. Taken as a whole, Bouali's treatise presents the *nūba* and *qṣīda* repertoires as a distant elaboration of the rules of Arabic—rules that are ultimately justified by the need to preserve the essence of the Arabic language in the face of the threat of dispersion and incoherence. At the same time, the body of Arabic musical theory is itself in need of recovery and further development, in part through scholarly intervention on the model of *Kashf al-qināʿ* and in part through the new technology of musical transcription.

Bouali's work provides a telling counterpoint to the Desparmet–Ben Sidi Saïd columns. The collaboration between the latter paired a scholar and a performer; Bouali combined these two roles in his own person in that he was himself an amateur practitioner—a *mūlūʿ*—as well as someone who, like Desparmet, was firmly ensconced in the Franco-Arab educational system. There is also the *shaykh* to whom he attaches himself, however, as both patron and student, in this case the recently decased Jewish musician known as Maqshīsh (Ichoua Medioni), who stands as a paragon of sophistication and as a representation of all that the repertoire lost over time. In this respect, Bouali was continuing a venerable dilettante tradition within Andalusi musical circles, even as he was helping the tradition take on new material and circulatory forms.

A similar pattern can be discerned when we turn to the third and most consequential print intervention of 1904, Yafil's *Majmūʿ* or *Dīwān*. In just under 400 pages, the *Majmūʿ* reproduces song texts for all fourteen *nūbāt* considered part of the Algerois tradition.[70] It also includes an appendix of texts for the *inqilābāt*. The first published songbook in the Algerian *nūba* traditions, for many years this collection would be the definitive printed compilation among performers and enthusiasts in Algiers and beyond, and practitioners cherish worn copies of this songbook to this day. It is also a work that gives voice to a revivalist idiom with particular clarity and that vividly highlights the complexities of indigenous collaborations with Europeans. In order to make sense of it, we will need to situate the songbook within Yafil's larger career, and in order to do this, we will need to look at the relationship between Yafil and Rouanet, and thereby return to the Hôtel de Ville in 1905.

Yafil and Rouanet

The names of Yafil and Rouanet emerge together in the historical record, and initially in a manner that places Rouanet in the dominant position, somewhat along the model of Desparmet and Ben Sidi Saïd. In many ways, the figure of Rouanet exemplifies the idiom of colonial revival in its mature form. By the time of the 1905 Congress, Rouanet was already a well-known journalist and musicologist, and listeners already knew of his role in "restoring Moorish music," in part through his recent contributions to the Paris-based musicological journals. His relationship with Yafil was also well-established, and European Orientalists who knew of the *Majmūʿ* credited Rouanet as Yafil's inspiration.[71] Rouanet's interest in music was not new, as he had previously been the director of the École de Musique du Petit Athénée in Algiers.[72] Nor was his interest in revival limited to musical matters: before his directorship of the Petit Athénée, he had been known as a journalist specializing in agricultural matters, acting in the 1880s as science editor of *La Gazette du colon*,[73] and writing in 1897 on the need for the colonial administration to take the lead in reviving and reforming the North African textile industry, which, "imported to Europe by the Saracens, is dying in North Africa, one of the regions of its origin."[74]

It is tempting to view Rouanet as having taken the lead in the turn-of-the-century musical efforts, with Yafil acting as a facilitator of a frankly colonialist project. However, to do so would miss crucial differences between the two men and the full complexity of their interactions in that their relationship represented the meeting of two musical projects that were only partly overlapping. Born in 1874 to a father who was a tobacco cutter-turned-restaurateur and to a mother of modest Algerois roots, by 1900 Yafil was a young, newly married Andalusi music enthusiast living in Mustapha and working in his father's working-class eatery, Makhlouf Loubia, near the Bazaar Malakoff adjacent to the governmental center of Algiers.[75] Growing up in and around this popular restaurant, the young Yafil had occasion to listen to Sfindja, who by around 1900 regularly sang at a nearby café (possibly the Café Malakoff, also known as the Galerie Malakoff; see fig. 3). In gathering the texts that came to make up the *Majmūʿ*, Yafil was a young music enthusiast engaged in a project that in some respects was similar to what aficionados had been doing for generations. What was new about Yafil was that he intended to publish the texts in printed form and market the compilation to the general public.[76] In addition, this would be only the first step in a much more ambitious project of musical publicization. In just twenty years, the modest restaurant worker would become one of the most prominent figures in the Algerian musical landscape and in Algerois public life.

Thus Yafil's songbook brought a manuscript-style compilation of the sort created and coveted by generations of Andalusi music enthusiasts into the world of print. In this respect, the work was by an indigenous Algerian writing primarily for other indigenous Algerians, both Muslim and Jewish, although this did not exhaust the text's projected audience. The complexity of the audience for the *Majmūʿ* is intimated by its linguistic deployments. The Arabic version reproduces hundreds of song texts, organized according to mode and movement, without French translation. The title page is solely in Arabic. But in addition there is a three-page French-language preface signed by Yafil in which he lays out the raison d'être of the compilation, namely the cause of salvage and leveling of access to musical knowledge:

> It seemed to us that there would be a real interest, for the natives and Arabists alike, to have between their hands a collection of *ghernata* [Granada] poetry as complete as possible and methodically presented.
>
> Realizing this project was not without difficulty of every order: we were required to knock on many doors and show an obstinate perseverance. Sometimes they were satisfied to give us one or two poems, sometimes they gave us more or less complete manuscripts with truncated poems, unrhymed verses, or false rhymes.
>
> Therefore it was not without a long labor of compilation and comparison, without patient research that we were able to constitute our collection, to class each melody in its *nouba*, to assign it its rational meter, to reconstitute it, in a word, in its true form as it was sung by the poets and musicians of Granada and of Cordoba in the age of Arab gentility.[77]

Yafil's French-language preface thus addresses a diverse audience, ranging from "the Arab public," to Arabists, to the more ambiguous "friends of popular Arabic poetry." The preface ends, however, with a direct comment toward the Arabists or Orientalists, who will find in it a collection

> without any literary pretension . . . the product of a modest intention to gather, in one volume, scattered poems which are difficult to find, which are exposed to all sorts of alterations and perhaps to an approaching disappearance when they are in fact one of the oldest and least contestable riches among the poetic treasures of Arabic literature.[78]

While native Algerians are not excluded from the preface, they are addressed in more intimate terms in the short, colloquializing Arabic-language introduction that follows.[79] This is true as well in the case of the *Dīwān*, the Judeo-Arabic version of the *Majmūʿ*. The existence of the Judeo-Arabic edition underlines the fact that Jews formed an integral part of the Algerian musical public, as well as the fact that Algerian Jews had very limited literacy in the traditional Arabic orthography.[80] It also underlines the complexity of Yafil's audience, which cut across the diverse social groups of urban Algiers. Finally, in the French, Arabic, and Judeo-Arabic introductions alike, Yafil sets up this entire audience against the figures of the parsimonious *shaykh* and connoisseur, who refuse to freely share their precious knowledge. Thus the public is constituted against an anti-public or counter-public that inverts the virtues of openness and free circulation.[81]

In this way, Yafil was explicit that the printing of the poems was designed to preserve an endangered repertoire and also to restore the repertoire to the public that loved it but that had been kept from it by the secretive practices of some of its possessors. Yafil's work hence demonstrates in particularly vivid form the restorative, popularizing power vested in Arabic printing in the 1904 interventions. In this respect, the printed compilation represented an insider's intervention into an already established musical practice. At the same time, Yafil's project was also oriented outward to Europeans who in the main were not deeply invested in Andalusi music as listeners. In particular, he addressed European Arabists who would be interested in the poems from the perspective of literary history.

This European audience was crucial to the other side of Yafil's activities at this time, which brought him into close collaboration with Rouanet. Having likely met around Sfindja, Rouanet and Yafil cooperated in transcribing a body of musical repertoire, in large part through the intermediary of Sfindja and the various members of his professional circle. Printed in a series of lavishly produced sets of sheet music that were themselves advertised inside the *Majmūʿ*, the *Répertoire de musique arabe et maure* complemented the printed compilation. Its many installments brought together a range of pieces, mainly *inqilābāt*, instrumental overtures (both the *tūshiyya* and *tshanbar*), and popular colloquial forms such as the *zindānī* and the *qādriyya*.[82] Thus the *Répertoire*, unlike the *Majmūʿ*, did not deal with any of the five core elements of the *nūba* structure until some of its final installments in the 1920s, focusing instead on the outer edges of the *nūba* complex.[83] The series was published over many years, extending well beyond Sfindja's death in 1908, but Rouanet, in his commentaries that accompanied each installment except for the final four, occasionally mentions Sfindja's performances as the direct source for the transcribed melody. In his general preface to each transcription, Rouanet acknowledges Yafil as the main force behind the *Répertoire*. Rouanet, however, is the explicit speaker, voicing their aims in creating the *Répertoire*:

> We wanted to set down, before they disappeared entirely, the melodies of every type that constitute the so very rich repertoire of the native musicians; to save from oblivion that which is left us of an art that was at one time very flourishing; to consign, in modern notation so that it might be put at the disposition of admirers [*amateurs*], an authentic music that is nearly unknown; to submit to musicologists elements, new for them, from the musical history of the peoples of the Orient; and to transcribe definitively for the Muslims the collection of the typical melodies of their race and their religion that everywhere followed the people of Mahomet and today constitute the lone vestiges of its artistic grandeur.[84]

The target audience for the transcriptions was therefore mixed, with a somewhat heavier emphasis on Europeans. Aside from the occasional transliterated lyrics and the neo-Mauresque calligraphy on the frontispiece reiterating the title of the transcribed piece in Arabic, the *Répertoire* was a decidedly francophone publication. Moreover, the fact that the series featured transcriptions in staff notation underlines its orientation toward Europeans. Although some Algerian practitioners read staff notation and bought the installments of the *Répertoire*, most practitioners did not need it. There are also hints of the way in which practitioners who read staff notation used, or did not use, the *Répertoire*: one Algerois musician born in the 1930s recounted to me that his father owned and made use of the transcriptions but would frequently point out differences between the version on the page and the version he was giving voice to at the piano.

The generic diversity of the *Répertoire*'s contents provided an opportunity for Rouanet to articulate the diverse rationales of revival in this period. His discussion of the *nūba* material and of the popular *zindānī* sets up a telling contrast. For Rouanet, because the *zindānī* "circulate in the street" among women and children, they are open to European influence. It is this danger that merits their transcription in order to save them from "oblivion and deformation." The *nūba* and *inqilābāt*, on the other hand, are able to resist degradation and influence because they remain "the monopoly of professionals" and "enter the public domain with difficulty."[85] At the same time, Rouanet's larger oeuvre, as well as the revivalist discourse more generally, suggests that the protected nature of the *nūba* is also a source of danger. Rouanet seems to suggest that the *shuyūkh* take the protection of the *nūba* too far, to the point that it is in danger of total burial.

Thus when Rouanet faced his audience in 1905, he was speaking from an already prominent position within the public project of revival, and Yafil and he were already closely linked. From this time forward, their names continued to be intertwined. The two of them would become central players in Algeria's nascent recording industry, with Rouanet acting as advisor to the early recording giant Gramophone and Yafil being linked to both Pathé Records and Gramophone.[86] In the period before the First World War, the recorded artists included Yamina as well as Sfindja in the last year of his life. Some of the discs were no doubt sold to scholarly-minded Europeans, others to members of the indigenous elite, and still others wound up in those cafés that could afford to replace live performance with the phonograph.[87] These early recordings were conceived in a way that was not far removed from transcription and print compilations: they laid claim to a documentary function, and one that in some cases dovetailed with print collections as well, as in the case of an anthology of popular song texts that Yafil printed in 1907 under the title *Majmūʿ zahw al-anīs al-mukhtaṣṣ bi-l-tabāsī wa-l-qawādis* (The collection of the companion's pleasure, specializing in discs and cylinders), which we will consider more closely in the following chapter.[88]

The documentary aspect of revival had a counterpart in the realm of live performance. Rouanet and Yafil collaborated in organizing an orchestra dedicated to Algerian music that was known for a time as Orchestre Rouanet et Yafil. This ensemble performed some of the first concerts of Andalusi music in the public squares of Algiers and was one of the groups recorded on disc by Gramophone in 1910.[89] Around 1912, the ensemble transformed into El Moutribia, the first amateur association devoted to Andalusi music in North Africa; its trajectory will be traced in more detail in chapter 6.[90] Drawing upon the 1901 Law of Associations, El Moutribia was explicitly not a professional ensemble but rather a grouping of mainly middle-class *mūlūʿīn*, most of them Jewish, whose performances represented a "migration of traditional music" from cafés and private homes "to the concert-hall."[91] El Moutribia was under Yafil's direction from its inception until his appointment as the first Chair of Arab Music at the Algiers Municipal Conservatory in 1923.[92] After this time, El Moutribia's direction was turned over to Mahieddine Bachetarzi, a young Muslim tenor who Yafil had discovered and signed on as a major new media star. El Moutribia would outlive Yafil's death in 1928, only to eventually cede its preeminence to the other amateur associations that sprung up after Yafil's passing.[93]

Rouanet continued to be involved in music, publishing major encyclopedia entries on Arab and North African music in 1921, and, like Yafil, serving as a consultant for the Scottish musicologist Henry Farmer during his preparation of an English translation of Salvador Daniel's classic *La musique arabe*.[94] But Rouanet's career was more broadly entangled in artistic and political matters. His vigorous defense of the colonial status quo in his 1931 rebuttal of former Governor-General Violette's *L'Algérie vivra-t-elle?* showed that his language of paternalist revival was not only directed toward textiles and musical life but by this time extended to the whole of Algeria as a political and social unit.[95] His relationship with Yafil, for that matter, effectively ended well before Yafil's death. The last four installments of the *Répertoire* were published, with much reduced opulence (though with much increased ambition with regard to their musical scope), under Yafil's name alone, after his migration to the conservatory. That this marked a break becomes clear through a sharp exchange of letters published in the columns of *La Dépêche Algérienne* in 1927. El Moutribia had just returned from a highly successful first tour to Paris, capped by a well-advertised public performance in Algiers. Rouanet fired the first shot:

> For several years now, I have formally requested that my person be in no ways implicated in a commercial enterprise that would aim to monopolize, for material ends, a domain that constitutes part of the Muslim folklore. I could not allow people to be left thinking that I approve of certain admittedly skillful forms of such exploitation of music that belongs to everyone due to its anonymity and great age. I did not wish to shout from the rooftops that I had composed Andalusi songs from the ninth century or from other distant epochs. I did not agree to call myself a great and illustrious composer in order to secure rights to melodies that are older than our "Au Claire de la Lune" or tunes that Mohammed Ben Ali Sfindja, Ben Farachou, and other masters of genuine fame had dictated to their students just as they had received them from their predecessors.[96]

Rouanet's thinly veiled accusation that Yafil had copyrighted parts of the Andalusi repertoire would be denied by Bachetarzi in his memoirs, but in fact governmental records show that Yafil had done as much.[97] Furthermore, Yafil's response vigorously defended his claim to be "sole propagator and owner of the Arab musical repertoire":

> M. Rouanet recognized, in writing, my sole ownership and exploitation of the Arab repertoire, which did not prevent him from deriving handsome profits from this art and from attributing to himself the most flattering comments which in reality are due solely to me. Considering that M. Rouanet went beyond his proper functions, I invited him to suspend his services, and it is thus that he fell back into oblivion. I hope that it will have sufficed to publish the present rectification, so that M. Rouanet ceases to attribute to himself merits

> that he never had and that therefore any controversy will be ineffective with regard to the ownership of a repertoire of which I am the sole proprietor and, in large part, the sole author.[98]

We will explore the unsettled notions of authorship and possession and their connections to the genealogical ethos further in the next chapters, but for the time being I would like to highlight two particular threads of the dispute. First, Rouanet took the patrimonial high ground, arguing both that Yafil had repeatedly debased himself by playing low repertoire and that he had no right to claim copyright over music that he inherited from Sfindja and others, who in turn had received it from their forebears. Second, Rouanet reserved some of his harshest words to respond to Yafil's charge that the journalist's role in the process of transcription was of little import—that Rouanet had merely been a "mechanical recorder of music" while in fact the living spirit of authorial genius had resided in Yafil. For Yafil, the technological apparatus is dead, while it is the genealogically situated musician who is alive and deserves the protection of copyright law.[99] Yet for commentators who were sympathetic to Rouanet's side of the story, the metaphor Yafil provided should be inverted. One journalist suggested that if anyone was a mechanical recorder, was it not Yafil, the "human phonograph," who simply played what was recorded on "the disc of memory" for Rouanet, the flesh-and-blood, thinking, highly unmechanical transcriber who took down what was printed there?[100] In Rouanet's and his defender's view, transcription and recording take down what is there, embedded in genealogical relationships. In Yafil's view, it is embodiment within those genealogical relationships that counts, while transcription and recording are simply media through which embodiment is externalized and brought under the protection of the law. This dispute brought out into the open a debate regarding embodiment, orality, and the powers of technologies that lay at the heart of the question of revival.

Returning to Sfindja

The story of this chapter has been about musical revival as an early twentieth-century project that brought together, sometimes uneasily and at cross-purposes, both indigenous Algerians and settler intellectuals. For European scholars and officials like Desparmet, Luciani, and Rouanet, musical revival fit into a larger project of colonial uplift. For middle- and upper-class indigenous Algerians like Bouali, Aboura, Ben Smaïl, Benteffahi, and Yafil, musical revival fit into a similar project, but one that could also be read as an indigenous *prise de conscience*. For them, revival was also a continuation of an older tradition of listening to and compiling Andalusi music. While in some respects their use of print, transcription, the discourse of restoration, recordings, copyright, and the amateur association radically changed the way in which Andalusi music could circulate, in other ways they were extensions or amplifications of already existing subjectivities and modes of participation.

In the following two chapters, this point will be explored further with regard to two key technologies and institutions: the songbook and the amateur association. For now, however, it is important to come back to that key figure in the discursive project of revival, the *shaykh*. For people like Rouanet, Yafil, and Bouali, as well as many of their successors, the embodied authority of the *shaykh* is double-edged: in order to save the repertoire, the person saving it requires the cooperation of the *shaykh*; at the same time, the repertoire must be saved precisely from the *shaykh*. The *shaykh* is, then, a complex enabling condition of the revivalist discourse. This is in fact a continuation of the notion that the *shaykh* possesses a repertoire that is the object of the patron's thwarted desire. This is one of the specific ways in which we can read the revivalist discourse as an amplification and refraction of the preexisting relations of musical production.

But with reference to the revivalist discourse, what are we to make of this enabling condition, particularly in light of the lives of actual *shuyūkh*? At the 1905 Congress, Sfindja was held up as a repository of the repertoire but also as the last of his kind. In many ways, what we know of him in this context is very much as a musical subaltern: he sings but does not speak.[101] But Rouanet's later accounts of the Congress in fact provide one tantalizing conversational fragment that is likely the only surviving report of Sfindja as a speaker. Interestingly enough, it is a threat. The master musician made it clear to Rouanet that "religious singing" was one part of the repertoire that he would not share during the 1905 lecture-demonstration and that he would not tolerate being shared by the other performers. He went so far as to promise Rouanet that he would leave the hall if any singer dared to perform "so much as the call to prayer." He was reported to say of such "religious singing": "This music is ours . . . it must die with us."[102]

This distantly recalled fragment of speech, taken at face value, considerably enriches our picture of the 1905 event. It suggests that the participants were far from passive subordinates. It also shows that the indigenous musicians were not necessarily a united interest: Sfindja threatens to leave if any other musician oversteps the acceptable boundaries between the sacred and the profane and between the Muslim and non-Muslim. It suggests that for the leading light of Algerian music, questions of genre and its appropriate audience were pressing. Finally, it suggests that the notion of taking repertoire to the grave was indeed being deployed, not only negatively in efforts to "rescue" repertoire but also positively in efforts to assert communal, musical, and personal boundaries.

Viewed from the Hôtel de Ville, from Belcourt, and from the Casbah, the musical milieu in which Yafil and Rouanet were acting was not unitary, and not even bifurcated. Instead, it was richly polyvocal, multilayered, and at times contradictory. It brought together, sometimes uneasily, settlers, Muslim and Jewish Algerians, European scholars, traditionalists, modernists, and the many who fell in between. In this sense, the political logic of musical revival was up for grabs: it could be a colonial modernist project, a Muslim reformist project, a proto-nationalist project, and perhaps a modernist project that responded to the local conditions of working- and middle-class Jewish performers.

But it is not that we should simply see the indigenous *mélomanes* as agents, alongside their European colonial counterparts. For it would be a mistake to read Sfindja and other *shuyūkh* only as objects of revivalist discourse or at best as subjects who resist revival. After all, Sfindja agreed to perform at the Congress, he cooperated with Yafil and Rouanet in their transcription project, and he recorded his voice a year before his death. It is not only a matter of Sfindja acquiescing to such demands. In fact, there are some ways in which we can read Sfindja himself as a revivalist. To get at such a notion of revival is to consider revival as a discourse that may have been available to people who entered into musical production from another position than did someone like Yafil or Bouali or Aboura. Sfindja, for example, was active in creating new melodies for poems whose original melodies were "lost." In Blida, Ben Sidi Saïd may very well have viewed Desparmet and the pages of *Le Tell* as appropriate vehicles for a musician-centered project of revival—one to which he would later contribute through his involvement in Blida's first amateur musical association, El Ouidadia. To speak of revival as the appropriation of Andalusi music by Europeans from Algerians, or by patrons from professionals, is to miss the way in which revival was a discourse and a project into which even a single individual could enter from several distinct points.

Indeed, revival as a discourse may not in fact have been new at all, even if Arabic print, sound recordings, and the association form were new. If the *nūba* was a forum around which listeners and performers could talk about rarity, then the *nūba* and its practitioners were always on the verge of disappearance. To engage the *nūba*, then, was axiomatically to engage in the animation of that which was rare, endangered, and thereby precious. It was, to turn Clifford Geertz's formulation to new purposes, revival "'all the way down.'"[103] This is not to dismiss the significance of the turn-of-the-century scene, the sensitivity of the musical milieu to various changes in the sociopolitical landscape, or the way revival inaugurated a century-long, ongoing project. As the following chapters demonstrate, these innovations had major consequences, even if they did not entirely erase the earlier musical practices from which they emerged and even if the wider stream of practice often encompassed them. Furthermore, the technologies of revival were themselves the delimitations of revival's outer edge: Sfindja was the last, in a sense, because he was the first to be recorded. I will return to this seeming paradox, but the point to keep in mind for the time being is that revival as a movement would come to build upon an ontological condition of revival. Hence even if the notion of "unmediated musical phenomena" might be problematic, Michael Frishkopf's comments about the relationship between recording technology and the notion of musical patrimony are apt:

> The supposed 'timelessness'—both in the Arab world and elsewhere—of premediated music can . . . often be dated precisely to the onset of technological mediation, due to media's ironically twinned effects of both rapidly transforming and preserving (usually for the first time) musical sound. Technologies of mass media . . . therefore always generate profound nostalgia for whatever unmediated musical phenomena they happen to encounter first, by fashioning, out of the flux of such phenomena, durable mediated objects later assumed to represent the infinite expanse of an unmediated past, before socially marginalizing those same objects within a new mediated music system centered on the moving target of current musical fashion.[104]

Revival, then, poses certain questions. From the Hôtel de Ville, revival appears as something dramatically new and public. The views from Belcourt and from the Casbah, however, cast some doubt on just how new this stance was. At the same time, the photograph of Sfindja, Benteffahi, and their listeners in the garden draws attention to the place of new technologies and apparatuses in marking out a sense of revival and carrying it forward into the future. We turn now to another kind of vessel for movement through time and space: the songbook.

5

Texts, Authority, and Possession

I was told that my host was a prominent local connoisseur of the Andalusi repertoire of Algiers. Though not a performer, this retired government functionary was said to possess a profound knowledge of the *nūba* form and its modes, a knowledge that he had displayed in recent years in a series of scholarly writings and conference talks. His knowledge was matched by an auditory passion so intense that he was known to weep on hearing certain modes. It was also rumored that he possessed a vast collection of rare recordings and documents. In short, it was essential that a novice scholar like myself meet him.

On my arrival at his aging villa on the edge of the city center, the *mélomane* led me into a shuttered salon. A stereo system dominated the room, surrounded by cases full of LPs, cassettes, and videotapes. We sat, and with minimal prodding from me, he launched into a detailed discourse on the routes that the musical tradition took from al-Andalus to North Africa, and in the course of the narrative he touched on the biographies of some of its twentieth-century masters. I was at an early stage of my research, and the time I had spent with musicians over the preceding weeks had introduced me to the importance of Edmond Yafil's 1904 song text compilation within the Algiers-Tlemcen musical practice. When I asked him if he knew much about this text, my host left the room. Some minutes later he returned carrying a thick, well-worn book that bore an old-fashioned frontispiece. It read, in Maghribi Arabic script, *Majmūʿ al-aghānī wa-l-alḥān min kalām al-Andalus*. Although I had heard a great deal about this book from musicians and connoisseurs, and seen a few photocopied pages from its preface, it was the first time that I had actually held a complete example. He hesitated when I asked him if I could get a photocopy. He would have to be the one to make the copy, he said, and I would have to pay. I explained that as a student conducting preliminary research, I had received only a modest grant. In this polite register, we soon agreed that he would make the photocopy later that week in exchange for the equivalent of close to fifty U.S. dollars, as well as copies of some secondary sources in my possession.

When I returned four days later, the photocopy was ready for me (see fig. 7), and although he grumbled that he was charging me far too little considering the document's importance, the aficionado accepted my payment with a merciful comment about my student status. He warned me, however, not to tell anyone in Andalusi musical circles that I had received the copy from him, particularly for so small a price: they might find it shocking, he said, that he had so easily parted with a treasure for which they would expect to pay at least five times the amount.

It was the end of the first of what were thankfully numerous exchanges with this particular enthusiast. Before I left—perhaps to encourage my return—he brought out another document for my perusal: a thick photocopied binder in Judeo-Arabic whose Hebrew letters read *Dīwān al-aghānī min kalām al-Andalus*. This, he explained, was the other version of Yafil's compilation, even rarer than its Arabic counterpart. I asked about where he had

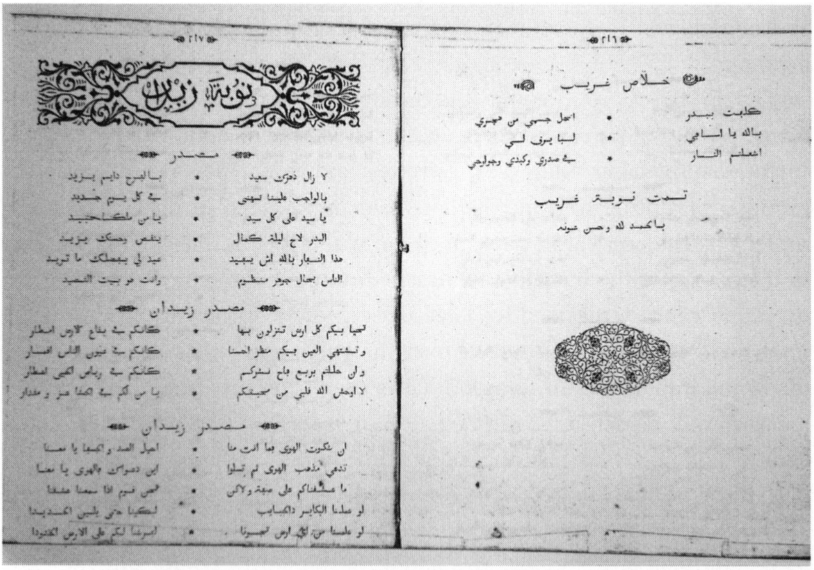

FIGURE 7. Two pages from Edmond Nathan Yafil's *Majmūʿ al-aghānī wa-l-alḥān min kalām al-andalus*, 1904. From right to left, the transition from the end of the *nūbat ghrīb* texts (a single *khlāṣ* at the top of the right-hand page) to the beginning of the *nūbat zīdān* texts (three *mṣaddarāt* are visible on the left-hand page). Only the last *mṣaddar* follows the repertoire's standard five-line *muwashshaḥ* form.

found it, but he would only tell me that he had procured the copy through a rabbi he had met overseas. "But for a copy of this," he said as I was leaving, "you will need to come back with a bigger grant."

It would be several years before I again laid eyes on a complete copy of Yafil's Arabic compilation other than the duplication I had bought from the connoisseur. Meanwhile, I had ample time to peruse the contents of my copy. On first reading the French-language preface to the *Majmūʿ*, the following lines jumped from the page:

> These poems were not yet collected or classified in books. There indeed exist, in the hands of certain Moors, manuscripts of *ghernata* more or less complete. But each owner is excessively jealous of his property; he refuses to share it and is satisfied to enrich it when he can with some new piece that he heard or that he obtained for a great sum from a native musician. In these circumstances, the Arab public cannot procure the text of the songs that it passionately loves and that remain the monopoly of the privileged few.[1]

A delicious irony: a document that was created explicitly to counter the practice of hoarding was itself being hoarded some hundred years after its publication. At first I wondered if my interlocutor was simply profiting from a foreign researcher he guessed was able to pay. But I soon heard that he was known for behaving in a similar fashion with everyone, and that he in fact was being far more open with me than was usual. I also realized that he was by no means unusual within the circles of *mélomanes* and performers—I only needed to recall that this was the first time I had seen the collection. Over time it became clear to me that hoarding or monopoly—what musicians and enthusiasts sometimes refer to in Arabic as *iḥtikār*—is a leitmotiv in the Andalusi musical practice I am discussing here, and that one of the things that gets hoarded—alongside recordings and actual pieces of the repertoire—are texts, high among them Yafil's compilation.[2]

The issue of hoarding arises in many different parts of this study, but in relation to compilations it is just one part of a much larger textual practice that demands sustained attention. As touched upon in chapter 3, inscription is a central part of the Maghribi-Andalusi musical traditions. As an expressive form emerging from urban centers, these traditions are examples of *la musique savante*, or learned music, and written texts have probably always played a part in their production and circulation. While writing takes many forms in the Andalusi musical community, from the scholarly treatise to the biographical dictionary, from manuscript to print to the internet, by far the central form is the handwritten or published compilation or songbook. The creation and possession of compendia of song texts, usually organized by mode and movement, are closely connected to the performance of this tradition. These compendia are closer to an index or a manual than they are to a poetic anthology.[3] One does not sit down and read a songbook; rather, one uses it.

How exactly one uses it is among the main concerns of the current chapter. As shown in chapter 3, songbooks are bearers of the building blocks for the *nūba*, what are often known in the musical practice as *ṣanāyiʿ* or *shghālāt*. In the absence of melodic notation, written song texts are the main way to move the repertoire through time and space, beyond its phenomenal performance. In a manner similar to an esteemed *shaykh*, a songbook bears the poetic kernel of the repertoire and along with it an aura of authenticity. A songbook is also eminently practical in that it can be consulted for use in performance, and as Youcef Touaïbia has pointed out, in some nineteenth-century manuscripts there were also elements of musical phrasing that entered into the presentation of the poems on the page.[4] Unlike the metonymic *shaykh*, the compilation divulges its contents to anyone who possesses it and is able to read. At the same time, a text alone is incomplete. One needs actual people, or at least traces of actual people, to provide the melodies and the larger musical structure in which the words may live.

A compilation, then, is a kind of text (or better, a text-artifact) that brings together other texts.[5] Such a compilation can be referred to by a range of terms: the French *cahier* (notebook) or *bouquin* (booklet), and the Arabic *zimām* (register), *kunnāsh* (scrapbook), *safīna* (vessel), *dīwān* (collection, treasury, or register), or *majmūʿ* (alternatively, *majmūʿa*; a collection).[6] However it is referred to, the compilation brings together texts that derive from the performance practice of present and past (even if, more immediately, they have been sourced from other compilations). But the compilation, unlike the component songs, is a necessarily written form of text that is attuned to durability and coherence—like the poetry itself, it is on the side of order, of *naẓm*, against the dispersion of *nathr*. Furthermore, it is a particularly "meta" form of text, since its component parts are already considered the basis for freestanding oral texts unto themselves, and since the compilation carries as its primary raison d'être the bringing-together of the songs to a specific social end. This basic metatextual character of compilations marks them as a particularly dense, layered variety of textual production that makes them a fitting metaphor for broader questions of authority and ingathering—indeed, the term *tadwīn*, from the same root as *dīwān*, has come to be used to refer to the broader act of documentation, codification, and safeguard of the repertoire, including but not limited to the written word.[7] It also shows that like other forms of metatextual discourse, compilations are given to questions of power and reflexivity. This helps to explain some of the density of meaning attributed to them in the musical practice that we are examining, as well as the compulsion to subject them to correction and replacement.[8] Furthermore, the compilation is a form of text that tends to point beyond its boundaries with particular forcefulness. A songbook presupposes a repertoire that exists "out there" in the world (even if many songbooks include some texts that have "lost" their melodies), so that it is not truly a compilation without the prior existence of the song texts. In this sense, a compilation is a form of text that opens itself in a disciplined, systematic fashion to its social context, and that thereby pretends to comprehensiveness.

This is not to reduce compilations to a single form. In what follows, not only do I pay attention to the relationship between the text-artifactual and the more broadly textual aspects of the compilation, but I also attempt to situate the compilation within a broader range of textual activities, including ad hoc notebooks, pedagogical practice, texts in performance, and sound recordings. I begin with an exploration of compilation production over the past hundred years among practitioners of the Algiers-Tlemcen Andalusi repertoire. This leads into a discussion of textual practice, and in particular the way in which compilations present *shuyūkh* as sources of authority: this section highlights compilations as what Carl Davila has called "powerful intervention[s]" into performance practice, and as a potentially powerful revivalist technology.[9] In turn, I show how compilations become integrated into the delineation and contestation of authority among the musical community's members. It is at this point that we will be able to return to the question of hoarding in greater depth and relate it to the wider questions of the genealogical ethos and diffusion, thereby elucidating the way in which compilations such as Yafil's have come to be embedded within the Andalusi musical community in variegated, uneven, sometimes contradictory ways that connect them closely to musical personhood and materiality.

Revival as Text

As the preceding chapter demonstrated, for the early twentieth-century musical reformers, revival was intertwined with the creation of written works. These included transcriptions in staff notation, musicological treatises and lectures, and, I would argue, sound recordings. Most of all, revival was closely connected to the creation of compilations, among them the turn-of-the-century print projects that in many respects worked from the form of manuscript songbooks but radically transformed their framing and circulation in that they were intended for mass diffusion. The previous chapter also pointed out the way in which this recontextualization of the songbook form was carried out using a vigorous, in some respects novel discourse of restoration. It is the idiom of endangerment, safeguard, and restoration, as well as the identities of specific agents like Yafil, that join the early twentieth-century textualization efforts to the rise of the amateur association and performance on the concert stage.

The reason why the idiom of *tadwīn* would provide the basis for a wider social movement that went well beyond the printed page is closely connected to the reason why revivalists would begin with the printing of song texts in the first place: in a musical practice that treats the systematic compilation of written song texts as a foundational act, and that treats the poem as a potential vessel for music, an attempt to work upon that practice must begin from work upon texts. It is for this reason that dating revival to the beginning of the twentieth century is both accurate in the sense that this was a self-consciously new project that fatefully used novel technologies and social forms, and inaccurate in the sense that connoisseurs and performers of the *nūba* had engaged in *tadwīn* for generations. Something like *tadwīn* likely underlies the creation and maintenance of anything understood as a repertoire, and in the Andalusi case this *tadwīn* had probably included the creation of written texts from an early date. One Algerois performer who I interviewed even speculated that the *nūba* arose in Granada as an act of *tadwīn* that brought together pieces that had previously been dispersed across al-Andalus, thanks to the ingathering of Muslims from across the Iberian peninsula in the waning years of Muslim political power.[10]

At the same time, the distinctive qualities of the early twentieth-century textualization efforts are important to recognize in order to take in the full breadth of the textual practice that followed. The print interventions of 1904 inaugurated a long, ongoing chain of efforts to bring song texts connected to the Andalusi complex into print—efforts that, as we will see, have justified themselves through an extension of the genre reach, the unavailability of earlier printed collections, extension or retraction of geographic focus, streamlining, correction, and the recovery of "lost" works. This chain of printed texts was responsive to the political changes that took place over the next hundred years, but its continuity also speaks to the way in which such a practice as Andalusi music transcends those upheavals. In many ways, the texts of today are in intimate dialogue with those of a century ago.

European scholar-officials, including French Arabists associated with the Franco-Arab school system, were among those who took the lead in the immediate aftermath of Yafil's *Majmūʿ*.[11] As discussed in the previous chapter, there was the work of Joseph Desparmet, including his collaboration with

Mahmoud Ben Sidi Saïd.[12] Jules Joly (1876–1920), an instructor in the Algiers *médersa*, edited and translated an *inqilāb*, *mṣaddar*, *bṭayḥī*, *inṣirāf*, and *darj* from diverse modes, as well as a satirical song in colloquial Arabic, which were published in the pages of the *Revue Africaine* in 1909.[13] These works continued the tradition of government-supported Arabists in Algeria engaging in poetic and musicological research within French-language scholarly venues.

Aside from his transcription efforts, Yafil likewise engaged in parallel textual activities after 1904. Three years later, he published another compilation, titled *Majmūʿ zahw al-anīs al-mukhtaṣṣ bi-l-tabāsī wa-l-qawādis*. This lithograph compilation reproduced the song texts for the discs that had been recorded up to that point as well as discs that Yafil planned to record.[14] In a sense, it was a bound set of liner notes, likely sold separately from the recordings themselves, gathering "compositions that had been scattered in other writings, with the aim of bringing near that which was difficult to grasp, of rounding out the benefit connected to the recently invented phonograph, and of providing entertainment and relaxation for body and soul."[15] Through its act of ingathering, the collection was very much an example of *tadwīn*, but it was one that brought Yafil into a different genre register from his previous work with *nūba* texts. Just as Yafil's and Rouanet's early sheet-music notations focused on the lighter parts of the *nūba* repertoire and its para-repertoire, much of it coded as feminine, the recordings that provided the basis for *Majmūʿ zahw al-anīs* were from the *khafīf* sectors of the urban genre map. Indeed, the term *zahw* in its title linked the compilation to the lowbrow *café-concert*, known in Arabic as *qahwat al-zahw* (pleasure café).

This monolingual 1907 printed collection is of interest on several other counts as well. It shows that recordings were being conceived in a way that linked them closely to print, and that the recording series itself may have been understood as compilations of sorts.[16] Although based on recordings rather than on the strict logic of a preexisting compound form like the *nūba*, *Zahw al-anīs* also takes a form very similar to the *Majmūʿ*—the text calls itself a *majmūʿ* (and refers to itself internally as a *dīwān*), it has a rhyming title, and it follows familiar manuscript conventions, complete with a colophon naming the compiler.[17] In addition, its internal order shows continuity with the *nūba* songbook tradition and with the broader socio-musical hierarchy in urban Algeria: it begins with three examples of a colloquial *mṣaddar ʿarbī*, continues with two colloquial songs marked *bṭayḥī*,[18] moves on to *ḥawzī*, then to non-*ḥawzī* examples of *qṣāyid*, and finally to *zindānī*, *istikhbārāt*, and *qādriyya*. In this way, it gives pride of place to the heavier elements, and by ending with the *zindānī* and *qādriyya* places those forms marked as lightest last. In other words, while it is a step away from the center of the *nūba* complex, *Zahw al-anīs* is still very much tied to that center by form, value, and presentational convention.

During the interwar period, there were at least three more printed collections that took up and elaborated the emphasis on *qṣāyid* evident in *Zahw al-anīs*. One of them, *Al-kanz al-maknūn fi-l-shiʿr al-malḥūn* (The hidden treasure of colloquial poetry)—written by the Islamic legal scholar Muḥammad Qāḍī of Tiaret and published in 1928 in Algiers by the Roudoussi [Rūdūsī] brothers' important Arabophone press—collected *qṣāyid* without any reference to their relationship to the *nūba* repertoire.[19] The two other interwar publications were conceived as a series, and drew an explicit link between the *qṣāyid* and the *nūba* repertoire. The first we have already encountered: Bekhoucha and Sekkal's 1934 *Nafḥ al-azhār*, consisting of 35 nature-themed "Andalusi poems" followed by 24 "Maghribi poems."[20] The second, much thicker volume, completed in Tlemcen in 1940 and titled *Al-ḥubb wa-l-maḥbūb* (Love and the beloved), was edited by Bekhoucha alone, and consists of *qṣāyid* only, with an exclusive focus on love themes.[21] Bekhoucha would continue this work of publishing *qṣāyid* after the Second World War, devoting each subsequent volume to a single poet.[22]

In many ways the focus of these interwar publications draws them inexorably away from the logic of the *nūba* songbook: rather than being organized by mode or movement, they are classed by author. Even *Nafḥ al-azhār*'s anonymous "Andalusi poems" are not presented by mode or movement but rather by the individual compiler's taste, as the term anthology would imply. In this sense, *Nafḥ al-azhār*, like Joly's and Desparmet's publications of *nūba* material, are based more on personal choice and availability than on the will to be exhaustive evident in many of the manuscript and print songbooks—an impulse that Foucault identifies with "western culture of the nineteenth century."[23] Yet considered in terms of their framing, the works by Bouali, Yafil, Rouanet, Qāḍī, Bekhoucha, and Sekkal are linked by a consistent discourse of danger and safeguard. The talk of "approaching disappearance" prominent in the writings of Yafil, Bouali, and Rouanet is taken up by Qāḍī,[24] by the author of the preface to *Nafḥ al-azhār*, and by Bekhoucha in his conclusion to *Al-ḥubb wa-l-maḥbūb*.

In these interwar works, there is also a clear note of national-religious import in their emphasis upon the twin symbols of Arabic and Islam. For Qāḍī, the compilation of colloquial poems promises to benefit "those of our Muslim brothers who are unable to read literary books," so that "the reader might recall his pure ancestors, learn about the condition in which they lived, and recognize his ability to perhaps in some respects be like them."[25] In *Nafḥ al-azhār*, "[what] animates this entire undertaking is fear for the loss of this art, its melodies and what they contain of the Arabic language . . . to make it available to its masters and to those people of Islam [*ahl al-islām*] who delight in it."[26] And for Bekhoucha, standing in the face of "the invasion of Egyptian song," the task was pressing:

> [even] if the time is late, our very highest goal is the perpetuation of this tradition through writing [*tadwīn*], its preservation from loss and oblivion, and the fulfillment of due service toward an aspect of our country's literary history. . . . While these poets are today famous, their names well-known, and their poems available, there will come a day when oblivion and neglect will weave their threads around them and wreak their havoc. These poets will enter the hidden pages of a forgotten history, as befell their peers among the *'ulamā'* and other historical figures who once filled our city but who are now left an utterly blank white page.[27]

The relationship with France and the French language in these works is complex. Like Bouali's *Kashf al-qinā'*, Qāḍī's *Al-kanz al-maknūn* is resolutely Arabophone (though in two very different registers of Arabic). Nevertheless, the tone of the introduction is defensive of the political status quo, describing recent expressions of resentment toward "the foreigner" as an "illness that has afflicted even civilized people" who are otherwise "aware that the foreigner brings great benefits." After all, Qāḍī writes, citing the Qur'an, "'land belongs to God,' not to his creation," and from a legal perspective, Algeria "belongs to the French state, since the French state took it by force just as our ancestors did in the past." Yet this does not mean that Algerians are not oppressed, but that the weak should leave the act of resistance "to someone stronger."[28]

Among the implied elements of oppression is the suppression of Arabic. Indeed, according to Qāḍī, it is thanks to colloquial Arabic that Algerians have not been struck dumb: when "the Arabic language weakened in our country, and the teaching of its poetic rules lessened," the innate Arab connection to Arabic "had to emerge in some way . . . just as water found underground must come to the surface even if the way is blocked."[29] It is then fitting that the one element of French in *Al-kanz al-maknūn* is the reproduction of Théophile Gautier's poem "La Source" (The Spring) at the end of the book, coupled with a colloquial Arabic translation that Qāḍī had completed as a student at the Tlemcen *médersa* in 1904.[30]

In terms of language, *Nafḥ al-azhār* and *Al-ḥubb wa-l-maḥbūb* are much closer to the model of Yafil's *Majmū'* in that much of the framing material is bilingual. As seen in chapter 1, the French introduction to Bekhoucha and Sekkal's 1934 collection ambiguously credits French influence for the current interest in the Arabic literary and musical heritage.[31] In both the French and the Arabic introductions, there is a mingling of emulation and competition with regard to French civilization, although the references to French thought are much more muted in the Arabic section. The authors identify al-Andalus and Islamic thought more generally as the precursor to European romanticism,[32] and the volume's emphasis on images of nature may reflect the broader cult of the outdoors that found expression in the interwar scouting movement.[33] The Arabic introduction asserts that while "we see many people of the book, particularly the Orientalists among them, rushing in pursuit of this weighty goal" of safeguarding this art, it is "we Muslim youth [also translatable as Muslim Scouts] who are the most suited for the task."[34]

The book is also framed by complementary quotations from two French writers who came from opposite ends of the political spectrum. The title page is graced with a quote from the arch-colonialist officer and intellectual Albert Sarraut: that "the renaissance of Islam is inexplicable except through the force of survivals from a brilliant past."[35] The final pages of the book reproduce the anti-colonialist, modernist music critic Emile Vuillermoz's glowing report on the Cairo Congress of Arab Music of 1932—a report that echoes Algerian anxieties regarding musical decay and disappearance but that also suggests, in the manner of Salvador Daniel, that Europe stands to learn much from the sophistication of Arab music.[36] *Al-ḥubb wa-l-maḥbūb* considerably extends the mingling of Arabic and European literary streams evident in Bekhoucha's first volume, with his French-language introduction drawing upon Benjamin Constant, Pierre Benoît, Théophile Gautier, Anatole France, and even Euripides and Ralph Waldo Emerson to form a contrast between the treatment of love in Arabic poetry and in the European tradition.

While the interwar works show that revivalist *tadwīn* through print continued to the edges of the Andalusi complex and came to be understood as an explicitly national, vindicatory act, it was not until after Algerian independence that a work on the scale and model of Yafil's *Majmūʿ* was undertaken. Among the recommendations of the FLN's Colloque national sur la musique algérienne held in the final days of 1964 was the call to establish a national music institute and to "redo the diwan Yafil" in an effort to "make an inventory of those beautiful works that resisted ruin and to again place them within a new edifice according to new methods."[37] The response was the Institut national de la musique (INM), founded in 1968, and its first major task: a massive textualization project that sought to replace Yafil's *Majmūʿ*. Relying on the cooperation of *shuyūkh* and connoisseurs in Algiers, Tlemcen, and Constantine, the three-volume *Al-muwashshaḥāt wa-l-azjāl* was produced by Djelloul Yelles and El Hafnaoui Amokrane, director and chief cultural consultant, respectively, at the INM. Printed by the state press between 1972 and 1982, the tenth and twentieth anniversaries of independence, the three volumes paralleled similar state-directed textualization projects in Morocco and Tunisia. While the various prefatory essays by Yelles and Amokrane are in many ways sophisticated elaborations of the discourse of salvage and revival familiar from the works of the colonial era, the editors placed Andalusi music within a decidedly nationalist musical narrative, even seeking predecessors to the proposed national conservatory system in the pre-Islamic Numidian period.[38] It is significant that unlike virtually all other print compilations before or since, *Al-muwashshaḥāt wa-l-azjāl* is a resolutely monolingual Arabic publication. For its authors, "our oral literature . . . displays the genius of a nation [*umma*] and highlights the hopes and aspirations of a people, the desires of the spirit of a society across the long centuries, and our desire for our foundational characteristics for the task of civilizational and intellectual reconstruction."[39]

The prefatory essays to the volumes also display a strong desire to conceptualize the national musical patrimony in class-conscious terms. Yelles and Amokrane present the *nūba* tradition as somewhere between an oral literature connected to the popular classes and a learned, written one connected to the elite, and they link this in-betweenness to ongoing academic debates about whether or not the *muwashshaḥ* and the *zajal* were popular or elite poetic forms in al-Andalus.[40] None of this is particularly surprising when we consider the nature of the independent Algerian state in this period: as will be explored further in chapter 7, the state is being presented here as the guardian of a patrimony that the experience of colonial rule had alienated from the Algerian nation, and which the postcolonial state is charged with returning to the masses in a form that frees it from a particular class connotation.[41]

We will return momentarily to the way in which the editors of *Al-muwashshaḥāt wa-l-azjāl* positioned their project vis-à-vis the existing relations of Andalusi musical production. For now, however, it is important to point out several ways in which the three volumes built upon and broke with earlier efforts at *tadwīn* through print. Like the earlier works, this one privileges the *nūba* material and treats the *inqilābāt* as the "eldest son" of the poems used for the central movements of the *nūba*.[42] However, *Al-muwashshaḥāt wa-l-azjāl* includes far more framing material that explains the functioning of the *nūba* than did earlier poetic collections, making it a repository not only of poems but also of information about how the repertoire works and what readers should make of it.[43] In this way, it is organized around a scholarly apparatus that reflects the musicological orientation of the editors, and, to a far greater degree than does Yafil's songbook, it separates knowledge of how the repertoire functions from the actual musicians who bear that knowledge.

As befits a state-centered work after independence, *Al-muwashshaḥāt wa-l-azjāl* attempts to take in the entirety of Algeria's Andalusi repertoire, including Constantine. Because it brings together works from related but distinct traditions that in some cases do not share texts and that classify those they do share along different axes, *Al-muwashshaḥāt wa-l-azjāl* eschews the traditional songbook's organization by mode and movement. Instead, the contents are organized alphabetically according to the incipit, and the traditional ordering by movement and mode (beginning, as is the pattern in most of the songbooks, with *dhīl*) is evoked in the index, where the rather diffuse contents of the volumes are organized into place-specific *nūbāt*. Thus by attempting to be a national work, *Al-muwashshaḥāt wa-l-azjāl* breaks out of the local bounds in which Andalusi musical and textual practice typically occurs.

With its three volumes and state imprimatur, *Al-muwashshaḥāt wa-l-azjāl* would seem to be a definitive work. But in part given its decidedly non-local character, it is not surprising that other compilation projects have appeared in the decades since, gathering mass and speed since the late 1990s. Among the most influential of this wave are the three editions of Sid Ahmed Serri's *Chants andalous: recueil des poèmes des noubate de la musique "Sanaa," musique classique algérienne,* which bring together all the song texts within the Algiers repertoire as it is practiced by this widely acknowledged living master.[44] Unlike *Al-muwashshaḥāt wa-l-azjāl, Chants andalous* directly addresses adherents of the Algiers school and makes no attempt to encompass all of the Andalusi musical traditions found in Algeria.[45] Because of this, *Chants andalous* is able to follow the mode-plus-movement format found in Yafil's *Majmūʿ* and in the traditional manuscript songbook. But more in keeping with *Al-muwashshaḥāt wa-l-azjāl, Chants andalous* also seeks to be a manual regarding the basics of how to make a *nūba*. In addition, it includes *istikhbārāt* and, in the second and third editions, *qādriyyāt* and *dlīdlāt*. *Chants andalous* goes so far as to vocalize all the song texts, so that Serri's understanding of the pronunciation of the words (a frequent source of disagreement between performers) is made explicit. In other words, *Chants andalous* seeks to transmit in one volume all the building blocks of the Andalusi tradition of Algiers as understood by Serri. Like other printed compilations, it also seeks to justify itself on the basis of the rarity of earlier compilations: the first objective that is listed in the French introduction is to "fill the void" left by the fact that "the almost century-old YAFIL [compilation] and the three volumes from the INM cannot be found, since they have not been reprinted."[46] Last but not least, the original publication of Serri's *Chants andalous* coincided with his creation of a vast series of recordings designed to transmit the entirety of the Algerois repertoire as he knows it—recordings that were made public with the third edition of *Chants andalous*, which includes both the recordings and the printed song texts.[47]

We will explore the differences among the three versions of Serri's collection momentarily. For now, however, it is important to situate *Chants andalous* within the latest generation of attempts to represent the Andalusi repertoire of Algiers and Tlemcen in printed form. This last edition of Serri's collection was published with the support of the Algerian Ministry of Culture on the occasion of Tlemcen's designation as "Capital of Islamic Culture 2011," organized by the Rabat-based Islamic Educational, Scientific, and Cultural Organization (ISESCO), which was founded in 1979 by the Organisation of the Islamic Conference (formerly the Organisation for Islamic Cooperation). Serri's collection was but one of a series of books and recordings focusing on the Andalusi repertoires that were printed by the Ministry of Culture and the ONDA (Office Nationale des Droits d'Auteur) on the occasion. The 2011 publications included a collection of all the song texts associated with the *nūba* repertoires of Tlemcen, Algiers, and Constantine, assembled on the basis of manuscript compilations;[48] a collection of song texts and recordings representing the quasi-totality of the Tlemcen *nūba* complex repertoire performed by leading soloists and association ensembles, including one from Algiers;[49] a collection of the Tlemcen *nūba* repertoire;[50] a collection of Tlemcani *qṣīda* song texts;[51] a two-volume historical and analytic treatment of the *nūba* complex in the Maghrib;[52] recordings of leading solo interpreters of the *nūba* complex from Constantine and Nedroma;[53] recordings of several Algiers *nūbāt* performed by ensembles from Algiers, Tlemcen, and Koléa;[54] and compilations of classic recordings by Cheikh Larbi and his son Redouane.[55]

In most respects, the flurry of publications inaugurated by the first edition of Serri's compilation has leaned toward the localizing impulse: they are documents that focus on Tlemcen, Algiers, or Constantine, with some room for their hinterlands as well. On the other hand, one of the publications follows the national scale found in *Al-muwashshaḥāt wa-l-azjāl*,[56] and the analytic history focuses on the Maghrib as a whole, with somewhat more attention to Algeria. In addition, the recordings of the Algiers repertoire as performed by contemporary ensembles include groups based in Tlemcen, and there are Algiers ensembles included in the set of recordings covering the Tlemcen repertoire—a nod to the national scale while respecting local specificity. Finally, all of the publications are linked by the fact that they were supported by the Ministry of Culture, whose imprimatur they bear.

While the 2011 works continue in the century-old tradition of printed compilation, they also represent a further intensification of the scholarly impulse. For example, the collection of Tlemcani repertoire by Salim El Hassar authenticates almost every *ṣanʿa* by naming the source, in the form of "According to the manuscript text of Shaykh Muḥammad Būʿalī."[57] Most of these texts are drawn from manuscript sources associated with a handful of leading musical figures in the Tlemcen tradition, dating from the middle of the nineteenth century until the middle of the twentieth. In some cases, El Hassar lists a recording of one of the masters as his sources. And on rare occasion, he names a printed work, such as *Nafḥ al-azhār* or the INM's *Al-muwashshaḥāt wa-l-azjāl*. Finally, El Hassar provides variants in footnotes and sometimes in the main part of the page, and in those few cases where it is known, he provides the name of the author of the lines. Taken as a whole, El Hassar's compilation, like some of the other 2011 works that we will touch on later, marks a very full embrace of the notion of authentication by way of *shuyūkh* as well as by poet when possible, and it brings such authentication to a very fine level of detail unseen in previous compilations.[58]

The works associated with the 2011 designation of Tlemcen as Capital of Islamic Culture are a fitting end to this textual chain, in that they come a century after Yafil's *Majmūʿ* and share a great deal with that foundational text while at the same time introducing significant innovations that in many cases respond to the wider political context. They are a literal extension and intensification of the revivalist project of bringing the repertoire into print, carrying along not only song texts but also understandings and subjectivities that are crucial to Andalusi musical practice, among them the relation of *shaykh* to text.

The *Shaykh* and the Text

While the preceding chain of texts brings to light some important differences between the compilations with regard to genre focus, organization, scale, and framing, it also points out their emergence from an older tradition of manuscript production and the continuity of various formal features. In addition, the printed texts give voice to a fairly stable discourse of danger, salvage, and revival. The resilience of this discourse raises several questions. Is it simply a trope, or do aspects of practice make the perception of danger and the urge toward salvage and revival through print virtually perpetual? Is unavailability a matter of compilations like Yafil's *Majmūʿ* and *Al-muwashshaḥāt wa-l-azjāl* going out of print, or are other factors at work? And why continue to go through the work of making song text collections?

In order to grasp the multiple patterns that have already been hinted at, we need to consider the way in which such printed texts emerge from a much broader textual tradition, including a still-living practice of manuscript production. A powerful impetus for the creation of revised songbooks is the impulse toward correction of errors. The notion that Yafil had made errors in his compilation that required correction and perhaps even the compilation's wholesale replacement arose almost immediately after the publication of the *Majmūʿ*.[59] During his lecture on poetic meter at the 1905 Congress of Orientalists, Desparmet took the opportunity to review the various recent works on Algerian popular song, citing his own recent publications in *Le Tell* and praising the works of various European scholars of North African music. He took the recently published *Majmūʿ*, however, as a negative inspiration:

> It is largely due to hurrying to publish the songs of Andalousia before their meter was determined that Yafil, the recent editor of *Klâm el Andles*—lacking any criterion for the establishment of his texts—was reduced to simply publishing the notebooks of the native singer and those of his colleagues.[60] Now who does not know what a *zmâm* or Arabic compendium is? Light poems, in particular, are transcribed from generation to generation by nearly illiterate musicians or by adolescents who are curious about sensual poetry. . . . They have but one aim: to slavishly copy their text, usually rather poorly written, thus recording along with their own mistakes those of their predecessors. A *zmam* can also be defined thus: the faithful accumulation of innumerable distortions that a text has undergone since [the life of] its author. One must not conceal (and Yafil's publication demonstrates it sufficiently) that they ought not to face publication on account of their age, unless one is able to free them from these successive layers of alterations that render them unintelligible enigmas for the natives alike. . . . Popular poetry, abandoned to gradual decomposition, is lost to us from a literary point of view if European criticism does not equip it with a decent method for safeguarding and, if necessary, scientifically restoring its integrity.[61]

Many of Desparmet's specific corrections of Yafil's text focus on questions of meter, Yafil's tendency to write in the colloquial register, his lack of attention to semantic coherence (perhaps reflecting a lack of competence in Arabic), and his ignorance of the Qur'an. He also suggests that some Muslims were shocked by the errors in the *Majmūʿ*.[62] At the same time, Desparmet acknowledges the possibility that certain orthographic irregularities may reflect the practice in al-Andalus and not simply an ignorance of classical Arabic.[63]

Twenty-five years later, writing in *Kitāb al-Jazāʾir* (The Book of Algeria), a landmark riposte to the centenary celebrations of French colonial rule,

Aḥmad Tawfīq al-Madanī compared the work of Yafil to that of the European aristocrat Baron d'Erlanger, who was then taking a leading role in "restoring" the Tunisian *mā'lūf*:

> Today in Algiers are found three musical associations: al-Muṭribiyya, al-Jazā'iriyya, and al-Andalusiyya. In Tlemcen, there is the ensemble of Sayyid al-Ḥājj al-'Arabī [Larbi] Bin Ṣārī, and outside these cities are many other musical ensembles. Together, they shoulder some of the burden of conserving this rich patrimony. The great artist Edmond Yafil recorded many of these pieces, and transcribed them in staff notation with the help of some of the leading musicians, but he did not record all the Algerian *nūbāt*, and those who are privy to the secrets of Algerian music say that the pieces that *mu'allim* Yafil did record contain many large errors. If only our fine Arab Algerian music had the luck to be taken up by someone like Baron d'Erlanger, or even by the Englishman Baron d'Erlanger himself, who spent hundreds of thousands to accomplish by himself what the large associations have been incapable of, and recorded the entirety of Tunisian Andalusi music with such exactness that people could not find any fault! The Arab music of Algiers is among the most brilliant and beautiful pages of Andalusi art, but it is one that will disappear with the new civilization. Who will extend his hand to conserve it and save it from shipwreck?[64]

Criticism of Yafil's compilation came from governmental circles as well. Writing in April 1940, one colonial official reporting on the state of the "Muslim" radio broadcasting in Algiers lamented that "few singers (probably only one or two) still know the entire repertoire, meaning that all the orchestras content themselves with repeating by rote the same pieces—the around one hundred incomplete melodies included in Yafil's collection, a very poorly done work crammed with giant errors."[65] Another report from September of that year described Yafil as the originator of an effort "inspired more by a spirit of lucre than by a disinterested artistic preoccupation."[66]

While the latter anonymous criticisms of Yafil cannot be separated from the official anti-Semitism of the Vichy regime, they fit into a larger pattern of critique of the songbook on linguistic grounds. In Desparmet's comments, in particular, we can hear a powerful association of print with a modern, scientific apparatus and an upbraiding of Yafil for perpetuating the blind copying that the French Arabist associated with the manuscript tradition. According to Desparmet, in an anticipation of the accusation that Yafil was simply a "human phonograph," this blind copying reproduces the errors of preceding manuscripts as well as of the singers whose performances themselves draw from and contribute to that same manuscript chain. This is textual and performative genealogy gone wrong, when what is required in Desparmet's view is attention to denotative meaning and the rules of grammar and poetic meter. In turn, such attention will allow for a return to or approximation of the otherwise lost original. The scientific spirit, in other words, can cut through the cobwebs of genealogical and inscriptual practice. And to make matters worse, Desparmet seems to be saying, Yafil broadcast these errors through the medium of print.

There are ways in which Desparmet's critique was taken up within the Andalusi musical community itself. For example, for Sid Ahmed Serri, Yafil's compilation constituted a focus for correction. Exactly fifty years before the publication of the first edition of *Chants andalous*, among the first things Serri did on joining Association El Djazaïria in 1946 was buy a copy of Yafil's compilation at the Roudoussi brothers' store. Serri recounted to me how several years later he loaned his copy to his work colleague, Ḥasan al-Madanī, brother of Aḥmad Tawfīq al-Madanī, both of whose skill in classical Arabic was attributed to their Tunisian upbringing. After Ḥasan al-Madanī made a first set of corrections, Serri's copy of the songbook continued to be edited by hand, both by Serri himself and by his fellow *mélomane* H'mida Elkateb. In turn, these corrections were often based on corrections suggested by other practitioners in Serri's circle.

So far, this sounds somewhat similar to the corrective project of Desparmet at the turn of the twentieth century. Yet while some such corrections are based on a notion of a standard, semantically clear, metrically rational Arabic, this is not the only kind of authority that was being drawn upon. If we look at the various differences between Yafil's songbook and Serri's *Chants andalous*, some of them are grammatical corrections, but some are simply alternative versions or reclassifications by mode or movement. The authority underlying such "corrections" often lies elsewhere than in a notion of Arabic grammaticality or metrical uniformity per se. Some of it is based on printed material and handwritten manuscripts that Serri has collected over more than half a century of musical practice—texts that themselves were traditionally built up through musical practice and its accompanying relationships. And much of the authority is based in how Serri himself learned the repertoire from peers and teachers. This genealogically authenticated repertoire in turn was textualized by Serri and his peers, recorded in their personal notebooks and on their internal "discs of memory." It was precisely these many kinds of texts that Serri was drawing upon in the creation of the first edition of *Chants andalous*.

The first edition was explicitly created to reflect Serri's own understanding of the Algiers repertoire. Yet this understanding quickly evolved as *Chants andalous* reached its second edition. Although the second edition closely follows the form of the first, it is more ambitious in scope. The dedication, instead of a single page tracing a connection to Benteffahi by way of the Fekhardji brothers, instead covers seven pages, and establishes a lineage from the late nineteenth-century Mnemmeche to Sfindja to Benteffahi to the mid-twentieth-century Fekhardji brothers, and finally to Serri himself at different stages of his long life. The song texts are likewise elaborated. The number of *istikhbārāt* are approximately double, and the texts for the five core movements of the *nūba* are similarly more numerous: in the case of *dhīl*, nearly every movement has additional song texts as well as additional lines within song texts that appeared in the first edition. While in the first edition Serri left out those poems whose melodies are lost, in the second edition he includes a variety of poems that have fallen out of the Algerois practice. Furthermore, there are various corrections, particularly with regard to the vocalizations and case endings, in most instances bringing the words in line with a standard written Arabic. Last but not least, the Arabic introduction to the second edition contains many updates that do not show up in the French introduction, which by and large stays close to the version found in the first. It still represents Serri's understanding of the repertoire, but it is an understanding that has expanded.

A strong influence on the second edition is Mourad Ouamara, a member of the younger generation of Andalusi music scholars who is listed on the inside title page as an artistic and literary consultant, linguistic editor, and commentator. It is Ouamara who collaborated closely with Serri in gathering song texts and verses that did not appear in the first edition and in bringing the Arabic of the compilation in closer line with a modern written standard. In the course of his commentaries, Ouamara inserts himself as a commentator on the *shuyūkh* as a class, including Serri himself, so that in a sense the second edition stands as a monument to Serri, with Ouamara being placed in the position of Serri's disciple. In Ouamara's subsequent recounting of their collaboration, after the teacher and student had reconnected after many years of separation, Serri "furnished me with some *kunnāshāt* and *dawāwīn*, and I set to work. I corrected, amended, revised, and commented upon that which required it, and I added items that the teacher [Serri] had left out so that it increased in length by a good third."[67] In turn, this mass of manuscripts provided the basis for Ouamara's subsequent project, published on the occasion of Tlemcen's 2011 festivities.[68] Closely modeled on the three volumes issued by the INM in that it takes in the traditions of Algiers, Tlemcen, and Constantine yet largely bypassing that work, Ouamara's 2011 collection draws directly on a vast collection of nineteeth- and twentieth-century manuscripts.

In addition, it draws on copies of Yafil's *Majmūʿ* that were emended by the early twentieth-century *shaykh* Mouzino and by Serri himself.[69]

Thus the creation of a compilation can be an occasion for drawing close to the *shuyūkh*, including by way of their own corrections and expansions of earlier generations of *tadwīn*. In somewhat similar fashion, Salim El Hassar's 2011 collection includes biographies of some of the key named sources for his texts as well as photographs and facsimiles of some of the manuscripts and transcriptions, thereby providing a sort of textual genealogy for his own compilation. The creators of *Al-muwashshaḥāt wa-l-azjāl*, too, make explicit their indebtedness to those "masters of this art who were convinced of the necessity of the work of making known and diffusing this precious patrimony" and who, having carried "the brilliant torch . . . in the darkest of circumstances that our country lived through" were themselves to be "eternalized" through the INM's publications.[70] And as shown in chapter 1, the creators of *Nafḥ al-azhār* invoked the authority of a genealogical chain linking Moulay Ziani to his predecessors.

This focus on genealogical transmission of texts has a close parallel in the realm of the transmission of melodies, which are often understood as primarily vessels for the poetic texts, just as poetic texts are often understood as vessels for melodies. For some traditionalists, staying within the received mold, or better yet, belief that one is staying within it, is crucial to the coherence of the tradition. Interestingly enough, this view embraces a certain margin of error and flexibility afforded by the dimension of belief and intention. In the words of one association head, speaking of whether the *nūba* the association plays today is the same as what it played in the past:

> We try to be faithful to the received version. . . . I will not say that it is 100 percent [the same], but it is a faithfulness that is complete. To my mind, perhaps there is an error in terms of a note here or there. But overall, the *mazmūm* that we sang in the '60s or '70s is the same as [today's] *mazmūm*. At least that's what we think. We never undertook the task of comparing the old version as sung by the same association. Certainly there are nuances, sometimes unintended, because a voice passes this way, for example—[a musician] is not free from error. . . . However, in a general way, the error is unintended. . . . Therefore we can say that the *mazmūm* of the '60s is the same as that of 2000.

In some respects, however, this genealogical impulse rubs against the impulse toward correction. The current work of Youcef Touaïbia, for example, whose website Groupe Yafil stands at the forefront of scholarship on the Andalusi tradition of Algiers, is very much in the spirit of Desparmet's work.[71]

For Touaïbia, textual criticism and attention to poetic meter is key to breaking through the devotion to genealogical authority that continues to animate much of the practice, although his project is less about standardization and unanimity so much as it is a structuralist project of understanding the logic of multiple versions. There is a skeptical spirit that enters into this project, particularly with regard to the faith that is placed in *shuyūkh* and in the transmission process. The message is twofold: what the *shaykh* does is not necessarily correct, and at the same time what certain *shuyūkh* have done correctly is often brought off track in the hands of their students.

But whether we are talking about a structuralist approach or a more normative one, we can conceive of the impulse toward revision in terms of an opposition between two kinds of authority, one in the vein of Desparmet that is modernist, scientific, restorative, and oriented toward meaning, the other in the vein of the traditionalist, genealogical, semantically obscure target of Desparmet's criticism. This opposition of slipshod manuscript to idealized print is in many ways a transformation of the opposition of the oral to the written: according to this trope, the manuscript copy too often reproduces the mistakes of the previous manuscripts and of the performers who made and used them.[72] In addition, it ties together with the complaint about the notion of the "human phonograph" and its "disc of memory." Ideally, authenticated print and its audiorecording analogue promise to bring the repertoire out of the grip of genealogical personhood. As one young musician and scholar told me—a man who happens to be the son of a late reform-minded musical *shaykh*—*tadwīn* is necessary because of the problem that "people think of authenticity as residing in individuals rather than in the music itself." The implication here is that individuals have the ability to withhold or distort knowledge, either knowingly or unknowingly, while, once properly researched and inscribed, the "music itself" (in other words, the music's inscribed form, both in terms of melody and words) is open to anyone who can read it. *Tadwīn*, then, can be an attempt to shift the location of this authoritative residence through the creation of texts that are both more accessible and, at least for some participants, more convincing than individuals in the sense that they have been repaired.[73] Its prototypical medium is print, and its idiom is that of the positivist scholar.

In the case of Serri's *Chants andalous*, the tension between the impulse toward correction and the genealogical ethos shows up in fairly explicit form in the second and third editions. As an example of such reflexivity, in the very first *mṣaddar* in *dhīl*, Ouamara offers the original text by the medieval Baghdadi poet Abū Nuwās in the footnote but keeps the song text as given "in the transmission [*al-riwāya*] from the *shuyūkh*."[74] He follows this with a telling note: "We undertook the correction of the poems as required by the laws of the [Arabic] language and meter. . . . However, from the perspective of performance, their recording was completed—as the teacher informed me—just as he received them from his *shuyūkh*." In other words, the editor treads a line between fidelity to standard Arabic and fidelity to the *shaykh*'s authority, while reproducing the logic of genealogical authority in his invocation of what "the teacher informed me." Although the written version does not go all the way toward correction, it is on the page that the room for correction is greatest. At the level of recording, on the other hand, the embodied, musical authority of the *shuyūkh* asserts itself. Thus the dilemma that the technologies of *tadwīn* promise to resolve is in fact smuggled into new media. The text and the *shaykh* both authenticate one another and call one another into question.

Shaykh, Text, Hoard

Thus far, we have seen how the genealogical ethos enters into the sometimes life-long building up of text, and the ways in which this ethos overlaps and sometimes conflicts with the impulse toward correction. In this sense, texts are understood to come from *shuyūkh* and to point toward them. At the same time, we can go further than this to say that the *shaykh* is in some ways treated as a text unto himself, or, more specifically, as a collection of texts. In this sense, there is a deeper isomorphism between the *shaykh* and the compilation that goes beyond a certain parallel authority that may or may not be in competition: both the *shaykh* and the compilation are repositories of song texts. From this, we get the rather unusual elocution that arises in Andalusi musical circles, wherein certain *shuyūkh* are referred to as "living libraries."[75] That is to say, the *shaykh* and the compilation not only resemble one another but also describe and define one another, standing as intermingling concentrations or hoards of repertoire. And although not all collectors of texts are *shuyūkh* and not all *shuyūkh* collectors of texts, the building up of a textual archive is certainly one of the things that can help to cement an individual performer's reputation for mastery. Likewise, the musical authority of a compiler can increase the value of his compilation. Seen from this angle, the *shaykh* is a compilation, a meta-text made through the process of ingathering, a node, passageway, or, in some cases, an endpoint in the flow of texts.[76]

Such isomorphism allows us to start to make sense of Yafil's puzzling claim of author's rights over much of the Andalusi repertoire touched upon in the preceding chapter. If we conceive of Yafil's recordings as Aḥmad Tawfīq al-Madanī conceived them—as extensions of print *tadwīn*—then Yafil's assertion of composers' rights over the recorded songs might be seen as a transmutation of traditional claims of editorial authority. Unlike the *shaykh*, who asserts that the song goes a certain way by performing it and teaching it in that manner, and by being acclaimed as a *shaykh* by those who hold his interpretation to be authoritative, Yafil asserted that the song goes a certain way by recording his performance of it and by shoring up his authority through the procurement of authors' rights. In this sense, his authority was overdetermined: not only did it rely on his interpretation's acceptance by educated listeners in Algeria, but it also relied on a quietly deployed legal apparatus of authorship and copyright guaranteed in Paris.

Of course, there was a problem in this move, a contradiction that would make such overdetermination potentially self-destructive. For unlike the traditional forms of musical authority that can always be challenged by a counter-authority, the institution of the author precludes counterclaims. According to the logic of copyright, there cannot be competing holders of authors' rights. Yafil's assertion of authors' rights, had it been successfully enforced by SACEM as well as accepted by the general public, would essentially have meant the end of the traditional forms of authoritative production and disputation.[77] In such a legal regime, the author trumps authority.

In fact, this eclipse did not come to pass for several reasons. First, Yafil's project was profoundly hybrid in nature. While he was helping to radically transform the social basis of the musical practice, he was not entirely removing the repertoire from its preexisting social matrix, in that his efforts were uneasily combining the notion of the author with the notion of the *shaykh*. Second, in his attempt to claim a place as both author and authority, the first position was not attained. The Algerois public—led by his erstwhile collaborator Rouanet, and, forty years later, even by his defender Mahieddine Bachetarzi—did not accept the imposition of the author on Andalusi musical practice.

Another key element in this "failure" is the way in which practitioners came to treat Yafil's compilation itself. The *Majmūʿ* became known as a hoarded object, often passed down from teacher to student, acting as a kind of proof-text. In the words of one Algerois musician with whom I spoke, "Yafil is the bible." As the use of his songbook demonstrates, Yafil was eventually acclaimed as a special authority, an ancestor of sorts, via his *Majmūʿ*. Yafil the historical personage has faded, while Yafil the textual personage came to be persistently powerful, if not precisely in the way he envisioned. On closer inspection, his claim of authorship is in fact not so far from the way in which the genealogical ethos worked in his day and since, or from the way in which his textual authority came to play out. In Foucault's terms, "Yafil" serves to "characterize the existence, circulation, and operation of certain discourses within a society"—in this case, poetic and musical discourses that lie at the heart of this community of value and practice.[78]

In calling it by the name of its eponymous compiler, the Algiers-Tlemcen practice closely mirrors the practice in the Moroccan *āla* tradition. There, the canonical compilation is called *Kunnāsh al-Ḥā'ik* (the collection or scrapbook of al-Ḥā'ik), named for its legendary editor Muḥammad al-Ḥā'ik, a *faqīh* (Islamic jurisprudent) from Tetuan who is believed to have lived in the eighteenth century.[79] A late nineteenth-century collection from the Moroccan sultan's court in turn abridged and reorganized *Al-Ḥā'ik*; in similar fashion, it is sometimes referred to using the name of its creator, *Al-Jāmi'ī*. Thus in Moroccan *nūba* practice, certain collections and collectors came to enjoy authoritative status. The printed collections that latter-day *āla* masters sometimes publish in an effort to document their own performance school all derive from and invoke *Al-Ḥā'ik*. In Morocco, then, over at least two centuries, ad hoc, performance-oriented *nūba*-text collection has worked from a single preeminent textual stream.[80]

The relevance to the case of Yafil's collection lies in the way the *Al-Ḥā'ik* collection likely arose and in its subsequent social life. We can speculate that there were many notebooks among *āla* performers, but that one among them, attributed to an individual called al-Ḥā'ik, came to take on authoritative status. This status was reflected in and reinforced by the fact that it came to be copied by many performers and that it also came to be the chief source for many performers' more ad hoc notebooks. This sort of attribution of editorial origin is closely akin to Foucault's discussion of medieval scientific discourse, in which the attribution of words to Hippocrates or Pliny "marked a proven discourse."[81] In this instance, the "proven discourse" is the repertoire itself. Something similar to the Moroccan context seems to have been at work for Yafil. In his case, however, printing was the crucial foundational act that turned a particular congeries of manuscripts into a named compilation.

The apparent tendency of more formalized compilations to take on a name points to several important facets of such texts. First, a songbook's textual authority mixes with the personal authority of its compiler, who is not identified as an author per se but rather as a gatherer of valued texts. Nevertheless, as shown by Salim El Hassar's practice of identifying the collections from which he derived his song texts, this position of editor or collector can take on a certain authorial aura, in part because of the pretensions of the songbook to embody the entirety of an otherwise anonymous repertoire, including "lost" texts whose melodies have been forgotten. Second, to elaborate a point touched upon in chapter 3, the song texts that are gathered together in the compilation are usually not attributed to any particular individual. Instead, they are *turāth*, attributed in a very general way to the poets of al-Andalus and of the urban Maghrib as an internally undifferentiated collective. To perform them is to quote from the distant past by way of the compiler and a particular modally defined *nūba*. Unlike the urtext in the Western European classical music tradition, then—where the modern-day editor attempts to use the earliest written sources to cut through the layers of interpretation and thereby touch the composer's original intentions—quotativity here is uncoupled from an explicit notion of an author, or rather the aura of authorship gets displaced to the collector, the compilation, the *nūba* form, and the concept of patrimony itself. And unlike the urtext, the intervening interpreters are not barriers but rather, for many people, the obligatory passages to the original.

In a similar fashion, songbooks have their generations, their genealogies. They, too, are embedded in genealogical relationships, serve as passageways toward some sense of the original, and can be carried along past the lifetimes of their editors, so that one day Serri's *Chants andalous* may very well be simply known as *Serri*. They, too, are built up through contact with other songbooks. They, too, are bearers of lost repertoire, carriers of the traces of what once circulated, and what stands to be recovered today.

It is this metonymy, isomorphism, and intermingling that helps explain some of the power of compilations. As illustrated in the account of the musician's dream at the beginning of chapter 2, inherited notebooks play an important role in the stories that performers and aficionados tell. Handwritten notebooks have often been transferred from a teacher to a respected student either as a gift during the scribe's lifetime or as an inheritance, and we can find numerous anecdotes of master musicians who inherited the notebooks of their teachers and for whom these texts function as a form of social capital. Cheikh Larbi of Tlemcen, for example, is said to have inherited the written notebooks of Boudelfa, with these notebooks acting as a metonym for the body of esoteric musical knowledge as a whole.

While it may seem to be ironic, the withholding of such collections from circulation starts to make sense when understood as a metonym. Once possessed and withheld, a compilation is not necessarily directly used in performance practice. While people may refer to it for song texts, and use it for the copying of song texts, often its authority works more passively. It might, indeed, just sit on a shelf—particularly among those connoisseurs who are not themselves musicians. Some musicians of the older generation who are known in somes places to hoard the *Majmūʿ* and other texts are not in fact even fully literate in Arabic and learned what they know of the repertoire orally or through French orthography.[82] For them, reading the compilation is exponentially less important than simply possessing it; as is the case for hoarded parts of the *nūba* among performers, the circulation of a rumor of the compilation's possession is an effective way to build up the reputation of the possessor. Again, this symbolic and positional aspect of possessing the *Majmūʿ* is underlined by the fact that many of its possessors were given their copy by someone in the position of authority. In other words, it derives its power not through the act of reading but largely through individual relationships of affection, discipleship, gift-giving, and the compilation's place within the larger performance practice.[83]

What, then, to do with a collection? Having one implies some kind of project: of preparing a history, or of having the ability to perform at least a part of what is contained there. Once received, there are two extremes along a spectrum of strategies available to its possessor. One is to preserve the notebook's status as a unique possession that can be passed on to the next generation. In this capacity, it might act as an individual's reference, or perhaps as a symbolic cachet that is maintained as a hidden source of authority. The mirror image of this option is to disseminate such a notebook through print. If such dissemination is successful, it can be a way of identifying, valorizing, and thereby preserving the authority of the compiler or of that compiler's lineage, as well as contributing to the public delineation of the repertoire's true contents.

We can find something like this latter strategy in the Moroccan *āla* tradition: a unique manuscript version of *Al-Ḥāʾik* copied by the performer Ahmed Zouiten of Fes came to be printed in mimeographed form after his death.[84] As we will see in the next chapter, printing such a manuscript notebook can be viewed as a close parallel to forming an association around a particular master, past or present. Like the association, print-textualization places that person's authority within the public sphere. In an important way, it routinizes and institutionalizes his charisma. Print makes the ineffable mastery of the *shaykh* more tangible and, hopefully, more durable.[85] And such an attempt at diffusion might in fact be preceded by its opposite: a person might spend a lifetime carefully building up a collection of texts that then go into the creation of an authoritative meta-collection aimed for publication.

Yet we have already seen that, like the association, print-textualization is never definitive. It may be challenged as a duplication of so many errors. And if a printed compilation is to serve its intended purpose, it should be put to use, and in being put to use the text may very well spawn a new generation of notebooks that in part derive from it. These derivations may in time be dissociated from the source compilation and be linked to a new personage. In theory at least, because printed texts get recycled through performance and through further forms of inscription such as handwritten notebooks, they may in time be replaced. Alternatively, new generations of inscriptions, connected to newer generations of individual authorities, may arise from such cycles of copying and circulation. In such a way, while each printed compilation may axiomatically claim to be authoritative, this claim is simply that: it is an assertion that can always be challenged by a new act of publication. Handwritten, practical manuscripts link the texts back to people, back to performance practice, and, further along, back to the genealogical. If practice offers a way out of print, it offers a way back in again, too. Furthermore, as the case of Yafil's collection demonstrates, print-textualization is never definitive due to the fact that print is mutable through its use and is vulnerable to cycles that veer between distribution and accumulation, abundance and scarcity. Like the early sound recordings described by Jonathan Sterne, textual media are as much about ephemerality as they are about permanence.[86]

For those who seek to overturn the practice of hoarding, printed texts should serve the cause of mass diffusion and the value of open access. Many of those who support such a vision are individuals who were kept from the inner circles of performers and enthusiasts through the hoarding of texts, and for them new printed compilations and particularly the internet are indeed powerful tools for escape from the unequal requirements of social exchange. As Ahmed Tantaoui, a Oujda-based scholar and singer in the Algiers tradition, explained to me:

> In my youth, I did not have the opportunity to use Yafil. There were *mélomanes* who refused to share it with me. This is the problem with Andalusi music. Because of this [refusal to share], I share everything that I have. The *shuyūkh* of the past did not want to share, they wanted to keep it to themselves. Most of the *shuyūkh* died and took their baggage with them. There were other books [beside the *Majmū‘* of Yafil]. *Al-muwashshaḥāt wa-l-azjāl*, which is based on Yafil but has even more than Yafil. There is *Al-ḥā'ik*. The *Chants andalous* of Serri. They [the *shuyūkh*] believed they had a treasure between their hands, but now, with the internet. . . . Three tomes of the *qṣīda* [compiled] by Mohamed El-Fasi . . . there are more than 350 *qṣīda*s [in them]. The old ones, if you asked for just one *qṣīda*, they would say no, I cannot [give it to you].

As striking as the poignancy of the performer's complaint is the sense that this hoarding is a thing of the past, a peculiarity of an older generation that has largely died off, and an object of musical nostalgia. In other words, lostness itself can come to be lost. The most striking support for this sense of generational shift that I have personally encountered came during an interaction with a musical elder in Oujda, the son of a major local *shaykh* of the mid-century Andalusi musical scene. After having spent many months in regular contact with him, I asked if I might be able to see his inherited copy of Yafil's *Majmūʿ*. He agreed, and a few days later brought it to the association headquarters to show me. It was the first time I had seen the compilation in this city where I had by then passed many months. The leader of another association happened to be visiting the headquarters at that moment, and while I was leafing through the worn pages printed in their archaic type, taking photos here and there, the visitor began to comment. With what sounded like a heavy dose of wistfulness, he explained that this could not have happened in the past—in the old days, he said, the *Majmūʿ* was a *tuḥfa*, a rare gem that could not just be shared and photographed so easily.

*

The notion that hoarding is a thing of the past is both true and false. In some situations, hoarding seems to have become rarer, in part because of changes in the accessibility of printed texts and in the political economy of musical performance.[87] On the other hand, changes in circulatory practice might simply be a swing of the pendulum, meaning that a new generation of musical practitioners could eventually give rise to new forms of valuation and new forms of circulation and withholding. In a long-term, difficult-to-standardize, gerontocratic practice such as the Andalusi musical tradition—and particularly one in which there are always a few "lost things" lurking in the wings—there is no guarantee of permanent accessibility.[88] As fugitive texts, songs can escape from the wider frame of compilations; likewise, compilations themselves can escape from possession. Or is the century-long project of *tadwīn* coming to a close? Is everything exposed? Will the associations reproduce the repertoire, but without zest, without energy or force?[89] Some seem to fear this, but it seems unlikely that this way of doing things will entirely disappear in any foreseeable future. One can always withhold what is now known, or one can withhold the "real" version, or one can discover things previously lost, or said to be lost. Finally, things differentiate simply through practice, and those differences get attributed to places of origin and carriers. *Tadwīn* can fail thanks to the simple fact of time. Verse (*naẓm*) can scatter into prose (*nathr*) and demand a new attempt at versification.

In turn, the hoarding of a compilation needs to be understood as part of a wider range of forms of textual hoarding. For example, some *shuyūkh* are known for refusing to share songs that are part of their repertoire. And, when they do share songs, some are known to withhold full song texts, at least for a time. One student of a leading Algerian master recounted to me that his teacher would sometimes give the first hemistich of a verse and then stop. This guarding of the repertoire, according to the student, was a way to ensure a certain following; the guarded knowledge, the student recalled his teacher explaining, is his capital. In talking about "the lost," practitioners have in turn come to use the image of *tadwīn* and publication as an idiom for loss. At least since the interwar period, commentators have spoken of "lost" pieces as *morceaux inédits*. Literally an unedited, unpublished, or never-released track or piece, a *morceau inédit* can be a *ṣanʿa* that was found through discovery of a hitherto unknown recording or through a living authority revealing such knowledge to a confidante. It can also refer to the body of still unknown repertoire glossed as *al-mafqūd*. Note that something *inédit* is not necessarily literally unpublished: Yafil's *Majmūʿ*, for example, contains many texts that are *inédits* in that their melodies are believed to be lost, either already in Yafil's day or since. Similarly, an old commercial recording that is entirely out of circulation could conceivably carry a *morceau inédit*. Thus edition or publication in this idiom is really a way to talk about a sung text—in other words, a *ṣanʿa*—being known to the community of practitioners at large. To become edited, published, or released, then, is to become known, revealed, brought into circulation. This metaphor is one very tangible way in which the early twentieth-century embrace of print and publicity came to be integrated into the broader idiom of Andalusi musical practice in the Algiers-Tlemcen tradition, even as the more explicit intentions of some of the revivalists seem to have been thwarted.

We will return to this image of hidden repertoire as capital. For the time being, the account that I have offered here attempts to understand the question of hoarding in relation to compilations. As concatenations of valued song texts, or rather of entryways into such texts, compilations are especially good candidates for withholding, and, unlike the songs themselves, are available to nonmusicians as well. Looking back on my interaction with the connoisseur recounted at the beginning of this chapter, I am struck that, for a reasonable fee, a locally respected aficionado invited me into the game. In this sense, the game of keeping and giving is a way of marking out the inner circle of authorities. Yet though he was willing to sell me a photocopy of the *Majmūʿ* and thereby confirm me as a fellow *mélomane*, he made it clear to me that his treasures did not end there: he made certain to show me the vanishingly rare Judeo-Arabic *Dīwān*, perhaps hoping that I would make it known elsewhere that he possessed this treasure.

In a way, then, both withholding and diffusion are aspects of *tadwīn*, making the hoard not only of the past but of the present as well. Hoarding unto lostness is one extreme that carries its own gravitational pull. Another extreme is the deformation through use that can come about with successful diffusion. Although these possibilities extend well beyond the pages of the songbook, it is between its covers that we can find a particularly powerful sense of these choices and of the continuum between them. The songbook carries forward both loss and recovery, both within its text and in the ways in which it is handled and remade by its possessors. From this angle, hoarding is not only of the past and the present, but of the future as well.

6

The Associative Movement

In 1971, the Algerian Ministry of Information published *Tlemcen*—a combination of coffee-table book, touristic brochure, historical overview, and policy paper. In a section devoted to the Andalusi musical tradition of that city, the book had this to say about the post-independence associations:

> The ambitions of these promoters [of the new amateur ensembles] are vast, in proportion to the grandeur of the cultural heritage that they wish to advance toward a new destiny by rendering it creative once again. Their object is to go beyond the anarchical, archaic, artisanal phase of transmission of the music. As one of the leaders of "gharnata" [Association Gharnata, founded in 1964] says: one must abandon the method of the *taleb* [*ṭālib*, the traditional religious disciple, student, or, sometimes, teacher] and inaugurate a rational apprenticeship that follows scientific procedures. It is a matter of putting in place the modern techniques that will permit the rational education of future artists.[1]

Packed into this passage are many of the hallmarks of modernist revival: the opposition of science to custom, enlightenment to obscurity, creativity to frozenness, order to chaos, rationality to blind faith, and modernity to tradition. Indeed, the amateur association is a fitting home for articulating these oppositions and for championing one against the other, in that they closely echo the sorts of arguments put forth by the original supporters of the association as a juridical form in turn-of-the-century France. The anticlerical, statist 1901 Law of Associations that forms the basis for the associative system in the Maghrib leaned heavily on an Enlightenment narrative that pitched the medieval guild against the modern association, with the latter presented as an inheritor of the spirit of the French Revolution—a rational, secular collective based on openness, free choice, and equality, fighting against the hierarchical, secretive, monopolistic nature of the guilds rooted in a feudal and religious past.

It is fitting, then, that associations have long been spaces for producing and reproducing such oppositions. From a modest beginning before the First World War, the amateur association became the central vehicle for Andalusi musical revival during the interwar period, and the associations that were established during this period form the basis for today's associative movement (*mouvement associatif*). Despite the existence of conservatories, professional ensembles, and informal circles of performers, amateur associations are the preeminent spaces of initiation for novices, of musical advancement for initiates, and of intensive sociability for all. For some musicians, involvement in associations is a lifelong commitment. Others weary of their internal tensions, outgrow them, or come to lack the time and energy necessary for the weekly rehearsals and seasonal performance commitments. But for many musicians, associations are a crucial step in the process of musical education, and associations even absorb nonperforming listeners into their governing boards and the ranks of their loyal listeners. In this sense, associations constitute veritable cross-generational meeting places for the Andalusi musical community. And a central part of the musical education that associations offer is the inculcation of the revivalist agenda: that Andalusi music is an endangered patrimony in need of salvage and enlightened renovation.

For many association members, as for the critics of "the method of the *taleb*" cited in the passage above, who presumably are referring to the use of rote repetition in the transmission of musical knowledge, the *shaykh* acts as a foil to the revivalist agenda. The critique of the spirit of the *shaykh* can in some cases become quite explicit. One group of enthusiasts, for example, complained to me of an association leader who minimizes his explanations of what he teaches as acting too much like a *shaykh* and not enough like an *ustādh* (the standard Arabic term for teacher). The other side of the coin, however, is that some people dismiss the associations as inauthentic and irrelevant. In Oujda, for example, I was repeatedly told to frequent "the old men" rather than the associations, with their young people and gender mixing. A guard at the municipal courthouse even laughed out loud when I told him I had come to look for documents relating to the history of Andalusi music in Oujda, and said I would find nothing there. "Why don't you go to the radio station," he said, pointing toward to the small building hidden among cypress trees across the main road. "Or go to the *kbār* [the old men] at the park, they have all the secrets. You won't find anything here." In other words, I was being pointed back to the park benches near the association headquarters, where the older veteran musicians, some of them members or former members of the associations, regularly gathered.

But in some respects still more confounding were the other sorts of comments I encountered that pointed to the presence of *shuyūkh* within the associative milieu. Many associations have been run by people who are described as *shuyūkh*, and not only in the sense that they act as teachers.[2] Associations frequently integrate the memory of *shuyūkh* through their names, iconography, and performance practices—in fact, as the following pages suggest, we can conceive associations as a sort of memory project that focuses on the institutionalization and production of musical authority. But perhaps the most disorienting comment I heard along these lines came from an older member of the Association Gharnata in Tlemcen, the very association that was being discussed in the 1971 publication. Sitting in the shadow of portraits of Cheikh Larbi and Redouane (see fig. 8), the man assured me that the parts of *nūbat raṣḍ al-dhīl* that I had just heard them play was "typical of Tlemcen. It came directly from Cheikh Larbi. We haven't changed anything, here we do it the traditional way. We are scientific, we don't change things."

What should we make of this state of affairs, in which the "method of the *taleb*" is the epitome of a "rational education," where science is tradition and tradition is lack of change? I would like to treat this comment not as a testament to the conservatism of this particular association or individual. At the risk of creating coherence where there is in fact contradiction, I suggest that this statement is not as paradoxical as it might sound—that it in fact sits at the confluence of several distinct streams of argument regarding the nature of musical authority that percolate through the associative domain. But before arriving at these streams, we need to trace the development of the association form within the Andalusi archipelago and understand more of its social texture. I begin with a close look at the local associative scene in the first decades of the twentieth century in Algiers before tracing the broad contours of associative contraction and expansion in the post-Second World War era. This is not an attempt to write an exhaustive history of the associations—like such an attempt with regard to the major *shuyūkh*, we would quickly become lost in the realm of localized biographies. Rather, the mixure of microhistory and broad overview that follows is designed to allow us to locate the link among associations, the genealogical ethos, and the project of *tadwīn*. If, like printed texts (or, as Saidani suggests, like recordings), associations can be treated as a technology of *tadwīn* and transmission, then this social form similarly tends to smuggle in the genealogical ethos that some claim it seeks to counter.[3]

FIGURE 8. Musicians in rehearsal at Association Gharnata in Tlemcen, 2009. From left to right, the instruments pictured are two violas, a *ṭār*, and a mandolin. Above the dry-erase board is an image of Redouane Bensari playing an *ʿūd*; above this is an image of his father, Cheikh Larbi, playing a *rabāb*.

El Moutribia and the Early Associative Milieu

In the Maghrib, as in France, the association is a ubiquitous social form and has long provided a key way for private citizens to collectively organize themselves in the public sphere. As a juridical category, the association dates back to the turn of the twentieth century, when the Law of Associations of July 1, 1901 established the ability of French citizens and subjects to form noncommercial corporate groups. This new social form, first promulgated in Paris, was applied in Algeria almost immediately, both among the settler population and among indigenous Algerians; as Omar Carlier has pointed out, musical and athletic associations were among the first kinds of associations that Algerians established, and this organizational form provided an important vehicle for indigenous self-expression and self-fashioning in the colonial public sphere, particularly during the interwar period.[4] Associations also continued to be a popular avenue of social participation in the post-independence era, and among the North African states today, Algeria is particularly "'association dense.'"[5]

To trace the association form back to the turn-of-the-century legislation, however, raises the question of what was particularly new about it. Some scholars of Algeria use the term "association" to describe a broad range of social groupings, including unions, clubs, and Sufi lodges.[6] And even those scholars who use the term to refer only to the state-recognized organizations that draw upon the turn-of-the-century legislation frequently point out continuity between the association and social forms with extra-legislative roots. Liverani, for example, describes the café as a "proto-associative space" and ascribes the club (*nādī*) a similar function.[7] Both Lakjaa and Goodman likewise see continuity between the association as a twentieth-century legal entity and the various corporate groups that have existed outside the temporal and juridical domain of the Law of Associations, with Goodman pointing out a tantalizing parallel between the decision-making processes in the *tajma'at* or Berber village assembly and those of the reformist theater associations of the interwar era.[8] More prosaically, the early twentieth-century legislation often allowed for recognition of groups that had already been in existence, and some of the terms used to describe pre- and post-legislation forms were shared: Ghouti Bouali, for example, used the Arabic term for association (*jam'īyya*) in place of the usual term for professional ensemble (*jawq* or, colloquially, *jūq*).[9] Clearly the turn-of-the-century legislation did not simply bring an entirely new social form into existence but rather built upon and joined an already existing field of social forms.

What was new, of course, was that there was state legislation that imposed a legal and political framework for the organization of extragovernmental social life. The debates that gave rise to the legislation are highly relevant in this regard. The Law of Associations of 1901 was the fruit of a longstanding controversy regarding the place of the Church and civil society within the French state.[10] The period since the formation of the Third Republic in 1870 had seen a proliferation of voluntary associations that were not officially recognized, in keeping with broader trends in Western Europe at this time.[11] At the same time, there was mounting concern in anticlericalist circles in France about the power of the Church, a concern that was exacerbated by the Dreyfus affair in second half of the 1890s.[12] The Law of Associations was both a discouragement of Church-based and political organizations that could accumulate wealth and allegedly threaten the state and an encouragement of voluntary, noncommercial groups. Supporters of the law relied heavily on an

Enlightenment narrative that pitched the medieval guild against the modern association, with the latter presented as an inheritor of the rational spirit of the French Revolution. More substantively, by bringing associations into the light of day, granting them official legitimacy, and potentially providing government subventions, the law selected the kinds of associations that state authorities found desirable or at least nonthreatening, and thereby granted the state a key role in the shaping of the French public sphere.[13] In turn, this created new incentives for social activists and enthusiasts of many stripes to insert themselves into the public sphere through the association form.

In its transplantation to the Algerian context, the associative form retained some of the functional and discursive elements that characterized it in the metropole while drawing upon distinctive traditions of sociability and impulses toward surveillance. In this sense, as Lakjaa cautions, the modern Algerian association was neither simply an annex of the French system nor just a holdover from precolonial forms of association. Its specificity emerges when we look more closely at the development of the first association for Andalusi music, El Moutribia. Yafil registered the association with the Algiers municipal authorities on July 14, 1912, but the act of registration on this politically potent date built upon a group that had already been in formation for some time.[14] An ensemble known as Orchestre Yafil or Orchestre Yafil et Rouanet was active in Algiers in the years immediately before the founding of El Moutribia. In itself, naming an ensemble after its leader was likely no different from the way in which people referred to professional ensembles. Yet, as we have seen, this ensemble was distinctive in at least three ways: it was named in part after a French musicologist who likely did not play in the group himself, it was known for its phonograph recordings and for its performances in public squares, and it was explicitly linked to the project of reviving Andalusi music. In this last respect, the ensemble seems to have been linked to Rouanet and Yafil's efforts to establish a free conservatory for Arab music. But in pursuing this modernist pedagogical objective, the association form would prove more attractive, perhaps because of the prestige that the new organizational framework enjoyed at the time of its introduction.[15] After 1912, Orchestre Yafil et Rouanet became Orchestre El Moutribia, or simply El Moutribia, and its members became known as the Moutribistes.

Why would someone join El Moutribia? First, the association form itself was a token of modernity. Its performance conventions differed from the familiar ones with regard to venue, interaction, and reception. Instead of requests made by audience members, many of El Moutribia's concerts were more rigidly fixed and took place on concert stages rather than in the more intimate settings of cafés and private homes. And although descriptions of

El Moutribia's earliest performances are lacking, the prescriptive aspects of Bouali's 1904 *Kashf al-qinā'* and the descriptions of associative practice in the interwar period suggest a model of leadership in line with the European orchestral conductor.[16] In addition, the introduction during the interwar period of a vocal soloist separate from the rest of the group broke from the usual practice in which vocalists were also instrumentalists and often vice versa. Finally, El Moutribia's ensemble, like those of the later associations, was quite a bit larger than the traditional *jūq*. Instead of a half-dozen musicians, the early association ensemble was typically double that size, and by the interwar period it was not unusual to find association ensembles counting thirty or forty players.[17]

Second, and more specifically, being part of El Moutribia was a way in which a lover of Andalusi music could publicly, collectively take part in the revivalist effort. While previously a performer who was willing to perform in public could play Andalusi music in a professional capacity, and an enthusiast could play in private or act as patron to a professional, the association form offered an alternative: a member could come to play Andalusi music in public not as a form of livelihood but rather as an expression of musical devotion and skill, an export of amateur musicality from the garden of the Lakehal family garden described in chapter 4 but to a space quite different from the café where Sfindja performed. In addition, the early El Moutribia may have offered an opportunity for professional musicians from Sfindja's and Yafil's circle to act as paid instructors in a classroom setting, although what the precise pedagogical arrangement was in this period remains obscure. In these respects, El Moutribia was not invading the cafés and displacing professional ensembles but rather was carving out new spaces for performance—spaces that, unlike the *cafés maures*, were not marked as primarily indigenous and "traditional." In doing this, El Moutribia represented a partial disengagement from the dominant relations of Andalusi musical production, while simultaneously engaging vigorously in the new market in sound recordings that it shared with professionals like Yamina and Sfindja. While this very likely affected the relationship between professionals and their patrons, it was not a direct challenge but instead an expansion of the relationships, organizational forms, kinds of discourse, and venues through which Andalusi music could take place. In the parlance of the Andalusi musical scene of today, the association was a crucial part of the migration of Andalusi music "out of the homes" and into public space.

When we recognize the way in which El Moutribia was a continuation of a collective effort to further the Andalusi musical cause, we can start to see its kinship with other circles of enthusiasts at this time that were not officially associations. In Tlemcen, Ghouti Bouali, the revivalist author of *Kashf al-qinā'* was closely linked to performers of the Andalusi repertoire both as a patron and as a fellow amateur performer. The brothers Mohamed and Ghaouti Dib, leaders of popular ensembles in turn-of-the-century Tlemcen, were professionals who are reported to have undertaken conservationist projects that never reached print.[18] And although Tlemcani musical activists would not form themselves into an association until the 1930s, the early twentieth-century scene was closely connected to the newly established, politically reformist Cercle des Jeunes Algériens in Tlemcen, a group that was not yet an officially recognized association but that shared a great deal organizationally and discursively with the association form.[19]

In Algiers as well, there were formations of musical enthusiasts who paralleled the efforts of El Moutribia. The elite amateurs and enthusiasts who gathered around Sfindja in the Belcourt neighborhood, including Mohamed Benteffahi and the Lakehal family, might be thought of as a loose formation of likeminded revivalists. Several of the music cafés in the Casbah were known for their "serious" music and attracted a clientele of *mélomanes*. There are also reports of a group of mainly Muslim enthusiasts establishing a short-lived rival or complement to El Moutribia in the years just before the First World War, although it is unclear if they ever declared themselves to the authorities.[20] Finally, some of the same elite Algerois families who were important patrons and amateur performers of Andalusi music were key members of the new *association cultuelle* dedicated to the maintenance of Muslim religious functions.[21] Thus even if El Moutribia was the sole association dedicated to music at this time, it existed within a burgeoning indigenous associative and proto-associative milieu. El Moutribia simply represented a more official, more sharply defined musical instantiation of a wider social phenomenon.

The embedding of El Moutribia and the associative form within a broader proto-associative milieu would prove important during the First World War, when El Moutribia's official activities seem to have gone on hold alongside Yafil's recording efforts.[22] During this time, Yafil gave private lessons to Muslim and Jewish students in his home on the edge of the Bab el Oued neighborhood, in the process gathering a devoted following of young enthusiasts. Among these was the young Mahieddine Bachetarzi, who Yafil discovered singing religious hymns at the Jāmi' Jadīd (the New Mosque, also known as Mosquée de la Pêcherie) shortly after the Armistice. This son of Algerois shopkeepers was drawn into Yafil's circle of young Andalusi music enthusiasts, and as the war ended he began to perform in *fêtes mauresques* organized by Yafil—a form of somewhat hybrid popular entertainment, mixing high and low genres, that had long been deployed for colonial festivities, and that was likely behind Rouanet's denunciation of Yafil on grounds of musical vulgarity.[23] Yafil also sought ways to record Bachetarzi's powerful, supple voice. According to his own recollection, Bachetarzi's recording career began in 1921, after a two-year delay brokered by the ḥanafī mufti and *mélomane* Boukandoura, his employer and mentor at the mosque.[24] Thus, although El Moutribia as an association was moribund during these years, private lessons, informal sociability, and impresario work made for a steady stream of musical activity around Yafil.

It was not until that same year that Yafil once again converted the wartime circle that he had cultivated into El Moutribia, with himself in the position of president and Bachetarzi now in the position of vice-president. This new incarnation of El Moutribia was different from its prewar incarnation in several ways. First, there was a greater prominence of Muslims, particularly through the leadership role of Bachetarzi, even if Jews remained a majority. Significantly, the post-Armistice Muslim members had a class background similar to that of many of the Jewish members: Bachetarzi was from a middle-class family of shopkeepers, and Allalou was from a humble family from the Algiers Casbah.[25] Furthermore, by now El Moutribia was no longer the sole association for Andalusi music in Algeria, even if it would remain alone in Algiers until after Yafil's death: by the mid-1920s there were associations that included music as at least part of their activities in Orléansville (today's Chlef), Miliana, and Oran.[26] In addition, there was Mohamed Ben Smaïl's l'Andaloussia just over the Moroccan border in Oujda.[27]

The interwar era also saw a widening of the space for Algerian political agency, reflected in part through the multiplication of predominantly indigenous associations that served as an important audience for the Moutribistes. The sharp increase in political participation by Algerian Muslim elites was in part due to the new Jonnart laws, named for the recently returned Governor-General.[28] Yafil himself, hardly an anticolonial agitator, was soon drawn into the tumultuous world of municipal political contestation, which, in the immediate aftermath of the Armistice, was dominated by Emir Khaled, grandson of the renowned resistance leader Emir 'Abd al-Qādir. It was under pressure from Emir Khaled—soon to be exiled as his grandfather had been—as well as other reformists in Algiers municipal politics that, in 1922, a chair of Arab music was created at the municipal conservatory. Due both to his musical prominence and the fact that, as a Jew, he carried French citizenship, Yafil was the obvious choice to fill the post.[29] In 1923, following his appointment, Yafil relinquished direction of day-to-day affairs at El Moutribia to Bachetarzi, even as the founder maintained a close connection, in part through the enrollment of many of the association members (including Bachetarzi) in his conservatory course.[30]

It was on Bachetarzi's initiative that El Moutribia began to expand its activities well beyond the Andalusi repertoire. From the beginning of the 1920s, El Moutribia's concert-hall events began to integrate skits into the musical program, and later full-fledged plays. For a time, Bachetarzi's theatrical activities even eclipsed his strictly musical ones. In 1919, Bachetarzi had been involved in the founding of the reformist Amicale des étudiants musulmans,[31] and his penchant for social critique quickly displayed itself in his popular Arabic-language theatrical activities.[32] With increasing boldness over the interwar period, Bachetarzi's melodramas tackled politically resonant issues such as alcohol, gender relations, and native collaboration with the colonial regime, with historical allusions to al-Andalus only occasionally taking center stage. Even beyond the dramatic content of the plays, the establishment of a public for popular Arabic theater was viewed as a worthy cause for opposition activists. Emir Khaled, for example, was active in trying to drum up an audience for the tentative, early theatrical experiments, none of which were explicitly political.[33] Parallel to the extension into theater, the Moutribistes' musical repertoire became highly mixed during this period as well, with Bachetarzi performing songs from the *nūba* tradition alongside arias from Italian opera, original compositions combining Arabic and French, and popular songs from Tin Pan Alley translated into colloquial Arabic.[34] That the original compositions were potentially a powerful mode of critique was not lost on the authorities: Bachetarzi later reported that on one occasion, after singing a song addressing the material poverty of Algeria's Muslims, he was advised by the director of the Office of Indigenous Affairs to stick to the "classical" Andalusi repertoire rather than sing new songs that "risk being misinterpreted."[35]

The spirit of critique that entered some of El Moutribia's performances in the 1920s did not exclude Europeans from the association's audience, whether in Algeria or in the metropole. Bachetarzi's and Yafil's first concerts in Paris in 1924 and 1926, which focused on the *nūba* repertoire, attracted both bourgeois French and working-class Algerian immigrant audiences. At the newly constructed Paris Mosque—where Bachetarzi performed the first call to prayer during its lavish inauguration in 1926—the *café maure* that was part of the complex drew a fashionable, international crowd attracted by the exotic décor and varied musical acts, which on occasion included Bachetarzi.[36] The connections that Yafil and Bachetarzi established during their early visits to Paris also led to a joint concert tour of Algeria with the violinist Jean de la

Casa Nocetti. These concerts—which combined songs from the *nūba* repertoire performed by Bachetarzi with pieces from the European classical tradition performed by Nocetti—drew large crowds of both indigenous Algerians and Europeans in the provincial cities.[37] El Moutribia in a sense provided the soundtrack for this integrationist moment, both in Algeria and in the metropole—a moment that also created discursive space for limited critique of the political status quo in the indigenous urban milieu.[38]

What is also clear from the interwar incarnation of El Moutribia is that this association had moved beyond its original focus on the Andalusi repertoire. When we consider the prominence of theater and the political significance of Bachetarzi's position at its helm, Société El Moutribia in the 1920s begins to look more like an open-ended institutional space than a tightly focused social formation. In fact, it comes to have the appearance of that other meaning of *société*—a business venture, in which there is a constant search for innovation in order to capture, maintain, and expand a market of consumers. The *nūba* continued to have a place of honor in its activities, but in many ways the repertoire of El Moutribia encapsulated the wider generic field of that moment, with the *nūba* continuing to occupy the apex of the hierarchy (or, alternatively, its base), but accounting for only a small part of its musical activity. The *nūba* material was among the repertoire that Moutribistes, including Bachetarzi himself, recorded, but Bachetarzi's reputation as a mass media star rested firmly on his topical compositions, not the Andalusi repertoire. In fact, viewed in retrospect, the early recordings of the Andalusi repertoire were something of an anomaly: later generations would see the *nūba* repertoire proper occupy a very marginal place in the recording industry, and there are virtually no mass media stars who made their name through recordings of the *nūba*. Similarly anomalous was Bachetarzi's dual role as mass media star and association head: although some association members would go on to careers as mass media figures, and some association figures would gain notoriety through live radio performances, the associative milieu would remain apart from the very idea of mass consumption and stardom. Rather, it would be better known as a non-mass but highly public form of intimate collectivity.

Interwar Scission

After Yafil's death in October 1928, almost precisely a year after his dispute with Rouanet spilled over into the columns of *La Dépêche Algérienne*, the capital witnessed a fairly sudden multiplication of musical associations. The hint of a first competitor in fact preceded Yafil's death: in 1927, a group of Muslim music enthusiasts, some of them drawn from the core of El Moutribia, gathered around Mouzino (Chaouel Durand, also known as Saul Durant), a veteran Jewish disciple and colleague of Sfindja, to form a group known as El Mossilia. Mouzino in his turn died in 1928, and the group was disbanded.[39] The second competitor, founded in early 1929, had a more auspicious start. Like El Mossilia, El Andalousia was in part a breakaway from El Moutribia, carrying with it many of its original core teachers; it also included at least one key figure associated with El Moussilia, the *mélomane* Larbi Zemirli. In a thinly veiled reference to Bachetarzi's generic experimentation, its founders publicly cited as the new association's aim "the propagation of the true Arab-Andalusi classical music which the tunes of the fox-trot and the refrains of the café-concert have the tendency at the present time to completely deform."[40] Like El Moutribia, El Andalousia had a Jewish majority, but *pace* Bachetarzi's recollections, it also included some Muslims, among them the brothers Mohamed and Abderrezak Fekhardji. These were the sons of a family that had owned one of the major cafés in the Casbah that had specialized in music at the turn of the century.[41] The fact that its founders justified El Andalousia on purist grounds also shows that genre differentiation and the attempt to separate the *nūba* from the wider field could be readily transposed into the associative idiom. In fact, the association form would provide an institutional framework through which the *nūba* repertoire could be partly encapsulated from its generic surround, carried through time, and somewhat distanced from the milieu of professional musicians.

The Fekhardji brothers' participation in El Andalousia was short lived: the following year, in 1930, they would be central to the founding of a new association, El Djazaïria. Although El Djazaïria can be seen as in part a breakaway from El Andalousia, in other respects it brought in a new category of performers who had not been previously part of any of the musical associations. Its establishment is often taken as a signal event in the history of the musical associations and of Andalusi music in Algeria more broadly.[42] A large part of its symbolic significance lies in the fact that it was the first predominantly Muslim association and closely associated with interwar social and political activities that the colonial authorities viewed with suspicion.[43] At its beginning, El Djazaïria was headquartered at the Nādī al-taraqqī/Cercle du Progrès, an important center for interwar reformist activities located at the Place du Gouvernement.[44] In the inter-associative competition over airtime on Radio Algiers in the coming years, the head of El Andalousia would even use the political tinge of El Djazaïria against them.[45]

While the proto-nationalist reputation of the association is certainly of great interest, to say that it was the first Algerian association for Andalusi music is clearly tendentious. In fact, as the foregoing narrative suggests,

El Djazaïria emerged from an Algerian associative milieu that was already twenty years in the making and that had included Muslims in important leadership positions even if the rank and file had been comprised mainly of Jews. El Djazaïria in turn would very quickly divide, showing that it was simply one association within a dynamic milieu rather than a definitive moment of founding. Furthermore, emphasis on religious categories and on the presence or absence of a nationalist or proto-nationalist discourse obscures the crucial dimension of social class that the founding of El Djazaïria brings to light. El Moutribia had been a predominantly working- and middle-class organization, even if its administrative core included some well-off Muslims and Jews. El Djazaïria, on the other hand, leaned toward the Algerois Muslim elite. Its first president was Mohamed Bensiam, who had been president of the *association cultuelle* in the years just before the First World War,[46] and its first vice-president was Ahmed Lekehal [Lakehal], from the same Belcourt family that had patronized both Sfindja and Egyptian reformist Muhammad 'Abduh at the turn of the century. After Bensiam, its president was Mohamed Benteffahi, who had likewise been part of the circle of Sfindja's patrons in Belcourt at the turn of the century.

A class-conscious interpretation of this moment in the associative movement can help clarify certain post-independence comments made by Bachetarzi regarding Jews and Muslims in El Moutribia. According to him, Muslims stayed away from adhering to El Moutribia despite his own best efforts to recruit them. In a passage in his memoirs, Bachetarzi suggests that during this period "young Muslims had an insurmountable repugnance toward performing in public."[47] What I would suggest is that we need to reread Bachetarzi's point in more specific terms: such repugnance is incomprehensible without paying attention to the class dimension and accompanying participant roles. In other words, a major dimension of El Djazaïria's sociological significance lay in the fact that it marked the decisive entry of a status elite into the realm of public performance—an elite that happened to be Muslim.[48]

Such attention to social class and relations of musical production is fruitful in thinking about not only what made El Djazaïria different from its predecessors but also how associations worked (and in fact continue to work) internally. Andalusi music associations are usually comprised of three basic elements: members, teachers, and an administrative council (in Arabic *maktab*, in French *conseil d'administration*). Because the interwar administrative councils could be quite large (a common feature of associations in this period more generally, as Goodman's work demonstrates), and because leading musicians often acted both as teachers and as council members, the lines between members, teachers, and administrative personnel were often blurry.[49]

In El Moutribia under Bachetarzi's leadership, for example, Bachetarzi was both artistic director and president, and several of the administration council members were professional musicians who likely served as pedagogues or at the very least as leading musicians in the ensemble.[50]

Nevertheless, there were some broad social distinctions that distinguished association administrators from the rank and file. Many of the administrative council members were drawn from business and professional elites, and many of them were not themselves musicians but simply enthusiasts who were eager to take part in the musical cause. In this sense, the association served as a home to nonperforming enthusiasts, thereby providing a space for people who would otherwise be patrons of professionals. Together with nonperforming rank-and-file members, such enthusiasts provided a built-in audience for the performances of the association ensemble.[51]

In the case of teachers as well, we can find traces of social distinctions internal to the association form. While Benteffahi of El Djazaïria and Mouzino of the early El Mossilia were figures in teaching roles who were from well-off families, many of the other teachers came from less well-off families and likely made a significant proportion of their living from musical performance and, thanks to the associations, from pedagogy. We know, for example, that Makhlouf Bouchara self-identified as a house-painter by trade, Laho Seror as a cobbler, and Mahieddine Lakehal as a weaver, while Sion Houzet was the son of a tailor.[52] Then there were people like the Fekhardji brothers and Bachetarzi, who hailed from somewhat modest backgrounds and came to make some or even much of their living from the associative milieu and from the new musical media and institutions. Just as the association form provided a new way for wealthy patrons to take part in musical activities, it also provided professionals an alternative outlet for their musical authority and novel paths toward a musical livelihood.

In all of the early associations, leading members put great stock in establishing a claim on lineages of musical authorities. Consider, for example, the following excerpt from El Moutribia's publicity dating from 1927, possibly penned by Yafil himself, that helped prompt Rouanet's inflammatory letter:

> The death of the famous Sfindja plunged the lovers of Arab music into a very great perplexity. Indeed, other than him, no one seemed to have the breadth of knowledge and requisite competence to save this music from oblivion. The pessimists saw it already summoned to an approaching disappearance. But Sfindja had trained students, and one among them, Yafil, who had been specially instructed by the old master, understood the danger and undertook the renovation of Arab music. A consummate musician, and loving Arab music for itself, the latter did not submit to its disappearance. Through a dogged,

> tenacious effort, he succeeded in putting the music to paper. The effort was long and costly; but, not recoiling from any sacrifice, Mr. Yafil accomplished marvels in his effort to gather as many songs as possible, which he promptly notated in musical form. This work accomplished, he understood that there was a still greater work to accomplish. Indeed, his effort would have been in vain if he had not sought to publicize the treasures of this antique music, with its so numerous variations and harmonious inflections and which he had so magnificently reconstituted. Toward this aim, he first created a free school, but the courses were quickly abandoned. Availing himself, then, of the truth that one more readily joins an association than signs up for a course, Mr. Yafil founded El-Moutribia.[53]

In a sense, then, the association provided a public space through which amateurs and professionals could lay claim to discipleship. In this passage, Yafil conceives El Moutribia as a sort of transposition of Sfindja's circle to the public sphere, a project for bringing musical devotion into the open and for building up the sense of discipleship. To this end, Yafil called upon various disciples of Sfindja in addition to himself to act as transmitters of repertoire.[54] In turn, after Yafil's death, Bachetarzi was reported to say during his graveside euology, "Your work, dear master . . . will not rest infertile, for I take here a solemn vow to pursue the aim of all your life's efforts, and to continue to be inspired by your example: to spread this music that you have so loved and to which you gave the best of yourself."[55] This was an eminently genealogical move: Bachetarzi was taking over the mantle from Yafil, who fashioned himself as having taken over the mantle from Sfindja. At the same time, we should note that the association form not only drew upon *shuyūkh* but also made them. For beginning with Bachetarzi and perhaps even Yafil, we can find a new phenomenon: people who took on a reputation as a *shaykh* without engaging solely (or even in some cases primarily) in musicianship in professional ensembles.

Yet as so often happens in genealogical territory, Yafil-Bachetarzi was not the only route back to Sfindja. One of the striking things about the founding of El Mossilia in 1927, El Andalousia in 1929, and El Djazaïria in 1930 is that each of them was formed around at least one mature musician who had been closely associated with Sfindja. Mouzino, Laho Seror, and Benteffahi were each linked to Sfindja's circle, just as Yafil had been. It was as if, in Sfindja's absence, the association members were seeking links back to him through the surviving members of his circle. The early incarnation of El Mossilia was based around Mouzino, a living link back to Sfindja; when El Mossilia was reestablished in 1932 as a breakaway from El Djazaïria, its two teachers, Mahieddine Lakehal (who had been previously linked to El Djazaïria) and

Makhlouf Bouchara (who had been previously linked to El Andalousia) not only embodied the mixed Muslim-Jewish character of the breakaway association but also represented a link back to Mouzino, who had been Mahieddine Lakehal's teacher.[56] And in turn, the members of the second incarnation of El Mossilia clearly linked themselves to the memory of Sfindja, as can been seen in a striking association photograph from 1933: like an embodied genealogical tree, we see the younger association members ranged behind the older teachers Makhlouf Bouchara and Mahieddine Lakehal, and the entire group graced by a framed photograph of Sfindja that is propped up by young men standing in the back row.[57]

These genealogically embedded musical authorities played an important role in the proliferation of breakaway associations. In the case of El Mossilia's emergence from El Djazaïria, it is not entirely clear if Lakehal and Bouchara had broken from their previous affiliations with El Djazaïria and El Andalousia, respectively, or if they were active in more than one group at once.[58] But the next offshoot from El Djazaïria would suggest that these were breaks rather than simple extensions of their pedagogical commitments. In 1935, an association called Gharnata (Granada) was formed, whose teachers included Mohamed Benteffahi and the Fekhardji brothers.[59] In this case, we know that this was an instance of scission because Gharnata's founding prompted a crisis in El Djazaïria's ranks, presumably due to the fact that the leading lights among the teachers had left. The next year, the problem was solved when El Djazaïria fused with Gharnata. The Gharnata name disappeared, but Benteffahi, the president of Gharnata, assumed presidency of El Djazaïria.[60]

The turbulent emergence of El Mossilia and Gharnata from El Djazaïria, and the prompt folding of Gharnata back into a reconfigured El Djazaïria, is not evidence of a special fractiousness unique to El Djazaïria. In fact, it is a familiar pattern for observers of associative life in Algeria and beyond. Liverani, writing about associations in Algeria at the end of the twentieth century, attributes both "associative decay"—in other words, the eventual existence of associations on paper only—and the multiplicative tendency of associations to a pervasive "atmosphere of distrust" arising from struggles over leadership. For Liverani, these struggles are compounded by the phenomenon of "familism," or "the presence of family members among the core membership group."[61] Although there are many gaps in our understanding of the micropolitics of the interwar Andalusi music associations, the twists and turns described here suggest that the patterns Liverani describes are nothing new.

Furthermore, the patterns of scission described here present certain features specific to the Andalusi music scene that need to be taken into account in thinking through the apparent tendency toward fragmentation. The 1930s saw an explosion of associative life in Algeria, particularly in the capital, and not only among indigenous Algerians but among the settler population as well. In Andalusi musical circles, this upsurge is visible in the fact that by 1936 there were nine active music associations in the Algiers region alone, up from one a decade earlier. In Tlemcen, in 1934, the Société des Lettres, des Arts et de la Musique (SLAM) emerged from a recently founded musical association called Union et Progrès,[62] which in turn had arisen from the longstanding circle of literary and musical enthusiasts linked to the pre-First World War literary and musical scene.[63] Among SLAM's founders was Mohamed Bouali, the son of the recently deceased Ghouti Bouali, author of *Kashf al-qināʿ* of 1904. In Constantine, the 1930s saw a parallel proliferation of associations specializing in *mā'lūf* that were closely tied to competing currents in reformist and proto-nationalist circles.[64] And in Tunisia, 1934 saw the founding of the first association for *mā'lūf*, al-Rāshidiyya.[65] The spread of the associative form may have encouraged people to form new ones, and may have lowered the barrier to establishing breakaway associations for people who were dissatisfied with the existing choices.

It is also important to note the rise of new forms of patronage during the interwar period, which in turn offered new sources for exposure, competition, prestige, and collective wealth.[66] Radio Algiers, for example, offered a novel venue for performance that became the locus of fierce rivalry over airtime among the Algiers associations of the 1930s. The more general proliferation of extra-musical associations among both settlers and indigenous Algerians is also helpful in explaining the proliferation of musical ones at this time, since the Andalusi associations were often engaged to perform at charitable functions hosted by associations whose chief pursuits were nonmusical.[67] National and international touring as well as conferences in settings such as Cairo, Paris, and Fes provided further incentives for proliferation. El Moutribia had shown the possibility of prestigious tours in Europe, and although the authorities chose to send the professional Larbi Bensari as Algeria's representative to the Cairo Congress of Arab Music in 1932, association members were aware of the opportunity, and at least one association (Al-Mizhar al-Būnī, from Bône [Annaba]) directly asked to be selected.[68]

Furthermore, the fact that respectable Algerois Muslims had established El Djazaïria and shown a willingness to take on a semi-public role as musical performers no doubt led the way for other constituents of the old Andalusi musical public to engage in associative life. The nearly immediate separation of El Mossilia from El Djazaïria, followed by a second breakaway (the short-lived Association Gharnata), suggests that El Djazaïria's founding represented an en masse entry of a particular class segment into the associative scene.

A single association may have simply been too limited to accommodate the entirety of this sector of the Andalusi musical public, especially if the establishment of El Djazaïria encouraged still other high-status Algerois Muslims to enter the associative fray.

Finally, this brings us to the question of associative scale and the genealogical ethos. If the association is a forum in which *mélomanes* could gather around living *shuyūkh*, and through them around the dead *shaykh*, then the association must not grow so large as to lose that intimacy. In other words, the scale of the associations was a good fit for the scale of Andalusi musical practice, and it made them (and make them still) very far from mass organizations in either numbers or ethos. In addition, the presence of the *shaykh* in the association provided a number of incentives toward scission. Because the relationship between members and teachers was a human one, and because people were not definitively tied down to the association to which they belonged, it was always possible for teachers and their allies to leave an association and form another. This is precisely what seems to have happened in the case of Makhlouf Bouchara and Mahieddine Lakehal, who left El Andaloussia and El Djazaïria respectively to help establish El Mossilia. The immediate circumstances of such exits from an association could be myriad: personality clashes, differing aesthetic visions, money, and the "familism" and "presidentialism" identified by Liverani. But the fact that such scission became a central part of Andalusi associative practice, and that the associations seemed to configure themselves around particular sorts of persons, brings us back to the essentially personalized kind of authority that Andalusi musical practitioners were trafficking in. For as we will explore more closely at the end of the chapter, the patterns of scission closely resemble the branching of a genealogical tree.

The Postwar Associative Movement: The Revival of Revival

The association system was well established by the mid-1930s, not only in Algiers but also in Tlemcen, Constantine, Blida, Bône, Tunis, and Oujda. In the Algiers-Tlemcen archipelago, the association had not replaced other forms of musical sociality: house concerts and informal gatherings continued to occur, professional ensembles largely independent from the associations persisted, informal gatherings continued to take place, and there were even some cafés where one could still go to hear live music. In addition, the conservatory classes and the establishment of an Algerian music orchestra at Radio Algiers in the mid-1940s would provide a new forum for the employment and production of professional musicians.[69] Yet in other respects, the association blended with many of these alternative social forms. Association headquarters themselves were often spaces of informal sociality, and at various moments associations met in cafés. Even though some *shuyūkh* remained aloof from the associations, many professionals played in both associations and separate professional ensembles. In some cases, such as Bachetarzi and some of the members of El Moutribia, elements from associations could double as professional ensembles, even if the social mores of the private concert did not always sit well with the association members' modernist and amateurist ethic. Finally, the new ensemble at Radio Algiers was headed in its first decade by none other than Mohamed Ferkhardji, a veteran of the associative movement.[70] Taken as a whole, the association both established a new social form for the production and consumption of Andalusi music and encapsulated and telescoped many of the social conventions that had preceded the association form. A novel forum for lovers of Andalusi music, it was at the same time oriented outward like other associations focused on scouting and sports. Associations publicized even their most internal activities to readers of the French-language newspapers, and journalists frequented their gatherings.[71] Associations were, in a sense, minor celebrities within the colonial public sphere of the interwar era.

The Second World War disrupted the activities of the associations,[72] particularly those such as El Moutribia and El Andalousia whose members were mainly Jewish and who faced persecution under Vichy. Following the Allied landing, various draft-age associationists, including Abderrezak Fekhardji, were also taken up into military service. But the active disruption to associative and other musical activities was fairly brief. By 1944 El Andalousia had reconstituted, and the radio orchestra was founded at this time.[73] By 1946, El Hayat (founded in 1936) and El Djazaïria were both active again.[74] Yet in some respects there were substantial changes between the pre- and postwar milieux that made the Second World War a real break. Benteffahi, a guiding force in El Djazaïria, died in 1944 in Tlemcen during a visit to his daughter, who was married to one of the founders of SLAM.[75] It took El Djazaïria until 1948 to find a new seat in the Bab el Oued neighborhood,[76] and until then the association met in the lower levels of cafés.[77] El Mossilia's immediate postwar activities were uneven, and El Moutribia's future was in question. Most of all, the establishment of new associations that had been a mainstay of the 1930s ceased.[78] In Algiers and Tlemcen, the years after the Second World War were dedicated to simply maintaining the already existing associations.

This state of affairs renewed the notion that Andalusi music required a revival. When El Djazaïria was finally able to reestablish a headquarters other than the cafés where its members had been meeting, the moment was marked by a concert headed by Abderrezak Fekhardji and performed in the presence of various figures from the Andalusi musical milieu.[79] In some ways, the statement of the association president, Rachid Kasdali, that there was a need "to revive our classical music" was simply an expression of the perennial discourse of salvage and restoration embedded in the modernist project.[80] Yet it also reflected the shakiness of the postwar associative movement and the way in which the associative movement had come to be equated with Andalusi music itself. The interwar period had established associations as the new context for Andalusi musical production, and the weakening of that context was a perceived weakening in the repertoire.

One solution to the challenges of the postwar years was to combine associative forces, in effect reversing the process of scission that had often led to their formation in the first place. In 1951, after several recent moves to new headquarters, El Djazaïria settled into El Mossilia's original location in the Casbah through an actual fusion with that earlier competitor.[81] Now called El Djazaïria-El Mossilia, on its letterhead listed as "an artistic musical association for the revival of Arab-Andalusi poetry," the organization apparently kept the core of El Djazaïria's committee configuration.[82] The moment of its fusion, which occurred in October of that year, briefly became the basis for an annual concert-celebration held at the association headquarters, which the Algiers press covered fairly consistently.

By this time, the young Sid Ahmed Serri was a central figure in the association. He had first joined El Djazaïria in 1946, where he met Abderrezak Fekhardji.[83] Serri's singing debut with the radio orchestra had come two years later, in December 1948.[84] By the time of the creation of El Djazaïria-El Mossilia, Serri was a regular soloist and commentator, and his musical talents garnered high praise in all the newspaper reports of the annual gatherings. The reports of the annual concert-celebrations marking the founding of El Djazaïria-El Mossilia provide valuable insight into the kinds of gatherings that were taking place among the members of this association in the final years of French rule—gatherings that suggested the club-like qualities of associations and their partial orientation to the organs of the public sphere. These were intimate affairs, with the listeners seated around tables in an atmosphere suffused with the scent of roses, jasmine, and tea. Aside from listening to performances from the *nūba* repertoire, the audience also heard statements from leaders of the association. During the 1952 gathering, for example, Abdelkader Jilali "defined the Andalusi musical heritage, exalted the universality of music and particularly of classical music, of which Ziriab [Ziryāb], leaving his native Baghdad, was the pioneer and 'prophet' for North Africa."[85]

In 1953, on the occasion of the twenty-third anniversary of the founding of El Djazaïria, the fused association held another small-scale concert. This time, the speech was given by the president, Rachid Kasdali, who "thanked the audience, [and] spoke of the pure and noble Andalusi music. A thrilling evocation of Andalusia stamped by this art that approaches perfection dominated the speech by Mr. Kasdali, who was eager to render homage to the association members who, for twenty-three years, have struggled to snatch from the claws of oblivion this magnificent art that is Andalusi music."[86]

In 1954, the anniversary celebration would follow the same pattern, counting El Djazaïria-El Mossilia's existence from the founding of El Djazaïria in 1930. This time, the hall was packed "with the oldest Algerois families" and numerous well-known individuals, and it was Serri who did the speaking:

> Expressing himself in literary Arabic, Mr. Ahmed Serri told of the vicissitudes of this music, vivid and joyous in the Alhambra, sad in exile, and that in our day risks being buried alongside the last masters, since it is only transmitted verbally.
>
> The orator recalled the glorious days of Zireb [Ziryāb]and Farabey [al-Fārābī], evoked the great masters—Lakhal, Teffahi, Swinza [Sfindja], Saïdi, Barhoum—and retraced the history of his association. He called for the audience to help 'El Mossilia' in its task and, after having paid homage to the Fakhardji brothers, implored Algerian composers to flee from this adulterated art that is called 'modern music,' in order to incline toward this pearl of incomparable brilliance that had the kingdom of Granada for its jewel-box.[87]

Serri's 1954 remarks are testament to the way in which the associations and their leading lights were discursively blended into the broader, extra-associative genealogies, and even into the imagined deep past of the musical tradition that was presented as a transparent linking of affect to historical circumstance. The language of revival could encompass many layers of the past in its users' efforts to fashion a musical future.

The Post-Independence Associations: Reconstitution and Homage

The war years of 1954–62 put many of the associations on hold, and only some of them would survive the upheavals. The Andalusi music scene did not go entirely underground during that time, however. With Mohamed Fekhardji's death in 1956, leadership of the radio orchestra went to his brother and El Djazaïria mainstay Abderrezak, and the newspapers continued to report concerts by El Djazaïria-El Mossilia through May 1955. In addition, some students continued to attend Arab music courses at the Algiers municipal conservatory, where Sassi (Alfred Lebrati) had taken over the post previously held by Yafil and Bachetarzi. There was even the establishment of a new association in the Algiers Casbah in 1957, although it specialized in *chaabi* repertoire rather than in the Andalusi repertoire proper.[88]

It would take several years after the end of the war for associative life to regroup, and some of the associations did not come back. For example, the departure of the bulk of the Algerian Jewish population in the years after independence seems to have spelled the end of El Andalousia. At the Colloque at El Riath at the end of 1964, in a close echo of the post-Second World War moment, participants lamented the sad state of the associative movement and the moribund state of Andalusi music overall.[89] Yet in Algiers there was musical activity in associative circles from the beginning of independence and even in the final years of fighting. Ahmed Serri reports having participated in the Andalusi orchestra of an association linked to the municipal conservatory from 1960 until 1964,[90] and many veterans of the associative movement of Algiers and Constantine were present at the discussions of the future of Algerian Andalusi music at El Riath at the end of 1964. And several months before this, at a major lecture on Algerian music by the Marxist intellectual Bachir Hadj Ali at the Salle Ibn Khaldoun in Algiers, members of El Djazaïria-El Mossilia, under the leadership of Abderrezaq Fekhardji and Ahmed Serri, provided Andalusi musical examples from the modes *raml al-māya*, *ʿarāq*, and *zīdān*.[91]

In Tlemcen, it took until 1966 for SLAM to reestablish its activities. In the meantime, however, Association Gharnata came on the scene. The circumstances of its founding strongly recall the establishment of SLAM in 1934 out of the already existing association Union et Progrès: Association Gharnata emerged from the Association Les Amis du Livre, which had been founded in 1927 and which after independence had lent its headquarters as an informal seat for the musical activities of Mohamed Bensari, a son of the recently deceased Cheikh Larbi.[92] In addition, the founders of Association Gharnata demonstrated close continuity with the interwar period and in turn with the early twentieth-century pioneers: Mohamed Bouali, who had been a founding member of SLAM in 1934 and was the son of Ghouti Bouali, was one of the founders of the new association, alongside another veteran of SLAM, Mustapha Belkhodja. In addition, its president from 1966 until 1976 was Mostefa Aboura's son Kheireddine, who worked in Tlemcen's town hall. The younger Aboura in turn lent his collection of discs, old musical instruments, manuscripts, printed books, and some of his father's transcriptions to an exhibition that was part of a local festival organized in Spring 1966 by Les Amis du Livre in cooperation with the municipal government of Tlemcen.[93]

The first decade after independence also saw the spread of the association form to Oran by way of the large network of Tlemcanis who had established themselves there in the years after the Second World War. Among the transplanted Tlemcanis who were active in the establishment of the Nadi el Andalousia and the Association Ennahda in the late 1960s were Abderrahmane Sekkal, co-author of the 1934 work *Nafḥ al-azhār*, and Mahmoud Bensari, another son of the late Cheikh Larbi. In 1970, a group of ambitious young enthusiasts of Tlemcani origin established Nassim El-Andalous.[94] It was also during this period that a musical club (*nādī*) was formed in the nearby city of Mostaganem.[95]

The first national festival of Andalusi music, the Festival de Musique Classique Algérienne, organized by the Ministry of Information and held during Ramadan, December 1967–January 1968, at the Algerian National Theater in Algiers, provided an important showcase for the new iteration of the associative milieu,[96] with the recently reconstituted SLAM receiving first prize.[97] Other major national festivals organized by the Ministry of Information followed, in 1969 and again in 1972. In addition, regional festivals began to be organized, including in Tlemcen starting from 1974. Like Radio Algiers in the 1930s, the establishment of a national and regional festival system in the late 1960s and the 1970s gave associations a prominent venue for performance as well as a forum for competition, standardization, scholarly debate, and innovation. By the 1970s, although festivals were not the only opportunity to perform publicly, they had become the main outlet for most of the associations. They also came to provide a space for Algerian musicians to interact with counterparts from other Maghribi and Arab countries. At the same time that festivals provided a forum for associations, professional ensembles continued to coexist with the associations on the festival stage, sometimes only convening for the occasion. These were also important spaces for the articulation of musical criticism by intellectuals, and for members of the post-independence Andalusi musical public to recognize themselves as such.[98] At the same time, festivals developed into a forum that emphasizes the display of a self-conscious notion of national and regional authenticity, made visible through a sartorial bifurcation between the festival stage and the non-festival soiree (whether professional or amateur): while the festival usually features clothing marked as traditionally Maghribi for both male and female performers, sometimes in the form of association uniforms (a practice dating back to the interwar period), the soiree typically features suits for the male performers.

The associations that had established themselves in the years after independence maintained their activities throughout the 1970s, and across the border in Oujda they helped to inspire the proliferation of associations other than the Association Andalouse. This decade also saw the establishment of annexes to the Algiers municipal conservatory in various outlying neighborhoods of the capital, which provided an avenue for recruitment of young musicians who would later join associations. The deeper changes that were at work lay in the realm of attitudes toward young people's participation in musical activities, and in particular attitudes toward women's participation. Parents began to enroll their young children, so that the associations were no longer the preserve of people in their twenties and upward. Although there had been some women in El Moutribia in the interwar era, both amateur and professional, young women did not begin to appear widely in the Algiers associations until the early 1970s, echoing the call at the El Riath conference for the integration of women into "this effort of [Andalusi musical] restoration and renovation," given "the primordial role that has devolved upon the woman within the family and society."[99] Today, women constitute roughly half of the young members in many of the associations throughout the Algiers-Tlemcen archipelago. It is rare, however, for women to continue to participate in associations after marriage, even if many women have emerged from the associations as professional performers, including leading female vocalists on the Andalusi scene today such as Beihdja Rahal, Lamia Maadini, Zakia Kara Terki, Rym Hakiki, and Nassima Chaabane. In this manner, the associative movement maintains the gendered and class-specific distrust of professional music-making detailed in chapter 2.

These changes were taking place within a restrained set of associations that had either been revived or established for the first time in the ten years after independence. In contrast, the early 1980s saw a new wave of associations arrive, encouraged by the liberalization reforms of the new administration of President Chadli Benjedid and a wave of interest in questions of national and transnational Maghribi patrimony.[100] In Algiers during this new moment in associative life, the aged Abderezzaq Fekhardji was a key symbolic node. Just as the earliest version of El Mossilia was formed around the still-living Mouzino, El Fekhardjia was formed around Abderrezak Fekhardji, and was in fact named after him and his late brother. This new act of naming an association after an individual would catch on: Association Ahbab Cheikh Sadeq El Bejaoui (the association of the devotees of Cheikh Sadeq El Bejaoui) in Bejaïa, Association El Bachtarzia in Koléa, Association Ahbab Cheikh Larbi Bensari in Tlemcen, Association Mustapha Belkhodja in Oran, and Association Ahbab Cheikh Salah in Oujda, among others. Not all of these acts of naming imply a direct connection with the named authority, although in a few of them the connection is quite close. Overall, however, they point to a strategic invocation of these authorities' memory, one that renders homage, borrows their authority, and, in the spirit of *tadwīn*, protects some of that authority against erosion. With a few exceptions, such as Association Ziryab and Association Ismaïliyya in Oujda (the latter being named after Mohamed Ben Smaïl), such invocations focus either on living but aged masters, as in the case of Abderrezak Fekhardji, or on figures who have died but are within living memory—Sfindja for the Algerois musicians of the interwar period, and, varying by locale, Cheikh Larbi, Cheikh Salah, Mustapha Belkhodja, and others for the musicians of today. Like French copyright law, with its valorization of the notion of the embodied author, the emphasis here is on the near distant, those who are within the reach of memory but threaten to escape it.

With the new wave of post-1980 associations came a new wave of scissions. In 1988, Ahmed Serri, after four decades of involvement in El Djazaïria-El Mossilia, left to pursue his efforts in other forums, both within the associative framework and without. Veterans of El Djazaïria-El Mossilia, for that matter, founded a number of associations in nearby cities, including Cherchell, Chéraga, and Koléa, as well as in France. In 1986, following Abderrezak Fekhardji's death in 1984, members of El Fekhardjia left to found Essoundoussia, from which arose still another association, El Inchirah. The devotion to the memory of Fekhardji brothers was brought with them, with one leader asserting to me that they are "the true Fekhardjia."

The violence and instability of the 1990s put another obstacle before the expansion of the associative movement, and put the activities of many associations on hold.[101] But it also saw the enrichment of the association and professional scene in Paris, and more recently the export of the association form to Montreal as well. In Paris, too, the pattern of homage is visible: the largest association is called Al Mawsili, pointing both to El Mossilia of Algiers and to its namesake, Iṣḥāq al-Mawṣilī, Ziryāb's erstwhile mentor in 'Abbasid Baghdad.[102] Here we see the way in which the associations themselves have come to be something like persons who can be honored in a manner similar to *shuyūkh*. In this respect, associations build upon persons and even come to take on qualities of persons, in some ways becoming known for their own versions of the repertoire in a manner similar to the notion that certain *shuyūkh* and cities have their own versions.

The *shuyūkh* of the past are invoked in other ways as well. As in the *mā'lūf* practice in the Libyan capital described by Philip Ciantar, the homage-concert to a past or aging master is a veritable institution within the contemporary associative movement, and such homage is an important way for disciples to publicly assert the genealogical relationship.[103] In one case—the journey of members of Association Nassim El-Andalous to Casablanca in the 1990s to visit Cheikh Larbi's legendary exiled son, Redouane—homage assumed the quality of a pan-Maghribi pilgrimage and a quest for the recuperation of lost repertoire and relationships. We can also find visual documents that echo the image of El Mossilia in 1933, such as a portrait of Association Nassim El-Andalous of Oran that features the ensemble members and two large framed black-and-white photographs, one of Cheikh Larbi and the other of his son Redouane, or an image from Association Ahbab Cheikh Salah in Oujda, in which we can see a visual representation of the genealogy from Cheikh Salah to his son Nasreddine to his students.

Associations, then, are built upon layers of memory of *shuyūkh*, both living and dead. In this way, the associative movement is profoundly cross-generational in symbolic terms, both looking backward toward ancestors and forward toward new generations of *pépinières* (seedlings) who might supply the ancestors of the future. The associative movement is also cross-generational in more practical terms, since some male members play a part in the associations throughout their lifetimes. Furthermore, it is important to note that associations are also cross-class formations: while members of the elite predominate in the governance committees and in some cases in the rank-and-file, and certain associations have been known to exclude people from modest backgrounds, living and dead *shuyūkh* are drawn from both the elite and from more modest layers of the urban socioeconomic terrain.[104] Yet the place of the *shaykh* within associative practice carries its share of ambivalence.

The Ambivalent *Shaykh*

Once again, those who are familiar with Sufi and more general Islamic knowledge practices might recognize a parallel between the religious *shaykh* and the musical *shaykh* as he appears in the associative context. Both are authorities who embody a prestigious form of sacred knowledge that is derived from past masters and that the present authorities in turn pass on to their own disciples. Various scholars have described how students of Sufi masters and religious scholars attempt to posthumously institutionalize the embodied charisma of the teacher through diverse forms of textualization and through the creation of hierarchical administrative structures.[105] Andalusi music associations follow a similar pattern: the late master is institutionalized through naming practices, public performances, photographs, printed texts, the establishment of a sonic archive, and the corporate structure of the association, even as such institutionalization raises problems of distance and loss. As one association member in Tlemcen told me:

> Before Boudelfa, after Boudelfa, with Cheikh Larbi, after Cheikh Larbi, there were things that became lost. And us too, we have probably lost [things]—and what are we doing, we are conducting research, taking from here and there, from this one's mouth, listening, using the cassette player. And it is in part thanks to the cassette player that we are in the process of learning. The absolute master today is there—it's the cassette player. We no longer have a true master like Cheikh Larbi or perhaps like Kheireddine Aboura.[106]

The parallel does not stop at the institutionalization of charismatic memory. Again, in a more oblique manner, the musical *shaykh*, like the traditional religious *shaykh* in the Maghrib, can also be an ambivalent figure. As explored in chapter 2, on the one hand, the musical *shaykh* is an object of reverence and a source of musical wisdom. On the other hand, the musical *shaykh* is sometimes from a somewhat lower social class than the very people who pay him reverence and is frequently a professional who mixes material livelihood with quasi-sacred social action—a mixture that many members of the associative movement actively avoid in their own musical lives, and which is not entirely disconnected from the common pattern of conflict between association musical directors and their governing board. The title of *shaykh* is associated with authority but also backwardness: one young female performer explained to me that the *shuyūkh* of the past were not educated, and "just listened and sang," while more recent teachers have done research and instilled the desire and ability to understand the words they sing. One veteran Tlemcani musician told me that "it was us amateurs who safeguarded this music, not the *shuyūkh*," in that the young amateurs of the associative movement knew how to correct things while the *shuyūkh* did not have such discernment, even as they were crucial sources of raw musical material. Hence the *shaykh* embodies the revivalist conundrum: he is the fount of authenticity, but according to many participants is too often a buried fount, or a compromised one.[107] In this view, a true association is a school, while many associations are simply social clubs or else "professional ensembles" masquerading as amateur associations.[108]

Here we are very close to the dispute between Yafil and Rouanet regarding "the disc of memory." According to the veteran Tlemcani musician and the young female performer cited above, it is not enough to simply repeat what the *shuyūkh* did. Rather, there must be discernment, critique, correction. In this view, contra the perspective of the musician at Association Gharnata cited earlier, it is not at all scientific to simply play what one hears on a recording of Cheikh Larbi. At the same time, musicians who advocate for such critique still hold to the importance of particular *shuyūkh*. For example, one musician with experience in several associations contrasted the "scientific approach" of some associations with the nonscientific one of others. According to him, the latter draw on multiple *shuyūkh* and stay close to the recordings without asking questions; the former kinds of associations, on the other hand, select one or two from a single, trustworthy lineage and then engage in inquiry, analysis, correction, and "purification" of what they hear on the recordings. For advocates of such an approach, these are "touch-ups," not changes; in the words of one young musician, "The tradition stays the same."

This is not the only view within the association scene. For some musicians, the impulse toward authentication through scholarship and the spirit of critique can go too far. This is not necessarily evidence of a slavish devotion to one's *shaykh*. Indeed, for a musician like Hadi Boukoura of Association des Beaux Arts in Algiers, who emphasizes self-education and his family's history of involvement in the associative movement more than a relationship with a *shaykh*, it is more important to stay close to whatever model one is working from, whether that be a living teacher or a sound recording. This position is somewhere between the view of Sekkal that a *shaykh* without a *shaykh* is not a *shaykh*, and the view that authenticity resides in the scientizing *mélomane* over the *shaykh*. Boukoura is in essence counseling a strategic blinkering of the eyes, opting for a workmanlike and aesthetic sense over one that emphasizes attachment to an original version.

But for many in the association scene, the questions about correction, scholarship, and authority are pressing, and often overlap with debates about the role of writing and specifically staff notation. For many advocates of the "scientific approach," notation is a crucial tool of analysis and a way to break with the "mouth-to-ear" of the traditional pedagogy of the *shuyūkh* and the associations and instead engage in correction and purification. It is also held up as a way to discipline the profusion of versions that is held to be endemic to Andalusi music and to separate it from the alleged clarity of European and Egyptian music.[109] In this way, writing is more than writing in its conventional sense: it is a way to talk about fixation, consolidation, codification—in short, *tadwīn* in its broadest sense. Even consultation of the written poetry is helpful in correcting errors that enter into recorded performances. Yet for many musicians I have encountered, even those who embrace the importance of *tadwīn*, writing is problematic in that it "destroys things": while writing may promote exactitude, "something" is lost, the playing turns "dry," it loses spirit (*rūḥ*) and sweetness. In addition, for some it also loses a sense of the organic music theory that is embedded in the practice: in the words of one critic, a score simply gives "a sequence of notes," without the sense of form that only a master can convey to a disciple. Through such claims, critics of writing are asserting the importance of the musical person as authority, either through recorded form or, if possible, in the flesh.[110] Indeed, it is the in-person relationship that is most desirable, in part due to the fact that much can be "lost" on recordings as well, in that recordings might represent incomplete versions of the material in question. While the living teacher might withhold a verse, for example, the living relationship holds out the possibility that a more complete knowledge might be recovered.[111]

Again, we can find a Sufi parallel: there is the need for contact with the master. Furthermore, the institutionalization of charismatic memory is a perennial source of fragmentation, since the death of the Sufi master frequently leads to the splintering of his followers into multiple organizations. To analogize this pattern with what we have seen among the Andalusi music associations is not to deny that the agonistic and fissionary tendencies here are similar to what one finds in vastly different musical worlds—see, for example, the tradition of rock band break-ups in Britain and North America. But while fragmentation may be built into repetitive collective music-making and other forms of institutionalized sociality, the resemblance between fissionary associative life and the traditional sacred realms of Maghribi society is striking.

Scission is usually interpreted in two contrasting ways among practitioners and observers. On the one hand, I have sometimes encountered laments about the breaking apart of an association, particularly associations that were previously dominant or even alone on the scene. These regrets have usually been voiced by people closely connected to the "mother" association who feel that it should have remained unified. I have also heard this kind of complaint from musical authorities who view the proliferation of associations as the work of people who falsely consider themselves capable of becoming transmitters of musical knowledge; from this criticism comes the recurring notion that state authorities ought to intervene to keep unqualified people from becoming teachers. Similarly negative takes on scission are sometimes voiced by outsiders to the associative movement, who see the proliferation of associations as a sign of weakness and selfishness and believe that unification of efforts would make for a healthier musical practice. One young musician explained to me: "We are conservative. The problem is that there are many versions. What we need to do is assemble everyone and figure out one version. If people keep doing what they're doing, even if you have only one version today in a few decades there will be thirty versions."[112]

In contrast to this nightmare vision of proliferating versions, of endless *nathr*, in which associations that allegedly received their pieces from the same chain of transmission play things differently from one another, stands a more benign view of the phenomenon. An association that gave rise to many other associations is sometimes understood as fecund: indeed, to call an association the "mother" of all the others is to say that it is a progenitor. One Algerois enthusiast pointed out to me that in the post-1980 moment of associative activity, the municipal conservatory gave rise to the Fekhardjia, which gave rise to Essoundoussia, which gave rise to Inchirah; El Djazaïria-El Mossilia, for its part, gave rise to the various associations in the vicinity of Algiers. In other words, the abundant progeny of these parent institutions is evidence of strength rather than of weakness. Some participants in the associative movement also point out that the existence of competing associations can raise the level of musical performance for everyone, just as the retrospective understanding of the interwar Algiers scene as a struggle between Jews and Muslims is sometimes understood in musically positive terms. And it is natural for pieces to change through acts of correction, innovation, simple drift, and confusion.

In these two contradictory interpretations of scission, then, we can hear an echo of the counterpoint between consolidation and fragmentation that we find in other realms of Andalusi musical practice. The model of musical personhood is all about the consolidation of musical knowledge. Taken to its extreme, however, consolidation is the hoard. But if consolidation is not to be self-defeating, it requires diffusion, transmission, circulation. And with this comes the inevitable danger of loss and deformation. Hence the extreme caution counseled by various musical authorities with regard to the mechanics and protocol of transmission, including within the ranks of the associations themselves, as well as the call for constant, disciplined critique.

At the same time, it is important to listen to another criticism of the associations that cuts deeper—the claim that associations are not the true locus of musical authenticity, and that what one critic called "the natural habitat" of this music has been lost. This complaint usually comes from people who are outside the associative milieu, and in some instances it stems from a perception that association leaders exploit the memory of *shuyūkh* for their personal gain when in fact the *shuyūkh* belong to everyone. Such a critique contains elements of class resentment, and those who make it also hint that associations are too closed and self-sufficient: rather than promoting an interface between musicians and a broad public in the context of weddings and other festivities, they turn Andalusi music into an insular performance of amateurs playing essentially for one another. One middle-aged critic in Oran, a music-lover from outside the associative movement, suggested that association leaders use the memory of *shuyūkh* "to attract people and make it look like they [the associations] have things." He drew an analogy to the realm of industry, proposing that *shuyūkh* outside the associations are populist artisans, like someone who makes pottery by hand, while the associations are like a factory with machinery that turns out thousands of pieces at a time: "The authenticity is more with the *shuyūkh* who are based in the popular neighborhood [*ḥōma*]—they aren't known except for among the people of the neighborhood. They play in the weddings, you have to go to them, and they'll give things. It's not the associations' right to say things go this way or that."

Another critic, this time in Oujda, counseled me to not only spend time with the associations but to seek out "the real old musicians." The terms of the opposition implied by this statement are telling: associations are linked chiefly to young people, while for this connoisseur the "old musicians" carry greater weight and prestige. And occasionally older musicians themselves, even those who are part of associations, express resentment over the preponderance of young women in the associative movement. Thus, while the association is often presented as modernist, rationalized, open, youthful, and disinterested, against the archaic, traditional, closed, aged, and avaricious *shaykh* and professional ensemble, the qualities attributed to the latter can in fact carry a positive valence of authenticity for some. Thus once again we face the agonistic relationship between *shaykh* and *mūlū'*—in this instance, not the *shaykh* who is embedded in the association through its name, but the *shaykh* who escapes the net of the associations and their *mélomanes*.

This critique in many ways rubs against the grain of what was presented in this chapter, in which the *shaykh* was central to the creation of the association form and in fact came to be produced and reproduced through associative activities. But this critique gets at an important point: that despite the close interweaving of *shaykh* and association, the relationship remains unsettled. Like a lost section of the *nūba*, the *shaykh* escapes the association's act of *tadwīn*, constantly pushing authenticity just outside the frame, constantly deferring any final agreement, standing as the precious but out-of-reach source. Just outside the bounds of the association are "the old men," sitting on their park benches, speaking with one another, reminiscing about their musical past as both professionals and association members, trading in their secrets.

7

The Politics of Patrimony

In the final days of 1964, just two and half years after Algeria had achieved independence from France, the Central Orienting Commission of the National Liberation Front (FLN) hosted a conference at the Hotel El-Riath at Sidi Fredj, just west of Algiers. It was here at this beach in 1830 that the first French troops had disembarked to launch the conquest of Ottoman Algiers. Now, some 134 years later, Algerians were gathering under the auspices of the revolutionary body that had led the independence movement and which now stood at the head of a free republic.

Of the many pressing issues that faced the new polity after eight devastating years of war, the conference participants gathered to discuss not agriculture, industry, Arabization, finance, housing, or reforestation, but music. For those present, there was nothing whimsical about this choice. In the words of the conference president, Abderrahmane Benhamida, who had only recently served as the first post-independence Minister of Education, Algeria is a country "rich in cultural patrimony," and "a revolution cannot be complete unless it ensures its own cultural revolution."[1] For the participants, years of war, generations of colonial oppression, a steady inflow of foreign sounds, and endemic elitism, commercialism, and greed had led to a profound need for musical renewal. In the words of the conference's secretary general,

> Let us not be afraid to say it plainly: Our musical patrimony is in danger, our classical music is moribund, our folklore agonizes, our national music is non-existent and remains to be created, and we are invaded by cheapness, adulterated songs and imported ballads, not to speak of frenetic parties organized for a privileged class at 5,000 Algerian dinars entrance fee at some seaside spa.[2]

The music under discussion over the three days of the conference covered a range of regions, styles, and languages: Bedouin music from the plains, Kabyle music from the mountains, *chaabi* from the Casbah of Algiers, and "modern music" from the airwaves and recording studios. But pride of place was given to what the conference-goers alternately called Algerian-Andalusi music, Algerian classical music, or simply *andalou*. The rapporteur for the committee on Andalusi music, Mahmoud Bouayed, standing before an audience that included Abderrezak Fekhardji, musical director of the Arab orchestra at Radio Algiers, and his disciple Sid Ahmed Serri, emphasized the fragility of this vocal and instrumental repertoire and its quasi-miraculous survival into the present:

> Transmitted by oral tradition for centuries, the repertoire has, alas, lost many parts of its whole, but what remains still constitutes a monument worthy of admiration, respect, and vigilance. Today, fifteen modes remain of the twenty-four originally known. And of these fifteen modes, twelve guarded their complete noubas. If we do not take care, the degradation will continue, and the few positive results attained by men of good will shall not suffice to avert the disaster. Already, each master who disappears brings with him a part of this patrimony.[3]

Nationalism is a familiar story for many scholars, and it is possible and even fruitful to hear Bouayed's words as an Algerian domestiation of a state-centered patrimonial ideology that originated elsewhere. Yet as the preceding chapters have demonstrated, this was an old, homegrown discourse that in many respects predated the rise of the nationalist movement. Indeed, as a member of an established family of *mélomanes* from Tlemcen, Bouayed had grown up within a milieu in which the hoarding *shaykh* was already a potent figure: the masters had been pulling parts of the patrimony into their graves for some time, and it is even possible to hear in Bouayed's statement that "the repertoire has, alas, lost many parts of its whole" a calque on an *inqilāb* in the mode *jarka*, whose title, "Yā asafī ʿalā mā maḍā," derives from its opening line:

> Alas for what has passed,
> the time that has perished,
> the days of pleasure and contentment:
> the evening has slipped away from us
> O lost dwelling-places of al-Andalus . . .[4]

Does learning to hear "Yā asafī" as a source for Bouayed's comments help? I believe it does, in that it introduces another way to think about the state in relation to Andalusi music. This chapter suggests that state institutions have been powerfully shaped by the actions of individuals and collectivities at its margins—individuals and collectivities long engaged in a project of revival that involved an amplification of already existing relations of musical production. In this analysis, the state does matter, but as a potentially powerful resource in the project of *tadwīn* rather than as a hegemon. This reading neither melts away the boundary between the inside and the outside of the state, nor rigidifies that boundary. It is in this space of ambiguity and specificity that the following pages dwell: the competition over legitimate connoisseurship, the shifting line between the "social" hoard and the "individual" hoard, the oblique critique of mainstream nationalist narratives regarding decolonization, the "redemption" of musical knowledge from its bearers, and the attempt to create a listening public that practitioners might deem worthy of the repertoire.

Patrimonial Anxieties

If it is true that the *nūba* had its roots in medieval courtly life, then in some sense representatives of the state have been involved in its production since its emergence as a form. Even if we confine ourselves to the historical record from the Maghrib, heads of state were patrons of musicians specializing in the *nūba* tradition in the nineteenth century. The last Dey of Algiers, for example, patronized Hadj Brahim, who Christianowitsch identified as the leading exponent of the *nūba* in mid nineteenth-century Algiers.[5] It was not, however, an exclusively courtly music: as far as can be surmised, heads of state engaged with *nūba* traditions as patrons and enthusiasts, albeit especially exalted ones. Furthermore, the state does not appear to have actively attempted to shape this kind of music, even if in the Moroccan case we can find examples of courtly performance affecting the broader musical practice.[6] The notion of a musical or broader "cultural" policy seems to be a peculiarity of a larger, more intrusive species of state that in the North African context was first introduced by the French, even if there are tantalizing hints of the involvement of the *'ulamā'* in efforts to preserve the Andalusi repertoire in Ottoman Algiers.[7]

The French colonial state, beginning in earnest in the 1850s, played a central role in the development of the patrimonial apparatus that would eventually come to include Andalusi music. But as suggested in chapter 4, French governmental engagement with Andalusi music per se was fairly oblique until the turn of the twentieth century. Salvador Daniel was closely tied to government circles through friendship and publication venues, and Christianowitsch interacted with officials at the Algiers Library and Museum. Later in the century, figures such as Delphin and Guin were government employees, and the same was true for turn-of-the-century figures like Sonneck, Desparmet, Aboura, Ben Smaïl, and Bouali. But it was only at the turn of the century, in large part due to the ethos of the Jonnart administration, that the government came to be a patron of the Andalusi revivalist scene, and a fairly modest one at that: government officials published Bouali's book, helped organize the Congress of Orientalists where Desparmet and Rouanet presented their work, paid Bouali's and Desparmet's salaries, and subscribed to Rouanet and Yafil's *Répertoire*.

State entanglement with Andalusi music intensified with the efflorescence of the associative movement during the interwar period. Some of this entanglement was due to government suspicion of associative activities. Association El Djazaïria captured the attention of officials on suspicion of engaging in political activity, and El Moutribia's theatrical experiments under the direction of Mahieddine Bachetarzi veered into the politically suspect territory of social critique, thereby training government surveillance on the tenor. On the other hand, Andalusi music was not in itself a controversial genre in the eyes of colonial authorities, who were more concerned with the satirical bite of colloquial theater and topical compositions.[8] More significant for governmental engagement with Andalusi music was the sense of the administrators' competition with both the associative movement itself and the neighboring French colonial regimes in Morocco and Tunisia, as well as the Spanish Protectorate in Morocco's north.[9] The authorities in Algeria were profoundly self-conscious regarding the morale and image of France's oldest Maghribi possession, and the policies of their counterparts to the east and west both heightened such self-consciousness and prompted new interventions in the aesthetic realm. In this sense, the colonial administrations considered the various *nūba* traditions to be fundamentally linked, sociologically parallel, and politically meaningful.

Two of the French administration's international initiatives that bracketed the 1930s give a sense of the changing concerns and interests that animated and shaped colonial policy at this time. The Congress of Arab Music, held in Cairo in 1932, brought musicians from across the Arab world face-to-face with leading European musicologists, and the gathering garnered considerable coverage in the European and Arab press.[10] Seven years later, in 1939, the Congress of Moroccan Music brought European musicologists and Maghribi performers to Fes. The reaction of the Algerian administration to these two events displays their swiftly evolving concern to simultaneously dampen any hint of nationalist activity and promote the French colonial mission via the state patrimonial project.[11]

In the lead-up to the Cairo Congress, the colonial authorities in Algeria were reluctant to send a delegation of musicians to a metropolis that they imagined to swarm with agitators seeking to spread "pan-Arab propaganda that works in concert with a Communist propaganda adapted to the Oriental mentality."[12] Nevertheless, the dispatch of the Algerian delegation, at whose musical head stood the esteemed Cheikh Larbi, was ultimately deemed desirable for a variety of diplomatic and political reasons. Among them was the wish to show that France's century-long presence was beneficial to Algerian artistic production. The group's financial delegate, Si Mohammed Ben Abdallah of Tlemcen, was charged with delivering the Arabic address for the Algerian delegation, and the proposed statement illustrates some of the considerations that militated for participation:

> In Algeria, the local music, which is above all of a Hispano-Mauresque cast with a few distant Turkish echoes, has not been neglected by the administration. It is for this reason that it charged trained scholars with the gathering and notation of all the popular melodies, a collection that today constitutes an imposing compilation. And it is for this reason that various associations in Algiers, including El Andalousia, El Moutribia, El Djezairia, give periodic concerts, teach the playing of instruments, the art of song, and have the honor to be broadcast. . . . These musical demonstrations are especially well loved by the listeners.[13]

It is testament to the degree of political anxiety in government circles that an official from the Office of Indigenous Affairs suggested that Ben Abdallah's remarks be "reduced to a few official banalities, in order to avoid all involuntary digressions of speech, susceptible to being unfavorably interpreted."[14] Yet Ben Abdallah's proposed comments were very much in keeping with the behind-the-scenes reasoning that decided the colonial officials in favor of sending the Algerian delegation to Cairo in the first place. An unsigned note looked forward to the Congress as an opportunity to find some direction in the larger project of "renewing Arab music":

> It would appear that, in the colony at least, the native music has for a long time been in a state of regression. The themes become more and more impoverished, the technical ability of its performers diminishes each day, and there remains nothing but some vague monotonous echoes of the beautiful melodies of Hispano-Mauresque inspiration that were once the charm of Algerian music. It would be desirable for the question to be examined by the [Cairo] conference, with a view to establishing a program for renewal and of conducting studies of the situation of the local music in the three [Maghrib] countries.[15]

In the end, the French authorities in Egypt who had encouraged Algerian participation were not disappointed. While the Arab participants were said to have strongly rejected the notion of bringing their musical traditions into congruity with European music theory, the Congress participants from Egypt and the other Arab countries were able to see that "France, far from annihilating the customs and traditions of the peoples who she protects, on the contrary puts all its efforts into developing and encouraging them. This Oriental demonstration will have therefore served our interests in an indirect but very appreciable fashion."[16] For the colonial authorities, then, the Cairo Congress turned out to be a public relations coup. What is more, the Algerian participants kept to themselves, without having any contact with "Egypt's doubtful elements."[17]

In 1939, the French authorities in Algeria were considerably less hesitant to send delegations to the Fes Congress, held during the festivities surrounding the birthday of the Prophet. Nevertheless, the fears and desires of the authorities remained. They were particularly self-conscious with regard to the French Protectorate in Morocco. The Protectorate authorities, under the command of Resident-General Louis Lyautey (1854–1934), had from the beginning adopted a paternalistic conservationism vis-à-vis Moroccan arts and institutions, with the Sultanate itself being the most dramatic example of the policy and ideology of museumification.[18] From textiles to musical arts to historic buildings, the French authorities in Morocco attempted to painstakingly differentiate themselves from the excesses of colonial conquest and domination in Algeria. Likely in a spirit of administrative competition, the Office of Indigenous Affairs in Algiers advised the director of the Governor-General's office that "[the] presence of Algerian artists at this Congress would indeed be most desirable, public opinion too often having the tendency to charge the native arts and letters in Algeria with decadence."[19] At the same time, it was inadvisable to send any of the associations to Fes, a city known to be "an acutely sensitive Muslim center, where influences that are hostile toward our domination are active."[20] Instead, the official provided a list of individual professional musicians who he deemed "indifferent to politics."[21]

As for the French Protectorate authorities in Morocco, like their counterparts in the northern Spanish zone they showed themselves to be deeply invested in the conservation of the Andalusi musical repertoire.[22] The congress came a decade after the Trois Journées de Musique Marocaine, a symposium in Rabat organized by the Protectorate's Service des Arts Indigènes in April 1928, at which the Association Andalouse of Oujda had performed to great effect.[23] In 1939, the Protectorate authorities' announcement regarding the congress summarized the project in vivid terms, describing it as part of a larger cultural renaissance:

> For several years, a specific effort has been made, under the encouragements of the Protectorate and the Makhzen [the Moroccan government], with a view toward safeguarding the classic themes of Andalusi music and Berber music from oblivion and alteration. The closer study that was recently made has notably permitted the reconstitution of the eleven *noubas* that are favored in the cultivated circles of the Arab bourgeoisie of Fes, Rabat, and Sale, and the identification of the indigenous orchestras that today carry the pure Andalusi musical traditions.

The announcement continued with a description of the parallel efforts to create "a complete written notation of the classical themes."[24] And a report on the Congress by the playwright and translator Guillot de Saix, reprinted in the left-wing *Alger Républicain*, put the cultural politics of the Protectorate authorities in even starker terms that echoed the medieval European parallel articulated nearly eighty years earlier by Salvador Daniel, and that invoked the ingathering of scattered objects so central to *tadwīn*:

> Through this first Congress, the government of the Protectorate intends to save the Moroccan soul in its most subtle, powerful form of expression—music—as it has already done for the other indigenous arts. . . . At the very foundation of Andalusi music is the poem of the ancient poets, similar to the Greek bards. Just as our *trouvères* and troubadours sang their verses, these are the remains of compositions that form the folklore that is still scattered through Morocco. It is important to establish a revised collection of the old texts of Haïk and of the entire popular repertoire that has not been conserved except piecemeal through the oral tradition.[25]

While the Fes Congress dovetailed with the larger aims of the upper-level colonial authorities, including the Spanish Protectorate authorities based in Tetuan, it also dovetailed with those of various elite North African *nūba* enthusiasts who were invited to attend (some of whom, of course, were themselves government employees). The scholarly presentations were fairly evenly divided between Europeans and North Africans. The former hailed from the Protectorate apparatus and the Paris musicological world, while the latter were drawn from Moroccan conservatories and the circles of both Algerian and Moroccan *nūba* enthusiasts. Among the Algerians were four from Tlemcen: Si Mohamed and Ahmed Ben Ghabrit, employees of the Protectorate authorities, members of the organizing committee for the Fes conference,[26] and key *mélomanes* and pioneers of the Tlemcen tradition in Morocco; Mohamed Ben Smaïl; and Mohamed Zerrouki, a scholarly *mélomane* who a few years earlier had spoken eloquently of the place of Andalusi music in modern Algeria at the Cercle des Jeunes Algériens. At the Congress, Ben Smaïl headed l'Andaloussia during several well-received performances, and was scheduled to make a presentation of the *nūbāt* transcribed in Tlemcen by the late Mostefa Aboura.[27]

Clearly there was extensive overlap between the aims of Algerians like Zerrouki and Ben Smaïl and the colonial authorities who helped organize the conference. However, there is also evidence that it was precisely this sort of overlap that unnerved the colonial officials. It was Zerrouki's Moroccan counterparts who at that same moment were making the Protectorate authorities concerned to preserve the Andalusi musical patrimony of Fes. For just as preparations for the Fes Congress were unfolding, officials in Rabat were seriously discussing the need to record the Moroccan Andalusi repertoire. One official wrote that due to the worldwide economic depression and the growth of the transistor radio, many musicians were unemployed, so that certain parts of the repertoire were becoming lost and other parts were known only by a few aging masters. Among them was Mohamed Brihi (al-Brīhī) of Fes, who was well past the age of sixty: "When he [Brihi] passes," one high-ranking official wrote, "a part of Andalusi music, so appreciated by the Moroccans, will be irredeemably lost, and it will not be possible to organize concerts that respond in their variety and quality to the legitimate demands of the Muslim listeners, who would not fail to accuse the administration of losing this 'national artistic patrimony.'"[28]

Thus in both Morocco and Algeria in the 1930s, we can find a growing sense among French colonial officials that they stood in competition with the patrimonial efforts of indigenous aficionados of Andalusi music. The increasingly vigorous engagement of colonial officials in Algeria with the local and national musical terrain was in part an attempt to catch up with the neighboring administrations and in part an attempt to tame the creative powers of the indigenous population. Looking back on the censored Arabic statement at the Cairo Congress, perhaps its offensiveness lay in the way that it highlighted the activities of the amateur associations rather than the support of the authorities. We can conceptualize the increasing interventionism of the French authorities in Algeria as an attempt to wrest some of the prestige and ebullience from the hands of the associations—organizations that sometimes also posed a deeper challenge to the colonial government with regard to Algeria's political future. In other words, colonial officials came to see themselves as guardians of indigenous patrimony because they saw that if they did not guard it, elements from outside the state apparatus would, potentially setting up their own state-like apparatus in the process. The patrimonial cause thus came to be an arena for the exertion and contestation of sovereign power.

The State as *Mélomane* at Midcentury

The complex relationship with *mélomanes* helped to increase governmental involvement in Andalusi music and in the process rendered that relationship more complex. On the one hand, government officials viewed themselves as locked in competition with the work of the associations and non-state revivalists. At the same time, one governmental strategy was to insinuate the state into the efforts of the non-state actors. Complicating this situation still further was the fact that non-state revivalists routinely turned to the state for support, and indigenous Algerians inside the state apparatus were often themselves *mélomanes*. In revivalist circles at midcentury, the state was not a distant monolith. Rather, there existed in many places a porous boundary between the state and the inhabitants of the Andalusi archipelago.

By the start of the Second World War, state officials in Algeria had developed a hands-on approach to musical intervention. One variety of intervention was the repeated attempt to blend European and North African Andalusi musical traditions in performance, some of which came from state officials and some from lower-level actors themselves. The public performances of 1927 that sparked Rouanet's denunciation of Yafil featured the Algiers municipal orchestra playing music written by Yafil as well as arrangements of Algerian Andalusi repertoire for European orchestra.[29] Nine years later, a live radio broadcast in Blida featured members of the local Société El-Ouidadia and assorted amateurs from the town, as well as a recitation of Victor Hugo's Orientalist poem, "L'an neuf de l'hégire."[30] In Morocco, where Protectorate cultural policy tended toward conservation rather than fusion, the gala concert that closed the Congress of Moroccan Music in Fes in 1939 nevertheless featured a European-style orchestra performing from transcriptions of *nūbāt* from the *āla* repertoire and "European music of Moroccan inspiration," in addition to performances by professional ensembles from Fes, Tlemcen, Algiers, Tunis, and the Sultan's court.[31] In some respects these look like anti-purist efforts. However, as touched upon in chapter 1, we can view purism and fusion as complementary: in order to undertake effective fusion, there must be a clear conceptual separation of the practices that are to be brought together.

Such efforts came to be furthered at Radio Algiers in the early years of the Second World War, with a clear nod to their political implications. The interventionist stance was articulated in embryonic form in a proposal stemming from the office of the Vichy-appointed Governor-General Abrial in September 1940. For the unnamed official, the Cairo and Fes congresses had "illuminated . . . the value of music as an aid to propaganda," and demonstrated

> the lively interest that various governments attach to the maintenance and renewal of local folklores. . . . One of the conclusions adopted by the Congress of Fes emphasized the need to gather Hispano-Mauresque music and codify it, before one can hope to attain a lasting artistic evolution guided in the direction of a modern-spirited musical creativity and an assimilation of French art.

While codification had already begun in the neighboring countries "thanks to the remarkable government-supported efforts pursued by the Baron d'ERLANGER in Tunis and by Mr. Alexis CHOTTIN in Rabat," in Algeria "this project of renewal has, until now, been the object of but a few scattered efforts without a future," chief among these alleged failures being the work of Yafil. In light of these deficiencies, the proposal continued, the Service for Muslim Broadcasts at Radio Algiers "has tried to become involved with this work of artistic renewal, with the view of putting it under the patronage of the administration and taking it out of the hands of private initiatives that are not inspired solely by the general interest." For "diverse technical and material reasons," however, the efforts had not succeeded. The wartime presence in Algiers of the French musician Jacqueline Maire therefore presented a unique opportunity to orchestrate Andalusi music for a French orchestra—an effort that Maire had already in fact begun, with the plan of performing the music with Mahieddine Bachetarzi as vocalist. This concert program promised to highlight two truncated *nūbāt*, ending with a modern orchestral composition "inspired by folklore." The proposal cited two goals:

> On the one hand it will reveal to French listeners a folklore that until now is little known because it is poorly presented by routine artists who play it on insufficient instruments with more sincerity than skill. It will show to the indigenous populations of the cities—very proud of their traditional music—all of this music's possibilities when it is performed by musicians worthy of the name. Furthermore, it will indicate once more, through actions, that the Algerian Administration is interested in these questions concerning art to the same degree as the governments of the neighboring Protectorates; that everywhere, it is French thought, it is French methods, it is French women and French men who are the upholders of all the good that Arab civilization has left behind.[32]

Thus the state intervention into Andalusi musical practice was not only a question of blending traditions in performance, nor only of taking over the project of *tadwīn*, but also of bringing modernist methods identified with France into the performative and textual space of the practice. In this spirit, the Centre d'Information et d'Etudes at the Direction des Affaires Musulmanes soon charged Maire "with the mission of collecting and transcribing the Algerian-Andalusi Arab folklore through the modern notational system and in collaboration with local Muslim musicians," at whose head stood Mahieddine Lakehal of Blida. The representatives of Radio Algiers viewed the collaboration as a success, citing the fact that "notables from numerous cities are already asking the favor of the collaboration of the French orchestra directed by Mrs. MAIRE on the occasion of the charity events being organized in various parts of the country."[33]

Radio Algiers' role in the newly emboldened interventionist efforts of the colonial administration was also important to discussions of Andalusi musical performance outside the realm of explicit fusion with European musical practice. A major report on the "Muslim broadcasts" at the radio, dated April 1940—several months before the rise of the Vichy regime—lamented the decadence into which "the urban music of Algiers" had plunged, a state of affairs made manifest through a variety of shortcomings. These included extensive linguistic ignorance among singers; the abandonment of traditional instruments such as the *rabāb* and *kuwītra* in favor of instruments such as the piano, banjo, and *darbūka* (the last viewed by the anonymous author of the report as an importation from the Arab East); the dispersion of the best performers among the myriad rival associations that had sprung up; and the failure of professional musicians to either make a living or, thanks to their mediocrity, retain a faithful audience, such that the public was beginning to turn to "Oriental music" (in other words, *sharqī*). Finally, the report lamented that only a few singers still knew the entire repertoire, meaning that orchestras were continually limited to repeating the errors found in Yafil's collection.

The report proposed six remedies. The first was to require associations and professional ensembles in Algiers to contribute their best members to an orchestra that would be created under Radio Algiers' supervision. The report excluded those associations and ensembles comprising a Jewish majority, claiming that in such cases the correction of "faults" (likely in pronunciation) would be "practically unattainable." The second remedy would be to require the abandonment of the new instruments in favor of the old. The third would establish a supervisor for radio concerts who would attend the rehearsals of the guest ensembles, correct their errors, and make sure that "classical pieces" be sung only by those with a good knowledge of literary Arabic; in addition, the supervisor would be in charge of "reviving" lost repertoire in a purified textual form. The fourth called for the establishment of subventions and awards for those who assist in "the renewal of native arts." The fifth suggested that guest teachers from the Moroccan conservatories introduce modes that are unknown in Algeria, or reintroduce modes that had been lost, thereby enriching the "limited" Algerian repertoire and providing an alternative to the

Middle Eastern music that was then gaining in popularity. Finally, the report proposed inviting selected ensembles from the Tlemcen and Constantine regions to play at Radio Algiers for the sake of stylistic variety.[34]

At least one of these recommendations bore fruit when, several years later, the Radio Algiers Arab orchestra was founded under the leadership of Mohamed Fekhardji, who by this time had separated himself from direct involvement in the associations.[35] But beyond any immediate results, the existence of these recommendations shows that the colonial government had by this time adopted a strongly interventionist stance vis-à-vis Andalusi music in the capital. The authorities were not only offering a new form of patronage, performance venue, and music, but were also setting themselves up as arbiters of purity and remunerators of obedience. Rather than the grudging acceptance of Algerian participation in the Cairo Congress shown in 1932 and a wariness regarding the associations, by 1940 there was at least the outline of an aggressive policy of paternalistic uplift, reform, and diffusion that did not hesitate to intrude into the associative and professional life of musicians. In other words, the state was beginning to take on the role of *mélomane*, and at least with respect to the rhetoric of musical reform, there was little difference between the servants of the Third Republic and Vichy.

But just as it was often impossible to separate indigenous aficionados from colonial authorities in the run-up to the Fes Congress, in that some of the authorities were in fact indigenous aficionados, the assumption of the role of *mélomane* by state actors associated with Radio Algiers at midcentury was in part a reflection of the entry of indigenous Andalusi music practitioners (including both performers and aficionados) into the state's orbit. Mohamed Fekhardji, who as head of the Radio Algiers Arab orchestra would have a profound effect on musical practice until his death in 1956, is the most obvious example. No less important was the presence of El-Boudali Safir, a young writer and teacher from Mascara who quickly rose to become secretary general for Arabic and Kabyle broadcasting in the post-Second World War era, and who oversaw the creation of the radio orchestras devoted to Andalusi music, "modern" Algerian music, and *chaabi*.[36] El-Boudali Safir quickly made a name for himself both as a musical organizer and as a commentator upon musical matters from within the state apparatus. In other words, by the 1940s Radio Algiers had come to incorporate indigenous Algerians into some key positions. As we will see in the following section, the incorporation of Andalusi performers and aficionados into the state apparatus at midcentury would play an important part in establishing continuity between pre- and post-independence debates and policies regarding musical production.

Mélomanes and *Citoyens*: Planning for Music at Independence

As the opening pages of this chapter suggest, it is no exaggeration to say that in post-independence Algeria music was among the very first objects of "cultural" debate. Andalusi music was seized upon as a national classical music, much as had been the case in Morocco and Tunisia. Although the term "Algerian classical music" was embraced, the Andalusi connection proved remarkably uncontroversial, and the sense that this was a natural candidate for a national classical canon was widely shared. In some respects, Andalusi music took the place of European classical music in the post-independence discourse, but this replacement was also an expression of kinship: Andalusi music was understood as the authentic, local equivalent of the European classical canon, and was even viewed as a genetic relative of that canon, so that Ziryāb's pedagogical techniques could be held up as a forerunner to modern Western European conservatory practices and the *nūba* could be presented as ancestor to the symphonic form.[37] For many people, Andalusi music was an aspect of the Algerian "personality" that represented an element of continuity with the precolonial past and was therefore deserving of solicitude.

At the same time, Andalusi music represented an element of continuity with the late colonial era. Such continuity was due in part to the presence of people who straddled the pre- and post-independence milieu. As shown in the preceding chapter, many of the people who had been active in the pre-independence musical circles took the lead in the post-independence moment. With regard to the state apparatus as well, certain individuals continued to exert a strong influence on musical policies and taste-making. El-Boudali Safir provides a striking example of this. Named as a cultural attaché at the French Ministry of Foreign Affairs in Paris in 1959, he returned to Algeria after independence and dove headlong into musical matters.[38] Among the first activities in which he engaged was the El Riath conference of 1964, where Safir was one of ten members of the committee on Andalusi music, alongside Serri and Fekhardji. Safir would also go on to play an important role in the organization of the first post-independence state-run Andalusi music festival in 1967.

The Colloque of 1964 at El Riath provides a particularly vivid picture of debates about music in the wake of 1962. The country was still in the throes of demographic, economic, and political instability, and six months after the conference Ahmed Ben Bella's government would be overthrown by Houari Boumédienne and his allies. In the midst of great uncertainty, the Colloque marked the first time since the end of the hostilities that Algerians officially gathered to specifically discuss and plan artistic policy. Such a focus on "cultural" matters did not come out of the blue. The Colloque convened in the wake of the promulgation of the Algiers Charter, which had been adopted at a major FLN gathering some eight months earlier. The Algiers Charter of 1964 was an important early articulation of independent Algeria's ideological and policy orientation as a socialist, anticolonial state, and it was a document that partially linked the Ben Bella and Boumédienne eras.[39] It laid out a vision of Algerian history that was both primordialist (reaching back, for example, to the ancient Berber kingdom of Numidia) and highly detailed with regard to the more recent history of French colonialism and decolonization. The concept of the past as a societal heritage weaves its way through the document, whose memorable opening line reads, "A revolution never constitutes a brutal and total rupture with the past." What the Charter calls "Algerian culture" plays an important role in the larger project of renewal that it advocates, and the document calls for that culture to be "national, revolutionary, and scientific." At the head of this program is the Arabic language, which the Charter describes as a "national patrimony" that holds the key to the authentic Algerian personality, and that ought to be the rightful possession of all as opposed to a luxury for a closed sector of society.[40]

The discussion of Arabic in the Algiers Charter foreshadowed the discussion of music a few months later.[41] But another crucial predecessor to the Colloque, and one that in some respects can be viewed as a source for the Algiers Charter itself, was a talk given by the Marxist intellectual Bachir Hadj Ali in February 1964 at the Salle Ibn Khaldoun, just one month before the FLN congress that adopted the Algiers Charter convened in the very same hall. As head of the Algerian Communist Party, which at that time was being legislated out of existence, Hadj Ali was in some ways on the left fringe of public discourse. At the same time, he was close to other Marxist intellectuals in the circle of President Ben Bella who would soon have a major role in shaping the Algiers Charter. That Hadj Ali would devote considerable attention to music in the midst of the instability of the Ben Bella period is noteworthy, and it is a topic that he would return to later in life after his release from a harrowing period in prison.[42] His 1964 talk, "What is a national music?," was a wide-ranging and sophisticated treatment of the Algerian musical question, with particular attention to the Andalusi repertoire. It was also an opportunity for the veterans of the associative movement to come out of the woodwork after years of violent political upheaval: Abderrezak Fekhardji, Sid Ahmed Serri, and other members of El Djazaïria-El Mossilia performed Andalusi repertoire following the conclusion of Bachir Hadj Ali's remarks.

The substance of the presentation dwelled on the question of music as an aspect of Algerian society, and, as the title suggests, the possibilities for the development of a national music. For this son of Kabyle migrants to the Algiers Casbah, the Andalusi repertoire represented the basis for a potential national music to be elaborated in the future. For Hadj Ali, this would be the work of "an independent and socialist Algeria." But first it was necessary "to save from shipwreck this musical heritage in order to make it the fundamental basis for future creations. Our music is being lost, like land washed away into the sea. We rightly reforest the mountains. We also need to save from degradation the subtlest expression of our soul."[43]

Hadj Ali identified several causes for the "disappearance of a part of our musical resources." First among these was the lack of writing. Oral tradition was simply "incapable of transmitting" music over the generations, either in its popular form or, even more, "in a work so monumental as the *noubats* of Granada."[44] Second, the Andalusi migrants found Algeria to be in a state of decline on their arrival.[45] This situation was later exacerbated by French colonialism and the resulting deterioration of the bourgeois and petit-bourgeois classes who had traditionally "cultivated" this music. "[This] music . . . declined with them," so that its small public became smaller still, the number of *nūbāt* shrank, movements were lost, instrument-makers disappeared, and "modern instruments" entered the ensembles to deleterious effect. An "individualist spirit" took over, and

> the great interpreters died without transmitting their repertoire, the secrets of their interpretation, the indications of rhythm, and the words of the melodies. The student was, for them, first and foremost a rival in a society where the learned music, reserved for a small circle of rich city-dwellers, was very much sought after and its performers paid generously.[46]

The lack of notation also led to the choking of the melodies in ornamentation, so that "today it is sometimes difficult to differentiate the *noubats cenaa* [*ṣanʿa*] from the light *noubats* (those of the *neqlabats*) and certain movements derived from the Turkish suites."[47] In addition, the loss of poetic texts and certain melodies led to the calquing of texts on melodies and vice versa, resulting in confusion. To make matters worse, Algerians had been inundated by other musics, including Western and Egyptian repertoires, a situation facilitated and exacerbated by radio, sound recordings, and cinema.[48] These negatively affected the Algerian traditions, with a few exceptions drawn from remote reaches of the country or from Hadj Ali's personal friend and musical hero, Hadj El Anka. Last but not least, previous efforts to "renew" this music using European methods had been doomed to failure, in large part because of the fact that they arose from a situation of colonial domination.[49]

For Bachir Hadj Ali, these problems called for specific solutions, many of them inspired by the Soviet and Eastern European examples. It was crucial to record the Algerian musical tradition in a "rational, systematically coordinated" manner, and in the case of the classical repertoire to call upon "living musical 'libraries'" like Larbi Bensari and Abderrezak Fekhardji.[50] In addition, he called for the establishment of a true national conservatory, where modern musical notation might be put to work and allow Algerian music to catch up with European music.[51] Radio, television, concerts, music education, and sound recordings also had their part to play, including by way of the establishment of a state publishing house for music and the promotion of the use of Algerian music in film soundtracks.[52] Through such strategies, "our people will familiarize themselves with their music. Thus new listening habits will be progressively created, the foundation for a great musical future." In turn, through such safeguard and popularization, as well as judicious attention to foreign musical traditions from Europe, Soviet Asia, China, Turkey, Lebanon, Syria, and Egypt,[53] Algerians will be able to build an authentic musical culture and give rise to new composers who might use the Algerian musical heritage just as Kachaturian did for the Armenian repertoire, or as Beethoven, Verdi, Smetana, and Glinka did for their countries.[54] Finally, for Hadj Ali, it was important to remind his audience that

> [the] presentation and concert of this evening are not shows. . . . [This] demonstration is intended to be an effort that fits into the growing movement for cultural renewal and rebirth. The rising interest in *la musique savante*, the very strong attachment to *chaabi*, testify to a musical reawakening in Algeria, a desire to return to the sources of our national culture. The effort with regard to music is a national task that interests all of us: musicians, musicologists, *mélomanes*, and all citizens. Music is not only a matter for specialists, but is an art of considerable social import. It derives its force from the collective élan of a people. And we form a people who are passionate about music.[55]

Bachir Hadj Ali was not one of the participants in the Colloque several months later, but the conversations of the conference participants closely echoed both his comments and the FLN-backed Algiers Charter. Participants in the three-day conference asserted that music was a key element of the "cultural revolution" that must accompany the larger Algerian revolution.[56] The report of the conference's secretary general emphasized that the work of those in attendance was part of a project of "cultural renewal" to be carried out on a national scale. People from all over the country had come "to debate an art, or better, a means of education and of combat in the cadre of a cultural renewal, taking stock of the national specificities and the construction of a new society, prosperous and happy, where music would no longer be an activity for profit and for lucre, nor the privilege of a caste, nor an instrument of simple moral degeneration and perversion."[57]

The dangers that the secretary general identified came from many sides. One was the unsuccessful effort to "bastardize and pervert" Algerian culture over the course of more than a century of colonial rule. The danger also came from Europe, the U.S., and, echoing Hadj Ali and, before him, Zerrouki, the wider musical market made possible by the radio and the long-playing record. The most immediate danger, however, was the war, which had led to the death of many performers and the collapse of ensembles. The work at El Riath, then, was "a mission of salvage."[58] The secretary general negatively compared Algeria's musical state to Tunisia and Morocco, countries that he said boasted rich and well-conserved traditional musical forms, chief among them Andalusi music, which in Morocco is almost "an official expression of Moroccan music."[59]

The story regarding Andalusi music that found voice at El Riath was largely the standard narrative of resilience coupled with losses sustained by historical vicissitudes and a lack of writing. But the secretary general's discussion of Andalusi music departed somewhat from the usual narrative by way of a tinge of socialist critique: the fact that it was the music "of a minority, of an elite of privileged urbanites, jealous of their culture, their traditions, and often their material comfort" was a problem that demanded attention. The implication was that Andalusi music was bourgeois, a fact which, along with colonialism, had led it to the brink of disaster. But so had the influx of rural people into the cities, as well as the "foreign invasion" of sounds that "find in these new [urban] circles, without urban cultural traditions, without deep musical roots, a particularly favorable terrain."[60]

Thus we can find an odd mix at El Riath. On the one hand, there is a rather puritanical, anti-elitist vision of music that meshed well with elements of the socialist and nationalist ethos that emerged from the war years and found echo in Bachir Hadj Ali's talk. On the other hand, there is a classic *mélomane* position that upholds the sophistication of the urbanite against the rootlessness of the rural migrant and that looks at the professional musician as potentially problematic. Interestingly enough, the secretary general, who was himself from the Algiers region, reserved special criticism for the Algiers school. He lamented the adoption of instruments such as the accordion in its Andalusi musical practice.[61] Furthermore, he asserted that in comparison with Tlemcen and Constantine, the Algiers school lacked unity, suffering from an overabundance of *shuyūkh*. "An effort at coordination, at unification is therefore necessary,"[62] and this unification would depend upon textual work: "We have to start from scratch, to make an inventory of the beautiful works that resisted ruin, and to again place them in the new edifice according to new methods (a remake of diwan Yafil)."[63]

Similarly, the committee to discuss "Algerian classical music," comprised of ten men from Algiers, Tlemcen, and Constantine, emphasized the tasks of safeguard and repertorial instruction and diffusion.[64] This diffusion was the inversion of the sort of diffusion or proliferation that the conference-goers decried, in that it would be tightly controlled and would rely on the state apparatus. In turn, state-directed diffusion would be in sync with the project of unification through a census of surviving works, systematic recording, "graphic fixation" through musical notation, and publication of "judiciously restored" song texts.[65] Instruction was to be achieved through audiovisual aids, conservatories, music schools, and the teaching of solfège in primary schools. Diffusion would rely upon radio, television, recordings, theater, printed material, state encouragement for associations, and national festivals and competitions. These efforts would require the creation of a national conservatory and regional conservatories, as well as a national institute of music that would be in charge of "gathering, recording, selecting, and establishing in their definitive form, and conserving, the works that are recognized as valuable and authentic in classical music and in popular music (Arab, Berber)." The committee members called, too, for the creation of a national recording library as well as a music museum and a national orchestra in the capital that would draw on the best of the regional groups. Finally, the men called for the integration of women into "this effort of restoration and renovation."[66]

The committee ended its report with thoughts concerning the future. They hoped that one day Andalusi music would give rise to a new music, a new national school of composition. The primary task at hand, however, was to conserve it in the purest form possible. "One does not demolish the Alhambra or the Great Mosque of Tlemcen to reconstruct them in concrete!" quipped the rapporteur, invoking the longstanding architectural metaphor for musical patrimony. Rather, Andalusi music must be guarded in a straightforward manner, purifying it of such elements as the oversized orchestra and chorus:

> It must remain the classical music, which is to say the source, the model, the reference. . . . To come back to it as to a pure spring, to give it back to a people who no longer needs ignore it, to leave behind the servile or excessive imitations of foreign musics that are certainly not its equal—this must be the golden rule of the composers whose birth and blossoming our long-frustrated people awaits with an immense and understandable hope.[67]

The evident sense of continuity between the post-independence discourse and the 1940 Radio Algiers report is likewise visible in the third crucial commentary on Andalusi music from the immediate postwar years, Sid-Ahmed Bouali's *Petite introduction à la musique classique algérienne*. Penned by a grandson of Ghouti Bouali, the *Petite introduction* was written on the occasion of Algeria's first national Andalusi music festival that took place in Algiers during Ramadan 1966–67. A poetic evocation of the repertoire's past and future, Sid-Ahmed Bouali's small book is a departure from the more explicit policy formulations of the Colloque and Bachir Hadj Ali's talk. Yet it is very much a continuation of these earlier works, and there is a close link in that its preface was written by Mahmoud Bouayed, the rapporteur for the Andalusi music committee in 1964. Behind Bouali's colorful exploration of the legends of the repertoire's medieval origins lies a strong impulse toward asserting the connection of the repertoire to the broader Arab past rooted in the Mashriq while at the same time asserting the distinctiveness of the Andalusi heritage and its millennial connection to the Maghrib.[68] In addition, Bouali explicitly links the Andalusi musical past to Europe, making Ziryāb a forerunner to the modern European conservatory tradition.[69] Bouali also uses the alleged past of Andalusi music as a way to negotiate the simultaneous link to the elite and to popular classes: according to him, the *nūba* began essentially as a courtly protocol but had already been claimed by commoners and become a "collective creation" in Granada in the two centuries before its fall.[70]

Bouali addresses some of the same concerns raised by Bachir Hadj Ali and the Colloque participants. Here again we find the narrative of decay: the repertoire was maintained in the cities of Maghrib, but the broader decline of the Muslim world and the fact that the music was not written led to its partial loss and to the proliferation of interpretations and localized, national traditions.[71] What is more, Bouali links this failure to notate the music to the tendency of musicians to hoard their knowledge.[72] In other words, rivalries and hoarding led to a failure to write things down, and together these tendencies led to the loss of a large part of the repertoire. As a result, Bouali proposes a continuation of the work of people like Mostefa Aboura and his son Kheireddine, whose transcriptions and collection of musical instruments he gives glimpses of in the pages of his pamphlet. Finally, echoing Bachir Hadj Ali, Bouali touches upon the need to catch up with European music. For Bouali, the tonal and rhythmic complexities of the Andalusi repertoire make wholesale adoption of European methods difficult, and in some ways he seems to suggest that this complexity and resistance to assimilation in fact protect the repertoire's uniqueness.[73] At the same time, the introduction of European-style harmony seems irresistible. In this light, Bouali sees the necessity for a "synthesis" that avoids the twin traps of rigid conservatism and total rejection of Algeria's musical tradition. Taking the lead from Béla Bartók, he ends his essay with the hope that Algerian composers might arise who can follow the Hungarian composer's dictum that "[one] never sings better than within one's genealogical tree." For Bouali, this recalls the image of the *shajarat al-ṭubū'*, the tree of modes, "the symbolic tree of Ziryab," which, "starting from its roots, from this land where our dead sleep, reaches upwards, with a tranquil assurance, to become a soaring, teeming greenness, finally flowers and fruits, heavy with flavors and scents, and shadows fitting for sleep."[74]

Finally, Bouali's work links itself explicitly to works by Europeans writing in the colonial period. His bibliography consists of works by Rouanet, Chottin, the schoolteacher Corcellet, and journalist Jean-Darrouy. None of this is to suggest that Bouali is a shill of the colonial era. In fact, his work is full of the hopefulness of the postwar moment, with its socialist, nationalist, and pan-Arabist tendencies. But his reliance upon these authors points out that for many people independence did not mean a break with the immediate past. And in fact Bouali saw himself as continuing the work of these authors, as well as of Mostefa Aboura. In keeping with the Algiers Charter, we can say that no revolution constitutes a complete rupture with the past.

The *Mélomane* against the State

Some of the suggestions from the Colloque, such as the establishment of a music museum, did not bear fruit. Others, such as the establishment of a national orchestra for Andalusi music, would wait forty years to come to fruition.[75] Still other aspects, however, became reality not long after the Colloque had taken place. The Institut National de la Musique (INM) was founded in 1968,[76] and its first major task was the massive textualization project that sought to replace Yafil's *Majmū'*, resulting in the three volumes of *Al-muwashshaḥāt wa-l-azjāl* discussed in chapter 5. The establishment of national and regional festivals beginning at the end of the 1960s[77]—an activity that was closely tied to El-Boudali Safir in his role as advisor at the state radio and television service—provided an outlet for and goad to associations, and government publications voiced support for their efforts.

But there were many ways in which the embrace of Andalusi music as a quasi-official national classical music did not take place to the satisfaction of its proponents. Such dissatisfaction has waxed and waned, in part following the shifting visions of the role of the state. The late 1960s and the 1970s, for example, saw several large-scale state-directed undertakings, including the creation and publication of *Al-muwashshaḥāt wa-l-azjāl* and several national festivals. This was the height of the era of President Boumédienne, with his highly centralized, paternalistic vision of governance. Many of the major initiatives since the 1980s—such as the proliferation of associations and the various projects to document the repertoire—have been efforts that come from outside the immediate state apparatus, reflecting the move away from heavy-handed state control in post-Boumédienne Algeria. This is not to say that the state has become absent, since associations are ultimately attached to the Ministry of Culture, and state authorities have played an important role in the publication of works such as the 2011 books and recordings on the occasion of Tlemcen's designation as Capital of Islamic Culture. But it is to say that Andalusi musical activities have on the whole followed the arc of more general developments in the relationship between the state and the wider society in post-independence Algeria.

Yet the earlier days of more centralized control evoke a certain gerontocratic wistfulness among many older practitioners, for whom the late 1960s and the 1970s were the halcyon days of Andalusi music. One older self-described *amateur* who sat next to me at a festival in Algiers spoke of the strength of the Andalusi musical movement in earlier years, recalling the festivals of the late 1960s and early 1970s with great passion. For him, it was "the years of difficulty" (in other words, the 1990s) and the increasing demographic pressures in Algeria's cities that put "the great project of restoration" on hold; but "little by little, things are picking up again." For the singer Beihdja Rahal, the audiences of the 1970s "knew how to listen to a whole *nūba*," unlike the audiences she encountered in the early 1990s, who needed to be educated in order to be able to understand the repertoire. Nor is this simply a question of perennial nostalgia for the past. People commenting on Andalusi music in the 1960s viewed what they saw around them as a dramatic revival of interest in Andalusi music, an expansion of its audience, and a generalized awareness of the project of restoration; for Mahmoud Bouayed and Mahieddine Bachetarzi, the rise of a vigorous public for Andalusi music in the 1960s was a pleasant surprise, in that it was a more sizeable and socially diverse audience than Bachetarzi had been accustomed to in the fifteen or twenty years before independence.[78]

But even in this heady moment of maximal state involvement there were hints of dissatisfaction. Take, for example, an early post-independence association only indirectly connected to Andalusi music, the Association Les Amis du Livre, which we first encountered in the preceding chapter. Originally founded in Tlemcen in 1927, Les Amis du Livre was central to the establishment of Association Gharnata in 1964, and its headquarters served as an informal seat for the musical activities of Mohamed Bensari, a son of Cheikh Larbi.[79] In addition, Les Amis du Libre was linked to Kheireddine Aboura, who exhibited his father Mostefa's musical collection at the cultural festival that the association organized in cooperation with the municipal government in 1966.[80] Thus Les Amis du Livre and its offshoot, Gharnata, were in many ways model associations that took the initiative to carry out grassroots organizing. But according to some of its former members, Les Amis du Livre collapsed in 1968, when FLN functionaries transferred the group's library from the association headquarters to a newly built local cultural center.[81] Although Les Amis du Livre was not primarily a musical association, its end and the bitterness that attends the memory of its dissolution highlight the tension over whether it is the state or the association that is the proper guardian of patrimony. The takeover of the association's holdings by the state in the name of patrimonial safeguard was for some members a case of state overreach. Such a narrative suggests a fundamental disagreement about whether it is the state or non-state actors who constitute the rightful and most trustworthy bearers of patrimony.

The reverse perspective on this matter is that associations are not fitting guardians of national patrimony. As shown in the preceding chapter, associations can work against the centralizing, standardizing impulse, since they tend to enshrine an association-specific interpretation of the repertoire. Furthermore, they are hardly mass organizations, either in numbers or ethos. Instead, associations tend to have active memberships of well under one hundred people and are based on face-to-face interactions between and among teachers and students. Nor have associations been immune to accusations of elitism: because music associations often draw their membership and leadership from the upper layers of urban society, some of them have come to resemble the closed milieux decried by Hadj Ali, the Colloque participants, and, for that matter, Yafil in his *Majmūʿ*. Speaking in an interview in 1979, for example, Ahmed Serri felt obliged to defend El Djazaïria-El Mossilia from such charges of elitism, even though the interviewer did not expressly voice them.[82]

Interestingly enough, Serri's defense of the associations in the 1979 interview underlines the fact that they are powered largely on the efforts and treasure of unpaid amateurs; in other words, he implies that the perception of elitism is in fact a result of a lack of sufficient government investment in the musical patrimony. This is in keeping with broader critiques of the state in Andalusi musical circles since that time. While in practice their efforts might appear complementary, association activists have often accused the state of inadequately supporting Andalusi music, either through failure to provide sufficient encouragement to the associations themselves or through failure to properly manage festivals and recordings. In this sense, the state is often described as shirking its role as patron and guardian of the patrimony, meaning that private connoisseurs and performers drawn from the local elite must step in. In other words, it is a question of the state hoard versus the private hoard as guarantor of repertorial continuity.[83]

Serri's more recent efforts to record the entirety of his Algerois repertoire illustrate the agonistic relationship between the state hoard and the private hoard quite vividly. Active members of contemporary Andalusi musical milieux frequently charge the state with failing to adequately recompense master musicians, with the result that they die without having divulged their secrets. In this case, the state is literally failing to pay the *shuyūkh* to relinquish their control over musical knowledge, not unlike Cheikh Larbi's rebuke to Zerrouki concerning the *rabāb* and the onions mentioned in chapter 2, or the complaints of the Moroccan enthusiasts regarding the elderly al-Brīhī. In the case of Sid Ahmed Serri's recordings, there was a long hiatus between his initial project and its publication in 2011 (see fig. 9). The delay hinged on the failure of the state authorities and Serri to agree to a price that might allow the latter to fully reimburse the musicians who accompanied him and the producers who recorded them. For defenders of such actions, withholding knowledge from the state and from the public is not a form of blackmail. As one veteran performer explained to me in defense of Serri's refusal to accept the state's initial offers, "It is up to the state to safeguard patrimony." According to this view, the repertoire is socially embedded and does not become freely available to the public without the financial and moral commitment of the state. The patrimony is in fact something that must be redeemed by the state.

In some respects this critique of the state long predates an independent Algeria. However, this critique seems to have taken on new life with the liberalization reforms of the Chadli Benjedid era (1979–92). For Ahmed Hachelaf, a key Algerian figure in the Maghribi and Arab music recording and public radio scene in Paris from the late 1940s until the 1980s, and a product of the *médersa* of Tlemcen and of Algiers whose career in many ways parallels that of El-Boudali Safir, the critique of the state revolved around the question of recordings. For Hachelaf, who together with his brother Mohamed ran the influential Club de Disque Arabe record label that was responsible for the reissue of classic recordings of Maghribi and other predominantly Arabic-language repertoires, the creation of recordings with a "guarantee of authenticity" was lacking in the Arab countries, meaning that the public was not able to enjoy the "safeguard" of its patrimony. This lack of sustained engagement

FIGURE 9. Eight of the forty discs recorded by Sid Ahmed Serri and released by the Algerian Ministry of Culture in 2011. Note that they begin with the mode *dhīl*, in keeping with the songbook convention.

with the "ingathering" of musical patrimony through research and recording was made worse by the growth of cassette production and "piracy" in the 1970s, which lowered the level of sound quality still further and prompted Hachelaf's call for a governmental ban on such activities.[84]

In many ways, Hachelaf's call for greater control sets up his own position as music producer as the ultimate position for the exercise of the *mélomane*'s sensibilities: it is in the studio that one has the ability to exercise control and impose good taste on performers of Arab music. Furthermore, this production process is explicitly not directed toward a commercial market. Rather, for Hachelaf, the ideal recording is noncommercial, highly controlled, state-sponsored, and affordable enough to compete with the cassette industry. This is a classic *mélomane*'s predicament: Andalusi music must be popularized, but in a tightly controlled manner that protects the music from cheapening and contamination. It must circulate, but not too freely. And in the absence of state commitment, responsibility for maintaining the musical patrimony falls to private citizens. In his case, the Club de Disque Arabe became a cache of recordings of the Algerian past that were otherwise unavailable, a sort of state archive waiting in the wings. Yet simply issuing a recording does not make it available: today, Hachelaf's reissues have again become difficult to find.

Redeeming Patrimony

In a way, we can conceptualize this as the tension between two forms of a single trilateral Arabic root, between *naẓm* (poetry, verse, order) and *niẓām* (government, state, power). The gist of Hachelaf's critique is that the state, the *niẓām*, should be the natural guarantor of patrimonial integrity (which we can conceptualize as *naẓm* against the threat of *nathr*) but that in fact it must be shamed and cajoled into performing its duty. If the state fails to fulfill this duty, non-state actors are obliged to step in. This is in fact a pattern that one can find in many patrimonial regimes, in which citizens take action to ensure the patrimony.[85] In this way, patrimony is something on whose behalf one acts. But what sort of something is it?

In many ways, patrimony looks like a special kind of author. It is an author who has spoken but, having spoken, cannot speak further, a sort of mute, impassive author immanent within the text-artifact. In this way it recalls the notion of public domain in copyright, which in the French and Algerian instance is the legal category by which one may register something as patrimony. If we recall the case of Yafil's assertion of author rights, legally speaking this was a legitimate claim that could likewise be legitimately challenged by another individual's claim that the work was in fact public domain. In this legal setting, the challenger would be replacing the original claim with the new claim in exactly the same way the "true" author or executor would act in the case of a challenge to the original claimant. In other words, in this legal regime, public domain is itself an author, but an impassive one on whose behalf individuals must act. It is as if to say, "We are part of this author; this author is us and is not us."

In the specific case of Andalusi music, this sense of the patrimony as an object outside the self enters deeply into the intimate musical space of performance practice. On the one hand, there is an understanding that this is, at least in theory, a fixed repertoire that must go a certain way and that must be internalized through repetition in the precise form in which the teacher gives it. Thus that precise form is closely tied to the musical transmitter. But for many practitioners, that transmitted object is emphatically not the same as the transmitter. It is alien, old, foreign. Just as patrimony can be conceived as an impassive author, it can also be conceived as a thing, person, or agent that is resistant, difficult, deceptive, and demanding of respect and redemption. In the words of Hadi Boukoura, musical director of the Association des Beaux-Arts of Algiers, "Andalusi music has a secret that people don't understand. If one gives it importance, it will give you importance as well. If you respect it, it will respect you too. But if not, it will break you."

When we move to the larger arena of patrimonial activism in which the intimate space of performance is held, the notion that Andalusi music is a cause on behalf of which its devotees act means that the *mélomanes*' critique of the state is in effect a political claim about the state itself. To shame the state into action closely resembles the Maghribi tradition of shaming the powerful individual into action: the supplicant performs a public sacrifice before the door of the targeted individual in an effort to secure that individual's intervention.[86] In the Algerian case, this shaming of the state is also a claim about the place of the Andalusi musical public and its musical patrimony within the national space. Shaming suggests that if the state takes up its duty, then that public and its patrimony will be recognized as essential to the national space. And it suggests that if the state leaves its duty unmet, then that public and its patrimony remain outside that national space, an unincorporated element that raises questions about the legitimacy of that state's rule.

None of this is to say that the Andalusi musical project constitutes an actual challenge to state power in the usual sense. Yet in the realm of musical matters, it is precisely such a challenge. Such a challenge is not a rejection of the state. In fact, the state is criticized precisely for neglecting its duties, and the state is appealed to and manipulated to carry out the project of the *mélomane*. Furthermore, in certain respects the partisans of Andalusi music, as representatives of *citadinité* or urbaneness, represent a sector of the broader public that came to see itself as marginalized by both the War of Independence and its aftermath, despite the persistence of the old urban elite and its place within the post-independence bureaucracy.[87]

In a similar vein, the Andalusi musical project implicitly challenges the narrative that treats the colonial period simply as an intrusion into a primordial national existence, and in doing so it is in keeping with the early post-independence rhetoric of the Algiers Charter with its claim that "no revolution is a total rupture with the past." In a national imaginary that would eventually treat the War of Independence as a radical, violent break from the colonial experience, the emphasis on genealogical and institutional continuity among Andalusi musical practitioners brings the historical imaginary back to the colonial public sphere from which the revival movement emerged, even if it also invokes an idealized medieval past. Granted, Andalusi musical revival was linked to the Algerian critique of the colonial status quo, and in its general outlines was more or less successfully assimilated to the post-independence nationalist narrative. But when we look more closely at the Andalusi musical milieu, it is clear that its ethos emphasizes institutions, people, and values that run against the nationalist grain. They are intensely local, genealogical, urbane, and intimate. Despite the best efforts at *tadwīn* on a national scale, they resist the homogenization and unitary voice associated with nationalism in general and with its Algerian variant in particular. They invoke the borderless, cosmopolitan terrain of the public and of genealogies rather than the bounded, epic terrain of the nation. And they exist in opposition to the notion of the urban masses or the rural peasant that figure so prominently in the nationalist imagination.

One might wonder if the tensions regarding the role of the state in the life of Andalusi music point toward a more general contradiction concerning the place of the musical tradition within the national scene. In Algeria, much as in Tunisia and Morocco, Andalusi music is taken to be the first among the traditional musical arts, and its preservation has long been framed within a nationalist framework. Because the patronage of Andalusi music was traditionally the purview of a certain sector of the bourgeoisie, its promotion as a national classical music demanded a concomitant effort to make it the possession of a wider swath of society. In short, it demanded popularization. But while most Algerians—or Tunisians or Moroccans, for that matter—are familiar with Andalusi music, it continues to be at least partly rooted among an old urban elite. This elite does not just claim Andalusi music: it in fact constitutes a core element of the Andalusi musical community. Indeed, the cachet of authenticity and of civilizational rootedness that Andalusi music enjoys largely depends upon the fact that its social life subsists in this sector, even if there are always parts of the Andalusi complex that escape the gravitational pull of the *thaqīl* and instead spin off, musically and socially, into the realm of the *khafīf*.

The call for the popularization of Andalusi music, then, carries a certain amount of bad faith, in that popularization carries the danger of devaluation of the repertoire. Popularization in this domain is really a form of uplift: the masses are ideally to rise to the level of the aficionados. For many musicians, it is a matter of cultivating an educated audience that can understand the complexity of the *nūba* form. Beihdja Rahal, for example, speaks of a decline in listening abilities from the 1970s until the 1990s. Gradually the ability to listen to an entire *nūba* was lost, so that when she began to perform professionally in Paris before Algerian audiences, she was "afraid to do a whole *nūba*, from the *mṣaddar*, because I was worried about the audience becoming impatient":

> People would come up saying they were disappointed that they couldn't dance. . . . I said, "This is a classical music. If you don't like it, don't come." We educated the public. It was one of my aims. When they see the name Beihdja Rahal, they know that they will hear a complete *nūba*. Of course, in the second half, they will hear *'arūbī* and *ḥawzī* as well.[88]

According to Rahal, the audience has changed in Algiers as well, so that it is more like the austere quiet she associates with Germany. "Now there is just an occasional *you-you* [ululation], it is very respectful, very *connaisseur*. It's a *nūba*, therefore it's classical, and therefore you need to be respectful." Thus the sorts of taking-in-hand said to be the responsibility of the state are also the responsibility of the performer and the educator. There is a strong sense that Andalusi music demands the moulding and maintenance of a certain sort of public. In this sense there is an inbuilt paternalism: the revivalist works not only upon the repertoire, but, channeling the state, also upon the repertoire's public. Thus the public that was lost may also be regained—a public comprised of people who recognize that if the *nūba* is a government, the *mṣaddar* is its king.

Conclusion: The Lost

> This music unknowingly cultivates nostalgia for "the lost paradise," or [the paradise] that is currently inaccessible, and which could be al-Andalus, or pre-1830 Algeria, or—why not?—the Algeria to come.
>
> BACHIR HADJ ALI, "El Anka et la tradition 'chaabi,'" 1979

As the preceding chapters have shown, the lost lies at the core of the narratives that the "people of al-Andalus" tell one another. The threat of loss shapes memorial practices and urges on the project of salvage, revival, and rationalization. The lost is both a black hole and a precious, elusive source, swallowing up repertoire and occasionally divulging that which was unknown. It is the out-of-sight base of the practice, the silence out of which the sound of the *nūba* and its children emerges. The lost is the ethos, pathos, aesthetic, and mystique of the Andalusi musical archipelago.

In these pages I have been wary of reducing the lost to an ideological effect: a response to the advent of new technologies, for example, a projection of nationalist or colonialist projects, a child of new practices of inventory and archiving, a variation on modernist themes of rupture, a goad for and brake on revivalist ambitions, or a result of shifts in the relations of musical production. It is, of course, all of these things, in the sense that the notion of the lost has been entangled with technological, political, discursive, and institutional changes of the past century and more. But to speak of entanglement is different from speaking of effects, responses, precipitates, or residues. While it might be tempting to tell a clear story of the lost's construction ex nihilo, we know both too little about the before and too much about the after to make such a tale satisfying.

Instead, I have preferred to trace the threads of the notion of the lost—threads that tie the living to the dead as well as separate them, that connect what is kept to what is given, that weigh things down, that rein in fragmentation, and that fade into a past that stands as a question mark beyond the temporal boundary of this study (see fig. 10). Such a strategy is attuned to the broader human processes of conceiving value, temporality, the social, the inalienable, and loss that in the Andalusi musical case seem to have been coemergent with the very notion of an Andalusi repertoire, patrimony, and process of genealogical transmission and proliferation. Sound recording, print, photography, transcription, copyright, the association, and turn-of-the-century discourses of salvage and revival all helped to reconfigure the ground on which Andalusi music was made, introducing new scales of memory and forms of evanescence along the way, and stoking the compulsions toward documentation and definition that Jacques Derrida has called "archive fever."[1] However, these new scales and forms were translations and amplifications of conditions and dilemmas that already existed regarding giving, keeping, and the embodied thingness of music, emerging as they did as consciousness of the temporality of practice itself.

At the risk of reducing it to a single source, we can say that in the Andalusi archipelago, the lost is a way to talk from a given present about the musical, social threads connecting to the past and future. These threads are in fact chains constituted by the carriers of the Andalusi repertoire—chains that can from one angle can be heavy and confining, but that are also the very texture of musical subjectivity and experience. For some of the people we have encountered in the preceding pages, the multiplicity of the strands is problematic and demands the impossible work of reducing them to a single, authoritative pathway or version. And in turn, for some practitioners, the future stands as a threat or promise of further multiplication, of fraying, of the undoing of the work of consolidation. In some ways, then, the lost stands for the conviction that the right strand indeed has an origin, and that the origin is singular. The lost is an image of a consolidation that once was, and that might be regained.[2] And hence the way in which the consolidation of *tadwīn* can turn into the consolidation of the hoard.

Many things get marked as lost among Andalusi music practitioners, but at its core is the notion of lost repertoire—actual pieces, usually song texts, whose melodies have vanished or have miraculously reemerged. As we have seen, this notion of the *mafqūd* has a long history, but attention to it has waxed and waned, with the past few decades of renewed scholarship bringing many "lost things" into circulation, as evidenced by the resurfacing of the Aboura collection with which this book began. I would like to close with an evocation of a few practitioners whose words summarize the mystique and ironies of the lost while also pointing out its close connection to patrimony, personhood, authority, transmission, and the stretching of projects of revival and archivization across generations.

Although ubiquitous, discourse about the lost is not without its critics. Consider the words of Hadi Boukoura, a member of the younger generation

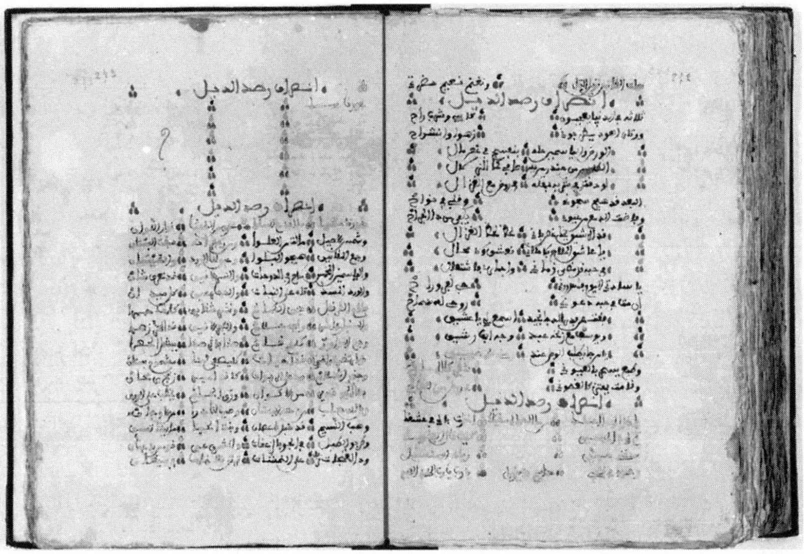

FIGURE 10. Two pages from a nineteenth-century songbook showing *inṣirāfāt* in the mode *raṣd al-dhīl*. The large question mark on the left margin suggests a missing *inṣirāf*, to be filled in at a later time. Leiden University Library, ms. Or. 14.169.

and the musical director of the Association des Beaux Arts in Algiers, recounting the comments of a leading master with whom he had spoken:

> He said to me, listen to me, Hadi, know this well: the most beautiful pieces have remained to today. These are the most beautiful. The less beautiful are called *al-mafqūd*. They disappeared. They are so tiresome, they are so monotonous, that people stopped singing them.

These remarks point toward another model of patrimony, in which there is a collective selection of that which is worth saving, and where the fantasy of restoration or recovery of the untouched is rejected in favor of a concept of continuity through use that recalls the kinds of inalienability associated with the pious endowments of Islamic law known as *waqf* or, in the Maghrib, *ḥabūs*.[3] Yet in another moment, the delight that accompanies the slaughter of a sacred cow can shift to reverence. Boukoura said a few minutes later, in response to a question I posed about hoarding:

> I consulted the Christianowitsch manuscript [of 1863]. At the end he had put a table, an inventory of the *shghālāt* of the period. . . . There were eighteen *mṣaddar*s in the mode *sīka*. Today there are three. This makes me sick at heart. Even if they're ugly, even if they're unattractive, annoying, monotonous, this makes me sick at heart. Too bad: fifteen pieces, there's an example [of hoarding]. I am against it. I am against it. One must give what one has. If you bring

> these *shghālāt* with you, who wins? Nobody. Nobody, nobody. I am against it. I am against it.

But giving takes work. In the case of Sid Ahmed Serri, whose project of *tadwīn* began in 1946 at the age of twenty and continues to this day, this task of divulging has involved the editing, printing, and unending revision of a songbook, the recording of the entirety of his repertoire, the cultivation of students who may receive it and pass it along, and the pursuit and achievement of governmental acknowledgment.[4] The ideal is total giving—a gift that cannot be returned, but that, like a debt, can only be passed on. In this sense, the threat of loss embodied in the figure of the already lost is the flip side of the kind of inalienability that comes from the publicization strategy being pursued here: the road to "social" inalienability can be cut off at the point where the hoard is trapped within the individual.

For Serri, the act of recording meant the accomplishment of a feat of memory that carried a quality of the supernatural: in his words, "When I began to record I said to myself, do I have the power to record all that I know? It was a miracle—it is a miracle." And having accomplished this feat, it means the risk of putting this corpus out for judgment, contestation, and adjustment, and seeking without fail to assert that the tradition goes this way and not that, thereby both addressing and potentially duplicating the problem identified at El Riath: that things "could become grave if one left each [musician] to settle into the conviction that he alone holds the truth" as received from his master.[5] There is no guarantee that Serri's version will be the version of the coming generations. Almost certainly there will be much that escapes this millennial project of *tadwīn*. There will be doubts that all was truly given, or that what was given was true to the original, or that it is beautiful, or that it represents anything greater than his own version. And there will be challenges to the center that come from what Marouf has described as the musical margins, which start their project of *tadwīn* from those spaces that may have escaped Serri's grasp.[6] But the alternative to disclosure, externalization, divestment, the full realization of value is burial, the hoard, oblivion, loss.

Serri himself, some forty-five years after the El Riath meeting, is at peace. It is late afternoon, the time to call believers to the *ʿaṣr* prayers, and, according to the humoral theories of old, the moment most propitious for *nūbat al-raml*. I have kept Sid Ahmed Serri in his study for a long time. He sighs deeply when I ask him my final question, about the future of Andalusi music:

> It is difficult to respond to such a question. I would very much like to be able to answer it. The only thing that is satisfying at the moment—and unfortunately it is not thanks to the authorities—the one consolation is that there

are associations coming into existence everywhere, even in places where *l'andalous* was never present. I would say that today there are thousands of young people who have given themselves over to learning this music. This is our hope—this is our hope.

But all these young people still need to be guided. They can't be left to go on like this, each one doing what he likes. The teachers teach them what they have heard on cds on the market, which are not very accurate. They do what they can. I don't know how this will turn out. But to channel them, guide them—I don't know how this will happen.

If the state doesn't take this problem seriously, then it will continue to be like this, split up, without any supervision. Everyone will be free to do as he likes, to interpret as he likes. This is the danger. I am not talking about *chaabi*. I'm not even talking about *ḥawzī*. These each person does his own way, there is no absolute rule. But when it comes to the classical *nūba*, there are rules that one must respect.

That's all. Will the work that I did one day circulate? Will it be taken into account by those who are teaching today? Who knows. That's all. As for my part, I have done everything I could. I will bring nothing with me. If I wanted to listen to something in my grave, then yes, I would bring it with me—along with a cassette player! That is all.

Notes

Introduction

1. On Aboura, see Benkalfat / Bin Qalfāt et al., *Al-mūsīqā al-klāsīkiyya fi-l-duwal al-maghāribiyya / La musique classique du Maghreb*, 1:39–40.

2. From a talk presented in 1928 titled "L'Andaloussia," conserved in the Aboura Collection. My thanks to Fayçal Benkalfat for his generosity in sharing this document with me.

3. Ben Smaïl, "Sur la musique et les musiciens arabes."

4. Prosper Ricard, *Essai d'action sur la musique et le théâtre populaire marocains*, 1.

5. Patrocinio García Barriuso, *Echos du Maghreb*, 13, 37.

6. Sid-Ahmed Bouali, *Petite introduction à la musique classique algérienne*, 1.

7. For an overview of Algerian history through the civil war years, see Ruedy, *Modern Algeria*.

8. Dib, *"Les Amis du livre": Fleuron du mouvement culturel algérien*, 59–60; Bouali, *Petite introduction à la musique classique algérienne*.

9. Carl Davila, The Andalusian Music of Morocco: Al-Āla: History, Society and Text.

10. Yafil, *Majmūʿ*, iv.

11. On the national and regional politics of Andalusi music, see Bouzar-Kasbadji, *L'emergence artistique algérienne;* Dwight F. Reynolds, "Musical 'Membrances of Medieval Muslim Spain"; Ruth F. Davis, *Mā'lūf: Reflections on the Arab Andalusian Music of Tunisia*; Langlois, "Music and Politics in North Africa"; Philip Ciantar, *The Mā'lūf in Contemporary Libya*; Shannon, *Performing al-Andalus.* In addition to these works, there is a significant literature on Andalusi musical traditions in the Maghrib, with emphases ranging from the musicological to the textual to the broadly social. For comparative perspectives on the *nūba* traditions of the Maghrib as a whole, see Guettat, *La musique classique du Maghreb*; Marouf, ed., *Le chant arabo-andalou*; Poché, *La musique arabo-andalouse*; Ṭānṭāwī, *Al-mūsīqā al-andalusiyya bi-l-gharb al-islāmī*; Benkalfat / Bin Qalfāt et al., *Al-mūsīqā al-klāsīkiyya fi-l-duwal al-maghāribiyya / La musique classique du Maghreb*. For Algeria, see Plenckers, "Changes in the Algerian Sanʿa Tradition and the Role of the Musicologist in the Process"; Rachid Guerbas, "Chant et musique de la Nawba ou Nûba algérienne"; Marouf, "Le système musical de la San'a ou le paradigme de la norme et de la marge"; the several editions of Serri, *Chants andalous*; Saidani, *La musique du constantinois*; Merdaçi, *Dictionnaire des musiques et des musiciens de Constantine*; Ghoul, *Patrimoine de musique arabo-andalouse*. For a focus on Moroccan *āla* and allied repertoires, see Schuyler, "Moroccan

Andalusian Music"; Binmūsa, *Al-īqā'āt al-khams*; Jam'iyyat Ribāṭ al-fatḥ, ed., *Athr al-mūsīqā al-andalusiyya fi-l-anmāṭ al-īqā'iyya al-maḥalliyya*; Carl Davila, *The Andalusian Music of Morocco*.

12. In Asad's words, a tradition is a set of "discourses that seek to instruct practitioners regarding the correct form and purpose of a given practice . . . discourses [that] relate conceptually to a *a past* . . . and *a future* . . . through *a present*." Asad, *The Idea of an Anthropology of Islam*, 14. See also Grewal, *Islam Is Another Country*, as well as the position mapped in Rabinow and Sullivan, "The Interpretive Turn," 19-24.

13. I should emphasize that this book does not pretend to be an exhaustive history of the Algiers-Tlemcen Andalusi tradition in the modern period. There are many institutions that I only briefly touch upon that certainly deserve a much deeper scholarly treatment, and one that would necessarily open up to a much wider range of musical genres. A few of these are the municipal conservatory of Algiers, the Institut national de la musique, and Radio Algiers and its counterparts in France.

14. This includes my own work. See, for example, Mourad Ouamara / Murād Bin 'Alī Wa'māra, ed., *Jāmi' al-safāyin wa-l-kunnāshāt fī ṣanā'i' al-azjāl wa-l-muwashshaḥāt / Recueil des poèmes Muwashshah⊠ât et Azdjâl*, 5.

15. See, for example, the work of Nadir Marouf, Yahia Ghoul, and Beihdja Rahal.

16. Thus my hope is that the "historical" sections will not be read simply as explanations of the "ethnographic" sections, or the latter simply as illustrations of the enduring power of the former. Instead, I hope that they add up to an enlarged sense of practice or lived structure in time. For the inspiration for such an approach that pays attention to structure, contingency, and transformation, see William H. Sewell, *Logics of History: Social Theory and Social Transformation* (Chicago: University of Chicago Press, 2005). In other words, echoing Lévi-Strauss, the approach taken here treats the past and society as two ways of talking about the same thing. Claude Lévi-Strauss, "Introduction: History and Anthropology," in *Structural Anthropology*, trans. Claire Jacobson and Brooke Grundfest Schoepf (New York: Basic Books, 1963), 18.

17. Charles L. Briggs and Richard Bauman, "Genre, Intertextuality, and Social Power," 142-43. Note the similarity of Brigg's and Bauman's understanding of genre and Asad's understanding of tradition.

18. There is a rich and growing literature on the notion of genealogy. For the Middle East and North Africa, see Kilani, *La construction de la mémoire*, 1992; Messick, *The Calligraphic State* 1993; Jean During, *Quelque chose se passe*, 1994; Armbrust, *Mass Culture and Modernism in Egypt* 1996; Shryock, *Nationalism and the Genealogical Imagination*, 1997; Bonte, Conte, and Dresch eds., *Émirs et présidents* 2001; Gill, "Melancholic Genealogies"; Ho, *The Graves of Tarim*, 2006; Shaery-Eisenlohr, "Territorializing Piety." On Hawaii, see Valeri, "Constitutive History." On genealogy and music outside the Middle East and North Africa, see Neuman, *The Life of Music in North India*; Weidman, *Singing the Classical, Voicing the Modern*; Neuman, "Pedagogy, Practice, and Embodied Creativity in Hindustani Music"; Rahaim, *Musicking Bodies*; Gillan, "'Dancing Fingers': Embodied Lineages in the Performance of Okinawan Classical Music"; Johansson and Berge, "Who Owns an Interpretation? Legal and Symbolic Ownership of Norwegian Folk Music"; Katz, *Lineage of Loss: Counternarratives of North Indian Music*.

19. There is a massive scholarly literature on nationalism; for a few classic works, see Benedict Anderson, *Imagined Communities*; Ernest Gellner, *Nations and Nationalism*; Eric Hobsbawm and Terence Ranger, eds., *The Invention of Tradition*; Partha Chatterjee, *Nationalist Thought and the Colonial World*; idem, *The Nation and its Fragments*. On music and nationalism, see Thomas Turino, *Nationalists, Cosmopolitans, and Popular Music in Zimbabwe*; Philip V. Bohlman, *The Music of European Nationalism*; Peter Wade, *Music, Race, and Nation*; Kelly M. Askew, *Perform-*

ing the Nation: Swahili Music and Cultural Politics in Tanzania; Janaki Bakhle, *Two Men and Music: Nationalism in the Making of an Indian Classical Tradition.*

20. There is likewise a massive literature on modernity and loss. For a sampling, see Marilyn Ivy, *Discourses of the Vanishing: Modernity, Phantasm, Japan*; Yelles, *Cultures et métissages en Algérie*, 45; Richard Bauman and Charles L. Briggs, *Voices of Modernity*; Julia Hell and Andreas Schönle, "Introduction," in *Ruins of Modernity*, 2.

21. George R. Trumbull IV, *An Empire of Facts: Colonial Power, Cultural Knowledge, and Islam in Algeria, 1870–1914.*

22. James McDougall, *History and the Culture of Nationalism in Algeria*; for a parallel critique of the metaphor of revival in the context of Hebrew-language politics in Mandate Palestine and the State of Israel, see Ron Kuzar, *Hebrew and Zionism*, 120. For works by historians who have argued, explicitly or implicitly, against a primordialist narrative of Algerian nationhood and its accompanying telos of inevitable decolonization, see Omar Carlier, "Medina and Modernity: The Emergence of Muslim Civil Society in Algiers between the Two World Wars"; Jonathan K. Gosnell, *The Politics of Frenchness in Colonial Algeria, 1930–1954*; and Todd Shepard, *The Invention of Decolonization: The Algerian War and the Remaking of France.*

23. Katherine Bergeron, *Decadent Enchantments: The Revival of Gregorian Chant at Solesmes.*

24. See Mark Slobin, "Rethinking 'Revival' of American Ethnic Music"; Neil V. Rosenberg, ed., *Transforming Tradition: Folk Music Revivals Examined*; Tamara E. Livingston, "Music Revivals: Towards a General Theory"; Britta Sweers, *Electric Folk: The Changing Face of English Traditional Music.* A corollary of this approach is the division into stock participant roles: for Livingston, core revivalists and source musicians, and for Slobin researcher/collector, elder statesman/repository, and popularizer/definer. Livingston, "Musical Revivals"; Slobin, "Rethinking 'Revival,'" 37.

25. For the concept of patrimony in France from the July Monarchy into the twentieth century, see Yvon Lamy, "Patrimoine et culture: L'institutionnalisation." For an introduction to the concept of patrimony, both in France and in the colonial Algerian context, see Nabila Oulebsir, *Les usages du patrimoine: Monuments, musées et politique coloniale en Algérie, 1830–1930*, 13–16. For discussion of the concept of patrimony within the context of music in Algeria, see Hadj Miliani, "Fabrication patrimoniale et imaginaires identitaires: Autour des chants et musiques en Algérie."

26. On the Louvre, see Andrew McClellan, *Inventing the Louvre*; on the new focus on remnants in the context of vandalism, see Bergeron, *Decadent Enchantments*, 1–24.

27. Oulebsir, *Les usages du patrimoine.*

28. Grangaud and Oualdi, "Tout est-il colonial dans le Maghreb? Ce que les travaux des historiens modernistes peuvent apporter."

29. Richard Schechner, *Between Theater and Anthropology.*

30. During, *Quelque chose se passe*; Feintuch, "Revivals on the Edge."

31. During, *Quelque chose se passe*, 134.

32. On the temporality of tradition, see ibid., 405.

33. Feintuch, "Revivals on the Edge," 3.

34. For musical ethnographies attuned to circulation, see McCann, "All That Is Not Given Is Lost," and Novak, *Japanoise.*

35. On "remainders of modernity," see Ivy, *Discourses of the Vanishing*, 9.

36. For an exploration of an Andalusi musical tradition through theories of value, which clearly have many threads of connection to theories of inalienability, see Davila, *The Andalusian Music of Morocco.*

37. Annette Weiner, "Inalienable Wealth"; idem, *Inalienable Possessions: The Paradox of Keeping-while-Giving*; idem, "Cultural Difference and the Density of Objects."

38. Elizabeth Emma Ferry, *Not Ours Alone: Patrimony, Value, and Collectivity in Contemporary Mexico*. For an exploration of the patrimony concept, though not through the framework of inalienable possessions, see Richard Handler, *Nationalism and the Politics of Culture in Quebec*. Although patrimony is in many respects similar to the concept of heritage that is more familiar to English speakers, patrimony and its cognates have a gendered and materialist connotation that are important for the argument of this book.

39. For a reading of inalienable possessions "as a theory, of sort, of object relations," see James Weiner, "Beyond the Possession Principle."

40. Peebles, "Inverting the Panopticon."

41. For contemporaneous concerns about orality, writing, and music in South India, see Amanda Weidman, *Singing the Classical, Voicing the Modern: The Postcolonial Politics of Music in South India*.

42. Sterne, *The Audible Past*.

43. For the classic statements of these positions, see John Ruskin, *The Seven Lamps of Architecture* (1849), 176–98; E. Viollet-Le-Duc, *On Restoration* (1875).

44. Penelope Papailias has written of local historians in Greece, "A notion of home as site of concealment, hoarding, possession, and (un)limited access . . . appears to be central to the concept of the archive." *Genres of Recollection*, 13.

45. In posing this question, I join in the conversation between Steven Feld and Annette Weiner regarding musical ephemerality and materiality. Steven Feld, *Jazz Cosmopolitanism in Accra*, 162–63.

46. This is related to Ochoa-Gautier's examination of sound inscription beyond the written page, in *Aurality*, 7.

47. Weiner already hinted at an answer to this when she included narratives as potential inalienable possessions. Weiner, *Inalienable Possessions*, 11, 64–65, 105–6.

48. Regula Burckhardt Qureshi, "Confronting the Social: Mode of Production and the Sublime for (Indian) Art Music"; idem, "Mode of Production and Musical Production: Is Hindustani Music Feudal?"; Martin Stokes, "Marx, Money, and Musicians."

49. Jean-Baptiste Say, *A Treatise on Political Economy, or the Production, Distribution, and Consumption of Wealth* (1880), 119, cited in Robert E. Moore, "From Genericide to Viral Marketing: On 'Brand,'" 333.

50. In other words, *pace* Terence Turner as cited by Graeber, performance is by definition portable, in that repeatability is what allows us to speak of musical performance in the first place, in that the performer must live up to a certain standard of execution. David Graeber, *Toward an Anthropological Theory of Valu*, 78.

51. Richard Bauman, "Verbal Art as Performance," 293.

52. On tradition and the judgment of "apt performance," see Talal Asad, *The Idea of an Anthropology of Islam*, 15.

53. Feld, *Jazz Cosmopolitanism in Accra*, 163. In the context of Andalusi music in Morocco, see Davila, *The Andalusian Music of Morocco*, 254.

54. Say wrote, "It was my intention to call these *perishable* products, but this term would be equally applicable to products of a material kind. *Intransferable* would be equally incorrect, for this class of products does pass from the producer to the consumer. The word *transient* does not exclude all idea of duration whatever, neither does the word *momentary*." *A Treatise on Political Economy*, 119.

55. Jane Fajans, "Exchanging Products; Producing Exchange," 7.

56. Karl Marx, *A Contribution to the Critique of Political Economy*, 125–37.

57. Ibid., 132.

58. Ibid., 133.

59. Mourad Yelles, *Cultures et métissages en Algérie: La racine et la trace*, 65.

60. On the notion of treasuries as state hoards, see Gustav Peebles, "Inverting the Panopticon: Money and the Nationalization of the Future."

61. Weiner, "Beyond the Possession Principle," 135.

62. On the contested concept, see Gallie, "Art as an Essentially Contested Concept," as well as Asad, *The Idea of an Anthropology of Islam*, which places contestation at the heart of the concept of tradition.

63. For an example of this widespread argument, see Saidani, *La musique du constantinois*, 311.

Part One

1. The French and Arabic terms do not carry quite the same resonance. *Patrimoine* tends to emphasize things that are available to the eyes and the touch, while *turāth* more easily assimilates the visual-tactile, the sonic, and the more abstract qualities associated with the English usage of heritage.

2. *Turāth* is also mobilized frequently in musical and nonmusical spheres in other Arabic-speaking countries. For Syria, see Christa Salamandra, *A New Old Damascus*; Jonathan H. Shannon, *Among the Jasmine Trees: Music and Modernity in Contemporary Syria.*

Chapter One

1. The full Arabic title can be glossed as The book of the scent of flowers and description of the rays of light and the voices of the birds and the melodies of the strings. Bekhoucha's name was sometimes spelled Bekkhoucha.

2. M. Bekhoucha and A. Sekkal, eds., *Anthologie d'Auteurs arabes / Kitāb nafḥ al-azhār*, 5.

3. Ibid., 5–6.

4. Ibid., 12.

5. On the chronotope see M. M. Bakhtin, "Forms of Time and of the Chronotope in the Novel." For recent applications to music, see Aaron A. Fox, *Real Country: Music and Language in Working-Class Culture*; David W. Samuels, *Putting a Song on Top of It: Expression and Identity on the San Carlos Apache Reservation*; Alexander Sebastian Dent, *River of Tears: Country Music, Memory, and Modernity in Brazil.*

6. We can also say that it is a traditionalizing practice that strategically invokes the quality of being a tradition, as proposed by Richard Bauman, "Contextualisation, Tradition, and the Dialogue of Genres: Icelandic Legends of the *Kraftaskáld*."

7. For a critical discussion of some of these terms, see Kay Kaufman Shelemay, "Musical Communities: Rethinking the Collective in Music," in particular 360–64. See also Will Straw, "Systems of Articulation, Logics of Change: Communities and Scenes in Popular Music," 369, cited in Shelemay, "Musical Communities," 362.

8. Bekhoucha and Sekkal, *Nafḥ al-azhār*, 12.

9. Carl Davila, *The Andalusian Music of Morocco.*

10. For an example of this view, see Mahmoud Guettat [Maḥmūd Gaṭṭāṭ], "Makānat al-mawrūth al-mūsīqī fī taḥdīd al-huwiyya (qaḍāyā al-mawrūth wa-l-taḥdīth al-mūsīqī)."

11. For a review of these medieval sources, see Davila, *The Andalusian Music of Morocco*, as well as Guettat, "Makānat al-mawrūth al-mūsīqī." While the thirteenth-century Tunisian author Aḥmad al-Tifāshī speaks of Andalusi singers performing a form that he refers to as a *nūba*, what this meant is unclear. For an alternative modern use of the term to mean a melody, see Richard C. Jankowsky, *Stambeli: Music, Trance, and Alterity in Tunisia*. On the *nūba* as fanfare, see al-Madanī, *Mudhakkirāt al-Ḥājj Aḥmad al-Sharīf al-Zahhār*.

12. This is a manuscript newly uncovered by Dwight Reynolds—*Al-ʿadhāra al-māyisāt fi-l-azjāl wa-l-muwashshaḥāt*, or what Reynolds translates as "The Swaying Virgins of *azjāl* and *muwashshaḥāt*." Dwight F. Reynolds, "Lost Virgins Found: The Early Arabic Songbook and an Early North African Exemplar."

13. The eighteenth-century description is in Thomas Shaw, *Travels, or Observations Relating to Several Parts of Barbary and the Levant* (1738), 203.

14. For the late Ottoman period, see Aḥmad Tawfīq al-Madanī, ed., *Mudhakkirāt al-Ḥājj Aḥmad al-Sharīf al-Zahhār, naqīb ashrāf al-Jazāʾir, 1168–1246 h., 1754–1830 m.*, 37–39. For post-1830 Algeria, see Alexandre Christianowitsch, *Esquisse historique de la musique arabe aux temps anciens* (1863); Francisco Salvador Daniel, *La musique arabe: Ses rapports avec la musique grècque et le chant grégorien* (1879); G. Delphin and L. Guin, *Notes sur la poésie et la musique arabes dans le Maghreb algérien* (Paris: Ernest Leroux, 1886). For nineteenth-century Morocco, see Ibrāhīm al-Tādlī al-Ribāṭī, *Aghānī al-siqā wa-maghānī al-mūsīqā aw al-irtiqāʾ ilā ʿulūm al-mūsīqā*. Copy dated 1336 H./1907 A.D., KA/489/D109.

15. *Māʾlūf* literally means composed or customary; *āla* literally means instrument; *ṣanʿa* connotes craft; and *gharnāṭī* means Granadan. The claim is sometimes made that *gharnāṭī* is specifically for the school of Tlemcen, and *ṣanʿa* is specifically for Algiers. It is a longstanding practice, however, to use these terms interchangeably in Tlemcen and its musical environs, and *gharnāṭī* and *gharnāṭa* have sometimes been used as alternative names for the *nūba* tradition in Algiers. See Edmond Yafil, *Majmūʿ al-aghānī wa-l-alḥān min kalām al-andalus* (1904), i. The attempt to assign separate, mutually exclusive terms for each of these can be read as an attempt to assert distinctiveness between these intimately related traditions, as well as an attempt to rationalize and freeze what are in fact fluid naming practices.

16. Alternatively, if one wishes, one can also speak of the *musique andalouse* of any of these places. In actual practice, Andalusi music can refer to a localized tradition, or to the totality of these traditions. See Jonathan Glasser, "Andalusi Musical Origins at the Moroccan-Algerian Frontier."

17. On the notion of genre adjuncts to the *nūba*, including their peri-urban associations, see Marouf, "Structure du répertoire andalous," 18.

18. Algiers and Béjaïa, with their longstanding Kabyle Berber populations, are prominent exceptions. Note that for the eighteenth-century English observer Thomas Shaw, the music of the Algiers region could be divided between the music of the rural "Arabs" or "Bedoweens," the music of the "Turks," and the music of the urban "Moors." It is his description of "Moorish" music that most closely matches the *nūba* repertoire. Shaw, *Travels*, 203.

19. In fact some places like Sefrou and Bouira have housed professional ensembles that play Andalusi repertoire, or, like Biskra, have come to house amateur associations in recent years. For that matter, some places that today are closely associated with Andalusi music are relative newcomers; Oujda may be such an example. The degree of association with the concept of *ḥaḍāra* is in many cases a matter of dispute.

20. For a schematic comparison of the three Maghribi traditions, see Guettat, "Makānat al-mawrūth al-mūsīqī."

21. Humberto R. Maturana and Francisco J. Varela, *The Tree of Knowledge: The Biological Roots of Human Understanding*, 75. For an anthropological domestication of the concept of structural coupling, see William A. Foley, *Anthropological Linguistics*.

22. And in this sense, the site of this study was delineated by the reach of this version of the *nūba*, even if the bulk of my ethnographic and archival work focused on particular parts of this site.

23. Already in 1900, scholarly-minded aficionados from Tlemcen such as Mostefa Aboura and Ghouti Bouali were making note of the differences they heard between their home tradition and that which they heard in Algiers. Ghouti Bouali [Al-Ghawthī Abū ʿAlī], *Kitāb kashf al-qināʿ ʿan ālāt al-samāʿ*, 107, 124.

24. To be fair, practitioners also sometimes hold up a quality of the rival city as worthy of emulation. See, for example, some Tlemcanis' comments on the virtuosity of Algerois musicians.

25. Interestingly enough, Fes is often held up in Tlemcen as a fount of authenticity. It is as if in Maghribi musical matters, as in spiritual matters, the source lies in the west. On the Maghrib's west as the main source of saints in Libya, see E. E. Evans-Pritchard, *The Sanusi of Cyrenaica*.

26. For something similar vis-à-vis Tunis and Testour, see Ruth F. Davis, *Mā'lūf: Reflections on the Arab Andalusian Music of Tunisia*, 71–89.

27. Saidani, *La musique du constantinois*, 234.

28. On Khaddūj al-Sabṭiyya, see Eugène Aubin, *Le Maroc d'aujourd'hui* (1904), 345.

29. On Cheikh Qaddūr Bin Gālī, see Joseph Desparmet, *La poésie arabe actuelle à Blida et sa métrique* (1907), 6n2. An alternative term that shows up in Judeo-Arabic is the Turkish *cank*, which, like *safīna*, can be a notebook of poems or a sailing vessel. See Edmond Nathan Yafil, *Dīwān al-aghānī min kalām al-andalus* (1904). For metaphors of seafaring in Andalusi repertoire, see Maya Saidani, *La musique du constantinois*, 14–18.

30. Such a link between travel and sacred learning has a long pedigree in Muslim societies. On Muslim travelers, see Dale F. Eickelman and James Piscatori, eds., *Muslim Travellers: Pilgrimage, Migration, and the Religious Imagination*; Houari Touati, *L'armoire à sagesse: Bibliothèques et collections en Islam*; Natalie Zemon Davis, *Trickster Travels: A Sixteenth-Century Muslim Between Worlds*.

31. In a very really sense, then, the movement of localized personages from place to place, and their memories' incorporation into new institutional and geographic contexts, is what renders North African musical places into mobile musical-discursive forms, thereby reterritorializing these places and turning them into what Deleuze and Guattari refer to as "territorial motifs." Gilles Deleuze and Félix Guattari, *A Thousand Plateaus: Capitalism and Schizophrenia*, 318. See also Jean During, *Quelque chose se passe: Le sens de la tradition dans l'Orient musical*, 131.

32. Alexis Chottin, *Tableau de la musique marocaine*, 93–94. Note the dissonance of Tlemcen being connected to Cordoba rather than to Granada. See also Guettat, "Makānat al-mawrūth al-mūsīqī," 24.

33. Office of the Governor-General, Centre d'Information et d'Études, "Note. A/S. d'un projet d'organisation d'un festival de musique andalouse transcrite et interprétée par un orchestre français," Algiers, Sept. 20, 1940, CAOM/9H/37/18.

34. Youcef Touaïbia, *Groupe Yafil*, http://yafil.free.fr/sommaire.html.

35. Mahmoud Guettat, *La musique classique du Maghreb*, 12, 187; Christian Poché, *La musique arabo-andalouse*, 13–14; Jonathan H. Shannon, "Performing al-Andalus, Remembering al-Andalus," 321; Touimy El Hadj Driss Benjelloun, ed., *Patrimoine Musical Arabe Marocaine*, 1. For the reading of the Andalusi label as an anticolonial strategy, see Leo Plenckers, "Changes in the Algerian Sanʿa Tradition and the Role of the Musicologist in the Process," 1256.

36. However, it should be noted that champions of such alternative names do not necessarily deny a connection to al-Andalus so much as emphasize the Maghrib's contribution. For advocacy of the national classical music line, without denying a link to al-Andalus, see FLN Commission centrale d'orientation, *Colloque national sur la musique algérienne, El-Riath, 25–26–27 decembre 1964*; Mohamed El-Fasi, "La musique marocaine dite 'musique andalouse.'"

37. Thus the nineteenth-century songbooks do not name the repertoire as Andalusi—though note that they do not generally name the repertoire at all.

38. For pre-1900 discussions of the repertoire as coming from al-Andalus, see Francisco Salvador Daniel, *Album de douze chansons arabes, mauresques et kabyles*; Ibrāhīm al-Tādlī al-Ribāṭī, *Aghānī al-siqā wa-maghānī al-mūsīqā aw al-irtiqā' ilā 'ulūm al-mūsīqā*; Christianowitsch, *Esquisse historique de la musique arabe*, 8. The early modern manuscript newly discovered by Dwight Reynolds does seem to point to a connection between the compiler and the Granadan exiles. Reynolds, "Lost Virgins Found."

39. For a similar point regarding musical imaginaries in Morocco, see Davila, *The Andalusian Music of Morocco*, 188. On projects of multiculturalism and things Andalusi (including music), see Shannon, *Performing al-Andalus*. The sense of al-Andalus in terms of the passing of an Arab-Islamic imperial power is not only Maghribi, but in the turn-of-the-century context was shared by many non-Maghribi Arabs, non-Arab Muslims, and European colonial standard-bearers. See Muḥammad Bey Farīd, *Min miṣr ilā miṣr*; Yaseen Noorani, "The Lost Garden of Al-Andalus"; Roger Benjamin, "*Andalusia in the Time of the Moors*: Regret and Colonial Presence in Paris, 1900"; Michael Laffan, "'Another Andalusia': Images of Colonial Southeast Asia in Arabic," 706. In only a few early twentieth-century Maghribi voices can we hear a faint anticipation of the contemporary trope of al-Andalus as a lost tri-religious paradise of tolerance and achievement. See Maktab al-akhbār al-tūnisiyya, *Ẓāhira murība fī siyāsat al-isti'mār al-faransī*. On the history of the image of al-Andalus as a site of tolerance, see Kenneth Baxter Wolf, "*Convivencia* in Medieval Spain.

40. Bronislaw Malinowski, "Myth in Primitive Psychology." For complications, see Glasser, "Andalusi Musical Origins at the Moroccan-Algerian Frontier."

41. For discussion of al-Andalus in the Maghribi imaginary, see Beebe Bahrami, "Al-Andalus and Memory"; Nasreddine Saidouni, "Al-andalusiyyūn (al-muriskiyyūn) bi-muqāṭa'at al-jazā'ir 'Dār al-sulṭān'"; Daniel J. Schroeter, "The Shifting Boundaries of Moroccan Jewish Identities." Note that it is not al-Andalus in general but the three cities of Granada, Cordoba, and Seville—and, in particular, their courtly centers—that serve as the storied source of Andalusi music, as well as of other arts (including some textile crafts) that Andalusis are said to have brought to the Maghrib in their migrations. For textiles, see A. Bel and P. Ricard, *Les industries indigènes de l'Algérie: Le travail de la laine à Tlemcen*, 353.

42. Maya Saidani [Māya Sa'īdānī], "Al-muṣṭalaḥāt al-khāṣṣa bi-l-turāth al-mūsīqī al-quṣanṭīnī bayn al-rīf wa-l-ḥaḍar," 89–90.

43. E. E. Evans-Pritchard, *The Nuer*, 108.

44. Note that the "old families" are not explicitly identified here as Andalusi, but are closely identified with the Andalusi migrations. This is in keeping with the sort of semiotic relay between Andalusi music enthusiasts and Andalusis, including with regard to their purported social characteristics, described in the section that follows.

45. 'Abbās Jarrārī, *Al-naghm al-muṭrib bayna al-andalus wa-l-maghrib*. Note that this effectively indigenizes the violin—or one might say it makes the violin as foreign to Western Europe as it is to North Africa.

46. Note that in this case, the speaker does not necessarily deny that the presence of women in the ensembles dates to recent decades. But he might argue that the presence of "civilization" makes Oujdis more receptive to such an innovation. Note the similarity to the metaphor of the onions, which again is an argument about receptivity due to preparation and pedigree.

47. Edmond Nathan Yafil and Jules Rouanet, eds., *Répertoire de musique arabe et maure: Collection de mélodies, ouvertures, noubet, chansons, préludes, etc., no. 17.*

48. The work of Brian Karl directly explores musical interactions between Spanish and Moroccan musicians, much of it taking place in Spain. Brian Karl, "Across a Divide: Mediations of Contemporary Popular Music in Morocco and Spain." See also Shannon, *Performing al-Andalus.*

49. This is not unlike the place of the Najd in genealogical play among Bedouin tribesmen in Jordan in the work of Andrew Shryock. Andrew Shryock, *Nationalism and the Genealogical Imagination: Oral History and Textual Authority in Tribal Jordan.*

50. For an exploration of musical punning, see Samuels, *Putting a Song on Top of It*, 8–9.

51. For an exploration of the notion of second nature, which I am interpreting here as primarily discursive, see William Cronon, *Nature's Metropolis: Chicago and the Great West.*

52. On the metaphorical linkage of al-Andalus to songbirds in the tradition of Constantine, see Maya Saidani, *La musique du constantinois*, 54.

53. On the animator, see Erving Goffman, *Forms of Talk*; Patrick Eisenlohr, "Materialities of Entextualization: The Domestication of Sound Reproduction in Mauritian Muslim Devotional Practice," 320–21.

54. Cited in Rabeh Sebaa, "Vibrations en ʿarubi et hawzi majeurs," 65.

Chapter Two

1. On the distinction between "the experiencing subject" and "discursive subject positions," see Katherine Pratt Ewing, *Arguing Sainthood: Modernity, Psychoanalysis, and Islam*, 5.

2. For participant (or participation) frameworks, structures, or roles, see Erving Goffman, *Forms of Talk*; William F. Hanks, "Exorcism and the Description of Participant Roles"; Judith T. Irvine, "Shadow Conversations: The Indeterminacy of Participant Roles."

3. As will be seen, "professional" can also be used in a metaphorical sense to refer to someone with a high skill level. For example, in referring to Yahia Ghoul, the Houston-based heart surgeon and founding member of Oran's Association Nassim El-Andalous, one association veteran explained that "he is an amateur only in name—in reality [i.e., with regard to his level of knowledge] he is a professional." For purposes of clarity, however, I will generally use professional to refer to someone who makes much of his or her livelihood from musical Performance.

4. A. J. Racy, *Making Music in the Arab World: The Culture and Artistry of Ṭarab*, 40–42.

5. Dār al-sharq, *Al-munjid fi-l-lugha*, 918.

6. This notion of interpellation or calling is derived from Louis Althusser, "Ideology and Ideological State Apparatuses (Notes Towards an Investigation)."

7. For the notion of apprenticeship in a North African musical context, see Philip D. Schuyler, "Music Education in Morocco," 22–27. Note that *mʿallim* is the term used for the musical and ritual master of ceremonies for Maghribi trance traditions of sub-Saharan origin, such as *gnāwa* and *sṭambēlī*. See Deborah Kapchan, *Traveling Spirit Masters: Moroccan Gnawa Trance and Music in the Global Marketplace*, and Richard C. Jankowsky, *Stambeli: Music, Trance, and Alterity in Tunisia*. See also Merdaci as cited in Maya Saidani, *La musique du constantinois*, 65.

8. On female musicians in and around the Andalusi milieu, see Fazilet Diff, "Musique andalouse et expressions féminines."

9. This is a fascinating question in itself. In the case of *msemma'āt* or *msemm'īyya*, which is a term associated specifically with Algiers, there is broad agreement that their numbers have diminished drastically, particularly since the violence and instability of the 1990s. Notwithstanding the widespread claim that the *msemma'āt* have disappeared, there are in fact some aged *msemma'āt* who are still employed for family gatherings in working-class neighborhoods in Algiers. For *meddāḥāt* in Oran in the 1990s, see Landoff's film, *A Little for My Heart, a Little for My God.*

10. On the *shaykha* in Morocco, see Deborah Kapchan, "Moroccan Female Performers Defining the Social Body." *M'allma* is a less problematic term.

11. Ghouti Bouali [Al-Ghawthī Abū 'Alī], *Kitāb kashf al-qinā' 'an ālāt al-samā'*, 96, 101. *Shaykh* can be replaced with the term for old man, *shayb*, and a similar opposition can be mapped onto the differentiation between the low *dum* and the high *tak* in the percussion; see Saidani, *La musique du constantinois*, 121. For the association of connoisseurs with men as opposed to women, and of older men as opposed to younger men, see Saidani, *La musique du constantinois*, 62, 100. Finally, see the use of *shabāb* as an alternative name for the *juwāq*, the piercingly high-pitched small flute traditionally used in some Andalusi music groups. Alexandre Christianowitsch, *Esquisse historique de la musique arabe aux temps anciens* (1863), 31.

12. On *shabb* as the inversion of *shaykh*, see Marc Schade-Poulsen, *Men and Popular Music in Algeria: The Social Significance of Raï*, 15.

13. Regula Burckhardt Qureshi, "Confronting the Social: Mode of Production and the Sublime for (Indian) Art Music," and "Mode of Production and Musical Production: Is Hindustani Music Feudal?" For a broader theorization that also draws on the North Indian case, see Katherine Butler Brown, "The Social Liminality of Musicians: Case Studies from Mughal India and Beyond." Brown's work draws upon and revises classic formulations by Alan P. Merriam, *The Anthropology of Music.*

14. Merdaci, "De Constantine à Constantine," 160.

15. Filippo Pananti, *Narrative of a Residence in Algiers* (818), 266–67, cited in Abū al-Qāsim Sa'dallah, *Ta'rīkh al-jazā'ir al-thaqāfī min al-qarn al-'āshir ilā al-rābi' 'ashar al-hijrī*, 2:456.

16. Elizabeth Blankley Broughton, *Six Years Residence in Algiers* (1839), 22.

17. Christianowitsch, *Esquisse historique de la musique arabe*; Francisco Salvador Daniel, *La musique arabe: Ses rapports avec la musique grècque et le chant grégorien* (1879); G. Delphin and L. Guin, *Notes sur la poésie et la musique arabes dans le Maghreb algérien* (1886); Bouali, Kitāb kashf al-qinā'; Edmond Nathan Yafil, *Majmū' al-aghānī wa-l-alḥān min kalām al-andalus* (1904); Edmond Nathan Yafil and Jules Rouanet, eds., *Répertoire de musique arabe et maure: Collection de mélodies, ouvertures, noubet, chansons, préludes, etc.*, nos. 1–25 (1904–?).

18. See, for example, Bouali's description of the audience for Maqshīsh in Tlemcen. Bouali, *Kitāb kashf al-qinā'*, 125.

19. See Glasser, "Musical Jews."

20. Christianowitsch, *Esquisse historique de la musique arabe.*

21. Laho Seror and Maklouf Bouchara are examples of Jewish professional musicians who identified themselves by their nonmusical work, at least at the time they were declaring such information to the authorities (Seror was a shoemaker, and Bouchara a house-painter). For these records, see Fonds ministérhiels, Dépôt des papiers publics des colonies: État Civil, Algérie, CAOM.

22. The link between *nūba* performers and textile workers has been commented on in Hadri

Bougherara's musical portrait of Tlemcen. Hadri Bougherara, *Voyage sentimentale dans la musique arabo-andalouse.* A. Bel and P. Ricard, *Les Industries indigènes de l'Algérie: Le travail de la laine à Tlemcen* (1913), 52. See also Nadir Marouf, "Le système musical de la San'a ou le paradigme de la norme et de la marge," 14–15.

23. Bel and Ricard, *Les industries indigènes à Tlemcen*, 193. In addition, see Saidani, *La musique du constantinois*, 70.

24. Bel and Ricard, 193, 359.

25. The analogy between textiles and music went beyond the *nūba* per se. See Delphin and Guin, *Notes sur la poésie et la musique arabes*, 35.

26. M. Bekhoucha and A. Sekkal, eds., *Anthologie d'Auteurs arabes / Kitāb nafḥ al-azhār* (1934), 9–10. For the possibility of using *ṣan'a* to refer to mode, see Saidani, *La musique du constantinois*, 243.

27. For the informed patron as a goad to expanding a performer's repertoire in Constantine, see Saidani, *La Musique du constantinois*, 60.

28. Mohammed Zerrouki, "Sur la musique orientale," 592–93.

29. Most of these manuscripts are in private collections, but see the manuscripts numbered 1811–1815 in the Bibliothèque nationale d'Algérie, as well as the Leiden manuscript 14169 cited in Amnon Shiloah, "Pe'ilutam shel musikayim yehudim ba-musika ha-klasit ha-algerit veba-sugot she-hist'afu mimena," 59. An exception to the collection created for performers and connoisseurs was the one created at the request of a military officer stationed in Tlemcen. See *Al-jawāhir al-ḥisān fī naẓm awliyā' tilimsān*, Bibliothèque nationale de France Or. 5254.

30. Rachid Guerbas, "Chant et musique de la nawba ou nûba algérienne," 26. For parallel anecdotes, see Saidani, *La musique du constantinois*, 61, 122.

31. Bouali, *Kitāb kashf al-qinā'*, 123–24.

32. Yafil, *Majmū' al-aghānī wa-l-alḥān*, iv.

33. Maya Saidani, "Le Zadjel Constantinois: Chant d'une andalousie déchue."

34. Mohamed Bekkhoucha / Muḥammad Bakhūsha, *Adab al-maghāriba wa-ḥayyātuhum al-ijtimā'iyya wa-l-dīniyya wa-ba'ḍ khurāfātihim / Savoir-vivre, vie sociale et religieuse des Marocains, Leurs contes*, 18. Bekkhoucha's brief description is very close to what Schuyler describes in "Music Education in Morocco."

35. Jean Lave and Etienne Wenger, *Situated Learning: Legitimate Peripheral Participation.* For an exploration of musical apprenticeship in Morocco, see Schuyler, "Music Education in Morocco." For an intimate look at musical apprenticeship in the context of ethnographic participant-observation, see Jankowsky, *Stambeli*; Amanda Weidman, "The Ethnographer as Apprentice: Embodying Sociomusical Knowledge in South India"

36. In Bouali's description of the situation that held in Algiers at the turn of the twentieth century, at least some of the supporting instrumentalists in a professional ensemble were understood to be the students of the *shaykh*. Bouali, *Kashf al-qinā'*, 124.

37. Cited in Saidani, *La musique du constantinois*, 85. Interestingly enough, some people parallel the "backward" refusal to transmit repertoire to a similar out-of-date attitude toward accumulation of wealth: the professional musicians of the past are sometimes said to have immediately spent their musical earnings. While this sounds like the opposite of hoarding, such a tendency has the same effect: certain *shuyūkh* left nothing for the next generation in both musical and monetary terms.

38. Jules Rouanet, "La musique arabe dans le Maghreb," 2913.

39. Yafil, *Majmū' al-aghānī wa-l-alḥān*.

40. Christianowitsch, *Esquisse historique de la musique arabe*, 16.

41. On competition among close musical peers in Constantine, see Saidani, *La musique du constantinois*, 66.

42. Bourdieu's notion of social, cultural, and symbolic capital, explored partly in *Outline of a Theory of Practice*, tends to sidestep the questions of production that are so central to Marx's understanding of the concept. To put it simply, Marx might ask what is being produced and whose labor is being harnessed in an instance that Bourdieu might say is a deployment of cultural capital. This calls for a theory of the production of the person or of subjectivity, while Bourdieu's use of the concept tends to evoke a game rather than a deployment of labor. See Read, *The Micro-Politics of Capital*.

43. For a parallel in Constantine, this time focused on the question of light versus heavy genres, see the case of Ben Tobal, in Saidani, *La musique du constantinois*, 67.

44. Bel and Ricard, *Les industries indigènes de l'Algérie*, 223; Bougherara, *Voyage sentimentale*, 14.

45. A related idiom can be found in the transmission and evaluation of the *ḥadīth* literature, sayings attributed to the Prophet Muhammad and his companions. The practice of transmitting, collecting, and evaluating the authenticity of *aḥādīth* (singular: *ḥadīth*) predates the rise of Sufism and constitutes a practice found among Sufi adepts and their critics. Here, however, the emphasis is on the evaluation of the trustworthiness of the chains of transmission of speech, rather than on the relationship of master and disciple per se. While elements of the *ḥadīth* model will return in later chapters, the *shaykh–mūlūʿ* dyad is closer to the Sufi pattern.

46. For similar comments among *āla* practitioners, see Davila, *The Andalusian Music of Morocco*, 213.

47. Ahmed Serri, *Chants andalous: Recueil des poèmes des noubates de la musique "Sanaa," musique classique algérienne* (2006), 6–11.

48. For a very similar trope in Egypt and the Levant, see Racy, *Making Music in the Arab World*, 20–25.

49. Bouali, *Kitāb kashf al-qināʿ*, 125.

50. Yafil, *Majmūʿ al-aghānī wa-l-alḥān*, iv; Jules Rouanet, in *Actes du XIVe Congres International des Orientalistes Alger 1905, Troisième Partie, Langues Musulmanes (Arabe Persan et Turc)* (1906), 92.

51. The verb for designating a successor, *yukhallif*, is the same used in Sufi circles and in the controversies regarding the successors of the Prophet Muhammad. This verb is derived from the same source as the term *caliph* (*khalīfa*).

52. See for example, Jules Rouanet, "La musique musulmane" (1927), 7; Aḥmad Tawfiq al-Madanī, *Kitāb al-Jazāʾir* (1931), 326. Interestingly enough, Rouanet's use of the shipwreck metaphor was part of a denunciation of musicians claiming author rights over *nūba* repertoire.

53. On unconscious metaphors, see George Lakoff and Mark Johnson, *Metaphors We Live By*.

54. For a parallel between Andalusi descent and the concept of sharifian descent, see Daniel J. Schroeter, "The Shifting Boundaries of Moroccan Jewish Identities," 151. We can think of this as a genealogical modality, not unlike the notion of a sensory modality in Alfred Gell, "The Language of the Forest: Landscape and Phonological Iconism in Umeda." The fact that it is about al-Andalus, rather than simply the Maghribi past, is not arbitrary: a lost place and a lost time combined is more powerful than either one alone for evoking the remoteness, value, unassailability, unity-in-multiplicity, and at the same time fragility of genealogical and repertorial authority. Indeed, we might hypothesize that chronotopicities that highlight origin narrative will also place great emphasis on the construction of traditionality and transmission. On tradi-

tionalization, see Richard Bauman, "Contextualisation, Tradition, and the Dialogue of Genres: Icelandic Legends of the *Kraftaskáld*."

55. Marcel Mauss, *The Gift: The Form and Reason for Exchange in Archaic Societies.*

Chapter Three

1. Alexandre Christianowitsch, *Esquisse historique de la musique arabe aux temps anciens*, 6.

2. Many of these insights can be traced back still further to the discussion of the linguistic sign in Ferdinand de Saussure, *Course in General Linguistics*, 65–78. See M. M. Bakhtin, "The Problem of Speech Genres"; Franco Fabbri, "A Theory of Musical Genres: Two Applications."; Joyce Burkhalter Flueckiger, "Genre and Community in the Folklore System of Chhattisgarh"; Charles L. Briggs and Richard Bauman, "Genre, Intertextuality, and Social Power," 142–43; Richard Bauman, "Contextualisation, Tradition, and the Dialogue of Genres: Icelandic Legends of the *Kraftaskáld*"; William F. Hanks, "Exorcism and the Description of Participant Roles"; Sue Tuohy, "The Social Life of Genre: The Dynamics of Folksong in China"; Karin Barber, *The Anthropology of Texts, Person and Publics*, 37; Anthony Guest-Scott, "Categories in Motion: The Use of Generic Multiplicity in Music Store Guitar Lessons."

3. For marginal genres, see Gary H. Gossen, *Chamulas in the World of the Sun: Time and Space in a Maya Oral Tradition*, 56–77.

4. Clifford Geertz, *The Interpretation of Cultures*, 452.

5. On "boundary work as metageneric practice," see Alexander Sebastian Dent, *River of Tears: Country Music, Memory, and Modernity in Brazil*, 115.

6. Steven Feld, "Sound Structure as Social Structure," 406.

7. For a history of the Arabic songbook form, including its Maghribi variants, see Dwight F. Reynolds, "Lost Virgins Found: The Arabic Songbook Genre and an Early North African Exemplar."

8. Virginia Danielson, *The Voice of Egypt: Umm Kulthum, Arabic Song, and Egyptian Society in the Twentieth Century*, 138–41, cited in Richard C. Jankowsky, *Stambeli: Music, Trance, and Alterity in Tunisia*, 110; Rasmussen, *Women, the Recited Qur'an, and Islamic Music in Indonesia*, 42–44; A. J. Racy, *Making Music in the Arab World: The Culture and Artistry of Ṭarab.*

9. The most common placement of the instrumental *jawāb* in a five-line text with a rhyme scheme of AAABB is as follows: instrumental repetition of the first and second A, and instrumental repetition of the first half of the first B. For a summary, see Youcef Touaïbia's notes in Serri, *Chants Andalous* (2002), xiii–xiv.

10. See, for example, Mohamed El-Fasi, "La musique marocaine dite 'musique andalouse,'" 90.

11. There are in fact Maghribi performers of *muwashshaḥ* poetry in the Levantine musical tradition, but these performances are marked as foreign, and specifically as coming from the Arab East (fitting under the umbrella term of *sharqī* or eastern music, in contradistinction to music that is understood as properly Maghribi). Note, too, that some of the poems in the North African Andalusi traditions are not in the *muwashshaḥ* form, or the allied *zajal* form, but are rather monorhyme *qaṣāy'id.*

12. The literature on the *muwashshaḥ* is vast. For an English-language introduction, see Samuel M. Stern, *Hispano-Arabic Strophic Poetry*; James T. Monroe, *Hispano-Arabic Poetry*; Salma Khadra Jayyusi, "Andalusī Poetry: The Golden Period"; James T. Monroe, "*Zajal* and *Muwashshaḥa*: Hispano-Arabic Poetry and the Romance Tradition"; Tova Rosen, "The Muwashshah."

13. For discussion of some of these terms, see Rosen, "The Muwashshah," 169.

14. Youcef Touaïbia credits the *muwashshaḥ* with "breaking the rigid vertical structure of the classical qasida." Fayçal Benkalfat et al., *Al-mūsīqā al-klāsīkiyya fi-l-duwal al-maghāribiyya / La musique classique du Maghreb*, 2:229. There is also a rich literature on the metric innovations introduced by the *muwashshaḥ*. Again, see the work of Touaïbia, as well as Desparmet, *La poésie arabe actuelle à Blida et sa métrique*.

15. On the concept of the lock in formalist readings of poetry and narrative, see Mary Douglas, *Thinking in Circles: An Essay on Ring Composition*. A related term, *qafla*, is used for the closing melodic phrase in the urban art music of Egypt and the Levant.

16. Rosen, "The Muwashshah," 167.

17. But according to Rosen, "It is debatable whether the muwashshah originally had refrains." Rosen, "The Muwashshah," 172. A tantalizing possibility is that the term *nūba*, which can be translated as "turn," is a gloss on the original Greek meaning of strophe.

18. For poetry and music in medieval al-Andalus, see Lois Ibsen al Faruqi, "Muwashshaḥ: A Vocal Form in Islamic Culture"; David Wulstan, "The Muwaššaḥ and Zağal Revisited"; Jozéf Pacholczyk, "The Relationship Between the Nawba of Morocco and the Music of the Troubadours and Trouvères"; Benjamin M. Liu and James T. Monroe, *Ten Hispano-Arabic Strophic Songs in the Modern Oral Tradition: Music and Texts*; Jozéf Pacholczyk, "Early Arab Suite in Spain: An Investigation of the Past through the Contemporary Living Tradition"; Owen Wright, "Music in Muslim Spain"; Dwight Reynolds, "Music."

19. James T. Monroe, "Poetic Quotation in the *Muwaššaḥa* and Its Implications: Andalusian Strophic Poetry as Song."

20. On *kharja* studies, see Samuel G. Armistead, "A Brief History of Kharja Studies"; Alan Jones and Richard Hitchcock, eds., *Studies on the Muwaššaḥ and the Kharja*.

21. Ali Jihad Racy, "Overview of Music in the Mashriq," in *The Garland Encyclopedia of World Music*, 6:550; Racy, *Making Music in the Arab World*; Mark S. Wagner, *Like Joseph in Beauty: Yemeni Vernacular Poetry and Arab-Jewish Symbiosis*.

22. I am grateful to Simon Shaheen and Nizar Fares for pointing this out.

23. Jallūl Yallis and al-ḥafnāwī Amuqrān, eds., *Al-muwashshaḥāt wa-l-azjāl*, 2:15.

24. S. M. Stern, "Andalusian Muwashshaḥs in the Musical Repertoire of North Africa"; Pacholczyk, "The Relationship Between the Nawba of Morocco and the Music of the Troubadours" and "Early Arab Suite in Spain: An Investigation of the Past through the Contemporary Living Tradition"; Liu and Monroe, *Ten Hispano-Arabic Strophic Songs*.

25. Yallis and Amuqrān, *Al-muwashshaḥāt wa-l-azjāl*, 2:11.

26. Stern, "Andalusian Muwashshaḥs in the Musical Repertoire of North Africa," 324. Note how such shedding takes advantage of the lyrical, piecemeal, nonnarrative nature of the *muwashshaḥ* form.

27. Ibid., 325.

28. Davila, *The Andalusian Music of Morocco*, 294.

29. For a theory that connects specific modes to particular poetic themes, see Maya Saidani, *La musique du constantinois*, 101–13.

30. In fact, *shughl* is sometimes differentiated from *ṣanʿa* through the notion that the former contains *tarāṭīn*. See Davila, *The Andalusian Music of Morocco*, 323. For many musicians and listeners who I have encountered, however, *shughl* and *ṣanʿa* are synonyms, as they are in the *āla* tradition as well. See ibid., 199n29. On the elision of *tarāṭīn* and repeated lines of poetry in *āla* compilations, see Davila, *The Andalusian Music of Morocco*, 154.

31. There is in fact some discrepancy about the equivalence of these two terms. For some, a *shghul* is a given sung text, while *ṣanʿa* refers to the totality of sung texts for a given mode. Note

that the musicality of the *ṣanʿa* means that some people simply translate it as melody, although in fact the dominant usage is that it is a sung poem, rather than its abstracted melody. For the glossing of *ṣanʿa* as melody, see Maya Saidani, *La musique du constantinois*, 169.

32. Nadir Marouf, "Le système musical de la Sanʿa ou le paradigme de la norme et de la marge," 24n11. For references to opera going back to the mid-nineetenth century, see Christianowitsch, *Esquisse historique de la musique arabe*, 6; Jules Rouanet in Edmond Nathan Yafil and Jules Rouanet, eds., *Répertoire de musique arabe et maure: Collection de mélodies, ouvertures, noubet, chansons, préludes, etc.*, no. 12; Aḥmad Tawfīq al-Madanī, *Kitāb al-Jazāʾir* (1931), 364; Aḥmad Safta, *Dirāsāt fi-l-mūsīqā al-andalusiyya*, 355.

33. That is to say, the typical *muwashshaḥ* in the Andalusi musical traditions is the kind known as *aqraʿ* or "bald" (so named because it has no *maṭlaʿ* at its head). Note, however, that the notion of common rhyme and non-common rhyme is often theoretical in the musical context, since the sung texts rarely have enough strophes to make such a pattern apparent. In other words, the notion of a common rhyme assumes a familiarity with the formal conventions of the *muwashshaḥ*.

34. Serri, *Majmūʿat ashʿār wa-azjāl*, 107–8.

35. Again, in actual fact, the notion of a common rhyme is virtual, since the *ṣanʿa* often lacks enough lines to convey the sense of a common rhyme.

36. For the inspiration for this turn of phrase, see Richard Bauman, *A World of Others' Words: Cross-Cultural Perspectives on Intertextuality*.

37. Even the account of modal relationships given here is up for dispute. For example, some practitioners understand *dhīl* to be the root and *muwwāl* to be the derivative. In addition, for another interpretation of the Algiers-Tlemcen distribution regarding the derivatives of *raml al-māya* and *ʿarāq*, see Fayçal Benkalfat et al., *Al-mūsīqā al-klāsīkiyya fi-l-duwal al-maghāribiyya / La musique classique du Maghreb*, 2:15.

38. The fact that *dhīl* usually comes first may be an artifact of a play on words. *Dil majmūʿa* is the Turkish term for a collection of poems, literally meaning "language collection." Such Turkish-language collections were current in Ottoman Algiers. Creators of the collections of Arabic poetry who were familiar with the Ottoman Turkish term may have taken it into account in deciding to place *dhīl* first among the modes. For such Turkish collections in Algeria during the Ottoman period, see J. Deny, "Chansons des janissaires turcs d'Alger (fin du xviiime siècle)."

39. The modes are not airtight with regard to poetic texts; in fact, there are many poems that are shared by different modes. The same is true with regard to the modes themselves: because some modes are understood to be related to one another, and because not every *nūba* has sufficient texts and melodies to be performed *in extenso*, there is some borrowing from compatible *nūbāt*.

40. In fact, the term *maqām* competes with *ṭabʿ* in the Maghribi musical lexicon. For the concept of *maqām* in the Mashriq, see Scott Marcus, "The Eastern Arab System of Melodic Modes in Theory and Practice: A Case Study of *Maqām Bayyātī*." See also Racy, *Making Music in the Arab World*.

41. Francisco Salvador Daniel, *La musique arabe: Ses rapports avec la musique grècque et le chant grégorien* (1879).

42. See in particular the work of Fayçal Benkalfat in Fayçal Benkalfat et al., *Al-mūsīqā al-klāsīkiyya fi-l-duwal al-maghāribiyya / La musique classique du Maghreb*.

43. Thomas Shaw, *Travels, or Observations Relating to Several Parts of Barbary and the Levant* (1738), 203.

44. See, for example, M. Bekhoucha and A. Sekkal, eds., *Anthologie d'Auteurs arabes / Kitāb nafḥ al-azhār*, 10.

45. For example, some veteran musicians recall having played *nūbat māya* at the end of the night of festivities, just before dawn. See Yafil and Rouanet, *Répertoire*, for the notion that *māya* is associated with this time of day, as well as Safir Al Boudali, "La musique classique algérienne ou l'eternel miracle du message andalou," 26. In addition, see Abdelkader Toumi's statement regarding the currency of the mode-hour connection in Constantine in 1960: Jürgen Elsner, "Présentation de la musique algérienne au congrès du Caire," 195. For a rich discussion of modes and their placement within wedding festivities in old Constantine, as well as legends about the effects of modes and of failure to respect their temporal placement, see Saidani, *La musique du constantinois*, 61–62, 209–11.

46. Ghouti Bouali, *Kitāb kashf al-qināʿ ʿan ālāt al-samāʿ*, 108.

47. Racy, *Making Music in the Arab World*, 98–100.

48. Bachir Hadj Ali, "Qu'est-ce qu'une musique nationale?" 178. For similar discussions in Constantine, see Saidani, *La musique du constantinois*, 209.

49. Bouali, *Kitāb kashf al-qināʿ*, 123–24.

50. The *istikhbār* is not confined to the Andalusi repertoire or its modes. For an introduction to its range in Algeria, see A. Hachlef, "Les preludes dans la musique arabo-andalouse en Algérie, istikhbar vocal." See also Leo J. Plenckers, "Modal and Formal Constraints in Improvisation: A Study to the Algerian *istiḫbār*."

51. Bouali, *Kitāb kashf al-qināʿ*, 108.

52. For disagreement regarding modal identities in Constantine, see Saidani, *La musique du constantinois*, 234.

53. See, for example, BNA Manuscript 1812.

54. See, for example, the blending of *raml al-māya, ʿarāq, ḥsīn*, and *mjennba* in BNA Manuscript 1812.

55. See Edmond Yafil, *Majmūʿ zahw al-anīs al-mukhtaṣṣ bi-l-tabāsī wa-l-qawādis* (1907); J. Joly, "Chansons du répertoire algérois" (1909). Interestingly enough, the *mṣaddar* seems to have been a term used for a similar form that existed outside the *nūba* repertoire. This is the *mṣaddar ʿarbī* in *Majmūʿ zahw al-anīs*, which follows the *muwashshab* form but uses a colloquial register that is marked as a rural or Bedouin pronunciation (hence the term *ʿarbī* or *ʿarūbī*).

56. See Ahmed Serri, *Chants andalous*.

57. Ibid.

58. See Yafil, *Répertoire de musique arabe et maure*, no. 29, where he refers to "nouba dil" as a "Sonate Style Arabe"; Marouf, "Le système musical de la Sanʿa ou le paradigme de la norme et de la marge," 19.

59. Interestingly enough, the colloquial elements that sometimes enter the *nūba* poetry do not seem to be primarily found in the *inṣirāf* or *khlāṣ* texts but also appear in the "heavy" early movements.

60. For the controversy over the *darj* in Algiers versus Tlemcen, see Touaïbia, "Le Derdj dans Nouba de Tlemcen" and Ghoul, "NEA_Y-Ghoul vs TECHNIQUE du Groupe Yafil signé Y-T (Partie 1)." For discussion of the rhythmic dimension of the first three movements, see Guerbas, "Chant et musique de la Nawba ou Nûba algérienne," 29–31.

61. For an exposition of the differences and similarities between Tlemcen, Algiers, and Constantine, see Nadia Mecheri-Saada, "Les documents algériens du Congrès du Caire."

62. The *inṣirāf* is notated in many different ways, including 2/4 in Christianowitsch, *Esquisse*; 21/32 in Rachid Guerbas "Chant et musique de la Nawba ou Nûba algérienne"; and 22/16, 6/8, and 3/4 in Fayçal Benkalfat/Fayṣal Bin Qalfāt et al., *Al-mūsīqā al-klāsīkiyya fi-l-duwal al-maghāribiyya / La musique classique du Maghreb.*

63. This rhythmic pulse is very widespread in Algerian and Moroccan musical practice and goes by a variety of names. Note that the transition from *inṣirāf* to *khlāṣ* is usually so gradual as to give the listener a sense of a blurred transformation, metamorphosis, or emergence. Serri's *Chants andalous* marks out particular potential *ṣanāyi'* for use in such transitions.

64. In Yafil and Rouanet, *Répertoire de musique arabe et maure*, no. 24.

65. Thomas Turino, *Music as Social Life: The Politics of Participation*. Davila describes a similar shift in *āla* performance in Morocco. See *The Andalusian Music of Morocco*, 187.

66. On *sha'bī* (in French, *chaabi*), see Bachir Hadj Ali, "El Anka et la tradition 'chaabi,'" and Fatīḥa Qāra Shantīr, *Al-sha'bī: Khiṭāb, ṭuqūs wa-mumārasāt*. On the circulation and transformation of elements of the Constantine *nūba* among *fqīrāt* from Annaba, see Saidani, *La musique du constantinois*, 288–90.

67. Yafil and Rouanet, *Répertoire de musique arabe et maure*, no. 6.

68. Technically, *malḥūn* references the poetry, while *ḥawzī* and *'arūbi* reference the sung text. Nevertheless, all of them can be used as genre names, as can the term *qṣāyid*. There is also some disagreement about the precise relationship between *ḥawzī* and *'arūbī*. While some argue that they are two subcategories of colloquial sung poetry, Yahia Ghoul suggests that *'arūbī* is a kind of *ḥawzī*. See Yahia Ghoul, *Patrimoine de musique arabo-andalouse: Le système rythmique dans l'école de Tlemcen*. For the view of *'arūbī* as separate from *ḥawzī*, see Dib, "Typologie du patrimoine hawzi et non hawzi (Poésie et rythmes)," 108–9.

69. The *istikhbār* introduces some interesting complications. Its unmetered nature and its sense of seriousness makes it the embodiment of the *thaqīl* both within the context of the *nūba* and outside it: from the point of view of the percussion, the *istikhbār* literally does not move. At the same time, it is largely free from textual enshrinement, and it is subordinated to what follows: one can do a *qṣīda* or an *inqilāb* without an *istikhbār*, but an *istikhbār* done alone is unidiomatic.

70. W. B. Gallie, "Art as an Essentially Contested Concept."

71. For a rich overview of these genre fields, see Jürgen Elsner, "Urban Music of Algeria."

72. In addition, particularly in the 1970s, one could add Indian film music and "Spanish music," meaning Andalucían guitar.

73. Frishkopf, "Introduction," 5.

74. Marc Schade-Poulsen, *Men and Popular Music in Algeria: The Social Significance of* Raï; Martin Stokes, "Marx, Money, and Musicians."

75. See Fatīḥa Qāra Shantīr, *Al-sha'bī: Khiṭāb, ṭuqūs wa-mumārasāt*.

76. See, for example, Bachir Hadj Ali, "El Anka et la tradition 'chaabi.'"

77. The alleged absence of quarter tones in the Andalusi traditions other than *mā'lūf* is also sometimes used to assert a kinship between the *nūba* and European classical music.

78. For discussion of the Andalusi origin narrative as being about fixedness, see Davila, *The Andalusian Music of Morocco*, 189.

79. See, for example, the orchestral works of the musical reformer Edmond Yafil in the 1920s that took their inspiration from the *nūba* repertoire, as well as the haunting pianistic experiments of Sariza and Ramaya from the post-Second World War era. I thank Hadi Kheir for drawing my attention to Ramaya. For more recent decades, see the works of Colette Merklen and Mutlu Torun based in *raml* and Miquèu Montanaro's collaboration with Association Al Maoussilia of Oujda.

80. For a discussion of Saoudi's composition within the wider question of innovation in the Andalusi tradition, see Fethi Salah, "Le 'Néo Andalou' à Alger: Procédés d'innovation structurale dans la tradition musicale."

81. For the identification of Sfindja as composer of its melody, see Yafil and Rouanet, *Répertoire de musique arabe et maure*, no. 16.

82. For a description of fin-de-siècle *nūba* practice in Algiers and Tlemcen, see Bouali, *Kitāb kashf al-qināʿ*, 122-25.

83. For a similar use of an image of "sedimentary patrimonialization" in relation to the Andalusi musical tradition of Algeria, see Marouf, "Le système musical de la Sanʿa ou le paradigme de la norme et de la marge," 21.

84. Mohamed Zerrouki, "La musique etudiée comme 'système d'expression,'" in CADN/193/3/C/10, in folder titled "Musique arabe et hébraïque."

Part Two

1. Karin Barber, *The Anthropology of Texts, Person and Publics*, 4, 201.

Chapter Four

1. The photo and identification are thanks to the Groupe Yafil website (http://yafil.free.fr/album_alger.htm) and Zakia Kara Terki.

2. See for example in Octave Depont and Xavier Coppolani, *Les confréries religieuses musulmanes* (1897).

3. On ʿAbduh's visit, see Ali Merad, "L'enseignement politique de Muhammad ʿAbduh aux algériens (1903)"; Rachid Bencheneb, "Le séjour du šayḫ ʿAbduh en Algérie (1903)."

4. Merad, " L'enseignement politique de Muhammad ʿAbduh," 99.

5. Rouanet was cited for his restoration of Arab music in a talk given at the same conference: Joseph Desparmet, "La poésie arabe actuelle à Blida et sa métrique," 463.

6. *Actes du XIVe Congrès*, 89–93. His talk was published as Jules Rouanet, "Esquisse pour une histoire de la musique arabe en Algérie-I-II-III" (1905–6).

7. *Actes du XIVe Congrès*, 92.

8. Rouanet, "Esquisse pour une histoire de la musique arabe III," 128.

9. Ibid., 129.

10. Ibid., 128.

11. Ibid., 141.

12. Ibid., 141–42.

13. "Chroniques Algériennes: Les M'tournis," *Le Temps*, February 8, 1902, 3.

14. The account would be read with great interest by aficionados of Andalusi poetry on the Mediterranean's other edge. See the work of Philippe El Khazen, ed., *Al-ʿadhāra al-māyisāt fi-l-azjāl wa-l-muwashshaḥāt* (1902).

15. On the Louvre, see Andrew McClellan, *Inventing the Louvre*. With regard to Weber and patrimonialism, see Julia Adams, "The Rule of the Father: Patriarchy and Patrimonialism in Early Modern Europe."

16. For the connection between patrimony and *ḥabūs*, see Oulebsir, *Les usages du patrimoine*, 15. For the challenge it posed to French colonial practices, see John Ruedy, *Land Policy in Colonial Algeria*. For an example of discursive continuity between *ḥabūs* and colonial patrimony, see section marked "Manuscrits," in "Rapport preliminaire sur la mission de Mr. A. Berbrugger, à Constantine," Algiers, 30 Nov. 1837, CAOM/F80/1733.

17. Pierre Bourdieu, *Outline of a Theory of Practice*, 46.

18. Oulebsir, *Les usages du patrimoine*, 134–38.

19. See E. Pelissier de Reynaud, *Annales algeriennes*, 1:79, quoted in Ruedy, *Land Policy in Colonial Algeria*, 14. See also Section marked "Manuscrits," in "Rapport preliminaire sur la mission de Mr. A. Berbrugger, à Constantine," Algiers, 30 Nov. 1837, CAOM/F80/1733; and "Notes sur la Bibliothèque et sur le musée d'Alger," 1845, CAOM/F80/1733.

20. Oulebsir, *Les usages du patrimoine*, 94–114.

21. For the use of the Roman past in colonial Algeria, see Jacques Frémeaux, "Souvenirs de Rome et presence française au Maghreb"; Patricia M. E. Lorcin, "Rome and France in Africa: Recovering Colonial Algeria's Latin Past"; Monique Dondin-Payre, "L'archéologie en Algérie à partir de 1830"; Camille Risler, *La politique culturelle de la France en Algérie: Les objectifs et les limites (1830–1962)*, 146–47; Oulebsir, *Les usages du patrimoine*. For examples of deciphering, see the epigraphic collaborations of Charles Brosselard with Hammou Ben Rostan in Tlemcen. Charles Brosselard, *Memoire épigraphique et historique sur les tombeaux de émirs Beni-Zeiyan, et de Boabdil, dernier roi de Grenade, découverts à Tlemcen* (1876), 195–96; Charles Brosselard, "Epitaphe d'un roi grenadin mort a Tlemcen."

22. On the royaume arabe as politics, see Osama W. Abi-Mershed, *Apostles of Modernity: Saint-Simonians and the Civilizing Mission in Algeria*, 159–200. In relation to patrimony, see Oulebsir, *Les usages du patrimoine*, 115–56.

23. See Oulebsir, *Les usages du patrimoine*, 155–57.

24. For evocation of Algiers in the late nineteenth century, see David Prochaska, "The Other Algeria."

25. On the fate of Franco-Arab secondary schools in the Third Republic, see Alain Messaoudi, "The Teaching of Arabic in French Algeria and Contemporary France," 305–6.

26. He would help implement significant reforms during his third tenure (1918–19). On Jonnart's career, see Oulebsir, *Les usages du patrimoine*, 335.

27. Ibid.

28. From LaBouthière, "La Renovation des Arts Musulmans Algériens," Sep. 1923, CAOM/10H60.

29. *Ḥuḍḍār* can be translated as conference-goers, audience, or as the civilized or enlightened ones. Note that the second syllable of Jonnart provided the end-rhyme for the poem. *Actes du XIVe Congrès*, 592–93.

30. See *Exposition d'art musulman: Août, Septembre, Octobre, Novembre 1893 Palais des Champs-Elysées* (1893), as well as the correspondence in ANF/F21/4079. In fact, this precedent to the musical revival was mentioned in Rouanet's 1905 presentation.

31. The French and broader European (and American) fascination with Muslim Spain grew out of a full century of Orientalist scholarship, writing, and painting that included the splendors of the Andalusi past within its purview. It was not until the end of the century, however, that decades of scholarly and literary attention to al-Andalus found a popular outlet via architecture, exhibitions, and performance. For this popularization of al-Andalus, see Roger Benjamin, "*Andalusia in the Time of the Moors*: Regret and Colonial Presence in Paris, 1900."

32. For India, see Amanda Weidman, *Singing the Classical, Voicing the Modern: The Postcolonial Politics of Music in South India*.

33. Indeed, there was a trend at this time toward a regionalist architectural emphasis in the metropole that would champion works reflecting the character of specific provinces. Oulebsir, *Les usages du patrimoine*, 233.

34. A fascination with al-Andalus and its remnants shows up in the account of the Egyptian Muḥammad Bey Farīd's travels in Spain, Morocco, and Algeria at the turn of the century. Muḥammad Bey Farīd, *Min miṣr ilā miṣr*. On images of al-Andalus in relation to Java, see

Michael Laffan, "'Another Andalusia': Images of Colonial Southeast Asia in Arabic." On somewhat later uses of al-Andalus in the Urdu poems of Iqbal and the Arabic-language poetry of the Egyptian Aḥmad Shawqī, see Yaseen Noorani, "The Lost Garden of Al-Andalus: Islamic Spain and the Poetic Inversion of Colonialism."

35. On British antiquarian views of the lower classes, see Richard Bauman and Charles L. Briggs, *Voices of Modernity: Language Ideologies and the Politics of Inequality*, and for a specifically musical discourse, see Britta Sweers, *Electric Folk: The Changing Face of English Traditional Music*. For France, see Robert Darnton, "Peasants Tell Tales: The Meaning of Mother Goose." For the broader notion of disappearance in the face of European power, see Patrick Brantlinger, *Dark Vanishings: Discourse on the Extinction of Primitive Races, 1800–1930*.

36. On "salvage ethnography" in the Algerian context, see George R. Trumbull IV, *An Empire of Facts: Colonial Power, Cultural Knowledge, and Islam in Algeria, 1870–1914*, in particular chapter 4.

37. J. Desparmet, "Nūbat al-Andalus."

38. Ghouti Bouali, *Kitāb kashf al-qināʿ ʿan ālāt al-samāʿ* (1904).

39. This is an ironic version of Kenneth Goldstein's notion of the technological engine of revival: Kenneth Goldstein, "A Future Folklorist in the Record Business," cited in Tamara E. Livingston, "Music Revivals: Towards a General Theory," 80.

40. See Joseph Desparmet, *La poésie arabe actuelle à Blida et sa métrique* (1907), 3, 27.

41. C. Sonneck, ed., *Chants arabes du Maghreb: Étude sur le dialecte et la poésie populaire de l'Afrique du Nord, vol. 1* (1902); idem, ed., *Chants arabes du Maghreb: Étude sur le dialecte et la poésie populaire de l'Afrique du Nord, vol. 2* (1904). His first major publication of song texts was M. C. Sonneck, "Six chansons arabes en dialecte maghrébin" (1899).

42. Neither piece is dated; however, the one that is dedicated to Israel Stora, honorary president of the Algiers *consistoire* (the state-recognized Jewish representative body), is likely from the late 1880s and must antedate 1894, the year of Stora's death. In this example, Bouaziz is listed as having notated the melody, while the piano transcription is credited to Keil, founder and director of the choral society called Les Enfants de l'Algérie. In another example, which may be from a later date, Bouaziz is listed as the transcriber. M. Bouaziz and Martz Keil, *A Monsieur I. Stora President Honoraire du Consistoire d'Alger: Inqilāb jarka / Djarka* (1886?); M. Bouaziz, *Musique arabe, mode Darj Lahcine.*

43. Edwin Seroussi, "Music," in *Encyclopedia of Jews in the Islamic World*, 511. In addition, see the advertisement in Mardochée Uzan, *el-Bah'r bidh'acli* (1892).

44. Francisco Salvador Daniel, *La musique arabe: Ses rapports avec la musique grècque et le chant grégorien* (1879). For a close reading of Salvador Daniel's life and projects, see Kristy Riggs, "On Colonial Textuality and Difference: Musical Encounters with French Colonialism in Nineteenth-Century Algeria."

45. For the ethnographically rich contemporary, see Alexandre Christianowitsch, *Esquisse historique de la musique arabe aux temps anciens* (1863).

46. On Saint-Simonians in Algeria, see Osama W. Abi-Mershed, *Apostles of Modernity: Saint-Simonians and the Civilizing Mission in Algeria*.

47. Francisco Salvador Daniel, *La musique arabe*, 125.

48. Francisco Salvador Daniel, *Album de douze chansons arabes, mauresques et kabyles*.

49. Katherine Bergeron, *Decadent Enchantments: The Revival of Gregorian Chant at Solesmes*.

50. Alexandre Christianowitsch, *Esquisse historique de la musique arabe*. For biographical

information on Christianowitsch, see Miloš Velimirović , "Russian Autographs at Harvard," 542n1, 551.

51. Christianowitsch, *Esquisse historique de la musique arabe*, 7.

52. Ibid., 1.

53. G. Delphin and L. Guin, *Notes sur la poésie et la musique arabes dans le Maghreb algérien* (1886). Another exception was the description of Maghribi musicians at the 1889 Exposition in Paris that appeared in Julien Tiersot's *Musiques pittoresques* (the author depicts them as an aural completion of Eugène Delacroix's *Noce juive au Maroc*). Julien Tiersot, *Musiques pittoresques: Promenades musicales, l'exposition de 1889*, 98.

54. For an extended discussion of Hanoteau, Boulifa, and Kabyle poem compilation, see Jane E. Goodman, *Berber Culture on the World Stage: From Village to Video*, 97–119.

55. On Bin Sidi Saïd, see Joseph Desparmet, *La poésie arabe actuelle à Blida et sa métrique* (1907), 7. On Desparmet, see Fanny Colonna, "Scientific Production and Position in the Intellectual and Political Fields: The Cases of Augustin Berque and Joseph Desparmet."

56. Desparmet, *La poésie arabe actuelle à Blida*, 4–5.

57. On Joseph Desparmet's career and context, see Henri Pérès, "Joseph Desparmet et son oeuvre (1863–1942)"; and Fanny Colonna, "Scientific Production and Position in the Intellectual and Political Fields."

58. On Bouali's sojourn in Tangier, see letter from Cherisey of the Tangier French Legation and Consulate to the Governor General in Algiers, Tangier, March 15, 1905, CADN/195B/517.

59. Bouali, *Kitāb kashf al-qināʿ*, 3.

60. Benali El Hassar, *Tlemcen: Cité des grands maîtres de la musique arabo-andalouse*, 202–3. Benali El Hassar has suggested that Bouali was locked in a debate with the *qāḍī*. The latter's treatise on music could answer the question of whether Bouali's treatise was in fact a response to the *qāḍī*.

61. See letter from Ghouti Bouali, Sidi-Bel-Abbès, March 23, 1906, to the Director of Indigenous Affairs, Algiers, in CAOM/9H/37/18.

62. It is Luciani who makes mention of Bensmaïa's positive review in an undated letter likely from 1904, in CAOM/9H/37/18. For Bensmaïa's circle, see R. Bencheneb, "Une correspondance entre savants maghrébins et orientaux au début du XXe siècle."

63. Bouali, *Kitāb kashf al-qināʿ*, 5.

64. See the various letters from 1904 and 1906, mainly between Bouali and the Office of Indigenous Affairs, CAOM/9H/37/18. Bouali's correspondence was initially with the historian, newspaper editor, and Algiers *médersa* teacher Muḥammad al-Ḥafnāwī but eventually involved Luciani himself. For more on al-Ḥafnāwī, see Saadeddine Bencheneb, "Quelques historiens arabes modernes de l'Algérie," 476; and Bencheneb, "Une correspondance entre savants maghrébins et orientaux," 196n21.

65. Bouali, *Kitāb kashf al-qināʿ*, 108.

66. Ibid., 124.

67. Ibid., 4.

68. Ibid., 23, 92.

69. Ibid., 110–22.

70. Note that not all of these were still being performed at that time; many of the texts' melodies were considered lost.

71. See 1904–1905 correspondence between Frédéric Raisin and Georges Colin, attached to Or. 14.169, Magmu'at al-Nawbat, Leiden.

72. Christian Poché and Jean Lambert, *Musiques du monde arabe et musulman: Bibliographie et discographie,* 137. By 1905, the building had been replaced by the Salle Barthe, a music and theater hall. See 1904–1905 correspondence between Frédéric Raisin and Georges Colin, attached to Or. 14.169, Magmu'at al-Nawbat, Leiden.

73. Poché and Lambert, Musiques du monde arabe et musulman, 137.

74. Jules Rouanet, "Pour les tapis algériens," 227. Turn-of-the-century Algiers was an incubator for visions of colonial uplift, and many of its sensibilities would be revived and elaborated during the interwar era both in Algeria and, to an even greater degree, in Protectorate-era Morocco. Rouanet's suggestions regarding the textile industry, for example, would eventually be put into practice by the colonial authorities in Morocco. See Saïd Chikhaoui, *Politiques publiques et société: Essai d'analyse de l'impact des politiques publiques sur l'artisanat au Maroc.*

75. Yafil's grandfather, Nathan Yafil, was a café owner according to records dating to 1845. CAOM, Fonds ministériels, Dépôt des papiers publics des colonies: État Civil, Algérie..

76. This effort was undertaken without any apparent support from the governmental authorities. Yafil's compilation was printed by Gojosso rather than the quasi-official Imprimerie Jourdane. Its printing likely required a considerable initial outlay from the young Yafil. Considering his modest social origins, the scale of his undertaking is impressive.

77. Edmond Nathan Yafil, *Majmūʿ al-aghānī wa-l-alḥān min kalām al-andalus,* i.

78. Ibid., iii.

79. A similar, though not identical, Judeo-Arabic preface is found in Edmond Nathan Yafil, *Diwān al-aghānī min kalām al-andalus* (1904).

80. As in many parts of the Arab world, Jews traditionally wrote Arabic in Hebrew orthography. The exclusion of Algerois Jews from the upper echelons of *nūba* practice was specifically attested to only by Christianowitsch, who was writing some forty years earlier. Yet Christianowitsch's vivid account certainly raises the possibility that Yafil was responding to some residual form of exclusion in musical circles. With the few materials at our disposal, however, it is impossible to make a strong case for such a subtext to the *Dīwān*. For a closer look at Christianowitsch, see Glasser, "Musical Jews." For a wider look at Jewish musicians and impresarios in North Africa and the Middle East, see Seroussi, "Music," 508–17.

81. On counter-publics, see Michael Warner, *Publics and Counterpublics.*

82. Edmond Nathan Yafil and Jules Rouanet, eds., *Répertoire de musique arabe et maure: Collection de mélodies, ouvertures, noubet, chansons, préludes, etc., nos. 1–25* (1904–?); followed by Edmond Nathan Yafil, *Répertoire de musique arabe et maure: Collection de mélodies, ouvertures, noubet, chansons, préludes, etc., nos. 26–29.*

83. Ibid., specifically nos. 24, 25, 27, and 28. Note that the focus upon framing material did not reflect the emphases of the indigenous enthusiasts—a further piece of evidence that the *Répertoire,* unlike the *Majmūʿ*, was oriented to genre outsiders.

84. Yafil and Rouanet, eds., *Répertoire de musique arabe et maure.*

85. Ibid., No. 21.

86. Allalou, *L'aurore du théâtre algérien (1926–1932),* 12; Hadj Miliani, "Le cheikh et le phonographe: Notes de recherche pour un corpus des phonogrammes et des vidéogrammes des musiques et des chansons algériennes," 44n5.

87. Competition between recordings and live performers was common. Musicians frequently refused to record out of fear for their livelihood; see Miliani, "Le cheikh et le phonographe," 44.

88. Edmond Yafil, *Majmūʿ zahw al-anīs al-mukhtaṣṣ bi-l-tabāsī wa-l-qawādīs* (1907). The

creation of compilations that directly referenced sound recordings was common in Egypt at this time. See Racy, *Making Music in the Arab World*, 148n2.

89. Ahmed Hachelaf and Mohamed Elhabib Hachelaf, *Anthologie de la musique arabe, 1906–1960*, 288.

90. The official declaration was Bastille Day, 1912. "Etat des sociétés existant dans la commune d'Alger," CAOM/F41, cited in Mohamed Guessal, "Les associations de musique classique maghrébine en Algérie: Histoire et répertoire," 151.

91. Bouzar-Kasbadji, *L'emergence artistique algérienne*, 52.

92. Nadya Bouzar-Kasbadji, L'emergence artistique algérienne au XXe siècle: Contribution de la musique et du théâtre algérois à la renaissance culturelle et à la prise de conscience nationaliste, 50.

93. For a parallel figure of a media-savvy musical renovator, albeit in Constantine several generations after Yafil, see Mohamed Tahar Fergani, in Maya Saidani, *La musique du constantinois: Contexte, nature, transmission et definition*, 69–71.

94. Jules Rouanet, "La musique arabe"; Jules Rouanet, "La musique arabe dans le Maghreb"; Henry George Farmer, "Preface," in Francesco Salvador Daniel, *The Music and Musical Instruments of the Arab with Introduction on How to Appreciate Arab Music*, trans. Henry George Farmer (1915), 38.

95. Jules Rouanet, *L'Algérie Vivra, Réponse aux «Notes d'un ancien gouverneur général»*.

96. Jules Rouanet, "La musique musulmane," *La Dépêche Algérienne*, September 25, 1927, 7.

97. He did not register himself simply as arranger, as suggested by Bouzar-Kasbadji in *L'emergence artistique algérienne*, 46, and by Mahieddine Bachetarzi, *Mémoires, 1919–1939*, 90. See the correspondence between representatives of SACEM and Moroccan Protectorate officials from 1931 to 1955. The letter from SACEM to the director of indigenous affairs, dated October 30, 1931, includes two long lists of copyrighted discs that were being played in Moroccan cafés; Yafil, listed as composer, dominates both lists, which seem to be comprised of songs that Yafil recorded. In 2005, the correspondence was located in the folder marked "droits de l'auteur" in CADN/494 in 2005. Titles of several of the works under Yafil's copyright are available through the SACEM search engine. See http://www.sacem.fr/oeuvres/oeuvre/index.do (accessed March 12, 2011).

98. Edmond Yafil, "La musique musulmane," *La Dépêche Algérienne*, October 1, 1927. For more on the controversy between Rouanet and Yafil, see Hadj Miliani and Jonathan Glasser, "What is an Author in Interwar Algeria? Recorded Music, Copyright, and the Problem of the Common."

99. For Yafil's invocation of Sfindja's memory, see *La Dépêche Algérienne*, Untitled announcement, September 20, 1927, 2.

100. *Notre rive: Revue nord-africaine illustrée*, October 1927, 7. Cited in Miliani and Glasser, "What is an Author in Interwar Algeria?" See also Pardo, "La musique arabe dans les écrits français," 130–33.

101. On the voice, song, and the subaltern, see Amanda Weidman, *Singing the Classical, Voicing the Modern: The Postcolonial Politics of Music in South India*, 150–91.

102. Rouanet, "La musique arabe dans le Maghreb," 2912.

103. Clifford Geertz, "Thick Description: Toward an Interpretive Theory of Culture, " in *The Interpretation of Cultures*, 29.

104. Frishkopf, "Introduction," 5.

Chapter Five

1. Edmond Nathan Yafil, *Majmūʿ al-aghānī wa-l-alḥān min kalām al-andalus* (1904), i.

2. This pattern has been attested in the Constantine tradition as well. See Maya Saidani, *La musique du constantinois: Contexte, nature, transmission et definition*, 131–35. For a parallel discussion of archival "black holes" in the Maghrib, see Sara Abrevaya Stein, *Saharan Jews and the Fate of French Algeria*, 149–56.

3. For a parallel use of text as index in a Maghribi musical practice, see Deborah Kapchan, *Traveling Spirit Masters: Moroccan Gnawa Trance and Music in the Global Marketplace*, 226.

4. Fayçal Benkalfat / Fayṣal Bin Qalfāt et al., *Al-mūsīqā al-klāsīkiyya fi-l-duwal al-maghāribiyya / La musique classique du Maghreb*, 2:233.

5. My definition of text is broader than it is in everyday speech: I follow Richard Bauman, Charles Briggs, and others in thinking of text as "a stretch of linguistic discourse . . . that can be lifted out of its interactional setting." Richard Bauman and Charles L. Briggs, "Poetics and Performance as Critical Perspectives on Language and Social Life," 73. The songbook, on the other hand, is what Michael Silverstein and Greg Urban term a text-artifact, "a more or less permanent physical object" that in this case assumes the form of manuscript or print. Michael Silverstein and Greg Urban, "The Natural History of Discourse," 2n1.

6. *Dīwān* usually refers to a collection of poems by a single author. However, when it is used in connection to *nūba* practice, it does not carry this single-author connotation. Yafil on one occasion refers to it in Judeo-Arabic as a *tshang*, likely from the Turkish *cank* or poetic compilation.

7. Hans Wehr, *Arabic-English Dictionary*.

8. For a similar point with regard to the compilation tradition in Moroccan *āla*, see Davila, *The Andalusian Music of Fes*, 272.

9. Ibid., 311.

10. For a similar logic by which a compound form can be understood as a kind of textual compilation, see the Constantinois notion of a *majmūʿ* as a suite rather than as a written collection. Saidani, *La musique constantinoise*, 164.

11. This is not to say that such involvement dated to the turn of the century only, since colonial officials had been occasional patrons of manuscript compilers in the Second Empire period. See the 1868 manuscript associated with al-Terrari, as well as ʿAbd al-ḥamīd Al-Ḥājiyyāt, ed., *Al-jawāhir al-ḥisān min naẓm awliyāʾ tilimsān*, which is a printing of the compilation commissioned by Charles Brosselard, prefect of Tlemcen, more than a century earlier from the schoolteacher Muḥammad Murābiṭ. The compiler's poem of praise for Brosselard, which is not included in the printed version, can be found in the original manuscript, BNF Or. 5254.

12. Joseph Desparmet, "La poésie arabe actuelle à Blida et sa métrique." These examples did not draw from the pieces from *nūbat al-dhīl* that he previously published in *Le Tell*.

13. J. Joly, "Chansons du répertoire algérois" (1909). The pieces were from diverse modes, but note the obedience to the basic order of a performance with the exception of the *darj* (an exception that possibly points to Constantine as a source for these particular songs). The topic of the non-*nūba* text is itself of interest: it details the foibles of the Algiers popular music scene, with particular attention to Yamina and her competitor Aïcha.

14. The creation of compilations that directly referenced sound recordings was common in Egypt at this time. See A. J. Racy, *Making Music in the Arab World: The Culture and Artistry of ṭarab*, 148n2.

15. Yafil, *Majmūʿ zahw al-anīs*, 68.

16. One can imagine that as the volume of recordings multiplied, it became impossible to print their words in such a fashion—in a sense, recordings came to be their own channel, separated from the discipline of print.

17. Yafil, *Majmūʿ zahw al-anīs*, 68.

18. These examples of an *mṣaddar* and *bṭayḥī* in colloquial register, neither of which show up in the collection of *nūba* material, suggests that the *mṣaddar* and *bṭayḥī* were understood to be distinct song forms and were not simply names for fixed positions within a *nūba* structure. Alternatively, it might point to a broader use of the concept of *nūba* in sung poetry beyond the Andalusi canon. What may have distinguished them formally, however, is not as yet clear. It may be that there was a specific mode associated with the term *ʿarbī*. Bouali's idiosyncratic listing of *ʿarbī* as its own *nūba* suggests this as a possibility. Bouali, *Kashf al-qināʿ*, 113. But note that *Majmūʿ zahw al-anīs* does not list any particular mode for the *bṭayḥī*.

19. For discussion of this press within the context of Arabic printing in Algiers, see Camille Risler, *La politique culturelle de la France en Algerie: Les objectifs et les limites (1830–1962)*, 109–10.

20. Again, note the pride of place granted the *nūba* material. The generic use of the term *qaṣīda* to mean poem, and to refer to both the "Maghribi" poems and the *nūba* poems, is unusual for the Algerian literature of this period.

21. M. Bekhoucha, *Al-ḥubb wa-l-maḥbūb*.

22. See the bibliography compiled by Abdelkader Bendamèche, *Florilège ou l'oeuvre réunie d'El-Boudali Safir*, 251–52.

23. Michel Foucault, "Of Other Spaces," 26. In contrast, some of the collections devoted to *qṣāyid* do seem to pretend to such exhaustiveness, in this case specifically authorial rather than repertorial.

24. Qāḍī, *Al-kanz al-maknūn*, 3.

25. Ibid., 3.

26. M. Bekhoucha and A. Sekkal, eds., *Anthologie d'auteurs arabes / Kitāb nafḥ al-azhār*, 9.

27. Bekhoucha, *Al-ḥubb wa-l-maḥbūb*, 216.

28. Qāḍī, *Al-kanz al-maknūn*, 5.

29. Ibid., 2–3.

30. Ibid., 220–21.

31. Bekhoucha and Sekkal, *Nafḥ al-azhār*, 5.

32. Ibid., 6–7.

33. For scouting in Algeria, particularly in the Muslim youth groups, see Chikh Bouamrane and Mohamed Djidjelli, *Scouts musulmans algériens (1935–1955)*, cited in Jane E. Goodman, "Acting with One Voice: Producing Unanimism in Algerian Reformist Theater," 178n4.

34. Bekhoucha and Sekkal, *Nafḥ al-azhār*, 9.

35. The quotation is drawn from Albert Sarraut, *Grandeur et servitude coloniales* (1931). For Sarraut's global imperialist career and intellectual development, see Martin Thomas, "Albert Sarraut, French Colonial Development, and the Communist Threat, 1919–1930."

36. Bekhoucha and Sekkal, *Nafḥ al-azhār*, 130–32. Without a doubt, it also invokes a radical separation between two civilizations and musical cultures, not unlike the dualistic trope described for South Indian music in Amanda Weidman, *Singing the Classical, Voicing the Modern: The Postcolonial Politics of Music in South India*.

37. FLN Commission centrale d'orientation, *Colloque national sur la musique algérienne, El-Riath, 25–26–27 decembre 1964*, 17, 31–32.

38. Jallūl Yallis and al-Ḥafnāwī Amuqrān, eds., *Al-muwashshaḥāt wa-l-azjāl*, 2:9.

39. Ibid., 2:7.

40. Ibid., 1:14–15.

41. In this way, the Algerian case closely parallels that of its fellow socialist, nonaligned African state of Tanzania, where cultural politics and particularly musical politics was similarly past-centered, anticolonial, and revisionist. Kelly M. Askew, *Performing the Nation: Swahili Music and Cultural Politics in Tanzania*. Chapter 5 is devoted to post-independence debates over cultural politics that closely parallel the Algerian debates, both temporally and thematically.

42. Yallis and Amuqrān, eds., *Al-muwashshaḥāt wa-l-azjāl*, 3:7.

43. Note that in the case of Yafil's work, such "instructions" about how to make a *nūba* showed up in the transcriptions he made with Rouanet, rather than in the *nūba* compilation, and were far from exhaustive.

44. Ahmed Serri, *Chants andalous*; Sid Ahmed Serri / Sīd Aḥmad Sarrī, *Majmūʿat al-qiṭaʿ allatī addāhā wa-sajjalahā li-l-turāth al-ustādh Sīd Aḥmad Sarrī / Maître Sid Ahmed Serri.*

45. A parallel in Moroccan *āla* is al-Ḥājj ʿAbd al-Karīm Rāyyis's *Min waḥī al-rabāb*, which abridges the canonical *Al-Ḥāʾik* on the basis of Rāyyis's own performance practice. Al-ḥājj ʿAbd al-Karīm Rāyyis, *Min waḥī al-rabāb: Majmūʿat ashʿār wa-azjāl mūsīqā al-āla.*

46. Serri, *Chants andalous* (2002), iv. Note that the Arabic preface has some differences in terms of the stated aims of the compilation; the third aim contains language that closely echoes that of Yafil regarding "manuscripts that remain guarded among a minority." Ibid., 7.

47. The form of these recordings is worth noting: because these take in the entirety of the repertoire as known by Serri, they present all of the song texts for each movement, meaning that the recordings replicate the form of a songbook, rather than the *nūba* performance convention.

48. Mourad Ouamara / Murād Bin ʿAlī Waʿmāra, ed., *Jāmiʿ al-safāyin wa-l-kunnāshāt fī ṣanāʾiʿ al-azjāl wa-l-muwashshaḥāt / Recueil des poèmes Muwashshaḥât et Azdjâl.*

49. Fayçal Benkalfat / Fayṣal Bin Qalfāt, Amin Qalfāt, and Rifāl Qalfāṭ, eds., *Majmūʿat ashʿār wa-azjāl mūsīqā: Al-ṣanʿa, al-ḥawzī, al-ʿarūbī, al-madīḥ, wa-l-samāʿ: Madrasat tilimsān / L'Ecole de Tlemcen.*

50. Salim El Hassar [Salīm al-ḥaṣṣār], *Al-mūsīqā al-ʿarabiyya al-andalusiyya min gharnāṭa ilā tilimsān / Musique arabo-andalouse de Grenade à Tlemcen.*

51. Mohammed Souheil Dib/Muḥammad Suhayl al-Dīb, ed., *Le répertoire poétique non andalou de Tlemcen (ḥawzî, ʿArûbî, Madḥ, Samâʾ et Gharbî) / Qaṣāʾid min: Al-ḥawzī, al-ʿarūbī, al-madīḥ, al-gharbī.*

52. Fayçal Benkalfat / Fayṣal Bin Qalfāt et al., *Al-mūsīqā al-klāsīkiyya fi-l-duwal al-maghāribiyya / La musique classique du Maghreb.*

53. Hadj Mohammed Ghaffour / Al-ḥājj Muḥammad Ghaffūr, *Majmūʿat ashʿār wa-azjāl mūsīqā al-ṣanʿa al-qiṭaʿ allatī addāhā wa-sajjalahā li-l-turāth al-ustādh al-ḥājj Muḥammad Ghaffūr*; Salim Fergani / Salīm Firgānī, *Majmūʿat ashʿār wa-azjāl mūsīqā al-māʾlūf al-qiṭaʿ allatī addāhā wa-sajjalahā li-l-turāth al-ustādh Salīm Firgānī.*

54. Fayṣal Bin Qalfāt / Fayçal Benkalfat, ed., *Mukhtārāt min al-mūsīqā al-klāsīkiyya li-madīnat al-jazāʾir maʿ jawq Raḍwān li-tilimsān, jawq al-jazāʾir al-ʿāṣima, jawq al-fann al-aṣīl li-l-qulayʿa.*

55. Al-ḥājj al-ʾArabī Bin *Ṣārī, Mukhtārāt min al-mūsīqā al-klāsīkiyya al-jazāʾiriyya maʿ al-ḥājj al-ʿArabī Bin ṣārī*; Raḍwān Bin *Ṣārī, Mukhtārāt min al-mūsīqā al-klāsīkiyya al-jazāʾiriyya maʿ al-shaykh Raḍwān Bin Ṣārī.*

56. Mourad Ouamara / Murād Bin ʿAlī Waʿmāra, ed., *Jāmiʿ al-safāyin wa-l-kunnāshāt fī ṣanāʾiʿ al-azjāl wa-l-muwashshaḥāt / Recueil des poèmes Muwashshaḥât et Azdjâl.*

57. El Hassar, *Al-mūsīqā al-ʿarabiyya al-andalusiyya.*

58. See for example Mourad Ouamara / Murād Bin ʿAlī Waʿmāra, ed., *Jāmiʿ al-safāyin wa-l-kunnāshāt fī ṣanāʾiʿ al-azjāl wa-l-muwashshaḥāt / Recueil des poèmes Muwashshaḥât et Azdjâl.*

59. It also continues to be repeated in the secondary literature. Mohamed Guessal, "Les associations de musique classique maghrebine en Algérie," 104.

60. *Confrères* can also be read as co-religionists.

61. Joseph Desparmet, *La poésie arabe actuelle à Blida et sa métrique*, 4–5.

62. Desparmet, "La poésie arabe actuelle à Blida," 463.

63. Ibid., 464n3b, 485n5b. Colin seriously considered the notion that one could detect traces of Granadan Arabic in the North African Andalusi repertoire, although he never seems to have completed the article he outlined. See *Orientaux*-Papiers G. S. Colin III Hispanique, Dossier no. 8: Langue des chants andalous du Maghrib, 218 fol. (F. 205–218), Bibliothèque nationale de France, Oriental manuscripts division.

64. Aḥmad Tawfīq al-Madanī, *Kitāb al-Jazāʾir* (1931), 365–66. For d'Erlanger's career, see Ruth F. Davis, *Maʾlūf: Reflections on the Arab Andalusian Music of Tunisia*, 43–50.

65. "Rapport sur les émissions musulmanes à Radio PTT," Algiers, Apr. 1940, CAOM/15H/32.

66. From Office of the Governor-General, Centre d'Information et d'Etudes, "Note. A/S. d'un projet d'organisation d'un festival de musique andalouse transcrite et interpretée par un orchestre français," Algiers, Sept. 20, 1940, CAOM/9H/37/18.

67. Mourad Ouamara / Murād Bin ʿAlī Waʿmāra, ed., *Jāmiʿ al-safāyin wa-l-kunnāshāt fī ṣanāʾiʿ al-azjāl wa-l-muwashshaḥāt / Recueil des poèmes Muwashshaḥât et Azdjâl*, 4.

68. Ibid.

69. Ibid., 6.

70. Yallis and Amuqrān, eds., *Al-muwashshaḥāt wa-l-azjāl*, 3:6.

71. Youcef Touaïbia, *Groupe Yafil*, http://yafil.free.fr/sommaire.html.

72. This is not to say that Touaïbia subscribes to this opposition in matter of fact: he shows, for example, that the nineteenth-century manuscript convention was far more faithful to musical phrasing than some of the twentieth-century printed efforts. Fayçal Benkalfat / Fayṣal Bin Qalfāt et al., *Al-mūsīqā al-klāsīkiyya fi-l-duwal al-maghāribiyya / La musique classique du Maghreb*, 2:233.

73. For an explicit language of textual repair in a Maghribi musical context, see Alessandra Ciucci, "'The Text Must Remain the Same': History, Collective Memory, and Sung Poetry in Morocco," 479. On the notion of repair among aficionados in Constantine, see Saidani, *La musique du constantinois*, 235.

74. Ahmed Serri, *Chants andalous*, 13n1.

75. See, for example, Hadri Bougherara, *Voyage sentimentale dans la musique arabo-andalouse*, 138.

76. This image of the passageway, derived from Marilyn Strathern, has been used by Marlene Schäfers to think through authorship as genealogy in Kurdish women's song. Marilyn Strathern, "Cutting the Network"; Marlene Schäfers, "In Pursuit of Permanent Traces: Constituting Authorship through Inscription."

77. For an analysis of a striking parallel within the world of Kabyle song, where public domain, authorship, and notions of patrimony jostle one another within the context of Algerian and Kabyle nationalism, SACEM, and village singers, see Jane E. Goodman, *Berber Culture on the World Stage: From Village to Video*, 145–61.

78. Michel Foucault, "What is an Author?" 124.

79. Among Andalusi music enthusiasts in the Algiers-Tlemcen tradition, *Al-Ḥāʾik* is occa-

sionally referred to as the Moroccans' *Yafil*. On the Moroccan compilation tradition, see Davila, *The Andalusian Music of Morocco*, 148–61.

80. This is not to say that there is a single stream. In fact, Davila has identified multiple streams.

81. Foucault, "What is an Author?" 125.

82. For a similar situation in the context of Moroccan *āla*, see Davila, *The Andalusian Music of Morocco*, 288–89, n39.

83. On the inherited compilation as a sign of membership in a lineage, see Saidani, *La musique du constantinois*, 131.

84. Aḥmad Zawītan, *Majmūʿat al-ḥāyik li-l-ṭarab al-andalusī.*

85. The use of print to preserve the memory of a past master closely parallels Sufi and scholarly practices detailed in Muhammad Qasim Zaman, "Commentaries, Print and Patronage: *ḥadīth* and the Madrasas in Modern South Asia"; see also Pnina Werbner, *Pilgrims of Love: The Anthropology of a Global Sufi Cult*, and Michael Gilsenan, *Recognizing Islam: An Anthropologist's Introduction*. The death of a religious *shaykh* frequently presents the challenge of translating his highly personalized, embodied charisma into a durable form that might outlive his immediate disciples, and printed manuals and hagiographies are frequently one possible solution to this problem.

86. Jonathan Sterne, *The Audible Past: Cultural Origins of Sound Production.*

87. Yafil's *Majmūʿ*, for example, has recently been made available as a pdf online through the site http://www.alkottob.com. I am thankful to Sid-Ali Hamouche for pointing this out to me.

88. On gerontocracy in the Maghrib, see Crawford, *Moroccan Households in the World Economy*.

89. Plenckers, writing in 1993, suggests this is already the case. Leo Plenckers, "Changes in the Algerian Sanʿa Tradition and the Role of the Musicologist in the Process," 1256.

Chapter Six

1. Ministry of Information, *Tlemcen*, 75–76.

2. For a similar observation regarding the master-teacher relationship within the context of the conservatory system for *āla* in Fes, see Davila, *The Andalusian Music of Morocco*, 166, 204.

3. Saidani, *La musique du constantinois*, 301–7.

4. Omar Carlier, "Medina and Modernity: The Emergence of Muslim Civil Society in Algiers between the Two World Wars." This is not to say that indigenous Algerians were absent from predominantly European organizations: recall that Mostefa Aboura was part of Tlemcen's symphonic band. Fayçal Benkalfat / Fayṣal Bin Qalfāt et al., *Al-mūsīqā al-klāsīkiyya fi-l-duwal al-maghāribiyya / La musique classique du Maghreb*, 1:39.

5. Andrea Liverani, *Civil Society in Algeria: The Political Functions of Associational Life* xxviii. Lakjaa has questioned the reading of Algeria as association-dense, pointing out that France has vastly more associations per capita than Algeria. However, it is worth recalling that during the colonial era and the post-independence period until the late 1980s, associations formed virtually the only authorized forum for collective self-expression. Lakjaa may be right to describe a certain comparative "quantitative weakness," but the qualitative strength is important to note. Abdelkader Lakjaa, "Vie associative et urbanisation en Algérie."

6. René Gallissot, "Mouvements associatifs et mouvement social: Le rapport état/société dans l'histoire maghrébine."

7. Liverani, *Civil Society in Algeria*, 15–16.

8. Jane E. Goodman, "Acting with One Voice: Producing Unanimism in Algerian Reformist Theater," 186–87; Lakjaa, "Vie associative et urbanisation en Algérie."

9. Ghouti Bouali, *Kitāb kashf al-qināʿ ʿan ālāt al-samāʿ* (1904), 124. See also the memories of pre-1901 associative formations in Constantine in Maya Saidani, *La musique du constantinois: Contexte, nature, transmission et definition*, 71.

10. For an overview of the legislative struggle the led to the 1901 Law of Associations, see Jean-Claude Bardout, *L'histoire étonnante de la loi 1901: le droit d'association en France avant et après Waldeck-Rousseau.*

11. Eric Hobsbawm, "Mass-Producing Traditions: Europe, 1870–1914."

12. For a contemporary account that emphasized the question of the Church, see Walter Littlefield, "France and the Associations Law" (1902).

13. Lakjaa has pointed out the paradox by which associations are ostensibly free from the state but are in turn supported by the state. Lakjaa, "Vie associative et urbanisation en Algérie," 6.

14. Mohamed Guessal, "Les associations de musique classique maghrébine en Algérie," 1on7. The El Moutribia 1930 letterhead dated its founding to 1911. See CAOM/64S/4.

15. For the turn from a free school to an association, see the narration of El Moutribia's rise in Untitled announcement, Sept. 13, 1927, *La Dépêche Algérienne.*

16. Bouali, *Kashf al-qināʿ*, 143.

17. A parallel expansion of the ensemble size can be found in Egypt during this time.

18. Koceil Amazigh, *Deux grands maîtres de la musique classique dans la tourmente de la nuit coloniale*, 26.

19. Mohamed Dib was among its founding members. Ibid. Note that the name of this group echoed the Young Turks who were then articulating a modernist agenda at the heart of the Ottoman Empire.

20. Carlier, "Medina and Modernity," 67.

21. Ibid., 66. See also see James McDougall, "The Secular State's Islamic Empire: Muslim Spaces and Subjects of Jurisdiction in Paris and Algiers, 1905–1957."

22. Allalou, *L'aurore du théâtre algérien (1926–1932)*, 14.

23. There had been a *fête mauresque* to celebrate Louis-Napoléon's visit, during which Youssef Eni-Bel-Kharraïa played, and a *fête mauresque*, perhaps organized by Yafil, that had closed the 1905 Congress of Orientalists. Francisco Salvador Daniel, *La musique arabe: Ses rapports avec la musique grècque et le chant grégorien* (1879), 31; *Actes du XIV. Congrès international des orientalistes Alger 1905, Troisième Partie, Langues Musulmanes (Arabe Persan et Turc)* (1906), 105.

24. Bachetarzi, *Mémoires, 1919–1939*, 28, 30.

25. Allalou, *L'aurore du théâtre algérien (1926–1932)*, i–ii.

26. See CAOM/F45, and letter of April 17, 1939 from Dir. Gen. des Affaires Indigènes et des Territoires du Sud, to the Oran préfet for Affaires Indigènes, CAOM/9H/37/18.

27. M. Lemaille, "Les algériens à Oujda en 1937," 260.

28. John Ruedy, *Modern Algeria: The Origins and Development of a Nation*, 129.

29. Nadya Bouzar-Kasbadji, *L'emergence artistique algérienne au XXe siècle: Contribution de la musique et du théâtre algérois à la renaissance culturelle et à la prise de conscience nationaliste*, 50; idem, "L'Algérie musicale entre orient et occident (1920–1939)," 94.

30. Seven of the sixteen students in Yafil's Arab music class at the conservatory in 1925 were

also on the administrative council of El Moutribia, meaning a fourth of the administrative council was enrolled in the conservatory class. The students ranged in age from 17 to 48, though most of them were in their twenties. There was one married woman among them. I am grateful to M. Yacine Touati, director of the Algiers Municipal Conservatory, for giving me access to these documents.

31. Bachetarzi, *Mémoires*, 26–27.

32. On Bachetarzi's interwar forays into politics, see Joshua Cole, "À chacun son public: Politique et culture dans l'Algérie des années 1930."

33. Bachetarzi, *Mémoires*, 41.

34. Ibid., 103–4.

35. Ibid., 109.

36. Ibid., 61, 88.

37. Ibid., 55–57.

38. Musical commentary by Arabophile settler intellectuals was another part of this integrationist moment. See the talk by journalist Jean-Darrouy, accompanied by a performance from Bachetarzi, as well as the public talk by the *lycée* teacher in Sidi-Bel-Abbès, Léon Corcellet, which was introduced by (and dedicated to) Mohammed Chérif, president of "Amis de l'Ecole Française." Léon Corcellet, *Conférence sur la musique arabe* (1928); Lucienne Jean-Darrouy, "La musique musulmane en Afrique du Nord" (1931); A. Maitrot de la Motte-Capron, "La Musique Méditerranéenne secrete et sacrée," (1941).

39. It is unclear if it was ever officially registered as an association.

40. From *La Presse Libre*, June 14, 1930, quoted in Bouzar-Kasbadji, *L'emergence artistique algérienne*, 80.

41. Guessal, "Les associations de musique classique maghrébine," 23.

42. Abdelhakim Meziane, for example, has called El Djazaïria the first Algerian association for Andalusi music Abdelhakim Meziane, "Le vieil Alger musical," May 20, 2009, Conferences of the 6th Andaloussiate festival, Complexe Culturel Laâdi Flici, Algiers.

43. El Djazaïria can in many respects be seen as closely parallel to the officially "Muslim" grouping al-Nahda in Constantine, founded in 1931 (although it does not appear that al-Nahda was officially an association). Saidani, *La musique du constantinois*, 71.

44. James McDougall, *History and the Culture of Nationalism in Algeria*, 66.

45. Krieff to Office des Affaires Indigènes, 10 Aug. 1933, CAOM/15H/32.

46. On Bensiam, see Allan Christelow, "Ritual, Culture and Politics of Islamic Reformism in Algeria," 262.

47. Bachetarzi, *Mémoires*, 155.

48. I say status elite rather than simply elite in order to point out that the socioeconomic standing of its members was in fact quite varied.

49. Goodman, "Acting with One Voice," 187.

50. See list in Guessal, "Les associations de musique classique maghrébine," 119. The professionals are listed as "lyric artists."

51. See, for example, the description of an outing by El Djazaïria in 1939, in which the association members provided both the audience and musicians for the outdoor concerts that punctuated the day's activities. Newspaper clipping, "«El-Djazairia» à Sidi-Ferruch," *Alger Républicaine*, August 21, 1939, in CAOM/4I/88.

52. In CAOM, Fonds ministériels, Dépôt des papiers publics des colonies: État Civil, Algérie.

53. Untitled announcement, September 13, 1927, *La Dépêche Algérienne*.

54. Allalou, *L'aurore du théâtre algérien*, 14.

55. "Les obsèques de M. Edmond Yafil," *La Dépêche Algérienne*, October 10, 1928, 7.

56. Bendamèche, *Les grandes figures de l'art musical algérien*, 1:116. Founded in 1932, El Mossilia's headquarters were briefly at 19 rue Randon, across the street from El Moutribia's office, before moving to 10 rue Medée in the Casbah. It is worth noting these locations in order to recall the spatial density of the associative scene and the fact that members of different associations were likely interacting (or attempting to avoid interacting) with great frequency. Ahmed Serri, "Aperçu historique sur la creation des assocations musicales et, en particulier, celles d'El-Djazairia-El-Mossilia," 56.

57. Bendamèche, *Les grandes figures de l'art musical algérien* 2:306, fig. 6.

58. Furthermore, it is not clear why the El Mossilia of 1932 is thought of as an offshoot of El Djazaïria, as opposed to an offshoot of El Andalousia.

59. Guessal, "Les associations de musique classique maghrébine," 69.

60. Ibid.

61. Liverani, *Civil Society in Algeria*, 56.

62. Bendamèche, *Les grandes figures de l'art musical algérien*, 1:65.

63. The layered nature of SLAM's emergence has led to some confusion about the year of its founding, with Bestandji claiming 1932. Tewfik Bestandji, "Anthologie de la musique arabo-andalouse d'Algérie, Çana'a et Gharnatî," 4. For claims that it was founded in 1934, see Guessal, "Les associations de musique classique maghrébine," 74; and Bendamèche, *Les grandes figures de l'art musical algérien*, 1:65. Bendamèche's assertion that Union et Progrès preceded SLAM, and that the earlier association's founders were also founders of SLAM, is a satisfying explanation of the source of confusion.

64. For an important source on Constantine, see Abdelmadjid Merdaçi, *Dictionnaire des musiques et des musiciens de Constantine*. For politically tinged rivalries between Constantine associations in the interwar era, including with regard to music, see the police reports from 1937 in CAOM/9H/37/18.

65. Ruth F. Davis, *Ma'lūf: Reflections on the Arab Andalusian Music of Tunisia*, 51.

66. The rooting of the voluntary organization within the 1901 Law of Associations would suggest that its character was noncommercial. El Moutribia, however, like its offshoots, had many of the characteristics of a business. The large sums of money that some associations took in at the door were mainly directed toward offsetting the costs of the tours and performances. They were nonprofit, but they were emphatically accumulative.

67. See, for example, El Moutribia's benefit concerts in the 1920s, whether for Oranais flood victims in 1928 or for Muslim charities. Bouzar-Kasbadji, *L'emergence artistique algérienne*, 73.

68. Letter from Djendi Hamida, "oukil judiciaire à Bône," president of "la société musicale et artistique musulmane 'El-Mizhar El-Bouni' (La Lyre bônoise)," to the Governor General of Algeria, March 1, 1932, CAOM 14H/4I/25/1.

69. Touaïbia places the founding of the Radio Algiers ensemble in 1946, while Bendamèche places it in 1943. Bendamèche, *Les grandes figures de l'art musical algérien*, 1:51

70. Bendamèche, *Les grandes figures de l'art musical algérien*, 1:51.

71. Newspaper clipping, "«El-Djazairia» à Sidi-Ferruch," *Alger Républicaine*, August 21, 1939, in CAOM/4I/88.

72. Serri, "Aperçu historique," 56.

73. "Societé Musicale «El-Andalousia»," *Alger Républicaine*, April 14, 1944, CAOM/9H/37/18.

74. Serri, *Chants andalous* (2002), vi.

75. Bendamèche, *Les grandes figures de l'art musical algérien*, 1:48.

76. A.N., *Alger Républicaine*, March 19–20, 1948?, in CAOM/4I/88.

77. Serri, "Aperçu historique," 57.

78. In Constantine, however, the immediate postwar years saw a flurry of new musical and theatrical associations. Merdaçi, *Dictionnaire des musiques et des musiciens*, 99; Guessal, "Les associations de musique classique maghrebine," 72, 109.

79. Serri, "Aperçu historique," 57.

80. A.N., *Alger Républicaine*, March 19–20, 1948?, in CAOM/4I/88.

81. Serri, "Aperçu historique," 57.

82. Letter from Association El Djazaïria-El Mossilia, Alger, 1951, CAOM/4I/88.

83. Ahmed Serri, *Chants andalous*, vi. He had first inscribed in El Andalousia but left out of dissatisfaction with the level of instruction there.

84. Ibid., vii.

85. Mohamed Ferhat, "Veritable festival de musique andalouse au thé-concert «El-Djazaïria-El-Mossilia»," *Alger Républicain*, October 20, 1952, in CAOM/4I/88.

86. Mohamed Ferhat, "23me anniversaire de la société musicale et littéraire «EL MOSSILIA-EL-DJAZAIRIA»," *Alger Républicain*, February 8–9, 1953, in CAOM/4I/88.

87. Mohamed Ferhat, "El Djazairia El Mossilia," *Alger Républicain*, February 9, 1954, in CAOM/4I/88.

88. CAOM 4I/88, Algiers.

89. FLN Commission centrale d'orientation, *Colloque national sur la musique algérienne, El-Riath, 25–26–27 decembre 1964*, 31.

90. Serri, *Chants andalous*, vii.

91. Bachir Hadj Ali, "Qu'est-ce qu'une musique nationale?"

92. Omar Dib, *"Les Amis du livre": Fleuron du mouvement culturel algérien, suivi de Le Mardi 04 juin 1957 à Tlemcen, un forfait contre l'humanité*, 58.

93. Ibid., 59–60.

94. Bestandji, "Anthologie de la musique arabo-andalouse," 5.

95. Bendamèche, *Les grandes figures de l'art musical algérien*, 2:112.

96. Sid-Ahmed Bouali, *Petite introduction à la musique classique algérienne*, 1.

97. Bendamèche, *Les grandes figures de l'art musical algérien*, 1:66–67.

98. See for example the important liner notes of El-Boudali Safir for the six LPs in Production R.T.A., *1er festival algérien de la musique andalouse 1967*.

99. FLN Commission centrale d'orientation, *Colloque national sur la musique algérienne*, 33.

100. Bestandji, "Anthologie de la musique arabo-andalouse," 3.

101. For an evocation of this moment in Tlemcen, see Reynolds, "Musical 'Membrances."

102. Note that there is also an Association Al Maoussilia in Oujda.

103. Philip Ciantar, *The Ma'lūf in Contemporary Libya*, 147–49. Note that the institution of the public homage, as well as the wall of memorial photographs, is widespread in Algeria outside musical circles as well.

104. It should also be noted that until independence many associations in Algiers crossed the ethno-religious boundaries separating Muslims from Jews.

105. Michael Gilsenan, *Recognizing Islam: An Anthropologist's Introduction*; Muhammad Qasim Zaman, "Commentaries, Print and Patronage: *ḥadīth* and the Madrasas in Modern South Asia"; Pnina Werbner, *Pilgrims of Love: The Anthropology of a Global Sufi Cult*.

106. This passage hints at the view that such reliance on recordings is simply not a replace-

ment for live, face-to-face communication with a master. See, for example, Saidani, *La musique du constantinois,* 65.

107. On the various kinds of liminality assocated with the Sufi *shaykh* in the Maghrib, see Abdellah Hammoudi, *Master and Disciple: The Cultural Foundations of Moroccan Authoritarianism.*

108. Such oppositions admittedly become complicated in those instances in which individuals wax nostalgic for the elitism of some of the old associations. The *mélomane* space *par excellence,* such associations are sometimes recalled as both casual spaces of sociality and forums for the cultivation of musical excellence.

109. At the same time, there are some who suggest that notation is simply a useful tool for conservation of a performance at a given moment in time, without becoming a reference for the group. This point of view treats the transcription as a time capsule.

110. It is also possible to invoke writing as a stop-gap measure of safeguard, while waiting for the state to invest greater efforts in musical preservation. See Saidani's position in *La musique du constantinois,* 75.

111. For the notion that recordings are often sites of withholding that fall well short of contact with a living musician, see Saidani, *La musique du constantinois,* 85.

112. For a suggestive exploration of resonances between discussions of orality, literacy, and standardization in Andalusi musical practice and in the classical Arabic literary tradition, including the canonization of the Qur'an in written form, see Davila, *The Andalusian Music of Morocco,* 297–300. For a treatment of the Algerian Andalusi practice in terms that borrow from Islamic debates regarding innovation, see Marouf, "Le système musical de la Sanʿa ou le paradigme de la norme et de la marge," 20–21.

Chapter Seven

1. FLN Commission centrale d'orientation, *Colloque national sur la musique algérienne, El-Riath, 25–26–27 decembre 1964,* 2–3.

2. Ibid., 6.

3. FLN, *Colloque national sur la musique algérienne,* 31.

4. For a version of this poem, see Serri, *Chants andalous,* 268. If the notion of a calque is right, then Bouayed was not the first: see the words of an anonymous poet lamenting the French conquest of 1830, in Heggoy, *The French Conquest of Algiers,* 20: "O regret times gone by! / I am grieved, o world, about Algiers!"

5. Alexandre Christianowitsch, *Esquisse historique de la musique arabe aux temps anciens* (1863), 2.

6. See the al-Jāmiʿī compilation tradition, in Carl Davila, *The Andalusian Music of Morocco,* 154–58. See, too, the poetic revival in Constantine during the reign of Salah Bey.: C. Sonneck, ed., *Chants arabes du Maghreb: Étude sur le dialecte et la poésie populaire de l'Afrique du Nord,* 55.

7. Mahieddine Bachetarzi, "Le Vieil Alger Musical," 12.

8. Mahieddine Bachetarzi, *Mémoires, 1919–1939,* 109.

9. On Spanish Protectorate involvement in Andalusi musical revival in Tetuan, see Eric Calderwood, "'The Daughter of Granada and Fez': Al-Andalus in the Colonial Imaginary and in Mediterranean Perspective." See also Davila, *The Andalusian Music of Morocco,* 143.

10. On the 1932 Cairo Congress, see CEDEJ, ed., *Musique arabe: Le Congrès du Caire de 1932.*

11. This challenges Nadya Bouzar-Kasbadji's claim that the colonial state had no ambitions to preserve traditional music in Algeria. Nadya Bouzar-Kasbadji, "L'Algérie musicale entre ori-

ent et occident (1920–1939)," 90. For French colonial music policies in the Maghrib and the larger empire, see Jann Pasler, "Musical Hybridity in Flux: Representing Race, Colonial Policy, and Modernity in French North Africa, 1860s-1930s," and "The Racial and Colonial Implications of Early French Music Ethnography, 1860s–1930s."

12. Letter from Henri Gaillard, Minister of France in Cairo, to M. Briand, Minister of Foreign Affairs, Cairo, Oct. 27, 1931, CAOM/14H/4I/25/1.

13. French translation from Arabic included in letter from President du Conseil, Le Directeur du contrôle to the Governor General of Algeria, Paris, Nov. 20, 1931, CAOM/14H/4I/25/1.

14. Note from OAI to Secretary General of the Government, Algiers, March 4, 1932, CAOM/14H/4I/25/1.

15. Reprinted in report titled "Renovation de la musique arabe," Algiers, Apr. 13, 1935, CAOM/14H/4I/25/1.

16. Letter from Legation of the French Republic in Egypt to M. A Tardieu, President du Conseil, Ministry of Foreign Affairs in Paris, Cairo, Apr. 14, 1932, CAOM/14H/4I/25/1.

17. Ibid.

18. For an extended discussion of French urban design in the Protectorate Morocco, see Gwendolyn Wright, *The Politics of Design in French Colonial Urbanism*, 108–9. Note that Lyautey's architectural vision was consciously in opposition to that of his political mentor, Jonnart. Wright, *The Politics of Design in French Colonial Urbanism.*

19. Letter from the Office of the Governor General, Direction Général des Affaires Indigènes et des Territoires du Sud, Services de l'Economie Sociale Indigène et du personnel, to Monsieur le Prefet, Directeur du Cabinet de M. le Gouverneur Général, Algiers, Feb. 18, 1939, CAOM/9H/37/18.

20. Ibid. Note that at this time Moroccan nationalism was seen as a far more developed threat to French interests than Algerian nationalism.

21. Ibid. Interestingly enough, some of these professional musicians were veterans of the associations, including El Djazaïria. It was the nonprofessionals in the associations, and the associations as collectivities, that seem to have posed the potential danger in the eyes of the authorities.

22. On cultural policy under the Spanish Protectorate, see the work of Eric Calderwood.

23. Prosper Ricard, *Essai d'action sur la musique et le théâtre populaire marocains* (1928). The 1928 event also highlighted the newly inaugurated radio and marked the first time that Maghribi music had been played on the airwaves.

24. Report titled "Variétés: Le prochain congrès de musique marocaine à Fes," CAOM/9H/37/18.

25. "Echos du Maroc, Fes. Congrès de la musique marocaine," *Alger Républicaine*, May 12, 1939.

26. Aline Gouget-Valière, *Premier recueil de chants marocains* (1939?), i.

27. For unknown reasons, this presentation did not take place; nor did Zerrouki's scheduled talk. Patrocinio García Barriuso, *Echos du Maghreb*, 45, 47.

28. From the Director of Political Affairs to the Director General of Public Instruction, Fine Arts, and Antiquities, "Enregistrement de musique andalouse," Rabat, June 17, 1938, CADN/193/3.

29. Untitled announcement, *La Dépêche Algérienne*, Sept. 20, 1927, 2.

30. "Note sur la soirée radiodiffusée de Blida," Dec. 13, 1936, CAOM/15H/31/101.

31. Barriuso, *Echos du Maghreb*, 25. The transcriptions were made by the Algerian-born musicologist and Protectorate functionary Alexis Chottin.

32. From Office of the Governor-General, Centre d'Information et d'Etudes, "Note. A/S. d'un projet d'organisation d'un festival de musique andalouse transcrite et interpretée par un orchestre français," Algiers, Sept. 20, 1940, CAOM/9H/37/18.

33. From the Direction des Affaires Musulmanes, Centre d'Information et d'Etudes, Emissions Musulmanes, to the Governor General, "Objet: Transcription et codification de la musique arabe andalouse algérienne.—Mission de Madame Jacqueline Maire," Algiers, Dec. 19, 1941, CAOM/15H/32/Radio Alger. Note that this discussion of Maire was occasioned by Lakehal's protests concerning the lack of equity between his pay and hers.

34. "Rapport sur les emissions musulmanes a Radio PTT Alger," Algiers, April 1940, CAOM/15H/32/Radio Alger.

35. Abdelkader Bendamèche, *Les grandes figures de l'art musical algérien*, 1:51.

36. For El-Boudali Safir's biography, see Abdelkader Bendamèche, ed., *Florilège ou l'oeuvre réunie d'El-Boudali Safir*, 11–31.

37. For the question of pedagogical technique, see Sid-Ahmed Bouali, *Petite introduction à la musique classique algérienne*, 19–20. For the *nūba* as forerunner of the symphony, see FLN Commission centrale d'orientation, *Colloque national sur la musique algérienne*, 31.

38. Bendamèche, ed. *Florilège ou l'oeuvre réunie d'El-Boudali Safir*, 11–31.

39. John Ruedy, *Modern Algeria: The Origins and Development of a Nation*, 203–5, 210.

40. La Charte d'Alger: Ensemble de textes adoptés par le premier congrés du parti du Front de Liberation Nationale (du 16 au 21 avril 1964), *Présidence de la République*, http://www.el-mouradia.dz/francais/symbole/textes/charte%20d'alger.htm.

41. Indeed, the Algiers Charter would be directly quoted in the liner notes to the recordings associated with the National Festival of Popular Arts. Saidani, *La musique du constantinois*, 295.

42. See Bachir Hadj Ali, "El Anka et la tradition 'chaabi.'" As Youcef Touïbia has pointed out, the fact that the Communist Party had limited room for self-expression in post-independence Algeria may help to explain the attention Hadj Ali and other communists paid to musical matters.

43. Bachir Hadj Ali, "Qu'est-ce qu'une musique nationale?" 183.

44. Ibid., 183–84.

45. Ibid., 184.

46. Ibid., 184–85.

47. Ibid., 185–86. Hadj Ali is referring here to the difference between the standard five-part *nūba* and the *nūbat al-inqilābāt*, in which various *inqilābāt* are brought together into a series. The elements of the "Turkish suites" that he is referring to are likely the *bashraf* and *tshanbar*, short instrumental preludes that are similar to the more standard *tūshiyya*, and that likely came into the Algiers practice by way of Constantine.

48. Ibid., 185–86.

49. Ibid., 186.

50. Ibid.

51. Ibid., 187–88.

52. Ibid., 188–89.

53. Ibid., 189.

54. Ibid., 192–93.

55. Ibid., 195.

56. FLN Commission centrale d'orientation, *Colloque national sur la musique algérienne*, 2.

57. Ibid., 6.

58. Ibid., 9.

59. Ibid., 10.

60. Ibid. 13.

61. Ibid., 13.

62. Ibid., 14.

63. Ibid., 17.

64. Ibid., 32.

65. Ibid.

66. Ibid. 32–33.

67. Ibid., 33.

68. Bouali, *Petite introduction à la musique classique algérienne*, 24.

69. Ibid., 20.

70. Ibid., 23, 24.

71. Ibid., 26.

72. Ibid., 26–27.

73. Ibid., 28.

74. Ibid., 30.

75. http://www.m-culture.gov.dz/mc2/fr/fiche_site.php?id=488, accessed Nov. 1, 2012.

76. Marc Schade-Poulsen, *Men and Popular Music in Algeria: The Social Significance of Raï*, 189. The INM has since been collapsed into the Institut National Supérieure de Musique.

77. Bendamèche, *Florilège*, 28.

78. Bouayed's preface in Bouali, *Petite introduction à la musique classique algérienne*, 2.

79. Omar Dib, *"Les Amis du livre": Fleuron du mouvement culturel algérien, suivi de Le Mardi 04 juin 1957 à Tlemcen, un forfait contre l'humanité*, 58.

80. Ibid., 59–60.

81. Ibid., 65–67.

82. Ahmed Serri, "Pour un véritable débat."

83. On debates about the state hoard versus the private hoard in nineteenth-century Europe, see Gustav Peebles, "Inverting the Panopticon: Money and the Nationalization of the Future."

84. Ahmed Hachelaf and Mohamed Elhabib Hachelaf, *Anthologie de la musique arabe, 1906–1960*.

85. If we look to France, we can find parallel examples of private citizens chiding the government for failing to protect the national patrimony See, for example, the restorers of the Panthéon clock. Emilie Boyer King, "Undercover restorers fix Paris landmark's clock: 'Cultural guerrillas' cleared of lawbreaking over secret workshop in Pantheon," *The Guardian*, Nov. 26, 2007.

86. See Lawrence Rosen, *Bargaining for Reality: The Construction of Social Relations in a Muslim Community*, 66–68, 75, 105, 122–24.

87. Some of this is a question of language, in that this elite is traditionally *francisant* rather than *arabisant*—that is to say, in the post-independence language divisions in Algeria, with their generational, class, and ethnic-regional inflections, most Andalusi music enthusiasts have been associated with an openness to and intimacy with the French language. For language ideologies regarding Arabic and French as lived within the political sphere, see James McDougall, "Dream of Exile, Promise of Home: Language, Education, and Arabism in Algeria."

88. For similar nostalgia for an era when audiences knew how to respect the *nūba*, see K. Darsouni in Maya Saidani, *La musique du constantinois*, 61.

Conclusion

1. Jacques Derrida, *Archive Fever: A Freudian Impression.*

2. This image resonates both with the discussion of unanimity proposed by Jane Goodman in "Acting with One Voice" and by Marouf in "Le système musical de la San'a ou le paradigme de la norme et de la marge," and with a long line of thought regarding patrilineality, much of it focused on North Africa. See, for example, Evans-Pritchard, *The Nuer* and *The Sanusi of Cyrenaica*; Gellner, *Saints of the Atlas*; Bourdieu, *Outline of a Theory of Practice*; Geertz, "The Meaning of Family Ties"; and, for a review of this literature and more, Crawford, *Moroccan Households in the World Economy*, particularly 89–111.

3. On the model of carrying forward rather than the model of loss, see Seeger, "UNESCO and the Safeguarding of Intangible Cultural Heritage."

4. For the idea of elders "divesting" their knowledge, see Weiner's discussion of Pintupi elders. Weiner, *Inalienable Possessions*, 105–6. For the notion of guardians of knowledge going public, see Muhammad Qasim Zaman, *The Ulama in Contemporary Islam: Custodians of Change.*

5. FLN Commission centrale d'orientation, *Colloque national sur la musique algérienne*, 14.

6. Marouf, "Le système musical de la San'a ou le paradigme de la norme et de la marge."

Bibliography

A Note on Discography

The following list of published sources includes various recordings that are cited in this book. These citations capture only a fraction of the published recordings of Andalusi music. Recordings of Andalusi music cover a wide range of regional styles, periods, and performance settings. For the Algiers-Tlemcen practice that is the focus of this book, the earliest recordings date back to the first decades of the twentieth century, some of which are available through the Groupe Yafil website, the sound archive of the National Library of France, and YouTube. In addition, some recordings from the first half of the century have been reissued through the Club de Disque Arabe series, the Trésors de la Musique Judéo-Arabe series, the Buda Musique label, and the Ministry of Culture publications associated with the 2011 designation of Tlemcen as "Capital of Islamic Culture." Unfortunately, the LP recordings of the first two national festivals of Andalusi music have not yet been reissued, and I am grateful to the generosity of the staff at the Algerian National Library for giving me access to these recordings. For performers of more recent decades, there have been many compact disc recordings (as well as reissues of LPs) featuring soloists, professional groups, and association ensembles, many of which are available outside Algeria. There are also a variety of websites that interface with the current recording world, including algeriacolor.com and the Andaloussiate blog.

Archival Sources

NATIONAL LIBRARY OF ALGERIA (BNA):

Manuscripts 1811–15

ARCHIVES NATIONALES DE FRANCE (ANF):

F^{21} Beaux-Arts: 4079-4085 Expositions artistiques diverses à Paris et en provinces

NATIONAL LIBRARY OF FRANCE (BNF):

Papers of G.S. Colin, Dossier no. 8: Langue des chants andalous du Maghrib
Al-jawāhir al-ḥisān fī naẓm awliyā' tilimsān. Copy dated 1271 H./1855 A.D., Or. 5254

CENTRE DES ARCHIVES D'OUTRE MER, AIX-EN-PROVENCE, FRANCE (CAOM):

Archives du Gouvernement Général de l'Algérie
- Series H: Affaires indigènes (1830/1960)
  - 9H Surveillance politique (1844/1958)
  - 10H Études et notices sur l'Algérie et l'Islam (1845/1957)
  - 14H Questions sociales concernant les indigènes (1846/1944)
  - 15H Presse indigène et radiodiffusion (1867/1956)
- Series S: Instruction Publique et Beaux-Arts (1839/1962)
  - 64S Centenaire d'Algérie (1930)

Archives du Département d'Alger
- Series I: Administration des indigènes (1837/1962)
  - 4I Service des liaisons nord-africaines (1936/1962)

Fonds ministériels
- Dépôt des papiers publics des colonies: État Civil, Algérie
- Series F^{80}: 1586-1589 Sciences et arts

CENTRE DES ARCHIVES DIPLOMATIQUES DE NANTES (CADN):

Fonds Protectorat du Maroc
- Cabinet Diplomatique
  - 494 Instituts internationaux

Direction de l'Intérieur
- 193
- 195B

AL-KHIZĀNA AL-ʿĀMMA, RABAT, MOROCCO (KA):

al-Tādlī al-Ribāṭī, Ibrāhīm. *Aghānī al-siqā wa-maghānī al-mūsīqā aw al-irtiqā' ilā 'ulūm al-mūsīqā.* Copy dated 1336 H./1907 A.D., KA/489/D109.

LEIDEN UNIVERSITY LIBRARY, NETHERLANDS:

Ms. Or. 14.169, Magmu'at al-Nawbat [Majmūʿat al-nawbāt].

Published Sources

Abi-Mershed, Osama W. *Apostles of Modernity: Saint-Simonians and the Civilizing Mission in Algeria.* Stanford, CA: Stanford University Press, 2010.

Abu-Lughod, Lila. "Writing Against Culture." In *Recapturing Anthropology: Working in the Present*, edited by Richard G. Fox, 137–62. Santa Fe: School of American Research Press, 1991.

Actes du XIVe Congrès International des Orientalistes Alger 1905, Troisième Partie, Langues Musulmanes (Arabe Persan et Turc). Paris: Ernest Leroux, 1906.

Adams, Julia. "The Rule of the Father: Patriarchy and Patrimonialism in Early Modern Europe." In *Max Weber's Economy and Society: A Critical Companion*, edited by C. Camic, P. S. Gorski and D. M. Trubek, 237–66. Stanford, CA: Stanford University Press, 2005.

Al Boudali, Safir. "La musique classique algérienne ou l'eternel miracle du message andalou." In *Le chant arabo-andalou*, edited by Nadir Marouf, 25–29. Paris: L'Harmattan, 1995.

Alger Républicaine. "Echoes du Maroc, Fes. Congrès de la musique marocaine." May 12, 1939.

———. 1939. "«El-Djazairia» à Sidi-Ferruch." August 21, 1939.

———.1944. "Societé Musicale « El-Andalousia»," April 14, 1944.

———. A.N. *Alger Républicaine*, March 19–20, 1948?

Allalou. *L'aurore du théâtre algérien (1926–1932).* Oran: Université d'Oran, 1982.

Althusser, Louis. "Ideology and Ideological State Apparatuses (Notes Towards an Investigation)." In *Lenin and Philosophy and Other Essays*, translated by Ben Brewster, 127–86. New York: Monthly Review Press, 1971.

Amazigh, Koceil. *Deux grands maîtres de la musique classique dans la tourmente de la nuit coloniale.* Tlemcen: Les Amis du Vieux Tlemcen, 1985.

Anderson, Benedict. *Imagined Communities.* New York: Verso, 1991.

Armbrust, Walter. *Mass Culture and Modernism in Egypt.* New York: Cambridge University Press, 1996.

Armistead, Samuel G. "A Brief History of Kharja Studies." *Hispania* 70/1 (1987): 8–15.

Arslān, Shakīb. *Al-ḥulal al-sundusiyya fi-l-akhbār wa-l-āthār al-andalusiyya.* Cairo: Al-maṭba'at al-raḥmāniyya, 1936–1939.

Asad, Talal. *The Idea of an Anthropology of Islam.* Washington: Center for Contemporary Arab Studies, Georgetown University, 1986.

Askew, Kelly M. *Performing the Nation: Swahili Music and Cultural Politics in Tanzania.* Chicago: University of Chicago Press, 2002.

Association Culturelle "Nassim el-Andalous." *Hommage à Cheikh Redouane Sari.* Oran: 11 rue Cheikh M'Barek El-Mili, 1993.

Aubin, Eugène. *Le Maroc d'aujourd'hui.* Paris: Librairie Armand Collin, 1904.

Austin, J. L. *How to Do Things with Words.* Cambridge, MA: Harvard University Press, 1962.

Bachetarzi, Mahieddine. *Mémoires, 1919–1939.* Algiers: SNED, 1968.

———. "Le vieil Alger musicale." *Jeunesse Action* 6 (1977): 12–26.

Bahrami, Beebe. "Al-Andalus and Memory: The Past and Being Present among Hispano-Moroccan Andalusians from Rabat." In *Charting Memory: Recalling Medieval Spain*, edited by Stacy N. Beckwith, 111–43. New York and London: Garland Publishing Inc., 2000.

Bakhle, Janaki. *Two Men and Music: Nationalism in the Making of an Indian Classical Tradition.* Oxford: Oxford University Press, 2005.

Bakhtin, M. M. "The Problem of Speech Genres." In *Speech Genres and Other Late Essays*, edited by Caryl Emerson and Michael Holquist, translated by Vern W. McGee, 60–102. Austin: University of Texas Press, 1986.

———. "Forms of Time and of the Chronotope in the Novel." In *The Dialogic Imagination: Four Essays by M. M. Bakhtin*, edited by M. Holquist, 84–258. Austin: University of Texas Press, 1981.

Barber, Karin. *The Anthropology of Texts, Person and Publics*. Cambridge: Cambridge University Press, 2007.

Bardout, Jean-Claude, *L'histoire étonnante de la loi 1901: le droit d'association en France avant et après Waldeck-Rousseau*. Lyon: Editions Juris, 2001.

Barriuso, Patrocinio García, *Echos du Maghreb*. Tangier: Editorial Tánger, 1940.

Bateson, Gregory. *Mind and Nature: A Necessary Unity*. New York: E. P Dutton, 1979.

Bauman, Richard. "Verbal Art as Performance." *American Anthropologist* 77, no. 2 (1975): 290–311.

———. "Contextualisation, Tradition, and the Dialogue of Genres: Icelandic Legends of the *Kraftaskáld*." In *Rethinking Context: Language as an Interactive Phenomenon*, edited by Alessandro Duranti and Charles Goodwin, 125–46. Cambridge: Cambridge University Press, 1992.

———. *A World of Others' Words: Cross-Cultural Perspectives on Intertextuality*. Oxford: Wiley-Blackwell, 2004.

Bauman, Richard, and Charles L. Briggs. *Voices of Modernity: Language Ideologies and the Politics of Inequality*. Cambridge: Cambridge University Press, 2003.

Bekhoucha, M. *Al-ḥubb wa-l-maḥbūb*. Tlemcen: N.p., 1937.

Bekkhoucha [Bekhoucha], Mohamed [Muḥammad Bakhūsha]. *Adab al-maghāriba wa-ḥayyātuhum al-ijtimā'iyya wa-l-dīniyya wa-ba'ḍ khurāfātihim / Savoir-vivre, vie sociale et religieuse des Marocains, Leurs contes*. Casablanca: Libraire Farraire, 1943 [1938].

Bekhoucha, M., and A. Sekkal, eds. *Anthologie d'Auteurs arabes / Kitāb nafḥ al-azhār*. Tetuan: Al-maṭba'a al-mahdiyya, 1934.

Bel, A. and P. Ricard. *Les Industries indigènes de l'Algérie: le travail de la laine à Tlemcen*. Algiers: Jourdan, 1913.

Ben Smaïl, Mohamed. "Sur la musique et les musiciens arabes." *France-Maroc: Revue mensuelle* 2 (1919): 43–44.

Benbabaali, Saadane, and Beihdja Rahal. *La plume, la voix et le plectre*. Algiers: Editions Barzakh, 2008.

Bencheneb, Rachid. "Le séjour du šayḫ 'Abduh en Algérie (1903)." *Studia Islamica* 53 (1981): 121–35.

———. "Une correspondance entre savants maghrébins et orientaux au début du XXe siècle." *Arabica* 31, no. 2 (1984): 189–217.

Bencheneb, Saadeddine. "Chansons satiriques d'Alger (1re moitié du XIVe siècle de l'Hégire)." *Revue Africaine* 74 (1933): 75–117.

———. "Quelques historiens arabes modernes de l'Algérie," *Revue Africaine* (1956): 475–99.

Bendamèche, Abdelkader. *Les grandes figures de l'art musical algérien*. 2 vols. Algiers: Editions Cristal Print, 2003.

Bendamèche, Abdelkader , ed. *Florilège ou l'oeuvre réunie d'El-Boudali Safir*. Algiers: ENAG Éditions, 2008.

Benjamin, Roger Benjamin. "*Andalusia in the Time of the Moors*: Regret and Colonial Presence in Paris, 1900." In *Edges of Empires: Orientalism and Visual Culture*, edited by Jocelyn Hackforth-Jones and Mary Roberts, 181–205. Oxford: Blackwell Publishing, 2005.

Benjamin, Walter. "The Work of Art in the Age of Mechanical Reproduction." In *Illuminations*, translated by Harry Zohn, 217–52. New York: Schocken Books, 1968 [1936].

Benkalfat, Fayçal/Fayṣal Bin Qalfāt, ed. *Mukhtārāt min al-mūsīqā al-klāsīkiyya li-madīna al-jazā'ir ma' jawq Raḍwān li-tilimsān, jawq al-jazā'ir al-'āṣima, jawq al-fann al-aṣīl li-l-qulay'a.* Algiers: Editions New Sound/ONDA, 2011.

Benkalfat, Fayçal/Fayṣal Bin Qalfāt, Amin Qalfāṭ, and Rifāl Qalfāṭ, eds. *Majmū'at ash'ār wa-azjāl mūsīqā: al-ṣan'a, al-ḥawzī, al-'arūbī, al-madīḥ, wa-l-samā': madrasat tilimsān/L'Ecole de Tlemcen.* Algiers: Editions New Sound, 2011.

Benkalfat, Fayçal/Fayṣal Bin Qalfāt, Mohammed Souheil Dib/ Muḥammad Suhayl al-Dīb, and Youcef Touaïbia/ Yūsuf ṭūwaybīyya. *Al-mūsīqā al-klāsīkiyya fi-l-duwal al-maghāribiyya / La musique classique du Maghreb.* 2 vols. Algiers: Editions New Sound/ONDA, 2011.

Bennouna, Malik, ed. *Kunnāsh al-ḥā'ik, li-Abī 'Abdallah Muḥammad bin al-Ḥusayn al-tiṭwānī al-andalusī.* Rabat: Maṭba'at al-ma'ārif al-jadīda, 1999.

Bergeron, Katherine. *Decadent Enchantments: The Revival of Gregorian Chant at Solesmes.* Berkeley and Los Angeles: University of California Press, 1998.

Berque, Jacques. *Les Arabes suivi de Andalousies: Essais.* Paris: Babel, 2009.

Bestandji, Tewfik. "Anthologie de la musique arabo-andalouse d'Algérie, *Gharnatî* tlemçenien, Amine Mesli et l'ensemble Nassim el Andalous, En hommage à Redouane Bensari dans la *Nûba* Çika." In *Algérie: Anthologie de la musique arabo-andalouse,* vol. 3: *Amine Mesli et l'ensemble Nassim el Andalous: La Nûba Çika.* Paris: Ocora Radio France, 1994.

Bin ṣārī, Al-ḥājj al-'Arabī. *Mukhtārāt min al-mūsīqā al-klāsīkiyya al-jazā'iriyya ma' al-Ḥājj al-'Arabī Bin Ṣārī.* Algiers: Editions New Sound, 2011.

Bin ṣārī, Raḍwān. *Mukhtārāt min al-mūsīqā al-klāsīkiyya al-jazā'iriyya ma' al-shaykh Raḍwān Bin Ṣārī.* Algiers: Editions New Sound, 2011.

Binmūsa, 'Abd al-Fattāḥ. *Al-īqā'āt al-khams.* N.p.: Maṭba'at al-naṣr, 1988.

Bohlman, Philip V. *The Music of European Nationalism: Cultural Identity and Modern History.* Santa Barbara: ABC-CLIO, 2004.

Bonte, Pierre, Édouard Conte, and Paul Dresch, eds. *Émirs et présidents: Figures de la parenté et du politique dans le monde arabe.* Paris: CNRS Editions, 2001.

Bouali, Ghouti [Al-Ghawthī Abū 'Alī]. *Kitāb kashf al-qinā' 'an ālāt al-samā'.* Algiers: Imprimerie Jourdane, 1904.

Bouali, Sid-Ahmed. *Petite introduction à la musique classique algérienne.* Algiers: SNED, 1968.

Bouamrane, Chikh and Mohamed Djidjelli. *Scouts musulmans algériens (1935–1955).* Algiers: Dar El-Oumma, 2000.

Bouaziz, M. *Musique arabe, mode Darj Lahcine.* Algiers: Leopold Palat, n.d.

Bouaziz, M., and Martz Keil. *A Monsieur I. Stora President Honoraire du Consistoire d'Alger: Inqilāb jarka/Djarka.* Algiers: Mme Tachet, 1886?

Bougherara, Hadri. *Voyage sentimentale dans la musique arabo-andalouse.* Paris: EDIF, 2002.

Bourdieu, Pierre. *Outline of a Theory of Practice.* Translated by R. Nice. Cambridge: Cambridge University Press, 1977.

Bouzar-Kasbadji, Nadya. *L'emergence artistique algérienne au XXe siecle: Contribution de la musique et du théâtre algérois à la renaissance culturelle et à la prise de conscience nationaliste.* Algiers: Office des publications universitaires, 1988.

———. "L'Algérie musicale entre orient et occident (1920–1939)." In *Musique arabe: Le Congrès du Caire de 1932,* edited by CEDEJ, 87–96. Cairo: CEDEJ, 1992.

Brantlinger, Patrick. *Dark Vanishings: Discourse on the Extinction of Primitive Races, 1800–1930.* Ithaca, NY: Cornell University Press, 2003.

Briggs, Charles L., and Richard Bauman. "Genre, Intertextuality, and Social Power." *Journal of Linguistic Anthropology* 2 (1992): 131–72.

Brosselard, Charles. "Epitaphe d'un roi grenadin mort à Tlemcen." *La Revue Africaine* 17 (1859): 66–71.

———. *Les Khouan: de la constitution des ordres religieux musulmans en Algérie.* Algiers: A. Bourget, 1859.

———. "Epitaphe d'un roi grenadin mort a Tlemcen." *Revue Africaine* 17 (October 1859): 66–71.

———. *Tlemcen et Tombouctou.* Algiers: A. Bourget, 1861.

———. *Memoire épigraphique et historique sur les tombeaux de émirs Beni-Zeiyan, et de Boabdil, dernier roi de Grenade, découverts à Tlemcen.* Paris: Imprimerie Nationale, 1876.

Broughton, Elizabeth Blankley. *Six Years Residence in Algiers.* London, 1839.

Brown, Katherine Butler. "The Social Liminality of Musicians: Case Studies from Mughal India and Beyond." *Twentieth-Century Music* 2, no. 1 (2007): 13–49.

Calderwood, Eric. "The Beginning (or End) of Moroccan History: Historiography, Translation, and Modernity in Ahmad b. Khalid al-Nasiri and Clemente Cerdeira." *International Journal of Middle East Studies* 44 (2012): 399–420.

———. "'In Andalucía, There Are No Foreigners': *Andalucismo* from Transperipheral Critique to Colonial Apology." *Journal of Spanish Cultural Studies* 14, no. 4 (2014).

———. "'The Daughter of Granada and Fez': Al-Andalus in the Colonial Imaginary and in Mediterranean Perspective." Paper presented at Crossing and Circulations in the Atlantic and Indian Oceans and the Mediterranean since 1450, Florence, Italy, December 6, 2014.

Carlier, Omar. "Medina and Modernity: The Emergence of Muslim Civil Society in Algiers between the Two World Wars." In *Walls of Algiers: Narratives of the City through Text and Image*, edited by Zeynep Çelik, Julia Clancy-Smith, and Frances Terpak, 62–84. Los Angeles: Getty Research Institute, 2009.

Chatterjee, Partha. *The Nation and its Fragments: Colonial and Postcolonial Histories.* Princeton, NJ: Princeton University Press, 1993.

———. *Nationalist Thought and the Colonial World: A Derivative Discourse.* Minneapolis: University of Minnesota Press, 1986.

Cheurfi, Achour. *Dictionnaire des musiciens et interprètes Algériens.* Algiers: Edition ANEP, 1997.

Chottin, Alexis. *Tableau de la musique marocaine.* Casablanca: Imprimeries Réunies, 1938.

Christianowitsch, Alexandre. *Esquisse historique de la musique arabe aux temps anciens.* Cologne: Dumony-Schauberg, 1863.

Christelow, Allan. "Ritual, Culture and Politics of Islamic Reformism in Algeria." *Middle Eastern Studies* 23, no. 3 (1987): 255–73.

Ciantar, Philip. *The Ma'lūf in Contemporary Libya: An Arab Andalusian Musical Tradition.* London: Ashgate, 2012.

Ciucci, Alessandra. "'The Text Must Remain the Same': History, Collective Memory, and Sung Poetry in Morocco." *Ethnomusicology* 56, no. 3 (2012): 476–504.

Cole, Joshua. "À chacun son public: Politique et culture dans l'Algérie des années 1930." Translated by Stéphane Bouquet. *Sociétés & Représentations* 38, no. 2 (2014): 21–51.

Colonna, Fanny. "Scientific Production and Position in the Intellectual and Political Fields: The Cases of Augustin Berque and Joseph Desparmet." Translated by David Prochaska and Jane Kuntz. In *Genealogies of Orientalism: History, Theory, Politics*, edited by Edmund Burke III and David Prochaska, 174–90. Lincoln: University of Nebraska Press, 2008.

Colwell, Rachel. "Listening Through and Against Tunisian *Ma'luf.*" Paper presented at The Musical Heritage of Moorish Spain, University of California Santa Barbara, February 20–22, 2015.

Corcellet, Léon. *Conférence sur la musique arabe.* Algiers: Imprimerie "La Typo-Litho," 1928.

Crawford, David. *Moroccan Households in the World Economy: Labor and Inequality in a Berber Village.* Baton Rouge: Louisiana State University Press, 2008.

Cronon, William. *Nature's Metropolis: Chicago and the Great West.* New York: Norton, 1991.

Danielson, Virginia. *The Voice of Egypt: Umm Kulthum, Arabic Song, and Egyptian Society in the Twentieth Century.* Chicago: University of Chicago Press, 1997.

Dār al-sharq. *Al-munjid fi-l-lugha.* Beirut: Al-maktaba al-sharqiyya, 1986.

Darnton, Robert. "Peasants Tell Tales: The Meaning of Mother Goose." In *The Great Cat Massacre and Other Episodes in French Cultural History*, 9–74. New York: Vintage Press, 1984.

Davila, Carl. "Fixing a Misbegotten Biography: Ziryab in the Mediterranean World." *Al-Masâq: Islam and the Medieval Mediterranean* 21, no. 2 (2009): 121–36.

———. *The Andalusian Music of Morocco: Al-Āla: History, Society and Text.* Wiesbaden: Reichert Verlag, 2013.

———. "Further Notes on Orality and the Anthologies of Ramal al-Māya." Paper presented at The Musical Heritage of Moorish Spain, University of California Santa Barbara, February 20–22, 2015.

Davis, Natalie Zemon. *Trickster Travels: A Sixteenth-Century Muslim Between Worlds.* New York: Hill and Wang, 2006.

Davis, Ruth F. *Ma'lūf: Reflections on the Arab Andalusian Music of Tunisia.* Lanham, MD: Scarecrow Press, 2004.

de Waal, Cornelis. *Peirce: A Guide for the Perplexed.* London: Bloomsbury, 2013.

Delphin, G., and L. Guin. *Notes sur la poésie et la musique arabes dans le Maghreb algérien.* Paris: Ernest Leroux, 1886.

Deleuze, Gilles, and Félix Guattari. *A Thousand Plateaus: Capitalism and Schizophrenia.* Translated by Brian Massumi. London: Continuum, 1987.

Dent, Alexander Sebastian. *River of Tears: Country Music, Memory, and Modernity in Brazil.* Durham, NC: Duke University Press, 2009.

Deny, J. "Chansons des janissaires turcs d'Alger (fin du xviiime siècle)." In *Mélanges René Basset*, 2:33–175. Paris: Ernest Leroux, 1925.

Depont, Octave, and Xavier Coppolani. *Les confréries religieuses musulmanes.* Algiers: Adolphe Jourdan, 1897.

Derrida, Jacques. *Archive Fever: A Freudian Impression.* Translated by Eric Prenowitz. Chicago: University of Chicago Press, 1996.

Desparmet, Joseph. "Nūbat al-Andalus." *Le Tell: Journal politique et des interêts coloniaux*, February 27, 1904, p. 2.

———. "La poésie arabe actuelle à Blida et sa métrique." In *Actes du XIV. Congrès international des orientalistes Alger 1905, Troisième Partie, Langues Musulmanes (Arabe Persan et Turc)*, 438–603. Paris: Ernest Leroux, 1906.

———. *La poésie arabe actuelle à Blida et sa métrique.* Paris: Ernest Leroux, 1907.

Dib, Mohammed Souheil/Muḥammad Suhayl al-Dīb, ed. *Le répertoire poétique non andalou de Tlemcen (ḥawzî, 'Arûbî, Madḥ, Samâ' et Gharbî)/Qaṣā'id min: Al-ḥawzī, al-'arūbī, al-madīḥ, al-gharbī.* 2 vols. Algiers: Editions New Sound/ONDA, 2011.

———. "Typologie du patrimoine hawzi et non hawzi (Poésie et rythmes)." In *Le Chant arabo-andalou*, edited by Nadir Marouf, 91–111.

Dib, Omar. *"Les Amis du livre." Fleuron du mouvement culturel algérien, suivi de Le Mardi 04 juin 1957 à Tlemcen, un forfait contre l'humanité.* Oran: Editions Dar El Gharb, 2006.

Diff, Fazilet. "Musique andalouse et expressions féminines." Paper presented at the Festival

International de la Musique Andalouse et des Musiques Anciennes, Algiers, Algeria, December 29, 2013.

Dondin-Payre, Monique. "L'archéologie en Algérie à partir de 1830: Une politique patrimoniale?" In *Pour une histoire des politiques du patrimoine*, edited by Philippe Poirrier and Loïc Vadelorge, 145–70. Paris: Fondation Maison des sciences de l'homme, 2003.

Douglas, Mary. *Thinking in Circles: An Essay on Ring Composition*. New Haven: Yale University Press, 2007.

During, Jean. *Quelque chose se passe: Le sens de la tradition dans l'Orient musical*. Paris: Editions Verdier, 1994.

El-Fasi, Mohamed. "La musique marocaine dite 'musique andalouse.'" *Hespéris Tamuda* 3 (1962): 79–106.

El Hassar, Benali. *Tlemcen: cité des grands maîtres de la musique arabo-andalouse*. Editions Dalimen, 2002.

———. "Mahmoud Agha Bouayad, un intellectuel, une époque, une oeuvre." *Le Quotidien d'Oran*, 2006.

El Hassar, Salim [Salīm al-ḥaṣṣār]. *Al-mūsīqā al-ʿarabiyya al-andalusiyya min gharnāṭa ilā tilimsān . . . dīwān shiʿrī li-l-ṣanʿa, muwashshaḥāt wa-azjāl/Musique arabo-andalouse de Grenade à Tlemcen . . . Corpus poétique de la çanaʿa Muwaschchahʾate wa Azdjal*. Algiers: ENAG Editions, 2011.

El Khazen, Philippe, ed. *Al-ʿadhāra al-māyisāt fi-l-azjāl wa-l-muwashshaḥāt*. Jūniyya: Maṭbaʿat al-arz, 1902.

Eickelman, Dale F. *The Middle East and Central Asia: An Anthropological Approach*. 3d ed. Upper Saddle River, NJ: Prentice Hall, 1998.

Eickelman, Dale F., and James Piscatori, eds. *Muslim Travellers: Pilgrimage, Migration, and the Religious Imagination*. Berkeley and Los Angeles: University of California Press, 1992.

Eisenlohr, Patrick. "Materialities of Entextualization: The Domestication of Sound Reproduction in Mauritian Muslim Devotional Practice." *Journal of Linguistic Anthropology* 20, no. 2 (2010): 314–33.

———. "As Makkah is Sweet and Beloved, So is Madina: Islam, Devotional Genres, and Electronic Mediation in Mauritius." *American Ethnologist* 33, no. 2 (2006): 230–45.

Elsner, Jürgen. "Urban Music of Algeria." In *The Garland Encyclopedia of World Music*, vol. 6: *The Middle East*, edited by V. Danielson, S. Marcus, and D. Reynolds, 465–77. New York: Routledge, 2002.

———. "Présentation de la musique algérienne au congrès du Caire." In *Musique arabe: Le Congrès du Caire de 1932*, edited by CEDEJ, 193–208. Cairo: CEDEJ, 1992.

Evans-Pritchard, E. E. *The Nuer: A Description of the Modes of Livelihood and Political Institutions of a Nilotic People*. Oxford: Oxford University Press, 1940.

———. *The Sanusi of Cyrenaica*. Oxford: Clarendon Press, 1949.

Ewing, Katherine Pratt. *Arguing Sainthood: Modernity, Psychoanalysis, and Islam*. Durham, NC: Duke University Press, 1997.

Faudree, Paja. "Music, Language, and Texts: Sound and Semiotic Ethnography." *Annual Review of Anthropology* 41 (2012): 519–36.

Fabbri, Franco. "A Theory of Musical Genres: Two Applications." In *Popular Music Perspectives: Papers from the First International Conference on Popular Music Research, Amsterdam, June 1981*, edited by David Horn and Philip Tagg, 52–81. Gothenburg: International Association for the Study of Popular Music, 1982.

Fajans, Jane. "Exchanging Products; Producing Exchange." In *Exchanging Products: Producing Exchange*, edited by Jane Fajans, 1–14. Sydney: University of Sydney Press, 1993.

Farīd, Muḥammad Bey. *Min miṣr ilā miṣr: riḥlat sanat 1901 bi-bilād al-andalus (isbāniyā) wa-marrākush wa-l-jazā'ir.* Cairo: Maṭba'at al-mawsū'āt, 1319 h.

Farmer, Henry George. "Preface." In *The Music and Musical Instruments of the Arab with Introduction on How to Appreciate Arab Music*, edited by Francesco Salvador Daniel, translated by Henry George Farmer, 37–40. London: W. Reeves, 1915.

al Faruqi, Lois Ibsen. "Muwashshaḥ: A Vocal Form in Islamic Culture." *Ethnomusicology* 19, no. 1 (1975): 1–29.

Feintuch, Burt. "Revivals on the Edge: Northumberland and Cape Breton: A Keynote." *Yearbook for Traditional Music* 38 (2006): 1–17.

Feld, Steven. "Sound Structure as Social Structure." *Ethnomusicology* 28, no. 3 (1984): 383–410.

———. "Aesthetics as Iconicity of Style, or 'Lift-up-over Sounding': Getting into the Kaluli Groove." *Yearbook for Traditional Music* 20 (1988): 74–113.

———. *Jazz Cosmopolitanism in Accra: Five Musical Years in Ghana.* Durham, NC: Duke University Press. 2012.

Feld, Steven, and Aaron A. Fox. "Music and Language." *Annual Review of Anthropology* 23 (1994): 25–53.

Feld, Steven, and Keith H. Basso, eds. *Senses of Place.* Santa Fe: School of American Research Press, 1996.

Fergani, Salim / Firgānī, Salīm. *Majmū'at ash'ār wa-azjāl mūsīqā al-mā'lūf al-qiṭa' allatī addāhā wa-sajjalahā li-l-turāth al-ustādh Salīm Firgānī.* Algiers: Editions New Sound, 2011.

Ferhat, Mohamed. "Veritable festival de musique andalouse au thé-concert «El-Djazaïria-El-Mossilia>>." *Alger Républicain*, October 20, 1952.

———. "23me anniversaire de la société musicale et littéraire «EL MOSSILIA-EL-DJAZAIRIA»." *Alger Républicain*, February 8–9, 1953.

———. "El Djazairia El Mossilia." *Alger Républicain*, February 9, 1954.

Ferry, Elizabeth Emma. *Not Ours Alone: Patrimony, Value, and Collectivity in Contemporary Mexico.* New York: Columbia University Press, 2005.

FLN Commission centrale d'orientation. *Colloque national sur la musique algérienne, El-Riath, 25–26–27 decembre 1964.* Algiers: F.L.N. Commission centrale d'orientation, section des affaires culturelles, 1966.

Flueckiger, Joyce Burkhalter. "Genre and Community in the Folklore System of Chhattisgarh." In *Gender, Genre, and Power in South Asian Expressive Traditions*, edited by Arjun Appadurai, Frank K. Korom, and Margaret A. Mills, 181–200. Philadelphia: University of Pennsylvania Press, 1991.

Foley, William A. *Anthropological Linguistics: An Introduction.* Oxford: Blackwell Publishing, 1997.

Foucault, Michel. "What is an Author?" In *Language, Counter-memory, Practice: Selected Essays and Interviews*, edited by Donald F. Bouchard, translated by Donald F. Bouchard and Sherry Simon, 113–38. Ithaca, NY: Cornell University Press, 1977.

———. "Of Other Spaces." Translated by Jay Miskowiec. *Diacritics* 16, no. 1 (1986): 22–27.

Fox, Aaron A. *Real Country: Music and Language in Working-Class Culture.* Durham, NC: Duke University Press, 2004.

Freadman, Anne. *The Machinery of Talk Charles Peirce and the Sign Hypothesis.* Stanford, CA: Stanford University Press, 2004.

Frémeaux, Jacques. "Souvenirs de Rome et presence française au Maghreb: Essai d'investigation." In *Connaissances du Maghreb: Sciences sociales et colonisation*, edited by Jean-Claude Vatin, 29–46. Paris: CNRS, 1984.

Frishkopf, Michael. "Introduction: Music and Media in the Arab World and *Music and Media in the Arab World* as Music and Media in the Arab World: A Metadiscourse." In *Music and Media in the Arab World*, edited by Michael Frishkopf, 1–64. Cairo: American University in Cairo Press, 2010.

Gallie, W. B. "Art as an Essentially Contested Concept." *The Philosophical Quarterly* 6, no. 23 (1956): 97–114.

Geertz, Clifford. *The Interpretation of Cultures*. New York: Basic Books, 1973.

———. Local Knowledge: Further Essays in Interpretive Anthropology. New York: Basic Books.

Geertz, Hildred. "The Meaning of Family Ties." In *Meaning and Order in Moroccan Society: Three Essays in Cultural Analysis*, 315–79. Cambridge: Cambridge University Press, 1979.

Gell, Alfred. "The Language of the Forest: Landscape and Phonological Iconism in Umeda." In *The Art of Anthropology: Essays and Diagrams*, edited by E. Hirsch, 232–58. London: Athlone Press, 1999.

Gellner, Ernest. *Saints of the Atlas*. London: Weidenfeld and Nicholson, 1969.

———. *Nations and Nationalism*. Ithaca, NY: Cornell University Press, 1983.

Ghaffour, Hadj Mohammed / Ghaffūr, Al-Ḥājj Muḥammad. *Majmūʿat ashʿār wa-azjāl mūsīqā al-ṣanʿa al-qiṭaʿ allatī addāhā wa-sajjalahā li-l-turāth al-ustādh al-Ḥājj Muḥammad Ghaffūr.* Algiers: Editions New Sound, 2011.

Ghoul, Yahia. *Patrimoine de musique arabo-andalouse: le système rythmique dans l'école de Tlemcen.* Sidi Bel-Abbes: Imprimerie A. Benkelfat, 2009.

———. "NEA_Y-Ghoul vs TECHNIQUE du Groupe Yafil signé Y-T (Partie 1)." *Andaloussiate Le Blog*, published September 6, 2014, http://www.andaloussiate.over-blog.net.

Gill, Denise. "Melancholic Genealogies: Horizontal Lineages and Contemporary Turkish Classical Musicians." Paper presented at the American Anthropological Association Annual Meeting, Washington, DC, December 3–7, 2014.

Gillan, Matt. 2013. "'Dancing Fingers': Embodied Lineages in the Performance of Okinawan Classical Music." Ethnomusicology 57, no. 3: 367–95.

Gilsenan, Michael. *Recognizing Islam: An Anthropologist's Introduction.* London: Croon Helm, 1982.

Glasser, Jonathan. "Edmond Yafil and Andalusi Musical Revival in Early 20th Century Algeria." *International Journal of Middle Eastern Studies* 44 (2012): 671–92.

———."Andalusi Musical Origins at the Moroccan-Algerian Frontier: Beyond Charter Myth." *American Ethnologist* 42, no. 4 (November 2015).

Goffman, Erving. *Forms of Talk*. Philadelphia: University of Pennsylvania Press, 1981.

Goodman, Jane E. *Berber Culture on the World Stage: From Village to Video*. Bloomington and Indianapolis: Indiana University Press, 2005.

———. "Acting with One Voice: Producing Unanimism in Algerian Reformist Theater." *Comparative Studies in Society and History* 55, no. 1 (2013): 167–97.

———. "The Man behind the Curtain: Theatrics of the State in Algeria." *The Journal of North African Studies* 18, no. 5 (2013): 779–95.

Goldstein, Kenneth. "A Future Folklorist in the Record Business." In *Transforming Tradition: Folk Music Revivals Examined*," edited by Neil V. Rosenberg, 107–22. Urbana and Chicago: University of Illinois Press, 1993.

Gosnell, Jonathan K. *The Politics of Frenchness in Colonial Algeria 1930–1954*. Rochester: University of Rochester Press, 2002.

Gossen, Gary H. *Chamulas in the World of the Sun: Time and Sace in a Maya Oral Tradition.* Cambridge, MA: Harvard University Press, 1974.

Gouget-Valière, Aline. *Premier recueil de chants marocains*. Rabat: N.p, 1939.

Graeber, David. *Toward an Anthropological Theory of Value: The False Coin of Our Own Dreams.* New York: Palgrave, 2001.

Grangaud, Isabelle, and M'hamed Oualdi. "Tout est-il colonial dans le Maghreb? Ce que les travaux des historiens modernistes peuvent apporter." *L'Année du Maghreb* 10 (2014): 233–54.

Grewal, Zareena. *Islam is a Foreign Country: American Muslims and the Global Crisis of Authority.* New York: NYU Press, 2014.

Guerbas, Rachid. "Chant et musique de la Nawba ou Nûba algérienne." *Horizons Maghrebins: Le Droit à la Mémoire* 47 (2002): 24–35.

Guessal, Mohamed. "Les associations de musique classique maghrebine en Algérie, histoire et répertoire." Ph.D. diss., Université de Paris Sorbonne, Paris IV, 2000.

Guest-Scott, Anthony. "Categories in Motion: The Use of Generic Multiplicity in Music Store Guitar Lessons." *Ethnomusicology* 52, no. 3 (2008): 426–57.

Guettat, Mahmoud [Maḥmūd Gaṭṭāṭ]. *La musique classique du Maghreb*. Paris: Sindbad, 1980.

———. "Makānat al-mawrūth al-mūsīqī fī taḥdīd al-huwiyya (qaḍāyā al-mawrūth wa-l-taḥdīth al-mūsīqī)." In *Anthropologie et Musiques*, 13–39. Algiers: Centre National de Recherches Préhistoriques Anthropologiques et Historiques, 2008.

Hachelaf, Ahmed and Mohamed Elhabib Hachelaf. *Anthologie de la musique arabe, 1906–1960.* Paris: Publisud, 1993.

Hachlef, A. "Les preludes dans la musique arabo-andalouse en Algérie, istikhbar vocal." In *Le stikhbar chanté en Algérie*. Paris: Les Artistes Arabes Associés 093, Club du disque arabe, 1994.

Hadj Ali, Bachir. "Qu'est-ce qu'une musique nationale?" *La Nouvelle Critique* 156–57 (1964): 175–96.

———. "El Anka et la tradition 'chaabi.'" *Annuaire de l'Afrique du Nord* 17 (1979): 905–11.

Hadj Slimane, Mokhtar. *La musique classique algérienne: recueil d'informations élémentaires sur la musique andalouse à Tlemcen.* Tlemcen, 2002.

Haj, Samira. *Reconfiguring Islamic Tradition: Reform, Rationality, and Modernity.* Stanford, CA: Stanford University Press, 2009.

Al-Ḥājiyyāt, 'Abd al-Ḥamīd, ed. *Al-jawāhir al-ḥisān min naẓm awliyā' tilimsān*. Algiers: SNED, 1974.

Hammoudi, Abdellah. *Master and Disciple: The Cultural Foundations of Moroccan Authoritarianism.* Chicago: University of Chicago Press, 1997.

Handler, Richard. *Nationalism and the Politics of Culture in Quebec.* Madison: University of Wisconsin Press, 1988.

Hanks, William F. "Exorcism and the Description of Participant Roles." In *Natural Histories of Discourse*, edited by Michael Silverstein and Greg Urban, 160–200. Chicago: University of Chicago Press, 1996.

Hardt, Michael, and Antonio Negri. *Empire*. Cambridge, MA: Harvard University Press, 2000.

Heggoy, Alf A. *The French Conquest of Algiers, 1830: An Algerian Oral Tradition.* Athens: Ohio University Press, 1983.

Hell, Julia, and Andreas Schönle. "Introduction." In *Ruins of Modernity*, edited by Julia Hell and Andreas Schönle, 1–16. Durham, NC: Duke University Press, 2010.

Hobsbawm, Eric. "Introduction: Inventing Traditions." In *The Invention of Tradition*, edited by Eric Hobsbawm and Terence Ranger, 1–14.

———. "Mass-Producing Traditions: Europe, 1870–1914." In *The Invention of Tradition*, edited by Eric Hobsbawm and Terence Ranger, 263–308.

Hobsbawm, Eric, and Terence Ranger, eds. *The Invention of Tradition*. Cambridge: Cambridge University Press, 1983.

Ho, Engseng. *The Graves of Tarim: Genealogy and Mobility Across the Indian Ocean*. Berkeley and Los Angeles: University of California Press, 2006.

Irvine, Judith T. "Shadow Conversations: The Indeterminacy of Participant Roles." In *Natural Histories of Discourse*, edited by Michael Silverstein and Greg Urban, 131–59. Chicago: University of Chicago Press, 1996.

Ivy, Marilyn, *Discourses of the Vanishing: Modernity, Phantasm, Japan*. Chicago: University of Chicago Press, 1995.

Jam'iyyat Ribāṭ al-fatḥ, ed. *Athr al-mūsīqā al-andalusiyya fi-l-anmāṭ al-īqā'iyya al-maḥalliyya*. Rabat: Manshūrāt jam'iyyat ribāṭ al-fatḥ, 1997.

Jankowsky, Richard C. *Stambeli: Music, Trance, and Alterity in Tunisia*. Chicago: University of Chicago Press, 2010.

Jarrārī, 'Abbās. *Al-naghm al-muṭrib bayna al-andalus wa-l-maghrib*. Rabat: Al-nādī al-Jarrārī, 2002.

Jayyusi, Salma Khadra. "Andalusī Poetry: The Golden Period." In *The Legacy of Muslim Spain*, edited by Salma Khadra Jayyusi, 317–66. Leiden: Brill, 1992.

Jean-Darrouy, Lucienne. "La musique musulmane en Afrique du Nord." *Société de Géographie d'Alger et de l'Afrique du Nord* 125 (1931): 34–50.

Johansson, Mats and Ola K. Berge. "Who Owns an Interpretation? Legal and Symbolic Ownership of Norwegian Folk Music." *Ethnomusicology* 58, no. 1 (2014): 30–53.

Joly, J. Chansons du répertoire algérois. *Revue Africaine* 53 (1909): 46–66.

Jones, Alan, and Richard Hitchcock, eds. *Studies on the Muwaššah and the Kharja: Proceedings of the Exeter International Colloquium*. Reading: Published by Ithaca for the Board of the Faculty of Oriental Studies, Oxford University, 1991.

Kapchan, Deborah. "Moroccan Female Performers Defining the Social Body." *The Journal of American Folklore* 107, no. 423 (1994): 82–105.

———. *Traveling Spirit Masters: Moroccan Gnawa Trance and Music in the Global Marketplace*. Middletown, CT: Wesleyan University Press, 2007.

Karl, Brian. "Across a Divide: Mediations of Contemporary Popular Music in Morocco and Spain." Ph.D. diss., Columbia University, 2011.

Katz, Max. *Lineage of Loss: Counternarratives of North Indian Music*. Middletown, CT: Wesleyan University Press, forthcoming.

Kilani, Mondher. *La construction de la mémoire*. Geneva: Labor et Fides, 1992.

King, Emilie Boyer. "Undercover Restorers Fix Paris Landmark's Clock: 'Cultural Guerillas' Cleared of Lawbreaking over Secret Workshop in Pantheon." *The Guardian*, November 26, 2007.

Kluckhohn, Clyde. "The Concept of Culture." In *Culture and Behavior*, 19–73. New York: The Free Press, 1962.

Kuzar, Ron. *Hebrew and Zionism: A Discourse Analytic Study*. Berlin: Mouton de Gruyter, 2001.

"La Charte d'Alger: Ensemble de textes adoptés par le premier congrés du parti du Front de Liberation Nationale (du 16 au 21 avril 1964)." *Présidence de la République.* http://www.el-mouradia.dz/francais/symbole/textes/charte%20d'alger.htm.

La Dépêche Algérienne. Untitled announcement. September 13, 1927.

———. Untitled announcement. September 20, 1927, 2.

———. 1928. "Les obsèques de M. Edmond Yafil." October 10, 1928, 7.

La Revue Africaine, May 1860, 239.

Laffan, Michael. "'Another Andalusia': Images of Colonial Southeast Asia in Arabic." *The Journal of Asian Studies* 66, no. 3 (2007): 689–722.

Lakjaa, Abdelkader. "Vie associative et urbanisation en Algérie." *Cahiers du CREAD* 53 (2000): 5–23.

Lakoff, George and Mark Johnson. *Metaphors We Live By.* Chicago: University of Chicago Press, 1980.

Lamy, Yvon. "Patrimoine et culture: L'institutionnalisation." In *Pour une histoire des politiques du patrimoine,* edited by Philippe Poirrier and Loïc Vadelorge, 45–65. Paris: Fondation Maison des sciences de l'homme, 2003.

Langlois, Tony. "Music and Politics in North Africa." In *Music and the Play of Power in the Middle East, North Africa and Central Asia,* edited by Laudan Nooshin, 207–28. Farnham: Ashgate, 2009.

Landoff, Brita. *A Little for my Heart, a Little for my God.* Film. New York: Filmmaker's Library, 1993.

Lave, Jean, and Etienne Wenger. *Situated Learning: Legitimate Peripheral Participation.* Cambridge: Cambridge University Press, 1991.

Le Temps. "Chroniques Algériennes: Les M'tournis." February 8, 1902, 3.

Lemaille, M. "Les algériens à Oujda en 1937." *L'Afrique française: Bulletin de la comité de l'Afrique française* 5 (1937): 255–60.

Leslie, Esther. "Walter Benjamin: Traces of Craft." *Journal of Design History* 11, no. 1 (1998): 5–13.

Lévi-Strauss, Claude. "Introduction: History and Anthropology." In *Structural Anthropology,* translated by Claire Jacobson and Brooke Grundfest Schoepf, 1–27. New York: Basic Books, 1963.

Linton, Ralph. "Nativistic Movements." *American Anthropologist* 45, no. 2 (1943): 230–40.

Littlefield, Walter. "France and the Associations Law." *The North American Review* 175, no. 551 (1902): 522–33.

Liu, Benjamin M., and Monroe, James T. *Ten Hispano-Arabic Strophic Songs in the Modern Oral Tradition: Music and Texts.* Berkeley and Los Angeles: University of California Press, 1989.

Liverani, Andrea. *Civil Society in Algeria: The Political Functions of Associational Life.* London and New York: Routledge, 2008.

Livingston, Tamara E. "Music Revivals: Towards a General Theory." *Ethnomusicology* 43, no. 1 (1999): 66–85.

Lorcin, Patricia M. E. "Rome and France in Africa: Recovering Colonial Algeria's Latin Past." *French Historical Studies* 25 (2002): 295–329.

al-Madanī, Aḥmad Tawfīq. *Kitāb al-Jazā'ir.* Algiers: al-Maṭba'a al-'arabiyya, 1931.

al-Madanī, Aḥmad Tawfīq, ed. *Mudhakkirāt al-Ḥājj Aḥmad al-Sharīf al-Zahhār, naqīb ashrāf al-jazā'ir, 1168–1246 h., 1754–1830 m.* Algiers: Al-sharika al-waṭaniyya li-l-nashr wa-l-tawzī', 1974.

el-Mahdi, Salah, and Mohamed Marzuqi. *Al-ma'had al-rāshidī li-l-mūsīqā al-tūnisiyya.* Tunis: Ministry of Culture, 1981.

Mahmood, Saba. *Politics of Piety: The Islamic Revival and the Feminist Subject*. Princeton, NJ: Princeton University Press, 2005.

Maitrot de la Motte-Capron, A. "La Musique Méditerranéenne secrete et sacrée." *Bulletin Provisoire de la Société de Géographie d'Alger* 168 (1941): 6–24.

Maktab al-akhbār al-tūnisiyya. *Ẓāhira murība fī siyāsat al-isti'mār al-faransī: hal tumaththilu mā'sāt al-andalus min jadīd fī shamāl ifrīqīyā: Al-ḥamla al-ṣalībiyya al-tāsi'a fi-l-mu'tamar al-afkharīstī*. Cairo?: Al-maṭba'a al-salafiyya, 1349 AH, 1930 CE.

Malinowski, Bronislaw. "Myth in Primitive Psychology." In *Magic, Science and Religion*, 93–148. Garden City, NY: Doubleday and Company, 1954 [1926].

al-Maqqarī, Aḥmad bin Muḥammad. *Nafḥ al-ṭīb min ghuṣn al-andalus al-raṭīb*. Beirut: Dār al-ṣādir, 1968.

Marçais, William. *Musées et collections archéologiques de l'Algérie et de la Tunisie. Musée de Tlemcen*. Paris: Ernest Leroux, 1906.

Marcus, Scott. "The Eastern Arab System of Melodic Modes in Theory and Practice: A Case Study of *Maqām Bayyātī*." In *The Garland Encyclopedia of World Music*, vol. 6: *The Middle East*, edited by V. Danielson, S. Marcus, and D. Reynolds, 33–44. New York: Routledge, 2002.

Marouf, Nadir, ed. *Le chant arabo-andalou*. Paris: L'Harmattan, 1995.

———. "Structure du répertoire andalous: Quelques problèmes de méthode." *Le chant arabo-andalou*, edited by Nadir Marouf, 11–22. Paris: L'Harmattan, 1995.

———. "Le système musical de la San'a ou le paradigme de la norme et de la marge." *Horizons maghrébins: Le droit à la mémoire* 47 (2002): 8–24.

Marx, Karl. *A Contribution to the Critique of Political Economy*. Edited by Maurice Dobb. Translated by S. W. Ryazanskaya. New York: International Publishers, 1970 [1859].

Maturana, Humberto R. and Francisco J. Varela. *The Tree of Knowledge: The Biological Roots of Human Understanding*. Trans. Robert Paolucci. Boston: Shambhala, 1998.

Mauss, Marcel. *The Gift: The Form and Reason for Exchange in Archaic Societies*. Translated by W. D. Halls. New York: W.W. Norton, 1990.

McCann, Anthony. "All That Is Not Given Is Lost: Irish Traditional Music, Copyright, and Common Property." *Ethnomusicology* 45, no.1 (2001): 89–106.

McClellan, Andrew. *Inventing the Louvre*. Cambridge: Cambridge University Press, 1994.

McDougall, James. *History and the Culture of Nationalism in Algeria*. Cambridge: Cambridge University Press, 2006.

———. "The Secular State's Islamic Empire: Muslim Spaces and Subjects of Jurisdiction in Paris and Algiers, 1905–1957." *Comparative Studies in Society and History* 52 (2010): 553–80.

———. "Dream of Exile, Promise of Home: Language, Education, and Arabism in Algeria." *International Journal of Middle East Studies* 43, no. 2 (2011): 251–70.

Mecheri-Saada, Nadia. "Les documents algériens du Congrès du Caire." In *Musique arabe: Le Congrès du Caire de 1932*, edited by CEDEJ, 51–68. Cairo: CEDEJ, 1992.

Merad, Ali. "L'enseignement politique de Muhammad 'Abduh aux algériens (1903)." *Orient* 28 (1963): 75–123.

Merdaçi, Abdelmadjid. *Dictionnaire des musiques et des musiciens de Constantine*. Constantine: Simoun, 2002.

———. "De Constantine à Constantine, un passage à la ville." In *Le Chant arabo-andalou*, edited by Nadir Marouf, 159–64. Paris: L'Harmattan, 1995.

Merriam, Alan P. *The Anthropology of Music*. Evanston, IL: Northwestern University Press, 1964.

Messaoudi, Alain. "The Teaching of Arabic in French Algeria and Contemporary France." *French History* 20 (2006): 297–317.

Messick, Brinkley. *The Calligraphic State: Textual Domination and History in a Muslim Society.* Berkeley and Los Angeles: University of California Press, 1993.

Meziane, Abdelhakim. "Le vieil Alger musical." Paper presented at the Conference of the 6th Andaloussiate festival, Complexe Culturel Laâdi Flici, Algiers, May 20, 2009.

Miliani, Hadj. "Comment constituer une tradition? Le cas des chants et des musiques." In *Non-material culture heritage in the Euro-mediterranean area*, 185–200. Rome: Acts of the Unimed-Symposium, 2000.

———. "Fabrication patrimoniale et imaginaires identitaires: Autour des chants et musiques en Algérie." *Insaniyat* 12 (2000): 53–63.

———. "Le cheikh et le phonographe: Notes de recherche pour un corpus des phonogrammes et des vidéogrammes des musiques et des chansons algériennes." *Turath* 8 (2004): 43–67.

Miliani, Hadj, and Jonathan Glasser. "What is an Author in Interwar Algeria? Recorded Music, Copyright, and the Problem of the Common." Paper presented at the Middle East Studies Association Annual Meeting, Washington, DC, November 21–24, 2014.

Ministry of Culture, People's Democratic Republic of Algeria. "Orchestre Symphonique Nationale." http://www.m-culture.gov.dz/mc2/fr/fiche_site.php?id=488, accessed November 1, 2012.

Ministry of Information. People's Democratic Republic of Algeria. *Tlemcen*. Algiers: SNED, 1971.

Monroe, James T. *Hispano-Arabic Poetry: A Student Anthology.* Berkeley and Los Angeles: University of California Press, 1974.

———. "Poetic Quotation in the *Muwaššaḥa* and Its Implications: Andalusian Strophic Poetry as Song." *La Corónica* (Spring 1986): 230–50.

———. "*Zajal* and *Muwashshaḥa*: Hispano-Arabic Poetry and the Romance Tradition." In *The Legacy of Muslim Spain*, edited by Salma Khadra Jayyusi, 398–419. Leiden: Brill, 1992.

Moore, Robert E. "From Genericide to Viral Marketing: On 'Brand.'" *Language and Communication* 23 (2003): 331–57.

Morgan, Prys. "From a Death to a View: The Hunt for the Welsh Past in the Romantic Period." In *The Invention of Tradition*, edited by Eric Hobsbawm and Terence Ranger, 43–100. Cambridge: Cambridge University Press, 1983.

Murphy, Philip J. "Annihilation in God and Living in the World: Sufi As-Samāʿ in Fez, Morocco." Paper presented at The Musical Heritage of Moorish Spain, University of California Santa Barbara, February 20–22, 2015.

Narotzky, Susana. "Provisioning." In *A Handbook of Economic Anthropology*, edited by James Carrier, 78–93. Cheltenham: Edward Elgar, 2005.

Neuman, Daniel. *The Life of Music in North India: The Organization of an Artistic Tradition.* Detroit: Wayne State University Press, 1980.

Neuman, Dard. "Pedagogy, Practice, and Embodied Creativity in Hindustani Music." *Ethnomusicology* 56, no. 3 (2012): 426–49.

Neuman, Dard. Genealogy, "Oral History and Musicology: Heterodox Appropriations of Classical Sources." Paper presented at the American Anthropological Association Annual Meeting, Washington, DC, December 3–7, 2014.

Noorani, Yaseen. "The Lost Garden of Al-Andalus: Islamic Spain and the Poetic Inversion of Colonialism." *International Journal of Middle East Studies* 31 (1999): 237–54.

Novak, David. *Japanoise: Music at the Edge of Circulation.* Durham, NC: Duke University Press, 2013.

Ochoa Gautier, Ana María. *Aurality: Listening and Knowledge in Nineteenth-Century Colombia.* Durham, NC: Duke University Press, 2014.

Ortner, Sherry B. "Patterns of History: Cultural Schemas in the Foundings of Sherpa Religious Institutions." In *Culture Through Time: Anthropological Approaches,* edited by Emiko Ohnuki-Tierney, 57–93. Stanford, CA: Stanford University Press, 1990.

———. "Theory in Anthropology since the Sixties." In *Culture/Power/History: A Reader in Contemporary Social Theory,* edited by Nicholas B. Dirks, Geoff Eley, and Sherry B. Ortner, 372–411. Princeton, NJ: Princeton University Press, 1994.

Ouamara, Mourad [Murād Bin ʿAlī Waʿmāra], ed. *Jāmiʿ al-safāyin wa-l-kunnāshāt fī ṣanāʾiʿ al-azjāl wa-l-muwashshaḥāt / Recueil des poèmes Muwashshaḥât et Azdjâl.* 2 volumes. Algiers: Editions New Sound/ONDA, 2011.

Oulebsir, Nabila. *Les usages du patrimoine: Monuments, musées et politique coloniale en Algérie, 1830–1930.* Paris: Maison des sciences de l'homme, 2004.

Pacholczyk, Jozéf. "The Relationship Between the Nawba of Morocco and the Music of the Troubadours and Trouvères." *World of Music* 25, no. 2 (1983): 5–15.

———. "Early Arab Suite in Spain: An Investigation of the Past through the Contemporary Living Tradition." *Revista de Musicología* 16, no. 1 (1993): 358–66.

Pananti, Filippo. *Narrative of a Residence in Algiers.* London, 1818.

Pandian, Anand. "Tradition in Fragments: Inherited Forms and Fractures in the Ethics of South India." *American Ethnologist* 35 (2008): 466–80.

Papailias, Penelope. *Genres of Recollection: Archival Poetics and Modern Greece.* New York: Palgrave Macmillan, 2005.

Pardo, Martial. "La musique arabe dans les écrits français. Une exemple: L'Algérie entre 1830 et 1930." Masters thesis, Université Paris IV, 1994.

Pasler, Jann. "Musical Hybridity in Flux: Representing Race, Colonial Policy, and Modernity in French North Africa, 1860s-1930s." *Afrika Zamani* 20 (2012): 21–68.

———. "The Racial and Colonial Implications of Early French Music Ethnography, 1860s–1930s." In *Critical Music Historiography: Probing Canons, Ideologies, and Institutions,* edited by Markus Mantere and Vesa Kurkela, 17–44. London: Ashgate, 2015.

Peebles, Gustav. "Inverting the Panopticon: Money and the Nationalization of the Future." *Public Culture* 20, no. 2 (2008): 233–65.

Pérès, Henri. "Joseph Desparmet et son oeuvre (1863–1942)." *Revue Africaine* 87 (1943): 251–66.

Plenckers, Leo J. "Changes in the Algerian Sanʿa Tradition and the Role of the Musicologist in the Process." *Revista de Musicología* 16, no. 3 (1993): 1255–60.

———. "Modal and Formal Constraints in Improvisation: A Study to the Algerian *Istiḫbār.*" In *Omani Traditional Music and the Arab Heritage,* edited by Issam El-Mallah, 83–114. Tutzing: Hans Schneider Verlag, 2002.

Poché, Christian. *La musique arabo-andalouse.* Arles: Cité de la Musique/Actes Sud, 1995.

Poché, Christian, and Jean Lambert. *Musiques du monde arabe et musulman: Bibliographie et discographie.* Paris: Geuthner, 2000.

Prochaska, David. "The Other Algeria." In *Renoir and Algeria,* edited by Roger Benjamin, 121–42. New Haven: Yale University Press, 2003.

Production R.T.A. *1er festival algérien de la musique andalouse 1967.* Zagreb: Production R.T.A. Mehradjane, 1967.

Qāḍī, Muḥammad. *Al-kanz al-maknūn fi-l-shiʿr al-malḥūn.* Algiers: Al-maṭbaʿa al-thaʿālibiyya, 1928.

Qāra Shantīr, Fatīḥa. *Al-sha'bī: Khiṭāb, ṭuqūs wa-mumārasāt*. Algiers: Manshūrāt abayk, 2007.

Qureshi, Regula Burckhardt. "His Master's Voice? Exploring Qawwali and 'Gramophone Culture' in South Asia." *Popular Music* 18, no. 1 (1999): 63–98.

———. "Confronting the Social: Mode of Production and the Sublime for (Indian) Art Music." *Ethnomusicology* 44 (2000): 15–38.

———. "Mode of Production and Musical Production: Is Hindustani Music Feudal?" In *Music and Marx: Ideas, Practice, Politics*, edited by R. Qureshi, 81–105. New York: Routledge, 2000.

Rabinow, Paul, and William M. Sullivan. "The Interpretive Turn: A Second Look." In *Interpretive Social Science: A Second Look*, edited by P. Rabinow and W. Sullivan, 1–30. Berkeley and Los Angeles: University of California Press, 1987.

Racy, Ali Jihad. "Overview of Music in the Mashriq." In *The Garland Encyclopedia of World Music*, vol. 6: *The Middle East*, edited by V. Danielson, S. Marcus, and D. Reynolds, 535–56. New York: Routledge, 2002.

Racy, A. J. *Making Music in the Arab World: The Culture and Artistry of ṭarab*. Cambridge: Cambridge University Press, 2003.

Rasmussen, Anne K. *Women, the Recited Qur'an, and Islamic Music in Indonesia*. Berkeley and Los Angeles: University of California Press, 2010.

Rahaim, Matthew. 2012. *Musicking Bodies: Gesture and Voice in Hindustani Music*. Middletown, CT: Wesleyan University Press.

Rāyyis, al-Ḥājj 'Abd al-Karīm. *Min waḥī al-rabāb: Majmū'at ash'ār wa-azjāl mūsīqā al-āla*. Casablanca: Maṭba'at al-najāḥ al-jadīda, 1989.

Read, Jason. *The Micro-Politics of Capital: Marx and the Prehistory of the Present*. Albany: State University of New York Press, 2003.

Reynaud, E. Pelissier de. *Annales algériennes*, vol. 1. Paris: Anselin et Taultier-Laguione, 1836–39.

Reynolds, Dwight F. "Musical 'Membrances of Medieval Muslim Spain." In *Charting Memory: Recalling Medieval Spain*, edited by Stacy N. Beckwith, 229–62. New York and London: Garland Publishing Inc, 2000.

———. "Music." In *The Literature of al-Andalus*, edited by María Rosa Menocal, Raymond P. Scheindlin, and Michael Sells, 60–82. Cambridge: Cambridge University Press, 2000.

———. "The Re-creation of Medieval Arabo-Andalusian Music in Modern Performance." *Al-Masaq* 21, no. 2 (2010): 175–89.

———. "Lost Virgins Found: The Arabic Songbook Genre and an Early North African Exemplar." *Quaderni di Studi Arabi* 7 (2012): 69–105.

Ricard, Prosper. *Essai d'action sur la musique et le théâtre populaire marocains*. Rabat: Imprimerie Nouvelle, 1928.

Riggs, Kristy. "On Colonial Textuality and Difference: Musical Encounters with French Colonialism in Nineteenth-Century Algeria." Ph.D. diss., Columbia University, 2012.

Risler, Camille. *La politique culturelle de la France en Algérie: les objectifs et les limites (1830–1962)*. Paris: L'Harmattan, 2004.

Rosen, Lawrence. *Bargaining for Reality: The Construction of Social Relations in a Muslim Community*. Chicago: University of Chicago Press, 1984.

Rosen, Tova. "The muwashshah." In *The Literature of al-Andalus*, edited by María Rosa Menocal, Raymond P. Scheindlin, and Michael Sells, 165–89. Cambridge: Cambridge University Press, 2000.

Rosenberg, Neil V., ed. *Transforming Tradition: Folk Music Revivals Examined*. Urbana and Chicago: University of Illinois Press, 1993.

Rouanet, Jules. "Pour les tapis algériens." *La Vie Algérienne et Tunisienne, Revue bimensuelle illustrée* 8 (1897): 227–29.
———. Esquisse pour une histoire de la musique arabe en Algérie-I-II. *Mercure musical* (1905): 553–62.
———. "Esquisse pour une histoire de la musique arabe en Algérie-III." *Mercure Musical* 15–16 (1906): 127–50.
———. "La musique arabe." In *Encyclopédie de la musique et dictionnaire du Conservatoire*, 2676–2812. Paris: Delagrave, 1922.
———. "La musique arabe dans le Maghreb." In *Encyclopédie de la musique et dictionnaire du Conservatoire*, 2813–2939. Paris: Delagrave, 1922.
———. "La musique musulmane." *La Dépêche Algérienne*, September 25, 1927, 7.
———. *La Dépêche Algérienne*, October 1, 1927 (dated September 30, 1927).
———. *L'Algérie Vivra, Réponse aux «Notes d'un ancien gouverneur général»*. Algiers: Société d'imprimerie de presse algérienne, 1931.
Rouighi, Ramzi. *The Making of a Mediterranean Emirate: Ifriqiya and its Andalusis, 1200–1400*. Philadelphia: University of Pennsylvania Press, 2011.
Ruedy, John. *Land Policy in Colonial Algeria: The Origins of the Rural Public Domain*. Berkeley and Los Angeles: University of California Press, 1967.
———. *Modern Algeria: The Origins and Development of a Nation*. 2d ed. Bloomington: Indiana University Press, 2005 [1992].
Ruskin, John. *The Seven Lamps of Architecture*. London: Smith, Elder, and Co., 1849.
Saadallah, Fawzi. *Yahūd al-jazā'ir: Majālis al-ṭarab wa-l-ghinā'*. Algiers: Dār Qurṭuba, 2010.
Sa'dallah, Abū al-Qāsim. *Ta'rīkh al-jazā'ir al-thaqāfī min al-qarn al-'āshir ilā al-rābi' 'ashar al-hijrī*. 2 vols. Beirut: Dar al-Gharb al-Islami, 1998.
Safta, Aḥmad. *Dirāsāt fi-l-mūsīqā al-andalusiyya*. Algiers: Al-mu'assasa al-waṭaniyya lil-kitāb, 1988.
Saidani, Maya. *La musique du constantinois: Contexte, nature, transmission et definition*. Algiers: Casbah Editions, 2006.
———. [Māya Sa'īdānī]. "Al-muṣṭalaḥāt al-khāṣṣa bi-l-turāth al-mūsīqī al-quṣanṭīnī bayn al-rīf wa-l-ḥaḍar." In *Anthropologie et Musiques*, 85–97. Algiers: Centre National de Recherches Préhistoriques Anthropologiques et Historiques, 2008.
———. "Le Zadjel Constantinois: Chant d'une andalousie déchue." Paper presented at the Programme des conférences of the 6ème Edition Andaloussiate: Nouba Printanière Festival, Algiers, May 13, 2009.
Saidouni, Nasreddine. "Al-andalusiyyūn (al-muriskiyyūn) bi-muqāṭa'at al-jazā'ir 'Dār al-sulṭān' athnā' al-qarnayn al-'āshir wa-l-ḥādī 'ashar li-l-hijra/al-sādis 'ashar wa-l-sābi' 'ashar li-l-mīlād." In *Dirāsāt andalusiyya: Maẓāhir al-tā'thīr al-ībīrī wa-l-wujūd al-andalusī bi-l-jazā'ir*, 43–73. Beirut: Dār al-gharb al-islāmī, 2003.
Salah, Fethi. "Le 'Néo Andalou' à Alger: Procédés d'innovation structurale dans la tradition musicale." In *Acts of the Conference on Music in the World of Islam*. Assilah, 2007.
Salamandra, Christa. *A New Old Damascus: Authenticity and Distinction in Urban Syria*. Bloomington and Indianapolis: Indiana University Press, 2004.
Salvador Daniel, Francisco. *Album de douze chansons arabes, mauresques et kabyles*. Paris: Richault et Cie Editeurs, N.d.
———. "Ruines et monuments de la musique." *Le Ménestrel* 44 (1866): 345–46.
———. *La musique arabe: Ses rapports avec la musique grècque et le chant grégorien*. Algiers: Adolphe Jourdane, 1879.

Samuels, David W. *Putting a Song on Top of It: Expression and Identity on the San Carlos Apache Reservation.* Tucson: University of Arizona Press, 2006.

Sarraut, Albert. *Grandeur et servitude coloniales*. Paris: Editions du sagittaire, 1931.

Saussure, Ferdinand de. *Course in General Linguistics*. Edited by Charles Bally and Albert Sechehaye, translated by Wade Baskin. New York: McGraw-Hill Book Company, 1959.

Say, Jean-Baptiste. *A Treatise on Political Economy, or the Production, Distribution, and Consumption of Wealth.* Translated by C. R. Prinsep. Philadelphia: Claxton, Remsen and Haffelfinger, 1880.

Schade-Poulsen, Marc. *Men and Popular Music in Algeria: The Social Significance of Raï.* Austin: University of Texas Press, 1999.

Schäfers, Marlene. "In Pursuit of Permanent Traces: Constituting Authorship through Inscription." Paper presented at the annual meeting of the Middle Eastern Studies Association, Washington, DC, November 21–24, 2014.

Schechner, Richard. *Between Theater and Anthropology*. Philadelphia: University of Pennsylvania Press, 1985.

Schofield, Katherine Butler. "Reviving the Golden Age Again: 'Classicization,' Hindustani Music, and the Mughals." *Ethnomusicology* 54, no. 3 (2010): 484–517.

Schroeter, Daniel J. "The Shifting Boundaries of Moroccan Jewish Identities." *Jewish Social Studies: History, Culture, Society* 15, no. 1 (2008): 145–64.

Schuyler, Philip D. "Moroccan Andalusian Music." *The World of Music* 20, no. 1 (1978): 33–43.

———. "Music Education in Morocco: Three Models." *The World of Music* 21, no. 3 (1979): 19–31.

Sebaa, Rabeh. "Vibrations en ʿarubi et hawzi majeurs." In *Le système musical de la canʿa ou "le paradigme de la norme et de la marge": Homage à Pierre Bourdieu*. By Nadir Marouf, 65–69. Oran: Dar El Gharb, 2003.

Seeger, Anthony. "UNESCO and the Safeguarding of Intangible Cultural Heritage." Paper presented the College of William and Mary, January 31, 2014.

Seroussi, Edwin. "Music." In *Encyclopedia of Jews in the Islamic World.* Edited by Norman A. Stillman, 498–519. Leiden: Brill, 2010.

———. "Andalusian Music (Morocco and Western Algeria): The Hebrew Version." Paper presented at The Musical Heritage of Moorish Spain, University of California Santa Barbara, February 20–22, 2015.

Serri, Sid Ahmed / Sarrī, Sīd Aḥmad. "Pour un véritable débat." In *Tilimsān: Al-dhikrā al-ʿāshira li-l-mihrajān al-waṭanī li-l-mūsīqā al-taqlīdiyya li-l-shabāb.* Tlemcen, 1984.

———. "Aperçu historique sur la création des assocations musicales et, en particulier, celles d'El-Djazairia-El-Mossilia." In *La ville dans tous ses états: Ouvrage collectif*, edited by Larbi Icheboudene, 53–58. Algiers: Casbah Editions, 1998.

———. *Chants andalous: Recueil des poèmes des noubates de la musique "Sanaa," musique classique algérienne.* Algiers: ENAG/Editions, 2002.

———. *Chants andalous: Recueil des poèmes des noubates de la musique "Sanaa," musique classique algérienne,* with the assistance of Mourad O. Algiers: ENAG/Editions, 2006.

———. *Majmūʿat al-qiṭaʿ allatī addāhā wa-sajjallahā lil-turāth al-ustādh Sīd Aḥmad Sarrī/Maître Sid Ahmed Serri.* Algiers: Editions New Sound/ONDA, 2011.

Sewell, William H. *Logics of History: Social Theory and Social Transformation*. Chicago: University of Chicago Press, 2005.

Shaery-Eisenlohr, Roschanack. "Territorializing Piety: Genealogy, Transnationalism, and Shiʿite Politics in Modern Lebanon." *Comparative Studies in Society and History* 51, no. 3 (2009): 533–62.

Shannon, Jonathan Holt. *Among the Jasmine Trees: Music and Modernity in Contemporary Syria.* Middletown, CT: Wesleyan University Press, 2006.

———. "Performing al-Andalus, Remembering al-Andalus: Mediterranean Soundings from Mashriq to Maghrib." *Journal of American Folklore* 120 (2007): 308–34.

———. *Performing al-Andalus: Music and Nostalgia across the Mediterranean.* Bloomington: Indiana University Press, 2015.

Shaw, Thomas. *Travels, or Observations Relating to Several Parts of Barbary and the Levant.* Oxford, 1738.

Shelemay, Kay Kaufman. "Musical Communities: Rethinking the Collective in Music." *Journal of the American Musicological Society* 64, no. 2 (2011): 349–90.

Shepard, Todd. *The Invention of Decolonization: The Algerian War and the Remaking of France.* Ithaca, NY: Cornell University Press, 2006.

Shiloah, Amnon. *Music in the World of Islam: A Socio-Cultural Study.* Detroit: Wayne State University Press, 2001.

Shryock, Andrew. *Nationalism and the Genealogical Imagination: Oral History and Textual Authority in Tribal Jordan.* Berkeley and Los Angeles: University of California Press, 1997.

Silverstein, Michael, and Greg Urban. "The Natural History of Discourse." In *Natural Histories of Discourse*, edited by Michael Silverstein and Greg Urban. 1–17. Chicago: University of Chicago Press, 1996.

Slobin, Mark. "Rethinking 'Revival' of American Ethnic Music." *New York Folklore* 9 (1983): 37–44.

Sonneck, C. "Six chansons arabes en dialecte maghrébin." *Journal Asiatique*, May-June, July-August, September-October, 1899.

Sonneck, C., ed. *Chants arabes du Maghreb: Étude sur le dialecte et la poésie populaire de l'Afrique du Nord.* Paris: J. Maisonneuve, 1902.

———. *Chants arabes du Maghreb: Étude sur le dialecte et la poésie populaire de l'Afrique du Nord*, vol. 2. Paris: E. Guilmoto, 1904.

Spivak, Gayatri. "Can the Subaltern Speak?" In *Marxism and the Interpretation of Culture*, edited by Cary Nelson and Lawrence Grossberg, 271–313. Urbana: University of Illinois Press, 1988.

Stein, Sarah Abrevaya. *Saharan Jews and the Fate of French Algeria.* Chicago: University of Chicago Press, 2014.

Stern, Samuel M. "Andalusian Muwashshaḥs in the Musical Repertoire of North Africa." *Actas del Premier Congreso de Estudios Árabes e Islámicos, 1962*, edited by F. M. Pareja, 319–27. Madrid: Maestre, 1964.

———. *Hispano-Arabic Strophic Poetry: Studies by Samuel Miklos Stern.* Edited by L. P. Harvey. Oxford: Clarendon, 1974.

Sterne, Jonathan. *The Audible Past: Cultural Origins of Sound Reproduction.* Durham, NC: Duke University Press, 2003.

Stokes, Martin. *The Arabesk Debate: Music and Musicians in Modern Turkey.* Oxford: Clarendon Press, 1992.

———. "Marx, Money, and Musicians." In *Music and Marx: Ideas, Practice, Politics*, edited by R. Qureshi, 139–63. New York: Routledge, 2000.

Strathern, Marilyn. "Cutting the Network." *Journal of the Royal Anthropological Institute* 2, no. 3 (1996): 517–35.

Straw, Will. "Systems of Articulation, Logics of Change: Communities and Scenes in Popular Music." *Cultural Studies* 5 (1991): 368–88.

Sweers, Britta. Electric Folk: The Changing Face of English Traditional Music.Oxford: Oxford University Press, 2005.

Ṭānṭāwī, Aḥmad. *Al-mūsīqā al-andalusiyya bi-l-gharb al-islāmī.* [Oujda?]: Wakālat al-jiha al-sharqiyya, 2008.

Terpak, Frances. "The Promise and Power of New Technologies: Nineteenth-century Algiers." In *Walls of Algiers: Narratives of the City through Text and Image*, edited by Zeynep Çelik, Julia Clancy-Smith, and Frances Terpak, 87–133. Los Angeles: The Getty Research Institute, 2009.

Thomas, Martin. "Albert Sarraut, French Colonial Development, and the Communist Threat, 1919–1930." *Journal of Modern History* 77 (2005): 917–55.

Tiersot, Julien. *Musiques pittoresques: Promenades musicales, l'exposition de 1889*. Paris: Librairie Fischbacher, 1889.

Touaïbia, Youcef. *Groupe Yafil*. Accessed May 31, 2015. http://yafil.free.fr/sommaire.html.

———. "Le Derdj dans Nouba de Tlemcen." Posted June 6, 2010. Accessed May 31, 2015. http://yafil.free.fr/partition_dossier_derdj_tlemcen.htm. sommaire.html

Touati, Houari. *L'armoire à sagesse: Bibliothèques et collections en Islam*. Paris: Aubier, 2003.

Touimy, El Hadj Driss Benjelloun, ed. *Patrimoine Musical Arabe Marocaine*. Casablanca: Maṭbaʿat al-Rāyyis, 1979.

Trumbull IV, George R. *An Empire of Facts: Colonial Power, Cultural Knowledge, and Islam in Algeria, 1870–1914*. Cambridge: Cambridge University Press, 2009.

Tuohy, Sue. "The Social Life of Genre: The Dynamics of Folksong in China." *Asian Music* 30, no. 2 (1999): 39–86.

Turino, Thomas. *Nationalists, Cosmopolitans, and Popular Music in Zimbabwe*. Chicago: University of Chicago Press, 2000.

———. *Music as Social Life: The Politics of Participation*. Chicago: University of Chicago Press, 2008.

———. "Peircean Thought as Core Theory for a Phenomenological Ethnomusicology." *Ethnomusicology* 58, no. 2 (2014): 185–221.

Turner, Victor. "Symbols in Ndembu Ritual." In *The Forest of Symbols: Aspects of Ndembu Ritual*, 19–47. Ithaca, NY: Cornell University Press, 1967.

Urban, Greg. "Entextualization, Replication, and Power." In *Natural Histories of Discourse*, edited by Michael Silverstein and Greg Urban, 21–44. Chicago: University of Chicago Press, 1996.

Uzan, Mardochée. *el-Bah'r bidh'acli*. Tunis: Mardochée Uzan et frère, 1892.

Valentine, David. *Imagining Transgender: An Ethnography of a Category*. Durham, NC: Duke University Press, 2007.

Valeri, Valerio. "Constitutive History: Genealogy and Narrative in the Legitimation of Hawaiian Kingship." In *Culture through Time: Anthropological Approaches*, edited by Emiko Ohnuki-Tierney, 154–92. Stanford, CA: Stanford University Press, 1990.

Velimirović, Miloš. "Russian Autographs at Harvard." *Notes* 17, no. 4 (1960): 539–58.

Viollet-Le-Duc, E. *On Restoration*. Translated by Charles Wethered. London: Sampson Low, Marston, Low, and Searle, 1875.

Wade, Peter. *Music, Race, and Nation: Música Tropical in Colombia*. Chicago: University of Chicago Press, 2000.

Wagner, Mark S. *Like Joseph in Beauty: Yemeni Vernacular Poetry and Arab-Jewish Symbiosis*. Leiden: Brill, 2009.

Wallace, Anthony. "Revitalization Movements." *American Anthropologist* 58, no. 2 (1956): 264–81.

Warner, Michael. *Publics and Counterpublics*. New York: Zone Book, 2002.

Waterbury, John. *The Commander of the Faithful: The Moroccan Political Elite—A Study in Segmented Politics*. New York: Columbia University Press, 1970.

Wehr, Hans. *Arabic-English Dictionary*. Edited by J. Milton Cowan. Ithaca, NY: Cornell University Press, 1976.

Weidman, Amanda. *Singing the Classical, Voicing the Modern: The Postcolonial Politics of Music in South India*. Durham, NC: Duke University Press, 2006.

———. "The Ethnographer as Apprentice: Embodying Sociomusical Knowledge in South India." *Anthropology and Humanism* 37, no. 2 (2012): 214–35.

Weiner, Annette. "Inalienable Wealth." *American Ethnologist* 12, no. 2 (1985): 210–27.

———. *Inalienable Possessions: The Paradox of Keeping-while-Giving*. Berkeley and Los Angeles: University of California Press, 1992.

———. "Cultural Difference and the Density of Objects." *American Ethnologist* 21, no. 2 (1994): 391–403.

Weiner, James F. "Beyond the Possession Principle: An Energetics of Massim Exchange." Review of Annette Weiner. *Pacific Studies* 18, no.1 (1995): 128–37.

Werbner, Pnina. *Pilgrims of Love: The Anthropology of a Global Sufi Cult*. Bloomington: Indiana University Press, 2003.

Witulski, Christopher. "'Because the People Will Like It!': Musical Innovation in Malḥūn." Paper presented at The Musical Heritage of Moorish Spain, University of California Santa Barbara, February 20-22, 2015.

Wolf, Kenneth Baxter. "*Convivencia* in Medieval Spain: A Brief History of an Idea." *Religion Compass* 3, no. 1 (2009): 72–85.

Wright, Gwendolyn. *The Politics of Design in French Colonial Urbanism*. Chicago: University of Chicago Press, 1991.

Wright, Owen. "Music in Muslim Spain." In *The Legacy of Muslim Spain*, edited by Salma Khadra Jayyusi, 555–82. Leiden: Brill, 1992.

Wulstan, David. "The Muwaššaḥ and Zağal Revisited." *Journal of the American Oriental Society* 102, no. 2 (1982): 247–64.

Yafil, Edmond Nathan. *Diwān al-aghānī min kalām al-andalus*. Algiers: Yafil, 1904.

———. *Majmūʿ al-aghānī wa-l-alḥān min kalām al-andalus*. Algiers: Yafil, 1904.

———. *Majmūʿ zahw al-anīs al-mukhtaṣṣ bi-l-tabāsī wa-l-qawādis*. Algiers: n.p., 1907.

———. *Répertoire de musique arabe et maure: Collection de mélodies, ouvertures, noubet, chansons, préludes, etc.* Nos. 26–29. Algiers: Yafil, 1925.

———. [No title.] *La Dépêche Algérienne*, October 1, 1927.

Yafil, Edmond Nathan, and Jules Rouanet, eds. *Répertoire de musique arabe et maure: Collection de mélodies, ouvertures, noubet, chansons, préludes, etc.* Nos. 1–25. Algiers: Yafil and Seror, 1904–?

Yallis, Jallūl [Djelloul Yelles], and al-Ḥafnāwī Amuqrān [Amokrane El Hafnaoui], eds. *Al-muwashshaḥāt wa-l-azjāl*. 3 vols. Algiers: SNED, 1972–82.

Yelles, Mourad. *Cultures et métissages en Algérie: La racine et la trace*. Paris: L'Harmattan, 2005.

Zaman, Muhammad Qasim. "Commentaries, Print and Patronage: *ḥadīth* and the Madrasas in Modern South Asia." *Bulletin of the School of Oriental and African Studies, University of London* 62, no. 1 (1999): 60–81.

———. *The Ulama in Contemporary Islam: Custodians of Change*. Princeton, NJ: Princeton University Press, 2002.

Zawītan, Aḥmad. *Majmūʿat al-ḥāyik li-l-ṭarab al-andalusī*. Casablanca: Maktabat al-rishād, 1972.

Zerrouki, Mohammed. "La musique arabe." *La revue internationale de musique* 12 (1952): 56–65.

Index